MUIRHEAD LIBRARY OF PHILOSOPHY

An admirable statement of the aims of the Library of Philosophy was provided by the first editor, the late Professor J. H. Muirhead, in his description of the original programme printed in Erdmann's *History of Philosophy* under the date 1890. This was slightly modified in subsequent volumes to take the form of the following statement:

"The Library of Philosophy was designed as a contribution to the History of Modern Philosophy under the heads: first of different Schools of Thought—Sensationalist, Realist, Idealist, Intuitivist; secondly of different Subjects—Psychology, Ethics, Æsthetics, Political Philosophy, Theology. While much had been done in England in tracing the course of evolution in nature, history, economics, morals and religion, little had been done in tracing the development of thought on these subjects. Yet 'the evolution of opinion is part of the whole evolution.'

By the co-operation of different writers in carrying out this plan it was hoped that a thoroughness and completeness of treatment, otherwise unattainable, might be secured. It was believed also that from writers mainly British and American fuller consideration of English Philosophy than it had hitherto received might be looked for. In the earlier series of books containing, among others, Bosanquet's *History of Æsthetic*, Pfleiderer's *Rational Theology since Kant*, Albee's *History of English Utilitarianism*, Bonar's *Philosophy and Political Economy*, Brett's *History of Psychology*, Ritchie's *Natural Rights*, these objects were to a large extent effected.

In the meantime original work of a high order was being produced both in England and America by such writers as Bradley, Stout, Bertrand Russell, Baldwin, Urban, Montague and others, and a new interest in foreign works, German, French, and Italian, which had either become classical or were attracting public attention, had developed. The scope of the Library thus became extended into something more international, and it is entering on the fifth decade of its existence in the hope that it may contribute to that mutual understanding between countries which is so pressing a need of the present time."

The need which Professor Muirhead stressed is no less pressing to-day, and few will deny that philosophy has much to do with enabling us to meet it, although no one, least of all Muirhead himself, would regard that as the sole, or even the main, object of philosophy. In view of Professor Muirhead's long and fruitful association with the Library of Philosophy to which he now also lends the distinction of his name, it seemed not inappropriate to allow him to recall us to these aims in his own words. The emphasis on the history of thought also seemed to me very timely; and the number of important works promised for the Library in the near future augur well for the continued fulfilment, in this and in other ways, of the expectations of the original editor.

H. D. LEWIS

MUIRHEAD LIBRARY OF PHILOSOPHY

General Editor: H. D. Lewis

Professor of History and Philosophy of Religion in the University of London

Action by SIR MALCOLM KNOX

The Analysis of Mind by BERTRAND RUSSELL

Belief by H. H. PRICE

Clarity is Not Enough by H. D. LEWIS

Coleridge as Philosopher by J. H. MUIRHEAD

The Commonplace Book of G. E. Moore edited by C. LEWY

Contemporary British Philosophy first and second Series edited by J. H. MUIRHEAD

Contemporary British Philosophy third Series edited by H. D. LEWIS

Contemporary Indian Philosophy edited by RADHAKRISHNAN and J. H. MUIRHEAD 2nd edition

Contemporary Philosophy in Australia edited by ROBERT BROWN and C. D. ROLLINS

The Discipline of the Cave by J. N. FINDLAY

Doctrine and Argument in Indian Philosophy by NINIAN SMART

Essays in Analysis by ALICE AMBROSE

Ethics by NICOLAI HARTMANN translated by STANTON COIT 3 vols

The Foundations of Metaphysics in Science by ERROL E. HARRIS

Freedom and History by H. D. LEWIS

The Good Will: A Study in the Coherence Theory of Goodness by H. J. PATON

Hegel: A Re-examination by J. N. FINLAY

Hegel's Science of Logic translated by W. H. JOHNSTON and L. G. STRUTHERS 2 vols

History of Aesthetic by B. BOSANQUET 2nd edition

History of English Utilitarianism by E. ALBEE

History of Psychology by G. S. BRETT edited by R. S. PETERS abridged one volume edition 2nd edition

Human Knowledge by BERTRAND RUSSELL

A Hundred Years of British Philosophy by RUDOLF METZ translated by J. H. HARVEY, T. E. JESSOP, HENRY STURT

Ideas: A General Introduction to Pure Phenomenology by EDMUND HUSSERL translated by W. R. BOYCE GIBSON

Identity and Reality by EMILE MEYERSON

Imagination by E. J. FURLONG

Indian Philosophy by RADHAKRISHNAN 2 vols revised 2nd edition
Introduction to Mathematical Philosophy by BERTRAND RUSSELL 2nd edition
Kant's First Critique by H. W. CASSIRER
Kant's Metaphysic of Experience by H. J. PATON
Know Thyself by BERNADINO VARISCO translated by GUGLIELMO SALVADORI
Language and Reality by WILBUR MARSHALL URBAN
Lectures on Philosophy by G. E. MOORE edited by C. LEWY
Matter and Memory by HENRI BERGSON translated by N. M. PAUL and W. S. PALMER
Memory by BRIAN SMITH
The Modern Predicament by H. J. PATON
Natural Rights by D. G. RITCHIE 3rd edition
Nature, Mind and Modern Science by E. HARRIS
The Nature of Thought by BRAND BLANSHARD
Non-Linguistic Philosophy by A. C. EWING
On Selfhood and Godhood by C. A. CAMPBELL
Our Experience of God by H. D. LEWIS
Perception by DON LOCKE
The Phenomenology of Mind by G. W. F. HEGEL translated by SIR JAMES BAILLIE revised 2nd edition
Philosophical Papers by G. E. MOORE
Philosophy in America by MAX BLACK
Philosophy and Illusion by MORRIS LAZEROWITZ
Philosophy and Political Economy by JAMES BONAR
Philosophy and Religion by AXEL HÄGERSTRÖM
Philosophy of Space and Time by MICHAEL WHITEMAN
Philosophy of Whitehead by W. MAYS
The Platonic Tradition in Anglo-Saxon Philosophy by J. H. MUIRHEAD
The Principal Upanisads by RADHAKRISHNAN
The Problems of Perception by R. J. HIRST
Reason and Goodness by BLAND BLANSHARD
The Relevance of Whitehead by IVOR LECLERC
The Science of Logic by G. W. F. HEGEL
Some Main Problems of Philosophy by G. E. MOORE
Studies in the Metaphysics of Bradley by SUSHIL KUMAR SAXENA
The Theological Frontier of Ethics by W. G. MACLAGAN
Time and Free Will by HENRI BERGSON translated by F. G. POGSON
The Transcendence of the Cave by J. N. FINDLAY
Values and Intentions by J. N. FINDLAY
The Ways of Knowing: or the Methods of Philosophy by W. P. MONTAGUE

The Muirhead Library of Philosophy
EDITED BY H. D. LEWIS

SOME MAIN PROBLEMS OF PHILOSOPHY

SOME MAIN PROBLEMS OF PHILOSOPHY

BY

GEORGE EDWARD MOORE
O.M., LITT.D., HON.LL.D., F.B.A.
Emeritus Professor of Philosophy and Fellow of Trinity College in the University of Cambridge

LONDON: GEORGE ALLEN & UNWIN LTD
NEW YORK: HUMANITIES PRESS INC.

FIRST PUBLISHED IN 1953
SECOND IMPRESSION 1958
THIRD IMPRESSION 1962
FOURTH IMPRESSION 1966
FIFTH IMPRESSION 1969

Reprinted in 1978 in the United States
of America by Humanities Press Inc. and in
England by George Allen & Unwin Ltd.

(U.S.A.) ISBN 0 391 00940 0
(England) ISBN 04 192009 0

Printed in the United States of America

Foreword

When I urged Professor Moore to publish these lectures which he gave some forty years ago he said to me 'But surely they are out of date.' Certainly they are out of date. Moore's own work in philosophy over these forty years is by itself enough to render them out of date. Anyone hearing these lectures at the time they were given might have guessed that they would soon be out of date. For in these lectures philosophy is done with a directness and honesty and inciciveness which at once gives hope that we may, working with Moore, soon cut a way out of the jungle into the light. It is the same hope we felt when we read what we still read—Moore's *Principia Ethica* and his *Philosophical Studies*. That hope was justified.

Amongst the problems which agitate philosophers there are two which, I think, strike the non-philosopher as especially remote, as typically frivolous. They are the problem of the external world and the problem of general ideas.

When the philosopher asks 'Do we really know what things are good and what are bad?', when he asks 'What is goodness?' the plain man sympathizes. When the philosopher asks 'Do we really know of the existence of mind?' 'How do we know the past?' 'What do we mean when we speak of consciousness or of what no longer exists?' the plain man may still manage to sympathize. But when the philosopher asks 'Do we really know that there is bread here and now in our mouths?' 'What do we mean when we speak of chairs and tables?' then the whole thing is apt to seem ridiculous to the plain man.

And when the philosopher then asks 'What is it to mean anything?' 'What is it to have a general idea of anything?' 'What is it to have a universal before the mind, to notice its presence in something before one?' 'What is it for a quality to be present in this and also in that?' then to the plain man it seems that the philosopher is getting himself into a difficulty by asking for the reduction to something more simple of what couldn't be simpler.

Moore manages to present these central, limiting, typical problems in such a way that the reader in spite of himself begins to feel them. And without this feeling of the difficulty there can be no full understanding of what it is to remove it. The idea that there is nothing much to make a fuss about is as fatal as the idea that nothing much can be done about it. For this reason alone Moore's introduction to philosophical difficulties can help us to judge and to understand the most modern attempts to resolve them. But further the ruthless clarity with which Moore shows us the pathless jungle before us helps us to realize what must be done to get through. There is no path. We must cut a way from tree to tree.

It often happens of course that one cannot tell where one wishes to go until one starts. But there are times when it is timely to ask 'Now where am I trying to go?' Moore has always reminded us of this. One thing he has always sought to keep before us is the difference between questions as to what is actually the case and questions as to what it is logically possible should be the case, the meanings of our words being what they are. In him too we find a habit of thought which, carried further by Wittgenstein, led to enormous advances—the study of the meaning of general terms by consideration of concrete cases.

JOHN WISDOM

Preface

I hope Professor Wisdom was right in thinking that this book was worth publishing. It consists of twenty lectures which I delivered at Morley College in London in the winter of 1910-11, the first ten being given before Christmas, and the second ten after. And I think I should have had less hope that they were worth publishing had I not thought (perhaps mistakenly) that, though much of them is no doubt 'out of date,' yet they also contain much which is as yet by no means out of date.

My audience were invited after each lecture to raise questions about what I had said in it, and it is to one of the resulting discussions that the first sentence of Chapter XV refers.

The lectures are now printed substantially in the form in which they were delivered. I have made a good many verbal changes, substituting for an expression which I used in the lectures another expression which I now think expresses my meaning better. But I could not make such changes everywhere : my old terminology still appears in many places ; and I have therefore added footnotes explaining where I now think it to be incorrect. In Chapters XIX and XX, however, I have made more extensive alterations, though only by omission—omission of several pages, which seem to me now both confused and confusing and not to make any substantial addition to what I was saying. I have, therefore, I believe, retained the substance even of these two chapters, and have added an Appendix to explain what seem to me to be the chief defects in what I have retained.

I am well aware that there are a good many positive mistakes in what is here printed ; and there is besides a good deal of repetition, since I often repeated at the beginning of a lecture part of what I had said in the preceding one, hoping, in some cases, to make my meaning clearer.

There are two matters about which I should have added footnotes, had I noticed them earlier ; and I should like to mention them briefly here. The first is the view which I express on p. 128, that it is possible that some material objects occupy merely points or lines or areas. This now seems to me to be a complete mistake : nothing, I should say, can be properly called either a material thing or a part of a material thing, unless it occupies a volume—though, of course, the volume may be extremely small. This point is, of course, connected with my mistake (pointed out on p. 34, note 2) in supposing that a surface can be properly called a "part" of a material thing. The second point about which I ought to have added a footnote concerns the relation between what I say about *propositions* in Chapter III and what I say about them in Chapter XIV, pp. 265-6, and again in XVII, p. 309. In III, p. 56, I say "There certainly are in the Universe such things as propositions", whereas in XIV (p. 256) I say that I am recommending a view about the *analysis* of belief which may be expressed by saying "There simply are no such things as propositions", and in XVII (p. 309) I say "I don't now believe that there are such things as propositions at all". Now this looks as if, when I wrote XIV and XVII, I had abandoned the very view which in III I had declared to be certainly true ; and certainly I had, *if* in III I had been using the expression 'There are such things as propositions' in the same sense in which I was using it in XIV and XVII. But I now feel doubtful whether in III I had been using that expression merely in that sense. I think it is possible that in III I was using it, partly at least, in such a sense that the truth of what it expresses would follow from the mere fact that such expressions as 'I believe the *proposition* that the sun is larger than the moon' are perfectly correct ways of expressing something which is often true—as they certainly are ; whereas in XIV and XVII I was using 'There are such things as propositions' in a way which is perhaps more doubtfully correct, namely in such a way that it would not express a truth unless such expressions as 'I believe the *proposition* that the sun is larger than the moon' can be correctly *analysed* in a certain way—which is a very different usage.

It is perhaps worth mentioning that Chapters I-X are the 'unpublished writings' of mine, to which Lord Russell refers in the Preface to *The Problems of Philosophy*.

I should like finally to acknowledge very gratefully my obligations to the Editor of the Muirhead Library, Professor H. D. Lewis. He not only took upon himself the labour of suggesting titles for my Chapters—titles which I was only too glad to adopt, with one or two slight alterations ; he also made such alterations at the beginning of each lecture as were necessary to adapt it for book-form ; and, finally, by taking the trouble to read through the whole of the page-proofs, he discovered misprints which had escaped my notice and which would have disfigured the book.

G. E. MOORE

February, 1953

Contents

Chapter I

WHAT IS PHILOSOPHY?

I want, as a start, to try to give you a general idea of what philosophy *is*: or, in other words, what sort of questions it is that philosophers are constantly engaged in discussing and trying to answer. I want to begin in this way for two reasons. In the first place, by doing this, I shall be giving you some idea of what the problems are which I myself mean to discuss in the rest of this course. And, in the second place, I think it is the best way of beginning any discussion of the main problems of philosophy. By attempting to give, first of all, a general sketch or outline of the whole subject, you point out how the different separate problems are connected with one another and can give a better idea of their relative importance.

I am going, then, first of all to try to give a description of the *whole* range of philosophy. But this is not at all an easy thing to do. It is not easy, because, when you come to look into the matter, you find that philosophers have in fact discussed an immense variety of different sorts of questions; and it is very difficult to give any general description, which will embrace *all* of these questions, and also very difficult to arrange them properly in relation to one another. I cannot hope really to do more than to indicate roughly the main sorts of questions with which philosophers are concerned, and to point out some of the most important connections between these questions. I will try to begin by describing those questions which seem to me to be the *most* important and the most generally interesting, and will then go on to those which are subordinate.

To begin with, then, it seems to me that the most important and interesting thing which philosophers have tried to do is no less than this; namely: To give a general description of the *whole* of the Universe, mentioning all the most important kinds of things which we *know* to be in it, considering how far it is likely that there are in it important kinds of things which we do not absolutely *know* to be in it, and also considering the most important ways in which these various kinds of things are related to one another. I will call all this, for short, 'Giving a general description of the *whole* Universe', and hence will say that the first and most important problem of philosophy is: To give a general description of the *whole* Universe. Many philosophers (though by no means all) have, I think, certainly tried to give such a description: and the very different descriptions which different philosophers have given are, I think, among the most important differences between them. And the problem is, it seems to me, plainly one which is peculiar to philosophy. There is no other science which tries to say: Such and such kinds of things are the *only* kinds of things that there are in the Universe, or which we know to be in it. And I will now try to explain more clearly, by means of examples, exactly what I mean by this first problem—exactly what I mean by a general description of the *whole* Universe. I will try, that is, to mention the most important differences between the descriptions given by different philosophers. And I wish, for a particular reason, to begin in a particular way. There are, it seems to me, certain views about the nature of the Universe, which are held, now-a-days, by almost everybody. They are so universally held that they may, I think, fairly be called the views of Common Sense. I do not know that Common Sense can be said to have any views about the *whole* Universe: none of its views, perhaps, amount to this. But it has, I think, very definite views to the effect that certain kinds of things certainly are in the Universe, and as to some of the ways in which these kinds of things are related to one another. And I wish to begin by describing these views, because it seems to me that what is most amazing and most interesting about the views of many philosophers, is the way in which they go beyond or positively contradict the views of Common Sense: they profess to know that there are in the Universe most important kinds of things, which Common Sense does not profess to know of, and also they profess to know that there are *not* in the Universe (or, at least, that, if there are, we do not know it), things of the existence of which Common Sense is most sure. I think, therefore, you will best realise what these philosophical descriptions of the Universe really mean, by realising how very different they are from the views of Common Sense—how far, in some points, they go beyond Common Sense, and how absolutely, in others, they contradict it. I wish, therefore, to begin by describing what I take to be the most important views of Common Sense: things which we all commonly assume to be true about the Universe, and which we are sure that we know to be true about it.

To begin with, then, it seems to me we certainly believe that there are in the Universe enormous numbers of material objects, of one kind or another. We know, for instance, that there are upon the surface of the earth, besides our own bodies, the bodies of millions of other men; we know that there are the bodies of millions of other animals; millions of plants too; and, besides all these, an even greater number of inanimate objects—mountains, and all the stones upon them, grains of sand, different sorts of minerals and soils, all the drops of water in rivers and in the sea, and moreover ever so many different objects manufactured by men; houses and chairs and tables and railway engines, etc., etc. But, besides all these things upon the surface of the earth, there is the earth itself—an enormous mass of matter. And we believe too, nowadays, that the earth itself, and all that is in it or upon it, huge as it seems to us, is absurdly small in comparison with the whole material Universe. We are accustomed to the idea that the sun and moon and all the immense number of visible stars, are each of them great masses of matter, and most of them many times larger than the earth. We are accustomed, too, to the idea that they are situated at such huge distances from us that any distance from point to point upon the surface of the earth is absurdly small in comparison. All this we now believe about the material Universe: it is surely Common Sense to believe it all. But, as you know, there was a time when it was by no means Common Sense to believe some of these things: there was a time when nobody believed some of them. There was a time when there were not nearly so many men upon the earth as there are now; and when those who were upon it did not know how many there were. They believed only in the existence of a comparatively small number of human bodies beside their own; of a comparatively small number of animals and plants; and they had no idea how large the surface of the earth was. They believed, too, that the heavenly bodies were small compared to the earth, and at comparatively short distances from the earth. But I think I am right in saying we *now* believe that these primitive views about the material Universe were certainly wrong. We should say that we *know* that they were wrong: we have *discovered* that they were wrong: and this discovery is part of our progress in knowledge. But though there are thus *some* things about which the views of Common Sense have changed: yet, so far as concerns the point that there are in the Universe *a great number* of material objects, it has, so far as we know, remained the same. So far as we know, men have believed this almost as long as they have believed anything: they have always believed in the existence of a great many material objects.

But, now, besides material objects, we believe also that there are in the Universe certain phenomena very different from material objects. In short, we believe that we men, besides having bodies, also have *minds*; and one of the chief things which we mean, by saying we have *minds*, is, I think, this: namely, that we perform certain mental acts or acts of consciousness. That is to say, we see and hear and feel and remember and imagine and think and believe and desire and like and dislike and will and love and are angry and afraid, etc. These things that we do are all of them mental acts—acts of mind or acts of *consciousness*: whenever we do any of them, we are conscious of something: each of them partly consists in our being conscious of something in some way or other: and it seems to me that the thing of which we are most certain, when we say we are certain that we have minds, is that we do these things—that we perform these acts of consciousness. At all events we are certain that we do perform them and that these acts are something very different from material objects. To hear is not *itself* a material object, however closely it may be related to certain material objects; and so on with all the rest—seeing, remembering, feeling, thinking, etc. These things, these acts of consciousness are certainly not themselves material objects. And yet we are quite certain that there are immense numbers of them in the Universe. Every one of us performs immense numbers of them every day and all day long: we are perpetually seeing different things, hearing different things, thinking of different things, remembering different things. We cease to perform them only while we are asleep, without dreaming; and even in sleep, so long as we dream, we are performing acts of consciousness. There are, therefore, in the Universe at any moment millions of different acts of consciousness being performed by millions of different men, and perhaps also by many kinds of animals. It is, I think, certainly Common Sense to believe all this.

So far, then, we have seen that Common Sense believes that there are in the Universe, at least two different kinds of things. There are, to begin with, enormous numbers of material objects; and there are also a very great number of mental acts or acts of Consciousness.

But Common Sense has also, I think, certain very definite views as to the way in which these two kinds of things are related to one another. But, before I explain what these views are, I must first mention something which we believe to be true of absolutely *all* the material objects which I have mentioned—and, indeed, not only of them but of *all* objects which we should commonly call material objects at all.

We believe, in fact, of all material objects, that each of them is, at any given moment, situated somewhere or other in something which we call *space*. And by saying that they are all of them in *space*, we mean, I think, at least two things. We mean, in the first place, that each of them is, at any given moment, at some definite *distance* from all the rest. It may be impossible practically to measure all these distances, or indeed to measure any of them absolutely exactly: but we believe that all of them could theoretically be measured, and expressed as so many miles or feet or inches, or such and such a fraction of an inch, down to those objects which are absolutely touching one another, and between which therefore the distance is nothing at all. We believe, for instance, that the earth is (roughly speaking) so many millions of miles distant from the sun in one direction, and many more millions of miles distant from the pole-star in another; and that just as there is, at any given moment, a definite distance between the sun and the earth, and between the pole-star and the earth, so there is also a definite distance between the sun and the pole-star, and similarly between any one of the heavenly bodies and all the rest. And so too between all the bodies on the surface of the earth, or any parts of these bodies: any two of them are, at any given moment, either touching one another, or else at some definite distance from one another—a distance which can be roughly expressed as so many miles or feet or inches or fractions of an inch. We believe, then, that it is true of all material objects that each is, at any given moment, at some definite distance from all the rest. This is one of the things which we mean by saying that they are all in space. But we mean, I think, *also* that each is distant from all the rest in some *direction* or other: in some one or other of a quite *definite* set of directions. And what this definite set of directions is, can, I think, be easily explained. We all know the shape of the figure which is called a sphere—the shape of a perfectly round ball. Now from the centre of a sphere a straight line can be drawn to each of the points upon its surface. Each of these straight lines, we should say, led in a different *direction* from the centre: this is what we mean by a direction. And moreover there are, we should say, absolutely no directions in which it is possible to move from the centre in a straight line *except* along one or other of these straight lines; if you are to move in a straight line from the centre of a sphere at all, you must go *towards* one or other of the points on its surface; and this is what I meant by speaking of a quite definite set of directions: all the possible directions in which you can go in a straight line from any given point form a quite definite set; namely, you must go along one or other of the straight lines leading from that point to some point on the surface of a sphere of which it is the centre. The second thing, then, which I say we believe about all material objects: is that starting from any point on any one of them, *all* the rest will lie upon one or other of this definite set of straight lines. If you consider all the straight lines which lead from any point to all the different points on the surface of a sphere enclosing it, absolutely every material object in the Universe will, at any given moment, lie on one or other of these straight lines; it will lie at some distance or other along one or other of them. There is, we should say, no other position in space which any material object could occupy; these straight lines will pass through every position in space; so that, if an object is in space at all it must be on one or other of them. This, therefore, is one of the things which we mean by saying that all material objects are situated in *space*. We mean, that is, when we talk of *the* space in which material objects lie and move, a space in which there are no other directions in which you can go from any point, except those which I have specified. We do, I think, certainly hold that all the material objects I have mentioned, do lie in such a space: that from any one of them all the rest must at any moment lie in one or other of these directions. And when we talk of 'material objects', we mean, I think, as a rule, only to include under this description objects of which this is true.

But, now, I introduced this account of what we believe about material objects, in order to explain what we believe about the *relation* of material objects to that other quite different sort of things, which I have called acts of consciousness or mental acts. Common Sense has, I said, some quite definite views about the way in which acts of consciousness in general are related to material objects, and I wish now to state what these views are.

We all, then, commonly believe, I think, that acts of consciousness are quite definitely *attached*, in a particular way, to some material objects, and quite as definitely not *attached* to others. And why I introduced my account of space, was in order to make more clear in what sense we believe acts of consciousness to be *attached* to certain material objects. We believe, I think, that our acts of consciousness —all those which we perform, so long as we are alive—are *attached* to our bodies, in the sense that they occur *in the same places* in which our bodies are. We all do, I think, constantly assume this in ordinary life, and assume it with the utmost certainty; although I believe most philosophers have held that, on the contrary, acts of consciousness do not occur in any place at all—that they are, simply, *nowhere*—*not* in space. But that we all do commonly assume it, that it is a belief of Common Sense, is, I think, pretty plain. I believe, for instance, that my acts of consciousness are taking place now in this room, where my body is. At the present moment I am hearing and seeing and thinking *here*, in this room. And when, just now, I travelled up to Waterloo by train, I believe that my mind and my acts of consciousness travelled with me. When the train and my body were at Putney, I was thinking and seeing at Putney. When the train and my body reached Clapham Junction, I was thinking and seeing at Clapham Junction. And so on with all the other places which I passed through. We all, I think, commonly assume, in this way, that our acts of consciousness take place, at any moment, *in the place* in which our bodies are at that moment. I do not mean to say that we have any definite idea as to exactly *where* in our bodies our acts of consciousness take place. I do not think we have. We should not be prepared to say whether they all took place at exactly the same spot in our bodies or whether different acts took place at different spots; nor should we be prepared to assign any particular spot as *the* spot at which a particular act took place. All that we do, I think, believe with certainty is that they all do take place somewhere or other in our bodies. At all events we all constantly talk as if we believed this. And I may illustrate the force of this belief which we now have, by contrasting it with a different belief which was formerly held. Some savages, I believe, used to hold that, sometimes when a man was dreaming, his mind or soul used to leave his body and go to some other place and watch what was going on in that place: that, therefore, while he was asleep, his acts of consciousness might be taking place at some place other than that where his body was. Now I think I am right in saying that it is no longer Common Sense to believe this. We commonly believe nowadays that, so long as we are alive, we can, at least normally, only think and see and hear and feel, *where* our bodies are. We believe, at least, that an immense number of acts of consciousness are attached, each of them, to some particular body, in the sense that they occur somewhere or other in that body. My acts of consciousness take place in my body; and yours take place in yours: and our minds (generally, at least) go with us, wherever our bodies go.

We believe, then, I think, that many acts of consciousness are attached to particular material objects, in the sense that they take place *where* those objects are. But I do not mean to say that this is the *only* sense in which we believe them to be attached to particular material objects. We also believe, no doubt, that many of them are *dependent* upon the changes which occur in our bodies. For instance, I only see, when certain changes take place in my eyes; I only hear, when certain changes take place in my ears; only think, perhaps, when certain changes take place in my brain. We certainly believe that many acts of consciousness are attached to particular bodies in this way also. But the simplest and most universal relation which we believe to hold between acts of consciousness and particular bodies is, I think, the one I have mentioned—namely, that they occur *where* those bodies are.

We believe, then, that acts of consciousness are attached to some material objects. But we believe, I think, no less certainly, that to the vast majority of material objects, *no* acts of consciousness are attached. We believe that they *are* attached to the living bodies of men—millions of different men—and, perhaps, of most animals; so that there is no lack of acts of consciousness in the Universe. But nevertheless to the vast majority of material objects we believe, I think, that *none* are attached. We are sure that chairs and tables and houses and mountains and stones do not really see or hear or feel or think or perform any other mental acts: we are sure that they are *not* conscious. We are sure too that the sun and moon and stars and earth are not conscious—that no conscious acts are attached to them, in the sense in which our conscious acts are attached to our bodies: *they* do not feel or hear or see, as *we* do. This, then, is one very important thing which we believe as to the relation between acts of consciousness and material objects: namely, that among the vast number of material objects in the Universe there are comparatively few to which acts of consciousness are attached; in other words, by far the greater number of the material objects in the Universe are *unconscious*. This, I think, may fairly be said to be the view of Common Sense nowadays. But this is another point in regard to which the present view of Common Sense differs a good deal from what it once was. There was, it seems pretty certain, a time when most men believed that acts of Consciousness *were* attached to logs of wood, and stones, and trees, and to the sun and moon and many other objects. They believed that spirits were at various times *in* these objects; and that while the spirits were in them, acts of consciousness often took place inside them: the spirit heard and saw and thought inside the log of wood, just as our minds hear and see and think inside our bodies. There was, then, a time when men commonly believed that consciousness was (for a time, at least) attached to many bodies, which we now believe to be unconscious. But even then, so far as I know, they always believed that there were, at any given time, many places in the Universe in which no acts of consciousness were going on. We, I think, only go much farther than this: we believe that, at any given time, the number of spots in which no act of consciousness is taking place is *immensely* larger than that of those in which an act of consciousness *is* taking place.

This, therefore, is one thing which we believe with regard to the relation between consciousness and material objects. But there are, I think, also two others which deserve to be mentioned. The first of these is this. We believe that we are at certain times conscious of certain material objects: we see, and feel, and think of them. But we believe with the utmost certainty that these material objects can and do continue to exist even when we are *not* conscious of them. We are, for instance, at this moment seeing certain material objects in this room. But we believe that they will continue to exist, even when we have all gone away and the room is shut up for the night and no one is seeing them. If I leave a room, for five minutes, in which a fire is burning, and then come back and find it burning still, I assume that it has been burning all the while I was away, and when no one was seeing it or feeling its heat, just as much as when I was there to see it. We all, I think, constantly assume with regard to material objects that they are, in this sense, wholly independent of our consciousness of them: they are all objects of a sort, which exist just as much when we are not conscious of them as when we are. We may, indeed, say of *all* material objects that they have three characteristics: (1) they are quite a different sort of thing from acts of consciousness; (2) they are all of them, at any given time, situated somewhere or other in space; and (3) they have this property which I have just mentioned—namely that they are a sort of thing, which exists when we are not conscious of it just as much as when we are. These three characteristics are not, I think, sufficient to define a material object: there may be other objects, which possess all three and yet are not material objects. But they are, I think, three of the most important characteristics which material objects have; and we should not call anything a material object, unless we meant to assert that it had all three.

A second thing, then, which we believe about the relation of consciousness to matter, is that matter is independent of our consciousness of it—that it exists even when we are not conscious of it; and we believe, too, that there are existing at any moment many more material objects, of which no man or animal is conscious, than material objects of which we are conscious. And the third thing which we believe about the relation of consciousness to matter is the following. We believe, namely, that there probably was a time when there were *no* acts of consciousness attached to any material objects on the earth: a time, when the earth was so hot that no living beings could exist upon it; and when therefore there could be no conscious beings on it either. And as regards human bodies and human consciousness we believe, I think, that this is not only probable, but certain. We believe that it is only for a comparatively limited time—*comparatively* limited, though amounting, perhaps, to several millions of years—that men have existed upon the earth: before that time, there were no bodies upon the earth which could be called human, and also no minds which could be called the minds of men; though there may have been minds and acts of consciousness belonging to other sorts of animals. And just as we believe that, at some time in the past, there were probably no conscious beings at all upon the earth, and certainly no beings with human consciousness; so we believe that there *may* come a time, in the future, when this will again be so. We should not indeed deny that, even when there was no consciousness on the earth, there *may* have been conscious beings elsewhere in the Universe, on other planets; we should not deny that there may be some now; nor should we deny that this may still be so, when (if ever) the time comes, when all consciousness upon the earth is again extinguished. But we should, I think, hold that there *may* have been, and may be again, long periods in the history of the material Universe, during which no consciousness was attached to any of the bodies in it—when no conscious acts were taking place anywhere in it. We believe, that is to say, that just as consciousness certainly is now attached to comparatively *few* among the material objects in the Universe, so there *may* have been in the past and *may* be again in the future, long periods when it was or will be attached to *none* at all. This is, I think, one belief of Common Sense with regard to the relation of consciousness to material objects; and, if it be so, it is certainly an important element in our general view of the Universe.

So far, then, the elements which I have tried to emphasize in the Common Sense view of the Universe, are these. Firstly, that there certainly are in the Universe two very different kinds of things, namely material objects and acts of consciousness. And secondly, as to the relation of these two kinds of things three points: the first (1) that conscious acts are attached to comparatively few among the material objects in the Universe; that the vast majority of material objects are unconscious. Indeed the only bodies to which we should say we know them with certainty to be attached are the living bodies of men, and perhaps other animals, upon the Earth. We should not deny that they *may* be attached also to other bodies on other planets: that there may on other planets be other living beings, which are conscious. But we should, I think, say that conscious acts certainly are not attached to the vast majority of the material objects in the Universe. This is one of our beliefs about the relation of acts of consciousness to material objects. A second is (2) that material objects are all of such a kind that they may exist, even when we are not conscious of them, and that many do in fact so exist. And the third is (3) that there *may* have been a time when acts of consciousness were attached to *no* material bodies anywhere in the Universe, and *may* again be such a time; and that there almost certainly was a time when there were no human bodies, with human consciousness attached to them, upon this earth.

And now there are only two other points in the views of Common Sense about the Universe, to which I wish to call attention.

The first is one, which I have constantly assumed in what I have already said, but which I wish now to mention expressly. It is this. That all material objects, and all the acts of consciousness of ourselves and other animals upon the earth, are in *time*. I say '*are* in time'; but, to speak more accurately I ought to say *either* have been in time *or* are so now *or* will be so in the future; *either* this, or else all three—*both* have been in time in the past, *and* are so now, *and* will be so in the future. For just one of the things which we mean by talking of 'time' is that there are such things as the past, the present and the future, and that there is a great difference between the three. None of the material objects in space and none of our acts of consciousness can, we hold, be truly said to *exist* at all, unless it exists *at the time at which we say so*; only those of them, for instance, which exist at the time at which I am now speaking can now be truly said to *exist* at all: of others it may be true that they *did* exist in the past or that they *will* exist in the future, but it cannot be true that they *do* exist. What I mean, then, when I say that all material objects and all our acts of consciousness are in time, is this: that each of them either did exist in the past, or exists now, or will exist in the future;

either this, or else, all three: *both* did exist at some time in the past, does exist now, and will exist in the future. And I mean, too, that to say that a thing 'did exist' is something different from saying that it 'does exist' and both these again from saying that it 'will exist'; and that each of these different statements is in fact true of some things. I am, for instance, quite sure that there have been in the past many acts of consciousness, both of my own and those of other men; I am quite sure that many are existing now; and I am very certain, though less certain, that many will exist in the future. And so too of material objects: many have existed in the past, many do exist now, and many (in all probability) will exist in the future. I say we all commonly believe that these things are so. We believe that the three statements 'It *did* exist'; 'It *does* exist'; 'It *will* exist': are each of them true of many material objects and many acts of consciousness; the first true of some; the second true of others; and the third of still others; and of many, again, all three. And we believe also, that one or other of these statements is true of *all* of them; either this, or else in some instances that all three of them are true of one and the same thing: the sun or the earth, for instance, both *did* exist, *do* exist, and (probably) *will* exist. This, I say, is certainly the belief of Common Sense.

And there is only one other belief of Common Sense which I wish to mention: namely, this. We believe that we do really *know* all these things that I have mentioned. We *know* that there are and have been in the Universe the two kinds of things—material objects and acts of consciousness. We *know* that there are and have been in the Universe huge numbers of both. We *know* that many material objects exist when we are not conscious of them. We *know* that the vast majority of material objects are unconscious. We *know* that things of both kinds *have* existed in the past, which do not exist now, and that things of both kinds do exist now, which did *not* exist in the past. All these things we should, I think, certainly say that we *know*. And moreover we believe that we *know* an immense number of details about particular material objects and acts of consciousness, past, present and future. We know most, indeed, about the past; but a great deal about the present; and much also (though perhaps this is only probable knowledge) about the future. Indeed the sphere of most of the special sciences may be defined as being to give us detailed knowledge about particular objects of the kinds which I have been trying to define: that is to say, about material objects which are or have been somewhere or other in space, and about the acts of consciousness of men upon the earth. Most of the special sciences confine themselves to some particular group among objects of these two kinds; and we believe that they have been very successful in giving us a great deal of real knowledge about objects of these kinds. Astronomy, for instance, tells us about the heavenly bodies—their size and movements and composition and how they act upon one another. Physics and chemistry give us detailed knowledge about the composition of different kinds of material objects, and how they and their minute parts act upon one another. Biology gives us knowledge about the differences between different kinds of animals upon the earth. Botany about the differences between different kinds of plants. Physiology about the processes which go on in living bodies. Geology gives us knowledge about the present state and past history of the different layers of rock or soil of which the crust of the earth is composed. Geography gives us knowledge about the present distribution of land and water upon the surface of the earth; about the positions of mountains and rivers; about the different soils and climates of different parts of the earth. History and biography give us knowledge about the actions of different men and collections of men, which have existed upon the surface of the earth; and also about their acts of consciousness, what sorts of things they saw and heard and thought and believed. Finally Psychology deals specially with the acts of consciousness of men and to some extent of animals also; it tries to classify and distinguish the different kinds of mental acts which we perform, and to decide how these different acts are related to one another. All these sciences which I have mentioned are, you will observe, occupied exclusively with giving us information about the two kinds of objects which I have tried to define—namely, material objects in space, and the acts of consciousness of men and animals on the surface of the earth. And we certainly believe that all of them have succeeded in acquiring a great deal of real *knowledge* about objects of these kinds. We distinguish sharply, in each case, between things which are now absolutely known; things which were formerly believed, but believed wrongly; and things which we do not yet know. In the case of all these sciences, there are, we believe, an immense number of things which are now definitely known to be facts; a great many, which were formerly believed, but are now definitely known to be errors; and a great many which we do not know and perhaps never shall know. In all our ordinary talk, in all newspapers and in all ordinary books (by which I mean books *other* than philosophical books) we constantly assume that there is this distinction between what we know, what we wrongly believe, and what we are still in ignorance about: and we assume that an enormous number of truths about material objects and the acts of consciousness of men belong to the first class —the class of things absolutely *known*—known, that is, by some man on the surface of the earth. All this is, I think, certainly nowadays part of the belief of Common Sense about the Universe.

I have tried, then, to enumerate certain general beliefs about the Universe, which may, I think, be fairly said to be beliefs of Common Sense: beliefs which we almost all of us nowadays entertain; and I do not mean to say that these are the only views of Common Sense about the Universe; but only that they *are* views which it does hold —*some* of its principal beliefs. But now all of these beliefs taken together do not amount to a general description of the *whole* Universe: they are not a general description of the *whole* Universe, in the sense in which I said that the first problem of philosophy was to give us such a description. They consist in saying that there certainly *are* in the Universe certain large classes of things, and that these things are related to one another in certain ways. But what they do not say, as they stand, is that these large classes of things are the *only* classes of things which are in the Universe, or which we *know* to be in it: they do not say that everything which we know to be in the Universe belongs to one or other of these classes; they do not deny, as they stand, that there may be in the Universe, or may even be *known* to be in it, important classes of things which *do not* belong to any of the classes I have mentioned. For instance, Common Sense says, according to me: There are in the Universe two classes of things: There are material objects in space, and there are the acts of consciousness of living men and animals upon the surface of the earth. But, in order to convert these statements into a general description of the whole Universe, we should have to add one or other of two things. We should have to say *either*: *Everything* in the Universe belongs to one or other of these two classes; everything is either a material object in space, or an act of consciousness of some man or animal on the earth. And this would plainly, if any one said it, profess to be a general description of the *whole* Universe. Or else we might say: Everything which we *know* to be in the Universe, does belong to one or other of these two classes; though there *may* be in the Universe other things, which we do not know to be in it. And this also, I think, might fairly be said to be an attempt to give a general description of the whole Universe. It would, indeed, consist in saying that, in a sense, *no* such description can be given; since it would say that there may be in the Universe things which we do not know of and therefore cannot describe. But it *would* profess to give a general description of everything that we *know* to be in the Universe; and would be a thing which no one would say unless his object were to solve our first philosophical problem—namely, to give the best general description he could of the *whole* Universe.

Starting, therefore, from the view of Common Sense that there certainly are in the Universe (1) material objects in space and (2) the acts of consciousness of men and animals upon the earth, we might most simply get a general description of the Universe in one or other of two ways: Either by saying, these two kinds of things *are* the only kinds in the Universe; or by saying: they are the only kinds we *know* to be in it, *but* there may possibly also be others. And as regards the first of these two views, I doubt whether any one, on reflection, would be willing to accept it quite as it stands. The most obvious objection to it is that by asserting that there are no acts of consciousness in the Universe, except those of men and animals on the earth, it denies the possibility that there *may* be or have been on other planets living beings endowed with consciousness. And this is a possibility which almost everybody would think it rash to deny. But still, by slightly modifying it to allow of this possibility, we get a view which might, I think, seem very plausible to many people. We might, for instance, say: There really is not, and never has been anything in the Universe, except material objects in space, on the one hand, and acts of consciousness, more or less similar to those of men and animals, attached to living bodies more or less similar to theirs, on the other hand. This is, I think, really a plausible view of the Universe; at least as plausible as many that have been proposed by philosophers. But, no doubt, the second view is more plausible still: it does seem more plausible to add the proviso: These are the only things we *know* to be in it; *but* there *may* be other kinds of things unknown to us. And this, I think, is a view which really has been held by many people, philosophers and others. They have held, that is, that the only kinds of things which we *know* to be in the Universe are material objects in space, and the acts of consciousness of men and animals on the earth; while adding also that there *may* be other kinds of things unknown to us.

No doubt, philosophers who have said this or something like it, have not meant by it quite what they said. Those who hold that there are and *have been* in the Universe material objects in space, and that there are and have been acts of consciousness, can hardly deny that there certainly are in the Universe *also* at least two other things beside these—things which are neither material objects nor acts of consciousness—namely, Space and Time themselves. It must be admitted on this view that Space and Time themselves really *are*—that they are *something*; and it is obvious that they are *neither* material objects *nor* acts of consciousness. And similarly there may be in the Universe other kinds of things known to us, besides Space and Time, which are neither material objects nor yet acts of consciousness. For my part, I think, there certainly are several other kinds of things, and that it is one of the objects of philosophy to point them out. But those philosophers who have spoken as if material objects and acts of consciousness were the *only* kinds of things known by us to be in the Universe, have, I think, not really meant to deny this. They have meant, rather, that material objects and acts of consciousness are the only kinds of things known to us, which are in a certain sense *substantial*: substantial in a sense in which Space and Time themselves do not seem to be substantial And I may say, at once, that, for my part, if we make suitable modifications of this sort, this view does seem to me to be a correct view. I hold, that is to say, that material objects in space, and the acts of consciousness of men and animals on the earth, really are the only *substantial* kinds of things *known* to us; though I should admit that there may possibly be others unknown to us; and though I think that there are certainly several *unsubstantial* kinds of things, which it is very important to mention, if we are to give a really complete general description of the *whole* Universe—Time and Space for instance.

One way, therefore, in which we might get a general description of the whole Universe, is by making additions to the views of Common Sense of the comparatively simple sort which I have just indicated. But many philosophers have held that any such view as this is very incorrect indeed. And different philosophers have held it to be incorrect in three different ways. They have either held that there certainly are in the Universe some most important kinds of things—*substantial* kinds of things—*in addition* to those which Common Sense asserts to be in it. Or else they have positively contradicted Common Sense: have asserted that some of the things which Common Sense supposes to be in it, are *not* in it, or else, that, if they are, we do not know it. Or else they have done *both*; both added and contradicted.

I wish now to give some examples of all three kinds of views. Both of those which *add* something very important to the views of Common Sense; and of those which *contradict* some of the views of Common Sense; and of those which do both.

To begin then with those which *add* something to the views of Common Sense.

There is, first of all, one view of this type which everybody has heard of. You all know, that enormous numbers of people, and not philosophers only, believe that there certainly is a God in the Universe: that, besides material objects and our acts of consciousness, there is also a Divine Mind, and the acts of consciousness of this mind; and that, if you are to give any complete description of the sum of things, of everything that is, you must certainly mention God. It might even be claimed that this view—the view that there is a God, is itself a view of Common Sense. So many people have believed and still do believe that there certainly is a God, that it might be claimed that this is a Common Sense belief. But, on the other hand, so many people now believe that, even if there is a God, we certainly do not *know* that there is one; that this also might be claimed as a view of Common Sense. On the whole, I think it is fairest to say, that Common Sense has *no* view on the question whether we do know that there is a God or not: that it neither asserts that we do know this, nor yet that we do not; and that, therefore, Common Sense has *no* view as to the Universe as a *whole*. We may, therefore, say that those philosophers who assert that there certainly *is* a God in the Universe do go *beyond* the views of Common Sense. They make a most important addition to what Common Sense believes about the Universe. For by a God is meant something so different both from material objects and from our minds, that to add that, besides these, there is also a God, is certainly to make an important addition to our view of the Universe.

And there is another view of this type, which also everybody has heard of. Everybody knows that enormous numbers of men have believed and still do believe that there *is* a future life. That is to say, that, besides the acts of consciousness attached to our bodies, while they are alive upon the earth, our minds go on performing acts of consciousness after the death of our bodies—go on performing acts of consciousness *not* attached to any living body on the surface of the earth. Many people believe that we *know* this: so many people believe it that, here again, as in the case of God, it might be claimed that this is a belief of Common Sense. But, on the other hand, so many people believe that, even if we have a future life, we certainly do not *know* that we have one; that here again it is perhaps fairest to say that Common Sense has no view on the point: that it asserts neither that we *do* know of a future life nor that we do *not*. This, therefore, also may be called an *addition* to the views of Common Sense; and certainly it is a most important addition. If there really are going on in the Universe at this moment, not only the acts of consciousness attached to the living bodies of men and animals on the surface of this earth, but also acts of consciousness performed by the minds of millions of men, whose bodies have long been dead—then certainly the Universe is a very different place from what it would be, if this were not the case.

Here, then, are two different views of the type which I describe as making important *additions* to the views of Common Sense, while not contradicting it. And there is only one other view of this type which I wish to mention. Some philosophers have held, namely, that there certainly is in the Universe, *something* else, beside material objects and our acts of consciousness, and something substantial too—but that we do not know what the nature of this something is—that it is something Unknown or Unknowable. This view, you see, must be carefully distinguished from that which I mentioned above as *not* going much beyond Common Sense: namely the view that there *may* be in the Universe, things which are neither material objects nor the acts of consciousness of men and animals, but that we do not know whether there are or not. There is a great difference between saying: There *may* be in the Universe some other kind of thing, but we do not know whether there is or not; and saying: There certainly *is* in the Universe some other important kind of thing, though we do not know *what* it is. This latter view may, I think, fairly be said to go a great way beyond the views of Common Sense. It asserts that in addition to the things which Common Sense asserts to be *certainly* in the Universe—namely, material objects in Space and the Acts of consciousness attached to living bodies—there *certainly* is something else besides, though we do not know what this something is. This view is a view which has, I think, been held by people who call themselves Agnostics; but I think it hardly deserves the name. To know, not only that there may be, but that there *certainly* is in the Universe something substantial besides material objects and our acts of consciousness is certainly to know a good deal. But I think it is a view that is not uncommonly held.

I have given, then, three examples of views which add to Common Sense without contradicting it and I now pass to the second type of views: those which contradict Common Sense, without *adding* to it; those which deny something which Common Sense professes to know, without professing to *know* anything, which Common Sense does *not* profess to know. I will call these, for the sake of a name, *sceptical views*.

Of this second type, there are, I think, two main varieties, both of which consist in saying that we do *not* know, certain things which Common Sense says we *do* know. No views of this type, I think, positively deny that there are in the Universe those things which Common Sense says certainly are in it: they only say that we simply do not know at all whether these things are in it or not; whereas Common Sense asserts quite positively that we *do* know that they are.

The first variety of this type is that which asserts that we simply do not know at all whether there are any material objects in the Universe at all. It admits that there *may* be such objects; but it says that none of us knows that there are any. It denies, that is to say, that we can know of the existence of any objects, which continue to exist when we are not conscious of them, except other minds and their acts of consciousness.

And the second view goes even further than this. It denies also that we can know of the existence of any minds or acts of consciousness except our own. It holds, in fact, that the only substantial kind of thing which any man can know to be in the Universe is simply his own acts of consciousness. It does not deny that there *may* be in the Universe other minds and even material objects too; but it asserts that, if there are, we cannot know it. This is, of course, an illogical position; since the philosopher who holds it, while asserting positively that no man can know of the existence of any other mind, also positively asserts that there are other men beside himself, who are all as incapable as he is of knowing the existence of any one else. But though it is illogical, it has been held. And it would cease to be illogical, if, instead of asserting that *no* man knows of the existence of any other mind, the philosopher were to confine himself to the assertion that *he* personally does not.

But now I come to the third type of views—views which depart *much* further from Common Sense than any that I have mentioned yet; since they *both* positively deny that there are in the Universe certain things, which Common Sense asserts certainly *are* in it, and *also* positively assert that there are in it certain kinds of things, which Common Sense does not profess to know of. Views of this type are, I may say, very much in favour among philosophers.

The chief views of this type may, I think, be divided into two classes: first, those whose contradiction of Common Sense merely consists in the fact that they positively deny the existence of space and material objects ; and secondly, those which positively deny many other things as well. Both kinds, I must insist, do positively deny the existence of material objects; they say that there certainly *are* no such things in the Universe; not merely, like the sceptical views, that we do not *know* whether there are or not.

First, then, for those views which merely contradict Common Sense by denying the existence of Space and material objects.

These views all, I think, start by considering certain things, which I will call the Appearances of material objects. And I think I can easily explain what I mean by this. You all know that, if you look at a church steeple from the distance of a mile, it has a different appearance from that which it has, when you look at it from the distance of a hundred yards; it looks smaller and you do not see it in many details which you see when you are nearer. These different appearances which the same material objects may present from different distances and different points of view are very familiar to all of us: there certainly are such things in the Universe, as these things which I call Appearances of material objects. And there are two views about them, both of which might be held quite consistently with Common Sense, and between which, I think, Common Sense does not pronounce. It might be held that some, at least, among them really are parts of the objects,[1] of which they are appearances: really are situated in space, and really continue to exist, even when we are not conscious of them. But it might also be held, quite consistently with Common Sense, that *none* of these appearances are in space, and that they all exist only so long as they appear *to* some one: that, for instance, the appearance which the church tower presents to me on a particular occasion, exists only so long as I see it, and cannot be said to be in the same space with any material object or to be at any distance from any material object. Common Sense, I think, does not contradict either of those views. All that it does insist on, I think, is that these appearances are appearances of material objects—of objects which do exist, when we are not conscious of them, and which *are* in space. Now the philosophers whose views I am now

[1] I should now say 'parts of the *surfaces* of the objects'. (1952)

considering have, I think, all accepted the second of the two views about appearances, which I said were consistent with Common Sense—namely the view that these appearances only exist, so long as the person to whom they appear is seeing them, and that they are *not* in space. And they have then gone on to contradict Common Sense, by adding that these appearances are *not* appearances of material objects—that there are no material objects, for them to be appearances *of*.

And there are two different views of this kind, which have been held.

The first is the view of one of the most famous of English philosophers, Bishop Berkeley. Berkeley's view may, I think, be said to have been that these Appearances are in fact not Appearances *of* anything at all. He himself says, indeed, that these Appearances are themselves material objects—that they are what we mean by material objects. He says that he is not denying the existence of matter, but only explaining what matter is. But he has been commonly held to have denied the existence of matter, and, I think, quite rightly. For he held that these Appearances do not exist except at the moment when we see them; and anything of which this is true can certainly not properly be said to be a material object: what we mean to assert, when we assert the existence of material objects, is certainly the existence of something which continues to exist even when we are *not* conscious of it. Moreover he certainly held, I think, that these appearances were not *all* of them in the same space: he held, for instance, that an appearance, which appears to me, was not at any distance or in any direction from an appearance which appears to you: whereas, as I have said, we should, I think, refuse to call anything a material object, which was not at some distance, in space, in some direction from all *other* material objects. I think, then, it may fairly be said that Berkeley denies the existence of any material objects, in the sense in which Common Sense asserts their existence. This is the way in which he contradicts Common Sense. And the way in which he *adds* to it, is by asserting the existence of a God, to whom, he thinks, there appear a set of appearances exactly like all of those which appear to us.

But Berkeley's view has not, I think, been shared by many other philosophers. A much commoner view is that these things which I have called the appearances of material objects, are in fact the appearances of *something*, but not, as Common Sense asserts, of material objects, but of minds or conscious beings. This view, therefore, both contradicts Common Sense, by denying the existence of material objects, and also goes beyond it by asserting the existence of immense numbers of minds, in addition to those of men and of animals. And it insists, too, that these minds are not *in space*: it is, it says, not true that they are at any distance in any direction from one another; they are, in fact, all simply *nowhere*, not in any place at all.

These views are, I think, startling enough. But there are other philosophers who have held views more startling still—who have held not only that space and material objects do not really exist, but also that time and our own conscious acts do not really exist either: that there are not really any such things in the Universe. At least, this is, I think, what many philosophers have meant. What they *say* is that all these four kinds of things, material objects, space, our acts of consciousness and time, are Appearances; that they are all of them Appearances *of* something else—either of some one thing, or else some collection of things, which is *not* a material object, nor an act of consciousness of ours, and which also is not in space nor yet in time. And, as you see, this proposition is ambiguous: whether it contradicts Common Sense or not depends on the question what these philosophers mean by calling these things Appearances. They might conceivably mean that these Appearances were just as real, as the things of which they are appearances; by asserting that they are Appearances of something else, they might only mean to assert that there is in the Universe something else *besides*—something to which these things are related in the same sort of way in which the appearance of a church-tower, which I see when I look at it from a distance, is related to the real church-tower. And, if they did only mean this, their views would merely be of the type of those that *add* to Common Sense: they would merely be asserting that, in addition to the things which Common Sense believes to be in the Universe, there is *also* something else *beside* or *behind* these things. But it seems to me quite plain that they do not really mean this. They do mean to maintain that matter and space and our acts of consciousness and time are *not* real in the sense in which Common Sense believes them to be real, and in which they themselves believe that the *something* else behind Appearances is real. And holding this, it seems to me that what they really mean is that these things are not real at all: that there are not really any such things in the Universe. What, I think, they really mean (though they would not all admit that they mean it) is something like this. There is a sense in which the pole-star, when we look at it, *appears* to be much smaller than the moon. We may say, then, that *what* appears—the *appearance*, in this case—is simply this: *that the pole-star is smaller than the moon.* But there simply *is* no such thing in the Universe as this which appears: the pole-star is *not* smaller than the moon: and, therefore, what appears to be in the Universe—namely, *that* it is smaller than the moon—is a simple nonentity—there is no such thing. It is in this sense, I think, that many philosophers have believed and still believe that not only matter and space but also our acts of consciousness and time simply do not exist: that there are no such things. They have believed that they are something which appears; but that what appears simply is *not* anything—that there is no such thing in the Universe. This, I think, is what they really mean, though they would not all admit that they mean it. And as to what they hold to be in the Universe, *instead of* the things which Common Sense holds to be in it, they have held different views. Some have held that it is a collection of different minds; others that it is one mind; others that it is something which is in some sense mental or spiritual, but which cannot be properly said either to be one mind or many.

These, then, are some of the views which have been held as to the nature of the Universe as a *whole.* And I hope these examples have made clear the sort of thing I mean by the first problem of philosophy—a *general* description of the whole Universe. Any answer to the problem must consist in saying one or other of three things: it must say *either* that certain large classes of things are the *only* kinds of things in the Universe, *i.e.*, that everything in it belongs to one or other of them; or else it must say that everything in the Universe is of one kind; or else it must say that everything which we *know* to be in the Universe belongs to some one of several classes or to some one class. And it must also, if it holds that there are several different classes of things, say something about the relation of these classes to one another.

This, then, is the first and most interesting problem of philosophy. And it seems to me that a great many others can be defined as problems bearing upon this one.

For philosophers have not been content simply to express their opinions as to what there is or is not in the Universe, or as to what we know to be in it or do not know to be in it. They have also tried to prove their opinions to be true. And with this, you see, a great many subordinate problems are opened up.

In order to prove, for instance, that any one of these views I have mentioned are true, you must both prove *it* and *also* refute all the others. You must prove either that there is a God, or that there is not, or that we do not know whether there is one or not. Either that there is a future life, or that there is not, or that we do not know whether there is one or not. And so on with all the other kinds of things I have mentioned: matter and space and time; and the minds of other men; and other minds, *not* the minds of men or animals. In order to prove that any particular view of the Universe is correct, you must prove, in the case of each of these things, either that they do exist, or that they do not, or that we do not know whether they do or not. And all these questions, you see, may be treated separately for their own sakes. Many philosophers, indeed, have not tried to give any general description of the *whole* Universe. They have merely tried to answer some one or more of these subordinate questions.

And there is another sort of subordinate questions, which ought, I think, to be specially mentioned. Many philosophers have spent a great deal of their time in trying to define more clearly what is the difference between these various sorts of things: for instance, what is the difference between a material object and an act of consciousness, between matter and mind, between God and man, etc. And these questions of definition are by no means so easy to answer as you might think. Nor must it be thought that they are mere questions of words. A good definition of the sorts of things you hold to be in the Universe, obviously adds to the clearness of your view. And it is not only a question of clearness either. When, for instance, you try to define what you mean by a material object, you find that there are several different properties which a material object might have, of which you had never thought before; and your effort to define may thus lead you to conclude that whole classes of things have certain properties, or have *not* certain others, of which you would never have thought, if you had merely contented yourself with asserting that there are material objects in the Universe, without enquiring what you meant by this assertion.

We may, then, say that a great class of subordinate philosophical problems consist in discussing whether the great classes of things I have mentioned do exist or do not, or whether we are simply ignorant as to whether they do or not; and also in trying to define these classes and considering how they are related to one another. A great deal of philosophy has consisted in discussing these questions with regard to God, a future life, matter, minds, Space and Time. And all these problems could be said to belong to that department of philosophy which is called Metaphysics.

But now we come to a class of questions which may be said to belong to other departments of philosophy, but which also have an evident bearing on the first main problem as to the general description of the Universe. One of the most natural questions to ask, when anybody asserts some fact, which you are inclined to doubt, is the question: How do you know that? And if the person answers the question in such a way as to shew that he has not learnt the fact in any one of the ways in which it is possible to acquire real knowledge, as opposed to mere belief, about facts of the sort, you will conclude that he does *not* really know it. In other words, we constantly assume in ordinary life that there are only a limited number of ways in which it is possible to acquire real *knowledge* of certain kinds of facts; and that if a person asserts a fact, which he has not learnt in any of these ways, then, in fact, he does not *know* it. Now philosophers also have used this sort of argument very largely. They have tried to classify exhaustively all the different kinds of ways in which we can know things; and have then concluded that, since certain things, which other philosophers have asserted or which they themselves formerly believed, are *not* known in any of these ways, therefore these things are not known at all.

Hence a large part of philosophy has, in fact, consisted in trying to classify completely all the different ways in which we can *know* things; or in trying to describe exactly particular ways of knowing them.

And this question—the question: How do we *know* anything at all? involves three different kinds of questions.

The first is of this sort. When you are asked: How do you know that? it may be meant to ask: What sort of a thing *is* your knowledge of it? What sort of a process goes on in your mind, when you *know* it? In what does this event, which you call a *knowing*, consist? This first question as to what sort of a thing knowledge is—as to what happens when we *know* anything—is a question which philosophy shares with psychology; but which many philosophers have tried to answer. They have tried to distinguish the different kinds of things, which happen in our minds, when we know different things; and to point out, what, if anything, is common to them all.

But there is, secondly, something else which may be meant; when it is asked what knowledge *is*. For we do not say that we *know* any proposition, for instance the proposition that matter exists, unless we mean to assert that this proposition is *true*: that it is *true* that matter exists. And hence there is included in the question what knowledge *is*, the question what is meant by saying that any proposition is *true*. This is a different question from the psychological question as to what happens in your mind, when you know anything; and this question as to what *truth* is has generally been said to be a question for *Logic*, in the widest sense of the term. And Logic, or at least parts of it, is reckoned as a department of philosophy.

And, finally, there is still another thing which may be meant, when it is asked: How do you know that? It may be meant, namely, what reason have you for believing it? or in other words, what *other* thing do you know, which *proves* this thing to be *true*? And philosophers have, in fact, been much occupied with this question also: the question what are the different ways in which a proposition can be proved to be true; what are all the different sorts of reasons which are good reasons for believing anything. This also is a question which is reckoned as belonging to the department of Logic.

There is, therefore, a huge branch of philosophy which is concerned with the different ways in which we know things; and many philosophers have devoted themselves almost exclusively to questions which fall under this head.

But finally, if we are to give a complete account of philosophy, we must mention one other class of questions. There is a department of philosophy which is called Ethics or ethical philosophy; and this department deals with a class of questions quite different from any which I have mentioned yet. We are all constantly in ordinary life asking such questions as: Would such and such a result be a good thing to bring about? or would it be a bad thing? Would such and such an action be a right action to perform or would it be a wrong one? And what ethical philosophy tries to do is to classify all the different sorts of things which *would* be good or bad, right or wrong, in such a way as to be able to say: Nothing would be good, unless it had certain characteristics, or one or other of certain characteristics; and similarly nothing would be bad, unless it had certain properties or one or other of certain properties: and similarly with the question, what sort of actions would be right, and what would be wrong.

And these ethical questions have a most important bearing upon our general description of the Universe in two ways.

In the first place, it is certainly one of the most important facts about the Universe that there are in it these distinctions of good and bad, right and wrong. And many people have thought that, from the fact that there are these distinctions, other inferences as to what is in the Universe can be drawn.

And in the second place, by combining the results of Ethics as to what *would* be good or bad, with the conclusions of Metaphysics as to what kinds of things there are in the Universe, we get a means of answering the question whether the Universe is, on the whole, good or bad, and how good or bad, compared with what it might be: a sort of question, which has in fact been much discussed by many philosophers.

To conclude, then, I think the above is a fair description of the sort of questions with which philosophers deal. And I shall try hereafter to say something about as many of the points which I have mentioned as I have space for. I propose to begin by considering some of the ways in which we know things. And first of all, I shall consider the question: How do we know of the existence of material objects, supposing that, as Common Sense supposes, we *do* know of their existence? And then, after considering *how* we know this, if we do know it, I shall go on to the question whether, in fact, we *do* know of their existence? trying to answer the principal objections of those philosophers, who have maintained that we certainly do not. In the course of this discussion we shall come upon a good many conclusions as to the sorts of ways in which we know things; and shall be in a better position to consider what *else* beside material objects we can know to exist.

I shall now, therefore, proceed to consider the most primitive sort of way in which we seem to have knowledge of material objects—that which we have by means of the senses—by seeing and hearing and feeling them.

Chapter II

SENSE - DATA

I have said that I shall now begin discussing the various ways in which we know of the existence of material objects—*supposing* that we do know of their existence. I do not want to assume, to begin with, that we *certainly do* know that they exist. I only want to consider what sort of a thing our knowledge of them is, *supposing* that it is really knowledge. I shall afterwards consider whether it *is* really knowledge.

And I said I should begin with the most primitive sort of way in which we commonly suppose that we have knowledge of them—namely, that kind of knowledge, which we should call knowledge *by means of the senses*—the knowledge which we have, for instance, by seeing and feeling, as when we feel an object over with our hands. This way of knowing material objects, by means of the senses, is, of course, by no means the only way in which we commonly suppose we know of their existence. For instance, each of us knows of the past existence of many material objects by means of memory; we remember the existence of objects which we are no longer perceiving by any of our senses. We know of others again, which we ourselves have never perceived by our senses and cannot therefore remember, by the testimony of other persons who *have* perceived them by their senses. And we know also, we suppose, by means of inference, of others which nobody has ever perceived by his senses: we know, for instance, in this way that there is another surface of the moon, different from that which is constantly turned to the earth. All these other ways of knowing material objects, I shall have presently to consider, and to contrast them with sense-perception. But all these other ways do seem, in a sense, to be *based* upon sense-perception, so that *it* is, in a sense, the most primitive way of knowing material objects: it seems, in fact, to be true, that if I had not known of *some* material objects by means of sense-perception, I could never possibly have known of any others in any of these other ways; and this seems to be true universally: no man could ever know of the existence of any material objects at all, unless he first knew of *some* by means of his senses. The evidence of the senses is, therefore, the evidence upon which all our other ways of knowing material objects seems to be based.

And what I want first to consider is what sort of a thing this evidence of the senses is; or in other words what it is that happens when (as we should say) we see, or feel, a material object, or perceive one by any other sense. And I propose to take as an instance, for the sake of simplicity, a single sense *only*—namely, the sense of sight: I shall use what happens when we *see*, as an illustration of what happens in sense-perception generally. All the general principles which I point out with regard to the sense of seeing, will, I think, be easily transferable, *mutatis mutandis*, to all the other senses by which we can be said to perceive material objects.

My first question is, then: What exactly is it that happens, when (as we should say) we *see* a material object? And I should explain, perhaps, to avoid misunderstanding, that the occurrence which I mean here to analyse is merely the *mental* occurrence—the act of consciousness—which we call *seeing*. I do not mean to say anything at all about the bodily processes which occur in the eye and the optic nerves and the brain. I have no doubt, myself, that these bodily processes *do* occur, when we see; and that physiologists really do *know* a great deal about them. But all that I shall mean by '*seeing*', and all that I wish to talk about, is the mental occurrence—the act of consciousness—which occurs (as is supposed) as a consequence of or accompaniment of these bodily processes. This mental occurrence, which I call 'seeing', is known to us in a much more simple and direct way, than are the complicated physiological processes which go on in our eyes and nerves and brains. A man cannot directly observe the minute processes which go on in his own eyes and nerves and brain when he sees; but all of us who are not blind can directly observe this mental occurrence, which we mean by seeing. And it is solely with *seeing*, in this sense—seeing, as an act of consciousness which we can all of us directly observe as happening in our own minds—that I am now concerned.

And I wish to illustrate what I have to say about seeing by a direct practical example; because, though I dare say many of you are perfectly familiar with the sort of points I wish to raise, it is, I think, very important for every one, in these subjects, to consider carefully single concrete instances, so that there may be no mistake as to exactly what it is that is being talked about. Such mistakes are, I think, very apt to happen, if one talks merely in generalities;

and moreover one is apt to overlook important points. I propose, therefore, to hold up an envelope in my hand, and to ask you all to look at it for a moment; and then to consider with me exactly what it is that happens, when you see it: *what* this occurrence, which we call the *seeing* of it, *is*.

I hold up this envelope, then: I look at it, and I hope you all will look at it. And now I put it down again. Now what has happened? We should certainly say (if you have looked at it) that we all *saw* that envelope, that we all saw *it*, *the same* envelope: *I* saw it, and you all saw it. We all saw *the same* object. And by the *it*, which we all saw, we mean an object, which, at any one of the moments when we were looking at it, occupied just *one* of the many places that constitute the whole of space. Even during the short time in which we were looking at it, it may have moved—occupied successively several different places; for the earth, we believe, is constantly going round on its axis, and carrying with it all the objects on its surface, so that, even while we looked at the envelope, it probably moved and changed its position in space, though we did not see it move. But at any *one* moment, we should say, this *it*, the envelope, which we say we all saw, was at some *one* definite place in space.

But now, what happened to each of us, when we saw that envelope? I will begin by describing *part* of what happened to me. I saw a patch[1] of a particular whitish colour, having a certain size, and a certain shape, a shape with rather sharp angles or corners and bounded by fairly straight lines. These things: this patch of a whitish colour, and its size and shape I did actually see. And I propose to call these things, the colour and size and shape, *sense-data*,[2] things *given* or presented by the senses—given, in this case, by my sense of sight. Many philosophers have called these things which I call sense-data, *sensations*. They would say, for instance, that that particular patch of colour was a sensation. But it seems to me that this term 'sensation' is liable to be misleading. We should certainly say that I *had* a sensation, when I saw that colour. But when we say that I *had* a sensation, what we mean is, I think, that I had the experience which consisted in my *seeing* the colour. That is to say,

[1] I am so extending the use of the word 'patch' that, *e.g.*, the very small black dot which I directly apprehend when I see a full-stop, or the small black line which I directly apprehend when I see a hyphen, are, each of them, in the sense in which I am using the word, a 'patch of colour'. (1952).

[2] I should now make, and have for many years made, a sharp distinction between what I have called the 'patch', on the one hand, and the colour, size and shape, *of* which it is, on the other; and should call, and have called, *only* the patch, *not* its colour, size or shape, a 'sense-datum'. (1952).

what we mean by a 'sensation' in this phrase, is my *seeing* of the colour, not the colour which I saw: this colour does not seem to be what I mean to say that I *had*, when I say I *had* a sensation of colour. It is very unnatural to say that I *had* the colour, that I *had* that particular whitish grey or that I *had* the patch which was of that colour. What I certainly did *have* is the experience which consisted in my seeing the colour and the patch. And when, therefore, we talk of *having* sensations, I think what we mean by 'sensations' is the experiences which consist in apprehending certain sense-data, *not* these sense-data themselves. I think, then, that the term 'sensation' is liable to be misleading, because it may be used in two different senses, which it is very important to distinguish from one another. It may be used *either* for the colour which I saw or for the experience which consisted in my seeing it. And it is, I think very important, for several reasons, to distinguish these two things. I will mention only two of these reasons. In the first place, it is, I think, quite conceivable (I do not say it is actually true) but *conceivable* that the patch of colour which I saw may have continued to exist after I saw it: whereas, of course, when I ceased to see it, *my seeing* of it ceased to exist. I will illustrate what I mean, by holding up the envelope again, and looking at it. I look at it, and I again see a *sense-datum*, a patch of a whitish colour. But now I immediately turn away my eyes, and I no longer see that sense-datum: my seeing of it has ceased to exist. But I am by no means sure that the sense-datum—that very same patch of whitish colour which I saw—is not still *existing* and still there. I do not say, for certain, that it is: I think very likely it is not. But I have a strong inclination to believe that it is. And it seems to me at least *conceivable* that it should be still existing, whereas my *seeing* of it certainly has ceased to exist. This is one reason for distinguishing between the sense-data which I see, and my seeing of them. And here is another. It seems to me *conceivable*—here again I do not say it is true but *conceivable*—that some sense-data—this whitish colour for instance—are in the place in which the material object—the envelope, is. It seems to me *conceivable* that this whitish colour is really on the surface of the material envelope. Whereas it does not seem to me that my *seeing* of it is in that place. My seeing of it is in another place—somewhere within my body. Here, then, are two reasons for distinguishing between the *sense-data* which I see, and my *seeing* of them. And it seems to me that both of these two very different things are often meant when people talk about 'sensations'. In fact, when you are reading any philosopher who is talking about sensations (or about sense-*impressions* or *ideas* either), you need to look very carefully to see which of the two he is talking about in any particular passage—whether of the sense-data themselves or of our apprehension of them: you will, I think, almost invariably find that he is talking now of the one and now of the other, and very often that he is assuming that what is true of the one must also be true of the other—an assumption which does not seem to be at all justified. I think, therefore, that the term 'sensation' is liable to be very misleading. And I shall, therefore, never use it. I shall always talk of *sense-data*, when what I mean is such things as this colour and size and shape or the patch which is *of* this colour and size and shape, which I actually see. And when I want to talk of my seeing of them, I shall expressly call this the seeing of sense-data; or, if I want a term which will apply equally to all the senses, I shall speak of the *direct apprehension of* sense-data. Thus when I see this whitish colour, I am *directly apprehending* this whitish colour: my seeing of it, as a mental act, an act of consciousness, just consists in my direct apprehension of it;—so too when I hear a sound, I directly apprehend the sound; when I feel a tooth-ache I directly apprehend the ache: and all these things—the whitish colour, the sound and the ache are *sense-data*.

To return, then, to what happened to us, when we all saw the same envelope. Part, at least, of what happened to me, I can now express by saying that I saw certain sense-data: I saw a whitish patch of colour, of a particular size and shape. And I have no doubt whatever that this is part, at least, of what happened to all of you. You also saw certain sense-data; and I expect also that the sense-data which you saw were more or less similar to those which I saw. You also saw a patch of colour which might be described as whitish, of a size not very different from the size of the patch which I saw, and of a shape similar at least in this that it had rather sharp corners and was bounded by fairly straight lines. But now, what I want to emphasize is this. Though we all did (as we should say) see *the same* envelope, no two of us, in all probability, saw exactly the *same sense-data*. Each of us, in all probability, saw, to begin with, a slightly different shade of colour. All these colours may have been whitish; but each was probably at least slightly different from all the rest, according to the way in which the light fell upon the paper, relatively to the different positions you are sitting in; and again according to differences in the strength of your eye-sight, or your distance from the paper. And so too, with regard to the size of the patch of colour which you saw: differences in the strength of your eyes and in your distance from the envelope probably made slight differences in the size of the patch of colour, which you saw. And so again with regard to the shape. Those of you on that side of the room will have seen a rhomboidal figure, while those in front of me will have seen a figure more nearly rectangular. Those on my left will have seen a figure more like this which you in front now see, and which you see is different from *this* which you then saw. And those in front of me will have seen a figure like that which you on the left now see, and which, you see, is different from *this*, which you saw before. Those directly in front of me, may, indeed, have all seen very nearly the same figure—perhaps, even, exactly the same. But we should not say we *knew* that any two did; whereas we should say we did *know* that we all saw the *same* envelope. That you did all see the same envelope, would, indeed, be accepted in ordinary life as a certainty of the strongest kind. Had you all seen me commit a murder, as clearly as you all saw this envelope, your evidence would be accepted by any jury as sufficient to hang me. Such evidence would be accepted in any court of law as quite conclusive; we should take such a responsibility as that of hanging a man, upon it. It would be accepted, that is, that you had all seen me, *the same man*, commit a murder; and not merely that you had all seen some man or other, possibly each of you a different man in each case, commit one. And yet, in this case, as in the case of the envelope, the sense-data which you had all seen, would have been different sense-data: you could not swear in a court of law that you had all seen exactly the *same sense-data*.

Now all this seems to me to shew very clearly, that, *if* we *did* all see the same envelope, the envelope which we saw was not *identical with* the sense-data which we saw: the envelope cannot be exactly the same thing as each of the sets of sense-data, which we each of us saw; for these were in all probability each of them slightly different from all the rest, and they cannot, therefore, *all* be exactly the same thing as the envelope.

But it might be said: Of course, when we say that we all saw the envelope, we do not mean that we all saw the *whole* of it. I, for instance, only saw *this* side of it, whereas all of you only saw *that* side. And generally, when we talk of seeing an object we only mean seeing some *part* of it. There is always more in any object which we see, than the *part* of it which we see.

And this, I think, is quite true. Whenever we talk roughly of seeing any object, it is true that, in another and stricter sense of the word *see*, we only see *a part of* it. And it might, therefore, be suggested that why we say we all saw this envelope, when we each, in fact, saw a different set of sense-data, is because each of these *sets of sense-data* is, in fact, a *part* of the envelope.

But it seems to me there is a great difficulty even in maintaining that the different sense-data we all saw are parts of the envelope. What do we mean by a *part* of a material object? We mean, I think, at least this. What we call a part of a material object must be something which occupies a part of the volume in space occupied by the whole object. For instance, this envelope occupies a certain volume in space: that is to say, it occupies a space which has breadth and thickness as well as length. And anything which is a *part* of the envelope at any moment, must be *in* some part of the volume of space occupied by the whole envelope at that moment: it must be somewhere within that volume, or at some point in the surfaces bounding that volume.

Are, then, any of the sense-data we saw *parts* of the envelope in this sense?

The sense-data I mentioned were these three—the colour—the whitish colour; the *size* of this colour; its *shape*.[1] And of these three it is only the colour, which could, in the sense defined, possibly be supposed to be a *part* of the envelope. The colour might be supposed to occupy a *part* of the volume occupied by the envelope—one of its bounding surfaces,[2] for instance. But the size and shape could hardly be said to *occupy* any part of this volume. What might be true of them is that the size I saw *is* the size of one surface of the envelope; and that the shape *is* the shape of this surface of the envelope. The side of the envelope which I say I saw certainly *has* some size and some shape; and the sense-data—the size and shape, which I saw as the size and shape of a patch of colour—might possibly *be* the size and shape of this side of the envelope.

Let us consider whether these things are so.

And, first, as to the colours. Can these possibly be parts of the envelope? What we supposed is that each of you probably saw a slightly different colour. And if we are to suppose that *all* those

[1] I had here forgotten that one of the sense-data mentioned was the *patch* which *has* that colour and shape and size—the *patch* which, I should now say, is the *only* 'sense-datum', having to do with the envelope, which I then saw. (1952).

[2] I should now say that any part of the *surface* of a volume is *not* a part of the volume, because it is not itself a volume. (1952).

colours are parts of the envelope, then we must suppose that *all* of them are in the same place. We must suppose that ever so many different colours all of them occupy the same surface—this surface of the envelope which you now see. And I think it is certainly difficult to suppose this, though not absolutely impossible. It is not absolutely impossible, I think, that all the different colours which you see are really all of them in the same place. But I myself find it difficult to believe that this is so; and you can understand, I think, why most philosophers should have declared it to be impossible. They have declared, chiefly, I think, on grounds like this, that none of the colours which any of us ever see are ever parts of material objects: they have declared that none of them are ever in any part of the places where material objects (if there are any material objects) are. This conclusion does, indeed, go beyond what the premisses justify, even if we accept the premiss that several different colours cannot all be in exactly the same place. For it remains possible that the colour, which some *one* of you sees, is really on the surface of the envelope; whereas the colours which all the rest of you see are *not* there. But if so, then we must say that though all of you are seeing the same side of the envelope, yet only one of you is seeing a sense-datum which is a part of that side: the sense-data seen by all the rest are *not* parts of the envelope. And this also, I think, is difficult to believe. It might be, indeed, that those of you who are seeing a colour, which is *not* a part of the envelope, might yet be seeing a size and a shape which really *is* the size and shape of one side of the envelope; and we will go on to consider whether *this* is so.

And, first, as to the size. I assumed that the sense-given sizes, which you see, are all of them probably slightly different from one another. And, if this be so, then certainly it seems to be absolutely impossible that they should *all* of them be the size of this side of the envelope. This side of the envelope can only really have *one* size; it cannot have several different sizes. But it may not seem quite clear, that you all do see different sizes; the differences between the different distances at which you are from the envelope are not so great, but what the patches of colour you all see might be, at least, of *much the same* size. So I will give a hypothetical instance to make my point clearer. Suppose this room were so large that I could carry the envelope two or three hundred yards away from you. The sense-given size which you would then see, when I was three hundred yards off, would certainly be appreciably smaller than what you see now. And yet you would still be seeing this same envelope. It seems quite impossible that these two very different sizes should both of them be *the* size of the envelope. So that here the *only* possibility is that the size which you see at some *one* definite distance or set of distances, should be the envelope's real size, *if* you ever see its real size at all. This may be so: it may be that some one of the sense-given sizes which we see is the envelope's real size. But it seems also possible that none of them are; and in any case we all see the envelope, just the same, *whether* we see its real size or not.

And now for the shape. Here again it seems quite impossible that *all* the shapes we see can be the envelope's real shape. This side of the envelope can have but *one* shape: it cannot be both rhomboidal, as is the shape which you on the left see, and also rectangular, as is the shape seen by those in front; the angles at its corners cannot be both right angles and also very far from right angles. Certainly, therefore, the sense-given shape which some of you see is *not* the shape of this side of the envelope. But here it may be said, it is plain enough that one of the sense-given shapes seen *is* its real shape. You may say: The shape seen by those in front *is* its real shape; the envelope *is* rectangular. And I quite admit that this is so: I think we do know, in fact, that the envelope really is *roughly* rectangular. But here I want to introduce a distinction. There are two different senses in which we may talk of *the* shape of anything. A rectangle of the size of this envelope, and a rectangle of the size of this blackboard, may both, in a sense, have exactly *the same* shape. They may have the same shape in the sense, that all the angles of both are right angles, and that the proportions between the sides of the one, and those between the sides of the other, are the same. They may, in fact, have the same shape, in the sense in which a big square always has the same shape as a small square, however big the one may be and however small the other. But there is another sense in which *the* shape of a big square is obviously not *the same* as that of a small square. We may mean by *the* shape of a big square the actual lines bounding it; and if we mean this, *the* shape of a big square cannot possibly be the *same* as *the* shape of a smaller one. The lines bounding the two cannot possibly be the *same* lines. And the same thing may be true, even when there is no difference in size between two shapes. Imagine *two* squares, of the same size, side by side. The lines bounding the one are *not* the same lines as those bounding the other: though each is both *of* the same shape and *of* the same size as the other. The difference between these two senses in which we may talk of *the* shape of anything, may be expressed by saying that the shape of the big square is the same *in quality*—qualitatively identical—with that of the small square, but is not *numerically* the same—not numerically identical: the shape of the big square is *numerically* different from that of the small, in the sense that they are *two* shapes, and not one only, of which we are talking, though both are the same in quality: both are *squares*, but the one is *one* square and the other is *another* square. There is, then, a difference between two different kinds of identity: qualitative identity and numerical identity; and we are all perfectly familiar with the difference between the two, though the names may sound strange. I shall in future use these names: qualitative identity and numerical identity. And now to return to the case of the envelope. Even supposing that the sense-given shape which you in front see is rectangular, and that the real shape of the envelope is also rectangular, and that both are rectangles of exactly the same shape; it still does not follow that the sense-given shape which you see is *the* shape of the envelope. The sense-given shape and the shape of the envelope, even if they are qualitatively the same, *must* still be *two* different shapes, *numerically* different, unless they are *of the same size*; just as *the* shape of a large square must be numerically different from *the* shape of a smaller one. And we saw before how difficult it was to be sure that any of the sizes which you saw were the *real* size of the envelope. And even if the sense-given size which some one of you sees *is* the real size of the envelope, it still does not follow that the sense-given *shape* which you see is numerically the same as the shape of the envelope. The two may be numerically different, just as in the case of two different squares, side by side, of the same shape and size, *the* shape of the one *is* not *the* shape of the other; they are two numerically different shapes. We may say, then, that if those of you who see rectangular shapes, do see rectangular shapes of different sizes, only one of these can possibly be *the* shape of the envelope: all the others may be *of* the same shape—the same in quality—but they cannot be *the* shape of the envelope. And even if some *one* of you does see a shape, which is of the same size as *the* shape of the envelope, as well as being of the same shape (and it is very doubtful whether any of you does) it would yet be by no means certain that this sense-given shape which you saw was *the* shape of the envelope. It might be a shape *numerically* different from *the* shape of the envelope, although exactly similar both in shape and size. And finally there is some reason to suppose that none of the sense-given shapes which any of you see are *exactly* the same, even in quality, as *the* shape of the envelope.

The envelope itself probably has a more or less irregular edge; there are probably ups and downs in the line bounding its side, which you at that distance cannot see.

Of the three kinds of sense-data,[1] then, which you all of you saw, when I held up the envelope, namely, the whitish colour, its size, and its shape, the following things seem to be true. First, as regards the colour, no one of you can be sure that the exact colour which you saw was really a part of the envelope—was really in any part of the space, which the real envelope (if there was a real envelope) occupied. Then as regards the size, no one of you can be sure that the size which you saw was the real size of the envelope. And finally as regards the shape, no one of you can be sure that the shape which you saw was really of exactly the same shape as that of the envelope; still less can you be sure that it *was the* shape of the envelope, that the bounding lines which composed it were numerically the same bounding lines as those which enclosed the envelope. And not only can none of you be sure of these things. As regards the sizes and shapes which you saw, it seems quite certain that some of you saw sizes and shapes which were *not* the real size and shape of the envelope; because it seems quite certain that some of you saw sizes and shapes different from those seen by others, and that these different sizes and shapes cannot possibly *all* be *the* size and shape of the envelope. And as regards the colours it seems fairly certain, that the colours which you saw cannot all have been *in* the envelope; since it seems fairly certain that you all saw slightly different colours, and it is difficult to believe, though not absolutely impossible, that all these different colours were really in the same place at the same time.

This seems to be the state of things with regard to these sense-data—the colour, the size and the shape. They seem, in a sense, to have had very little to do with the real envelope, if there *was* a real envelope. It seems very probable that *none* of the colours seen was really a part of the envelope; and that *none* of the sizes and shapes seen were the size or the shape of the real envelope.

But now I wish to mention one other sense-datum, of a kind that we all saw, which might be thought to have more to do with the real envelope. Besides the patch of colour and its shape and size, we did, in a sense, all see the *space* which this patch of colour occupied. The patch of colour seemed to occupy a certain area; and we can by abstraction distinguish this area from the patch of colour occupying

[1]The *patch* itself, which *has* that colour and shape and size, again forgotten! (1952).

it. This area was also a sense-datum. And in this area we can distinguish parts—this part, and this part, and this. And it might be thought with regard to parts, at least, of this area, that two things are true. Firstly, that part at least of the sense-given area which each of you saw, is really numerically identical with some part of that seen by all the rest. And secondly, that *this* part, which you all saw, is also a part of the area occupied by the real envelope. In other words, you might comfort yourselves by supposing, that even if the colour presented by your senses is *not* a part of the real envelope, and even if the shape and size presented by your senses are not the shape and size of the real envelope, yet at least there is presented by your senses a *part* of the *space occupied by* the real envelope. And against this supposition I confess I cannot find any argument, which seems to me very strong. We are all, I think, very strongly tempted to suppose that this is so. That, for instance, this space which I touch is really seen by all of you—this very same place—and that it also is part of the space which the real envelope occupies. The best argument I can think of against this supposition is the following; and I think it is enough to render the supposition doubtful. If we are to say that part of this sense-given area which I see is really numerically the same with part of those which you see, and that it is also numerically the same as part of the area occupied by the real envelope, then we must either again accept the hypothesis that all the different colours which we see as occupying the area are really in the same place and in the same place as the real envelope, or else we must say that the colours only *seem* to be in this sense-given area and are not really there. But there is the former objection to supposing that several different colours are all really in the same place. And as to the only remaining possibility, namely, that they only *seem* to be in this sense-given area; it may be objected that so far as the sense-given area is concerned, the colours we see *really do* occupy it—that they not only seem to be but *really are* there—that there can be no doubt about this. If we are talking of the area really presented by the senses as occupied by the colours, *this* area, it may be said, undoubtedly *is* occupied by the colours: it *is* nothing but the space over which the colour is spread. So that, if the area, which I see, really is numerically the same as those which you see, then it will follow that all the different colours we see really are in the same place. This argument, I say, does not seem to me to be absolutely conclusive. It does seem to me possible that the colour I see only *seems* to be in the sense-given area, which I see. But it is, I think, sufficient to suggest a doubt whether any part of this sense-given area seen by me really is numerically the same as any part of any of those seen by you.

Well now: Chiefly, I think, for reasons of the sort which I have given you, an overwhelming majority of philosophers have adopted the following views. Reasons of the sort which I have given are not the only ones which have been alleged as reasons for holding these views, but they are, I think, the ones which have really had most influence in getting them adopted, and they are, it seems to me, by far the strongest reasons for adopting them. However that may be, whatever the reasons, an overwhelming majority of philosophers have, I think, adopted the following views; and I wish you to realise these views as clearly as possible.

They have held with regard to absolutely *all* the sense-data[1] and every part of any sense-datum, which we ever apprehend by any of our senses, the following things.

They have held (1) that absolutely no part of the sense-data, which I ever apprehend, exists at all except at the moment when I am apprehending it. They have held, that is to say, that except at the moment when I am apprehending it, there simply *is not* in the Universe any particular sense-datum which I ever apprehend. If, for instance, I look at this envelope again and now turn away my eyes for a moment, then while I saw that particular patch of whitish colour, there *was* that particular patch of colour in the Universe: there certainly *was*, for I saw it. But now that I no longer see it, that particular patch of colour has ceased to exist. It no longer *is* in the Universe, any more than my seeing of it is. They are both of them, both the colour and my seeing of it, things which *were*, but which are no longer: both of them equally and in the same sense have completely ceased to be. These philosophers would not deny, indeed, that there *may* still be in the Universe a patch of colour *exactly like* that which I saw. For instance, some one else might at this moment be seeing a patch of colour exactly like it. But this other patch of colour, though exactly like, they would say, is certainly not the same: they may be exactly the same in quality, but they are *not* numerically the same. *The* patch of colour which I saw cannot be now existing even though another exactly like it may be. And they would say this with regard to absolutely all the sense-data, which any of us ever apprehends. Each of them only *is*, so long as the person apprehending

[1]These three propositions about what philosophers have held are only true if the word 'sense-datum' be understood in the sense explained in footnote 2 on p. 30, *i.e.* in such a sense that 'patches' are sense-data, but their colour, size and shape, are not. (1952).

it *is* apprehending it. And they would say this not only with regard to sense-data like colours, sounds, hardness, smoothness, heat, cold, aches, which seem to us to occupy space—to be localised. They would say it also with regard to the sense-given spaces which these things seem to occupy. For instance, the sense-given area, occupied by this patch of colour: I see it now, and while I see it, it *is*: that particular area is one among the contents of the Universe. But now that I turn my head away, *it*, that particular area I saw, has entirely ceased to exist. With my seeing of it, *it* also has ceased to be. I may indeed be still seeing an area exactly like it: this area for instance, which I now see, seems to be exactly like, and only distinguishable by the fact that it is occupied by a different colour. But these two areas, they would say, though perhaps exactly like, are not the *same*. They are no more the *same* than is this part of the total area which I now see the same as *that* part. *The* particular sense-given area which I just now saw has entirely ceased to be.

This, then, is one view, which an overwhelming majority of philosophers have held with regard to sense-data. They have held that every sense-datum, of *every* kind, and every part of every sense-datum, is something which only *is* or *exists*, so long as the person apprehending it is apprehending it.

(2) And they have held too this second view. Namely, that no two of us ever apprehend exactly the same sense-datum. They would allow that we might, perhaps, apprehend sense-data exactly *alike*; but they would say that even though exactly alike—the same in quality—they cannot ever be *numerically* the same. That this is so with regard to sense-data which exist at different times, would, indeed, follow from the first view. If this particular patch of colour which I see now, has *now*, when I turn away my head, entirely ceased to be, it follows that nobody can be seeing it now. But it is worth while to emphasize that this is the view actually held by most philosophers. It is held, for instance, that if somebody were to come and look at this envelope, immediately after I had looked at it, standing at exactly the same distance from it and in the same direction, having exactly the same power of eye-sight, and the light also not having changed at all, so that he saw a patch of colour exactly similar to that which I had just seen; nevertheless the patch of colour which he saw would not be *the same* as that which I had just seen. It would be numerically different from it, in the same sense, in which, supposing you see two spots of colour, of exactly the same size and shape side by side, the one spot, though exactly like the other, is yet *not* the

same, is numerically different from it. And it is held too, that no two persons can see the same sense-datum, or any part of the same sense-datum, even *at the same time*: a point which does not follow from the last view. For though it might be true that all the sense-data, which any of you now sees in looking at this envelope ceased to exist the moment you ceased to see it; yet it might be true that, *while* you were seeing and while, therefore, it exists, some other of you might be seeing at least a part of one of them too. But this is what is denied by this second view. It is denied that any two of you are at this moment seeing, even in part, the same sense-data. It is asserted that every part of every sense-datum which any one of you sees now, is numerically different from any part of any sense-datum seen by any other of you.

And the third view, which is held by an overwhelming majority of philosophers about sense-data is this.

They hold, namely (3) that none of the sense-data apprehended by any one person can ever be situated either in the same place with, or at any distance in any direction from, those apprehended by any other person. In other words, they hold that any sense-datum apprehended by me cannot possibly be in the *same place* as any sense-datum apprehended by any one of you: and that this is true of any pair of persons you like to take. That is to say, this patch of colour seen by me is neither in the same place with, nor at any distance in any direction from, any that is seen by any of you: the two simply have no spatial relations of any kind to one another. With regard to the different sense-data seen by me at any one moment, they would indeed admit that these have, in a sense, spatial relations *to one another*. This corner of the patch of colour which I see really is at a certain distance, in a certain direction, from this corner; and at another distance in another direction from this other corner. But they would say that all the different sense-data within my field of vision at any one time have distance and direction from one another only within a *private space of my own*. That is to say, no point in this private space of mine is either identical with, nor at any distance from, any point within the field of vision of any other person. The sense-given field of vision of each of us, at any moment, constitutes a private space of that person's own;—no two points in any two of these spaces, can be related to one another in any of the ways in which two points in any *one* of them are related.

These three views have, I think, been held by an overwhelming majority of philosophers. They have held, that is (1) that absolutely every sense-datum that any person ever directly apprehends exists only so long as he apprehends it, (2) that no sense-datum which any one person directly apprehends ever is directly apprehended by any other person, and (3) that no sense-datum that is directly apprehended by one person can be in *the same space with* any sense-datum apprehended by any other person—that no sense-datum that is seen or heard or felt by me can possibly be either in the same place with or at any distance from any that is seen or heard or felt by any one else. These three things are, I think, the chief things that are meant, when it is said that all sense-data exist only *in the mind of* the person who apprehends them; and it is certainly the common view in philosophy that all sense-data do only exist *in our minds*. I do not think myself that this is a good way of expressing what is meant. Even if all these three things are true of all the sense-data which I ever directly apprehend; it does not seem to me to follow that they exist only in my mind, or indeed are *in* my mind in any sense at all except that they are apprehended by me. They are, so far as I can see, not in my mind in the sense in which my apprehension of them is in my mind: for instance, this whitish colour, even if it does only exist while I see it, and cannot be seen by any one else, does not seem to me to be *in* my mind in the sense in which my seeing of it is *in my mind*. My seeing of it is, it seems to me, related to my mind in a way in which this which I see is not related to it: and I should prefer to confine the phrase '*in* the mind' to those things which are related to my mind, in the way in which my seeing of this colour, and my other acts of consciousness are related to it. But whether they could be properly said to be in my mind or not, certainly all the sense-data, which I ever directly apprehend, are, if these three things are true of them, *dependent* upon my mind in a most intimate sense. If it is really true of all of them that they exist only while I am conscious of them, that nobody else ever is directly conscious of them, and that they are situated only in a private space of my own, which also exists only while I am conscious of it, and of which no one else is ever directly conscious—then certainly nothing could well be more thoroughly dependent on my mind than they are. Most philosophers have, I think, certainly held that all sense-data are dependent on our minds in this sense. This has been held both by philosophers who believe that there are material objects and that we know of their existence, and by those who believe that there are no such things as material objects, or, that, if there are, we do not know it. It has, in fact, an overwhelming weight of authority in its favour. And I am going to call it for the moment *the accepted view.*

And as regards the question whether this accepted view is true or not, I confess I cannot make up my mind. I think it may very likely be true. But I have never seen any arguments in its favour which seem to me to be absolutely conclusive. The strongest arguments in its favour, as I said, seem to me to be arguments of the sort which I have given you. This one, for instance : That if we are to say that any portion of the sense-given spaces apprehended by each of us at the same time, really is numerically the same portion of space, then we must hold *either* that the very same portion of space may be occupied at the same time by several different colours *or* that it only really is occupied by the colour which *one* of us sees and only *seems* to be so by those which the rest of us see *or* that it only *seems* to be and is not really occupied by any of the colours which any of us see. There do seem to me objections to saying any of these three things; but, on the other hand, the objection to none of them seems to me perfectly conclusive: it seems to me *possible* that any one of them *might* be the truth. One argument which has been urged by some philosophers as being conclusive seems to me to have absolutely no weight at all. It has been urged, namely, that we can see directly, without the need of any argument, if we will but think of it, that all sense-data are a sort of thing which can only exist while the person perceiving them is perceiving them: it is urged that this is a self-evident truth like the truth that $2+2=4$. This argument seems to me to have no weight at all. It seems to me that it is simply false that what it says is self-evident. I can perfectly well conceive that the very same sense-data, which I see at one time, should exist even when I am not seeing them: and I cannot, by merely considering the possibility, determine whether it is true or not. And moreover, I think, that the apparent strength of this argument has been largely due to the confusion I spoke of above—the confusion between the sense-data which I see and my seeing of them. Many philosophers have, as I said, not only called both of these two very different things 'sensations', but have treated them as if they were the same thing. And, of course, when I cease to see a given sense-datum, I do cease to see it: my seeing of it certainly does cease to exist. They have, then, argued, treating the sense-datum as if it were the same thing as my seeing of it, that the sense-datum ceases to exist too. But this is surely mere confusion. We are, then, I think, if we are to find conclusive arguments in favour of this accepted view, thrown back upon such questions as whether many different colours can all occupy the same space; and whether, when the space we are talking of is the sense-given space presented with the colours, it can be true that these colours only *seem* to occupy this sense-given space, and do not *really* occupy it. And no arguments of this kind seem to me to be perfectly conclusive, though they do seem to me to have weight. And on the other side, in favour of the contrary view, there seems to me the fact that we all have a very strong tendency to believe it. I find it very difficult not to believe that when I look at this, and turn away my head, the colour which I just saw is not still existing; that the space in which I saw it is not still existing too; and that the colour is not still *in* that space. And so too, I find it very difficult to believe that this space, which I see—this very same portion of space—is not also seen by all of you. I point at it; and what I point at seems to be a part of the sense-given space which I see; and I cannot believe that by pointing at it I do not make plain to you also, which portion of space I am pointing at. We all constantly assume that pointing at a thing is of some use; that if I point at a thing, that serves to show you *which* thing I am talking about; that you will see the same thing, which I see, and will thus know what it is that I see. And it certainly seems as if *the* thing at which I am pointing now is part of the sense-given space which I see; and that, therefore, if you see *what* I am pointing at, some portion of the sense-given space which each of us sees *must* be the same. But on the other hand, I can imagine that I am mistaken about this. I can imagine that what I am sure that you see is *not* a part of my *sense-given* space; and that what you see, when you see the place I am pointing at, is *not* a part of your sense-given space either: and that the supposition that some portion of our sense-given spaces must be identical, arises from our confusion of sense-given space with the real space, which we do really all of us see—but see in another sense. I can, therefore, not find any arguments, either, which seem to me conclusive *against* the accepted view: the view that all the sense-data I see, including every portion of my sense-given space, are private sense-data of my own, which exist only while I directly apprehend them, and no part of which can be directly apprehended by any one of you. And what I wish to do in the rest of this lecture is this. I wish for the moment to *suppose* that this accepted view is true; to *suppose* that absolutely all the sense-data of each of us are private to that person, in the sense I have explained; and then to consider what, supposing this view is true, can be the nature of our knowledge of material objects by means of the senses, if we have such knowledge at all.

I return, then, to my original question: What happens, when we all see this envelope?

I began, you may remember, by saying that a *part* of what happened to me was that I *saw* certain sense-data—a particular whitish patch of colour, of a certain size and shape, and also the area which this patch of colour did, or seemed to, occupy. This, the seeing of certain sense-data, was also a part *at least* of what happened to you. But now, having for the moment accepted the philosophical view that all the sense-data seen by any one of us are seen by *that* person alone, we have got this far further: namely, that, *if* we do in fact all see the same envelope, this seeing of the envelope cannot possibly consist *merely* in our seeing of those sense-data; this seeing of sense-data, which I declared at first to be *at least* a part of what happens when we see the envelope, must, we now find, be a *mere part* of what happens; it cannot possibly be the whole, if we all do really see the *same* envelope: for we *do not*, according to the accepted philosophical view, see the same sense-data; the sense-data which we see are not, even as regards the least part, the same. It remains, then, to enquire, what else *beside* the seeing of sense-data, can have happened when we saw the envelope. But before we go on to consider this I want to insist upon one point, with regard to this first part of what happened—namely this, which I have called the seeing of certain sense-data. I said before, that, if I wanted to use a term which would apply not only to the sense of sight but to any other sense, I should use the term 'direct apprehension' of sense-data. And the point I wish now to insist on is *what* exactly this way of perceiving[1] things, which I call *direct apprehension*, is. It is certainly one of the most important ways we have of perceiving things. And I want, in future, to be able to refer to it by the name 'direct apprehension' and therefore I want you to realise as clearly as possible what sort of a thing *this* way of perceiving which I call 'direct apprehension' is. It is, as I said, that which happens when you actually see any colour, when you actually hear any sound, when you actually feel the so-called 'sensation' of heat, as when you put your hand close to a fire; when you actually smell a smell; when you feel the so-called sensation of hardness, in pressing against a table; or when you feel the pain of a toothache, etc., etc. In all these cases you *directly apprehend* the sense-datum in question—the particular colour, or sound, or smell; or those peculiar sense-data, which we

[1]There is another, very different, use of 'perceive', in which we are said to perceive *that* so and so is the case, *i.e.* to perceive, *not* a 'thing', but a fact or truth (see below, p. 77, footnote). I can be said both to see a man, and also to see *that, e.g.*, he has a beard.

are more apt to call 'sensations', such as that peculiar something we call 'heat', and which we directly apprehend when we put our hands close to a fire, and those peculiar somethings which we call hardness or smoothness, or the pain of a toothache. And in all these cases, so far as I can see, what I mean by 'direct apprehension', namely, the act of consciousness, is exactly the same in quality: that is to say, the actual seeing of a colour, considered as an act of consciousness, differs in no respect at all from the actual hearing of a sound, or the actual smelling of a smell. They differ only in respect of the fact, that whereas the one is the direct apprehension of *one* kind of sense-datum, the other is the direct apprehension of *another* kind: the one, for instance, of a colour, the other of a sound. And *what* they are is perhaps best realised by considering the difference between what is happening when you *are* directly apprehending a given sense-datum and what happens when you cease to apprehend it. For instance, you look at this envelope, and you actually see a particular colour: you directly apprehend that particular colour. But, then, if you turn away your eyes, you no longer directly apprehend it: you no longer actually see the colour which you saw. But you *may* still be thinking of it—thinking of just that colour which you saw a moment ago: you may, therefore, in a sense still be conscious of it, though you are no longer directly apprehending it. Here, therefore, is one way of having before the mind, which is *not* direct apprehension: the way which we call 'thinking of' or remembering. That is to say, you may still be thinking of *the* colour which you saw, and therefore having it before your mind in a sense, although you are no longer directly apprehending it. No doubt, when you think of it, you are still directly apprehending *something*: you may, for instance, be directly apprehending an image of it—one of those faint copies of sense-data, which are called images. But you are no longer directly apprehending *the* coloured patch which you saw; the image which you are directly apprehending, though it may be like, is not *the same*; and the relation which you now have to the image is obviously different from that which you have *now* to the sense-datum, which you *saw* but do *not* now see; while this relation which you *now* have to the image, is *the same* as that which you *had* to the sense-datum, just now when you actually saw it. You directly apprehend the image *now* in exactly the same sense as you just now directly apprehended the sense-datum, *of* which it is an image: but you are no longer now directly apprehending *the* sense-datum which you were directly apprehending a moment ago.

I hope, then, you understand what I mean by 'direct apprehension.' And one reason I have insisted on the point is this. I think many philosophers have assumed more or less unconsciously that *this* way of having things before the mind, which I call 'direct apprehension' is the *only* way in which we ever have anything before our minds. They have assumed, that is to say, that the only thing which ever happens, in our minds, whenever we have anything before our minds, merely consists in the fact that we directly apprehend certain sense-data or certain images, or both at the same time. And there is, I think, obviously a certain excuse for this assumption. For this kind of having before the mind—the direct apprehension of sense-data and images—is certainly far easier to observe and to understand the exact nature of than any other. If you try to observe what is going on in your mind at any moment, it is easy to see that you are directly apprehending certain sense-data, or certain images, or both; but it is not by any means easy to see that anything else is happening in your mind at all. At least that is what I find. And even if you are convinced, as you may I think be convinced, that something else is *in fact* happening, it is very difficult to see exactly what the nature of this something else is: far more difficult than to see what the direct apprehension of sense-data or of images is.

It is, therefore, I think, very natural to suppose that all knowledge consists *merely* in the direct apprehension of sense-data and images; and many philosophers have, I think, constantly assumed this. But now observe what results if we combine this view with that view with regard to sense-data which I have called the accepted view—a view which is, of course extended to all images, and which does, in fact, much more obviously apply to images than to sense-data. It then follows that no one does in fact ever have before his mind anything at all except certain sense-data and images, which are quite private to himself, and which can never be before anyone else's mind. And the question then arises how any one of us can possibly know that there *is* anything else at all in the Universe except his own private sense-data and images; how he can possibly know, for instance, that there are in the Universe, either the minds of other people, or material objects, or the sense-data and images of other people. And obviously, on these hypotheses, these are questions which must be answered in the negative. On these hypotheses, nobody can possibly know of the existence of anything at all except his own sense-data and images. But, then, on the same hypotheses, nobody can even think that there *might* be anything else: for to think that there might possibly be something other than your own sense-data and images, certainly does not merely consist in directly apprehending a certain number of sense-data or images or both.

There must, therefore, be some other ways of knowing of the existence of things besides the mere direct apprehension of sense-data and images. And, in fact, it seems to me quite certain that sense-data and images are not the only kinds of things which we directly apprehend. For instance, suppose I look at this envelope again, and directly apprehend the whitish colour; it seems to me that if I try to observe what is happening in my mind, I can *also* directly apprehend not only the whitish colour but *also* my own direct apprehension of it: that is to say, that just as my seeing of the colour consists in my direct apprehension of *it*, the colour, so, if I happen to observe *my seeing* of it, this observation consists in the direct apprehension of my seeing of it—of something, that is to say, which is neither a sense-datum, nor an image, but the direct apprehension of a sense-datum. I think, therefore, we certainly sometimes directly apprehend not only sense-data and images, but also our own acts of consciousness: and we may, I think, directly apprehend other things also.

But there are, I think, certainly other ways of knowing, which do not merely consist in the direct apprehension of anything. And if we do ever know of the existence of material objects by means of our senses, our knowledge of their existence, on the accepted view with regard to sense-data, must, I think, partly consist in one of these other ways of knowing. But it is very difficult to analyse exactly what these other ways of knowing are; and that, I think, is one chief reason why many philosophers have supposed that we do not know of their existence at all.

In order to shew quite clearly that there are ways of knowledge other than direct apprehension, and also, in at least one instance, as clearly as I can what sort of a thing such knowledge is, I will return to an instance which I mentioned just above, the instance of memory.

I look at the envelope again and I see the whitish colour. I turn my head away, and I no longer see it. But I remember that *I did see it a moment ago*. I *know* that I did see it. There is nothing that I know more certainly than this. Moreover I know that that whitish colour *was*: that there was such a thing in the Universe. I know, therefore, *now* of the past existence of that whitish colour; and yet I am certainly not directly apprehending it *now*. I may, indeed, possibly be apprehending now an image more or less like it. And, according to the view that all knowledge consists merely in the direct apprehension of sense-data and images, it is very natural to suppose that my memory of what I just now saw consists merely in my direct apprehension of an image of it now. But if you consider a moment, I think you can easily see that this cannot possibly be the case. If it were the case, I could not possibly know that the image which I now see was at all different from the colour which I saw a moment ago. And yet this is just what we all constantly do know whenever we remember anything. We know that there *was* something in the past different, in some respects, from anything which we are directly apprehending now. Memory, in fact, always carries with it the possibility of our knowing this: that there *was* something which we are not now directly apprehending and different in some respects from anything which we are now directly apprehending.

And it seems to me that, on the view we have accepted with regard to sense-data, our knowledge of the existence of material objects by means of the senses must be analogous to memory at least in this: it must consist in our knowing that there *exists something* different from any sense-datum or image which we are directly apprehending at the moment. This would seem to be the minimum which we must know, if we are to know of the existence of any material object by means of the senses. We must know, when we directly apprehend certain sense-data, that there exists *also* something *other* than these sense-data—something which we do not directly apprehend. And there seems no sort of reason why we should not know at least this, once we have dismissed the prejudice that we cannot know of the existence of anything *except* what we directly apprehend. Of course, *merely* to know this, would be to know very little. If the *something*, whose existence we know of really is, *in fact*, a material object, we might be said to know of the existence of a material object, even if we did not know *that it was* a material object. But, we must know much more than this, if we are to know *also that* this something *is* a material object. And moreover, if we are to know that we all saw *the same* envelope, we must know that the something, of whose existence we each of us know, is *the same something*. But there seems no reason again why we *should not know* many things of this kind. In the case of memory, we certainly do know, with the utmost certainty, a very great many things, about the *something* which we remember, beyond the mere fact that it *was* and was different from anything which we are now directly apprehending.

The *seeing* of a material object—or the perceiving one by any other sense—would therefore, on this view, be something quite different from the *seeing* of sense-data. The seeing of sense-data consists in directly apprehending them. But the seeing of a material object does *not* consist in directly apprehending *it*. It consists, *partly* in directly apprehending certain sense-data, but partly also in *knowing, besides and at the same time*, that there exists *something* other than these sense-data. And so, too, if we ever *see* that a material object is round or square, or in a particular position in space; this also would consist, *not* in directly apprehending these things, but in knowing, when we do directly apprehend certain sense-data, certain things about something quite other than these sense-data.

I will now try, first of all, to describe more clearly exactly what sort of a thing I take this perception of material objects to be. And will then go on to consider what sort of reasons we may have for supposing that this sort of perception really is *knowledge*; for supposing, that is, that there really does exist something *other* than the sense-data, which we directly apprehend, and that this something has certain properties and is a material object.

Chapter III
PROPOSITIONS

I have tried to begin describing what sense-perception *is*; or, in other words, what it is that happens in our minds, when (as we should say) we get knowledge of the existence of a material object by means of our senses. Events undoubtedly do happen in our minds which we should describe in this way, *i.e.*, as the getting knowledge of the existence of a material object by means of our senses. When, for instance, I hold up this envelope and you all look at it: we should say that we all *saw it*, the same object, the same envelope; that, by seeing it, we got knowledge of its existence; and that this object, the envelope which we all see, and know to exist, is a material object. I tried, then, to begin describing what sort of an event this was which happened in the mind of each of us; *without* assuming either that we did, in fact, all know of the existence of the same object, when it happened, *or* that, if we did, the object was a material one. I have only tried to describe what sort of a thing this event, which we *call* knowledge of the existence of a material object by means of the senses, certainly *is*, without deciding whether it really deserves to be called what we do call it—namely, knowledge of the existence of a material object.

And I pointed out, first of all, that every such event *partly* consists in a peculiar way of having before our minds certain kinds of things which I called *sense-data*—for instance, a visible patch of colour, a visible area, which is or seems to be occupied by the patch of colour, and a visible size and shape which are the size and shape of the visible patch and of its area: these were all *sense-data*.[1] And the peculiar way in which we had these sense-data before our minds I called 'direct apprehension'. Every act of sense-perception consists then, partly at least, in the direct apprehension of certain sense-data. And this part of what happens in sense-perception is, I think, far the easiest to notice, when you try to discover what happens by observing your own mind. About the existence of this kind of thing, which I called the direct apprehension of sense-data there seems to be no

[1]See footnote 2, p. 30.

doubt at all, nor about what sort of a thing it is. You can very easily observe *it*: but the difficulty is to discover that anything else happens *at all*, and, if so, what the exact nature of this something else is.

But now, with regard to this part of what happens—this direct apprehension of sense-data—I said that an overwhelming, majority of philosophers had held certain views. They have held, namely (1) that no part of the sense-data which I ever directly apprehend *is* or exists at all, except at the moment when I am directly apprehending it; (2) that no part of the sense-data which I ever directly apprehend, is ever directly apprehended by any one else; and (3) that no part of the sense-data which I ever directly apprehend is in the *same space* with any part of those which are directly apprehended by any one else. And by saying that they are not in the *same space*, I meant, as always, that they are *neither* in the same place *nor* at any distance in any direction from one another; or, if we are talking of the sense-given spaces themselves, we must say, to be accurate, that no part of *my* sense-given space *is the same part of space* as any part of the sense-given space of any one else, nor at any distance in any direction from any such part. These three views, taken together, I spoke of as *the* accepted view with regard to sense-data, though of course they are not accepted quite by everybody. They are, I said, often expressed by saying that all sense-data exist only *in the mind* of the person apprehending them; or by saying that sense-data are not *external* objects: and I think there is no great harm in expressing them in this way, although when such expressions are used, something else may be meant as well, which is, I think, more doubtful than are these three views. We may say, then, that it is and has long been the accepted view that all sense-data exist only in the mind of the person who directly apprehends them, or are *not* external objects —meaning by these expressions merely the three views, which I have tried to formulate more exactly above. And I wished to call your attention to this accepted view, and to make you grasp it as clearly as possible for two reasons. Firstly, because it seems to me that many of the strangest views of philosophers, those which depart most widely from Common Sense, are founded, in the first instance, upon this view. Had not this view been thought of, no philosopher would ever have thought of denying the existence of matter or of inventing all sorts of other things to take its place. And secondly, I wish to call your attention to it because I think that so far as philosophical views are founded upon this view, they are not badly founded. In other words, I think there really are very strong arguments in favour of this view, arguments of a sort that I tried to give you. And though these arguments do not seem to me absolutely conclusive, yet they are so strong that I think none of us can really be sure that this accepted view with regard to sense-data is not a correct one: though if any of you can find, either for or against it, any more conclusive arguments than I can find, I should be only too glad to hear them. The question whether this accepted view about sense-data is true or not, may, I think, fairly be called one of the main problems of philosophy.

But now, in speaking of this accepted view, I ought perhaps to have explained that some philosophers, whom I meant to reckon as holding it, would not perhaps assert it quite in the unqualified form which I have given it. And I wish now to mention these possible qualifications, both for the sake of accuracy and because these qualifications can only serve, I think, to bring out more clearly the general nature of the view and the immenseness of the range of facts to which it is supposed to apply. The first qualification is this. There are some philosophers who hold that sense-data exist in my mind, not only when I directly apprehend them, but also very often when I *do not* directly apprehend them: and so too, of course, in the minds of all of us. And these philosophers might, I think, perhaps hold (I do not know whether they would) that the very same sense-datum which I directly apprehend at one moment, may go on existing *in my mind* even when I cease to apprehend it, and that this may happen very often indeed. This, then, if it were held, would be to hold that there were exceptions to the first of my three rules, and even possibly *many* exceptions to it: it would involve holding that some sense-data, which I directly apprehend, may go on existing when I do not directly apprehend them. But the philosophers I am thinking of would certainly hold that this, if it happens at all, can only happen *in my mind*: no sense-datum, which I ever apprehend, can exist, *after* I cease to apprehend it, *except in my mind*. And they would hold, too, that of these sense-data, which exist in my mind, when I do not directly apprehend them, *both* the other two rules are just as true as of those sense-data which I do directly apprehend: *both* that nobody else can directly apprehend them, *and* that they cannot be in the same space with the sense-data in anybody else's mind. So that I think you can see that this qualification, though, strictly speaking, it does admit *many* exceptions to my first rule, is yet not very important for our present purpose. And the second qualification is this: Some philosophers would, I think, admit that in a few abnormal cases, there may be two or more different minds—two or more different *persons*—in or attached to *the same living human body*, and that in such cases these different persons *may* be able to apprehend directly *the same* sense-data; and they would perhaps say also, that this, which may happen abnormally to human minds in living human bodies, may happen constantly in the case of *other spirits* in the Universe. And this, of course, if it were held, would involve exceptions, and perhaps many exceptions, to both my second and third rule. But this qualification also is, I think, plainly unimportant for our present purpose. For these philosophers *would*, I think, admit that in the case of *our* minds, the minds of each of *us*, normal human minds, attached, each of them, to a different living human body, *no* exceptions to these two rules ever occur.

With these qualifications, I think it is fair to say that my three rules with regard to sense-data are accepted by the vast majority of philosophers; and these qualifications only, I think, serve to make it plainer what an enormous range of facts the three rules are supposed to apply to. They are supposed to apply to all the sense-data directly apprehended by all the human minds, attached like ours, each of them, to a different living human body, with the possible exception that sense-data, directly apprehended at one moment by *one* mind, may exist in *that* mind even when not directly apprehended by it.

But now, *if* this accepted view is true, it follows, I said, that if we do ever perceive a material object or any part of one, and if we do all of us now perceive the same material object—if, for instance, we do all see this same envelope—this event cannot *merely* consist in the fact that we directly apprehend certain sense-data: it must consist, in part, of something else too. For, according to the accepted view, no part of the sense-data which any one of us directly apprehends can be either a part of a material object nor a part of the space occupied by a material object, nor can any part of the sense-data directly apprehended by any one of us be the same as any part of those directly apprehended by any other of us. If, therefore, I do ever perceive a material object, then, on the accepted view, something else must happen besides the fact that I directly apprehend certain sense-data. And I tried, at the end of my last lecture, to give a brief account of what this something else might be. But I said I should try to explain more fully at the beginning of this lecture, *what* this something else might be; and this is what I shall now try to do. Only I am afraid that this explanation will take me much longer than

I thought it would. Instead of occupying only the beginning of this lecture, it will ocupy the *whole* of this lecture; and I shall not be able to finish what I have to say about it even in this lecture : I shall have to leave over a part of the subject until next time. The fact is I want to make as clear as possible exactly what sort of a thing the knowing of material objects by means of the senses can be, if it does *not* merely consist in the direct apprehension of sense-data. And I think the way of doing this, which will in the end prove shortest and clearest, is to try and give an account of *all* the different ways we have of knowing things: trying to distinguish different sorts of things which might be said to be ways of knowing from one another, and giving them separate names. And I think I can best do this by first calling your attention to an entirely new class of facts—a class of facts which I have not yet mentioned at all.

The fact is that absolutely all the contents of the Universe, absolutely everything that *is* at all, may be divided into two classes—namely into *propositions*, on the one hand, and into things which are not propositions on the other hand. There certainly are in the Universe such things as propositions: the sort of thing that I mean by a proposition is certainly one of the things that *is*: and no less certainly there are in the Universe some things which are *not* propositions: and also quite certainly absolutely everything in the Universe either is a proposition or is *not*, if we confine the word 'proposition' to some one, quite definite, sense: for nothing whatever can both have a quite definite property and also *not* have that very same property. This classification, therefore, of all the things in the Universe into those which are and those which are not propositions, is certainly correct and exhaustive. But it may seem, at first sight, as if it were a very unequal classification : as if the number of things in the Universe, which are *not* propositions, was very much greater than that of those which are. Even this, as we shall presently see, may be doubted. And, whether this be so or not, the classification is, I think, by no means unequal, if, instead of considering all that *is* in the Universe, we consider all those things in the Universe which we *know*. For, however it may be with the Universe itself, it is, I think, certain that a very large and important part of *our knowledge* of the Universe consists in the knowledge with regard to propositions that they are true.

Now the new class of facts which I want to call your attention to, are certain facts about propositions and about our knowledge of them.

And, first of all, I want to make it as plain as I can exactly what I mean by a proposition. The sort of thing, which I mean by a proposition is, as I said, something which certainly is. There certainly are things in the Universe, which have the properties which I shall mean to ascribe to a thing when I call it a proposition. And when I call a thing a proposition I shall mean to ascribe to it absolutely no properties, except certain definite ones which some things certainly have. There may be doubt and dispute as to whether these things have or have *not* certain *other* properties besides those which I ascribe to them; and also as to whether what I mean by a proposition is quite the same as what is usually meant. But as to the fact that some things *are* propositions, in the sense in which I intend to use the word, I think there is no doubt.

First of all, then, I do *not* mean by a proposition any of those collections of *words*, which are one of the things that are commonly called propositions. What I mean by a proposition is rather the sort of thing which these collections of words *express*. No collection of words can possibly be a proposition, in the sense in which I intend to use the term. Whenever I speak of a proposition, I shall always be speaking, *not* of a mere sentence—a mere collection of words, but of what these words *mean*.

I do not then mean by a proposition any collection of words. And what I do mean can, I think, be best explained as follows. I will utter now certain words which form a sentence: these words, for instance: Twice two are four. Now, when I say these words, you not only hear *them*—the words—you *also* understand what they mean. That is to say, something happens in your minds—some act of consciousness—*over and above* the hearing of the words, some act of consciousness which may be called the understanding of their meaning. But now I will utter another set of words which also form a sentence: I utter the words: Twice four are eight. Here again you not only hear the words, but also perform some other act of consciousness which may be called the understanding of *their* meaning. Here then we have an instance of two acts of consciousness, each of which may be called an apprehension of the meaning of certain words. The one of them was an apprehension of the meaning of the words: Twice two are four; the other an apprehension of the meaning of the words: Twice four are eight. Both of these two acts of consciousness are alike in respect of the fact that each of them is an act of apprehension, and that each of them is the apprehension of the meaning of a certain set of words which form a sentence. Each of them is an apprehending of the meaning of a sentence: and each of them is an *apprehending* in exactly the same sense: they are obviously exactly alike in *this* respect. But no less obviously they differ in respect of the fact that *what* is apprehended in the one case, is different from what is apprehended in the other case. In the one case *what* is apprehended is the meaning of the words: Twice two are four; in the other case *what* is apprehended is the meaning of the words: Twice four are eight. And the meaning of the first set of words is obviously different from that of the second. In this case, then, we have two acts of apprehension, which are exactly alike in respect of the fact that they are acts of apprehension, and acts of apprehension, too, of exactly the same kind; but which differ in respect of the fact that *what* is apprehended in the one, is different from *what* is apprehended in the other. Now by a proposition, I mean the sort of thing which *is apprehended* in these two cases. The two acts of consciousness differ in respect of the fact that *what* is apprehended in the one, is different from *what* is apprehended in the other. And *what* is apprehended in each case is what I mean by a proposition. We might say, then, that the two acts of apprehension differ in respect of the fact that one is an apprehension of one proposition, and the other the apprehension of a different proposition. And we might say also that *the* proposition apprehended in the one is the proposition *that* twice two are four—*not* the *words*, twice two are four, but the *meaning* of these words; and that *the* proposition apprehended in the other is the different proposition that twice four are eight—again *not* the words, twice four are eight, but the meaning of these words.

This, then, is the sort of thing that I mean by a proposition. And whether you agree or not that it is a proper use of the word, I hope it is plain that there certainly *are* things which are propositions in this sense. As a matter of fact this is, I think, one of the senses in which the word is commonly used. Often, no doubt, we may mean by a proposition a sentence—a collection of words; but quite often also, I think, we mean by a proposition *not* the words but their meaning. This, then, is how I am going to use the word 'proposition'. And I hope it is plain that there certainly are such things as propositions in this sense. It is quite plain, I think, that when we understand the meaning of a sentence, something else does happen in our minds *besides* the mere hearing of the words of which the sentence is composed. You can easily satisfy yourselves of this by contrasting what happens when you hear a sentence, which you *do* understand, from what happens when you hear a sentence which you do *not* understand: for instance, when you hear words spoken in a foreign language, which you do not understand at all. Certainly in the first case, there occurs, beside the mere hearing of the words, another act of consciousness—an apprehension of their meaning, which is absent in the second case. And it is no less plain that the apprehension of the meaning of one sentence with one meaning, differs in some respect from the apprehension of another sentence with a different meaning. For instance the apprehension of the meaning of the sentence: Twice two are four, certainly differs in some respect from the apprehension of the meaning of the sentence: Twice four are eight. They certainly differ in some respect, which may be expressed by saying that one is the apprehension of one meaning, and the other the apprehension of a different meaning. There certainly *are* such things as the two different meanings apprehended. And each of these two meanings is what I call a proposition. In calling them so, I do not mean to assert anything whatever as to the manner in which they are related to the apprehension of them. All that I mean to assert is simply that each of them is something which can and must be distinguished from the act of apprehension in which it is apprehended. Each act of apprehension is alike in respect of the fact that it is an act of apprehension, and an act of apprehension of the same kind. But they differ in that whereas one is the apprehension of one proposition, the other is the apprehension of a different proposition. Each proposition, therefore, can and must be distinguished both from the other proposition, and also from the act which is the apprehending of it.

But now, if we use the word 'proposition' in this sense, it is plain, I think, that we can say several other things about propositions and about the apprehension of them.

In the first place, it is, I think, plain that we apprehend a proposition in exactly the same sense in three different cases. When we hear certain words spoken and understand their meaning, we may do three different things: we may *believe* the proposition which they express, we may *disbelieve* it, or we may simply *understand* what the words mean, without either believing or disbelieving it. In all these three cases, we do I think obviously apprehend the proposition in question in exactly the same sense: namely, we understand the meaning of the words. The difference between the three cases merely consists in the fact, that when we believe or disbelieve, we *also* do something else *beside* merely apprehending the proposition: beside merely apprehending it, we also have towards it one attitude which is called belief, or another different attitude which is called disbelief. To believe a proposition, to disbelieve one, or simply to understand it, in the sense in which we do these things when we hear words spoken that express the proposition, consist then, all three of them, at least in part, in apprehending this proposition in exactly the same sense. In all three cases we do apprehend a proposition in exactly the same sense, though where we believe or disbelieve we *also* do something else besides. This sense in which we apprehend a proposition, in all these three cases equally, is obviously one sense of the word apprehension; and it is a sense to which I wish to direct your attention, as I shall presently have more to say about it.

One point then with regard to propositions and our apprehension of them, is that there is a definite sort of apprehension of them, which occurs equally, whenever we either believe, disbelieve, or merely understand a proposition on actually hearing spoken words which express it.

And a second point is this. It is, I think, also plain that we often apprehend propositions in exactly the same sense, when instead of *hearing* words which express them, we *see* written or printed words which express them—provided, of course, that we are able to read and understand the language to which the words belong. This understanding of the meaning of written or printed sentences, which occurs when we actually read them, is, I think, obviously an apprehension of propositions in exactly the same sense as is the understanding of sentences, which we hear spoken. But just as we apprehend propositions in exactly the same sense in both these two cases —whether we hear spoken sentences which express them, or *see* these sentences written or printed—so also, obviously, we very often apprehend propositions in exactly the same sense, when we *neither* hear nor see any words which express them. We constantly think of and believe or disbelieve, or merely consider, propositions, at moments when we are neither hearing nor seeing any words which express them; and in doing so, we are *very often* apprehending them in exactly the same sense in which we apprehend them when we do understand the meaning of written or spoken sentences. No doubt when we do thus apprehend propositions, without either hearing or seeing any words which express them, we often have before our minds the *images* of words, which would express them. But it is, I think, obviously possible that we should apprehend propositions, in exactly the same sense, without even having before our minds *any images* of words which would express them. We may thus apprehend a proposition, which we desire to express, before we are able to think of any sentence which would express it. We apprehend the proposition, and desire to express it, but none of the words we can think of will express exactly *the* proposition we are apprehending and desiring to convey.

Our second point, then, with regard to propositions and our apprehension of them is this: namely, that in exactly the same sense in which we apprehend them, when we hear certain words spoken of which we understand the meaning, we also often apprehend them, when we neither see nor hear any words which express them, and probably often without even having before our minds any *images* of words which would express them.

And a third point is this. Namely, that the propositions which we apprehend in this sense, and in all these different cases, are obviously quite a different sort of thing from many of the things which we apprehend. When, for instance, I directly apprehend a sense-datum —a patch of colour, for instance—the patch of colour is obviously not the same sort of thing as these propositions of which we have been talking: *it*, the patch of colour, is not itself a proposition. The most obvious way of expressing the difference between a proposition, and what is not a proposition, is by saying that a proposition is the sort of thing which is commonly expressed by *a whole* sentence. I say the *sort* of thing; because, as we have seen, we may apprehend many propositions which are not *actually* expressed at all. And I say *commonly* expressed by a whole sentence, because I am not sure that some whole sentences, for instance an imperative, such as 'Go away', express a proposition at all; and because also propositions are sometimes expressed by single words. For instance, when a man calls 'Fire', he is expressing a proposition: he is expressing the proposition which *might* be expressed by the whole sentence: There is a fire taking place. But, if we say that a proposition is the sort of thing that is commonly expressed by a whole sentence, we indicate, I think, pretty clearly the sort of thing that a proposition is. Things which are not propositions, if expressed at all, are usually expressed by single words or collections of words, which do not make complete sentences. Thus, supposing I utter the whole sentence: This patch of colour, which I now see, exists. One part of this sentence, namely, the words 'This patch of colour which I now see', may perhaps be said to 'express' or mention this patch of colour, which I do now directly apprehend, and which is *not* a proposition; and obviously that particular set of words, which mention this colour, do not by themselves form a complete sentence: the words 'This patch of colour, which I now see' *are* not a complete sentence by themselves. And similarly, whenever we utter a complete sentence, while the whole sentence does, as a rule, express a proposition, some of the words or sets of words of which it is composed express something which is *not* a proposition. For instance, consider again the sentence: Twice two are four. This whole sentence, as we saw, does express a proposition. But, if we take some one of the words of which it is composed, for instance the word 'two', this word by itself does not make a complete sentence and does not express a proposition. But it *does* express *something*. What we mean by the word 'two' is certainly something. This something, therefore, *is*—is something, and yet is not a proposition. In fact, whenever we do apprehend a proposition we always also apprehend things which are *not* propositions; namely, things which would be expressed by *some* of the words, of which the whole sentence, which would express the proposition, is composed.

A third point, then, with regard to propositions and our apprehension of them, is that propositions are by no means the only kind of things which we apprehend; but that whenever we do apprehend a proposition, we always *also* apprehend something else, which is *not* a proposition.

And a fourth point with regard to propositions is this. Namely, that propositions, in the sense in which I have been using the term, are obviously a sort of thing which can properly be said to be *true* or *false*. Some propositions are true propositions and other propositions are false propositions. And I mention this point, because some philosophers seem inclined to say that nothing can be properly said to be true or false, *except* an act of belief: that, therefore, *propositions*, not being acts of belief, cannot properly be said to be so. And I do not here wish to deny that an act of belief may be properly said to be true or false; though I think it may be doubted. We do undoubtedly speak of true and false beliefs; so that *beliefs*, at all events, may be properly said to be true or false. But the fact is, I think, that, as with so many other words, we use the word 'belief' in two different senses: sometimes, no doubt, we mean by a belief an *act* of belief, but very often, I think, we mean by it simply the proposition which is believed. For instance, we often say of two different people that they entertain *the same belief*. And here, I think, we certainly do not mean to say that any act of belief performed by the one is the *same act* as an act of belief performed by the other. The two acts of belief are certainly different—numerically different: the one act is the act of one person, and the other is the act of a different person; and we certainly do not mean to assert that these two acts are identical—that they are not *two* acts, but one and the same act. What we do, I think, mean, when we say that both persons have the same belief, is that *what* is believed in both of the two different acts is the same: we mean by a belief, in fact, *not* the act of belief, but *what* is believed; and what is believed is just nothing else than what I mean by a proposition. But let us grant that acts of belief may be properly said to be true and false. Even if this be so, it seems to me we must allow that propositions, in the sense I have given to the term, can be properly said to be true and false *also*, though in a different sense. For what I mean by a proposition is simply *that* in respect of which an act of belief, which is a *true* act, differs from another, which is a false one; or that in respect of which two qualitatively different acts of belief, which are both false or both true, differ from one another. And obviously the quality in virtue of which one act of belief is true, and another false, cannot be the quality which they both have in common: it cannot be the fact that they are both of them acts of belief: we cannot say that the one is true, simply because it is an act of belief, and the other false, for the same reason—namely, simply because it is an act of belief. What makes the one true and the other false must be that in respect of which they differ; and that in respect of which they differ—whatever it may be—is just that which I mean by the proposition which is apprehended in each of them. Even, therefore, if we admit that nothing but an act of belief can be properly said to be true or false, in *one* sense of these words, we must, I think, admit that there is another corresponding sense in which propositions are true and false. Every true act of belief partly consists in the apprehension of a proposition; and every false act of belief also partly consists in the apprehension of a proposition. And any proposition apprehended in a true act of belief must be different from any proposition apprehended in a false act of belief. Consequently all the propositions apprehended in true acts of belief must have some common property which is not possessed by any of those which are apprehended in false acts of belief. And there is no reason why we should not call *this* property '*truth*'; and similarly the property possessed in common by all propositions apprehended in false acts of belief '*falsity*'.

Propositions are, then, a sort of thing which may be properly said to be true or false. And this gives us one way of distinguishing what is a proposition from what is *not* a proposition; since nothing that is *not* a proposition can be true or false in exactly the same sense in which a proposition is true or false. There are, indeed, we may say, two other senses of the words 'true' and 'false', which are closely allied to those in which propositions are true or false. There is, to begin with, *if* acts of belief can be properly said to be true or false at all, the sense in which an act of belief is true or false. An act of belief is true, if and only if the proposition believed in it is true; and it is false, if and only if the proposition believed in it is false. Or, putting the matter the other way, we may say: A proposition is true, if and only if any act of belief, which was a belief in it, would be a true act of belief; and a proposition is false, if and only if any act of belief, which was a belief in it, would be false. I do not pretend to say here which of these two ways of putting the matter is the better way. Whether, that is to say, the sense in which acts of belief are true and false, should be defined by reference to that in which propositions are true and false; or whether the sense in which propositions are true and false should be defined by reference to that in which acts of belief are true and false. I do not pretend to say which of these two senses is the more fundamental; and it does not seem to me to matter much which is. What is quite certain is that they are two different senses, but *also* that each *can* be defined by reference to the other. One sense, then, of the words true and false, *beside* that in which propositions are true and false, is the sense in which acts of belief are true and false. And there is obviously, also, another sense of the words, which, though different from these two, is equally closely related to both of them. Namely, the sense in which any set of words—any sentence, for instance—which *expresses* a true proposition is true; and any set of words which *expresses* a false proposition is false. Or here again, putting the matter the other way, we may say: Any proposition which is such that any verbal statement which expressed it *would* be a true statement, is true; and any proposition which is such that a verbal statement which expressed it *would* be a false statement, is false. We may, therefore, say that another sense of the words true and false is that in which anything that *expresses* a true proposition is true; and anything which *expresses* a false proposition is false. And obviously in this sense not only words, but also other things, gestures, for instance, may be true or false. If, for instance, somebody asks you: 'Where are my scissors?' and you point to a particular place by way of answer, your gesture—the gesture of pointing—expresses a proposition. By pointing you obviously express the same proposition as if you had used the words 'Your scissors are there', or had named the particular place where they were. And just as any words you might have used would have been true or false, according as the proposition they expressed was true or false, so your gesture might be said to be true or false, according as the scissors really are in the place you point to or not. There are, therefore, these three senses of the words true and false: The sense in which propositions are true or false; the sense in which acts of belief are true or false, according as the propositions believed in them are true or false; and the sense in which anything that *expresses* a proposition is true or false, according as the proposition expressed is true or false. And obviously these three senses are not *the same*, though each can be defined by reference to the others. That is to say, neither an act of belief nor the *expression* of a proposition, can be true or false in exactly the same sense in which a proposition is true or false. And the same, I think, is true universally: nothing but a proposition can be true or false in exactly the same sense in which propositions are so. And why I particularly wanted to call your attention to this, is for the following reason. Some people seem to think that, if you have before your mind an image of an object, which is *like* the object—a copy of it—in certain respects, you may be said, merely because you have this image before your mind, to have a *true* idea of the object—an idea which is *true*, in so far as the image really is like the object. And they seem to think that when this happens, you have a *true* idea of the object, in exactly the same sense as if you believed a true proposition about the object. And this is, I think, at first sight a very natural view to take. It is natural, for instance, to think that if, after looking at this envelope, I have before my mind (as I have) an image, which is like, in certain respects, to the patch of colour which I just now saw, I have, *merely* because I directly apprehend this image, a true *idea* of the patch of colour which I just now saw. It is natural, I say, to think that merely to apprehend this image *is* to have a true idea (true, in certain particulars) of the patch of colour which I saw; and that, in apprehending this image, I have a true idea of the patch of colour, in exactly the same sense as if I had a true belief *about* the patch of colour. But it is, I think, easy to see that this view, however natural, is wholly mistaken. The fact is that if *all* that happened to me were *merely* that I directly apprehended an image, which was in fact like some other object, I could not be properly said to have *any* idea of this other object *at all*—*any* idea, either true or false. Merely to apprehend something, which is *in fact* like something else, is obviously not the same thing as having an idea *of* the something else. In order to have an idea *of* the something else, I must *not only* apprehend an image, which is *in fact* like the something else: I must also either know or think *that* the image *is* like the something else. In other words, I must apprehend some *proposition about* the relation of the image to the object: only so can I be properly said to have an *idea* of the object at all. If I do apprehend some proposition about the relation of the image to the object, then, indeed, I may be said to have an *idea* of the object: and if I think that the image is like the object in respects in which it is *not* like it, then I shall have a *false* idea of the object, whereas if I think that it is like it in respects in which it is in fact like it, then I shall have, so far, a *true* idea of the object. But if I apprehend *no proposition at all* about the relation of the image to the object, then obviously, however like the image may *in fact* be to the object, I cannot be said to have any idea of the object at all. I might, for instance, all my life through, be directly apprehending images and sense-data, which were *in fact* singularly accurate copies of other things. But suppose I never for a moment even suspected that there were these other things, *of* which my images and sense-data were copies? Suppose it never occurred to me for a moment that there were any other things at all beside my sense-data and images? Obviously I could not be said to have any idea at all about these other things—any idea at all, either true or false; and this in spite of the fact that my sense-data and images were, *in fact*, copies of these other things. We must, therefore, say that merely to apprehend an image (or anything else), which is, in fact, like some other object, but without even thinking that the two are like, is *not* to have a true idea of the object in the same sense as when we apprehend a true proposition about the object. No mere image or sense-datum can possibly *be* either a true idea or a false idea *of* anything else, however like or unlike it may be to the something else. Or, if you choose to say that it is, *in a sense*, a true idea of an object, if it be like it, and an untrue one, if it be unlike it, you must at least admit that it is a *true* idea in quite a different sense from that in which a proposition about the object, if true, *is* a true idea of it. Nothing, in short, can be true or false in the same sense in which propositions are true or false. So that, if we never apprehended any propositions we should not be capable of ever making any mistakes —a mistake, an *error*, would be impossible. Error always consists in believing some proposition which is false. So that if a man merely apprehended something, which was *in fact* unlike something else, but without believing either that it was like or unlike, or anything else at all about it, he could not possibly be said to make any mistake at all: he would never hold any mistaken or false opinions, because he would never hold any *opinions* at all.

Now I have insisted on these four points with regard to propositions, chiefly in order to make as plain as possible *what* sort of a thing a proposition is: what sort of a thing I mean to talk about, when I talk of a proposition. But now I come to the two points about propositions to which I wish specially to direct your attention.

The first of them is this. You may remember that I called your attention to a particular way of apprehending propositions: *the* way in which you apprehend one, when you hear a sentence uttered and understand its meaning: *the* way, for instance, in which you apprehend the proposition that Twice two are four, when you hear me say 'Twice two are four', and understand what these words mean. Now I want a special name for *this* way of apprehending propositions, because, as we shall presently see, there is another quite different sort of thing which might also be said to be a way of apprehending propositions. I want, therefore, a special name for *this* way of apprehending them—the way I have hitherto been talking of, and which I have just tried to define—so that you may always, by means of the name, recognise that it is *this* way that I am talking of, and not any other way. And I propose, for this purpose, to call *this* way of apprehending them, the *direct apprehension* of them. But now at once a question arises. I have already given the name *direct apprehension* to something else. I have given the name *direct apprehension* to the relation which you have to a patch of colour, when you actually see it, to a sound when you actually hear it, to a toothache, when you actually feel it, etc.: I have said that the actual seeing of a colour *is* the direct apprehension of that colour; that the actual hearing of a sound *is* the direct apprehension of that sound, etc. The question, therefore, now arises: Is this relation to a proposition, which I now propose to call direct apprehension of a proposition, the same as the relation which I formerly called *direct apprehension*—namely, the relation which you have to a colour, when you actually see it? Or in other words: Is the relation, which you have to a proposition, when you hear words which express it uttered, and understand the meaning of these words, the same relation as that which you have to a colour, when you actually see it? I confess I cannot tell whether this is so or not. There are, I think, reasons for supposing that what I call the direct apprehension of a proposition is something different from the direct apprehension of a sense-datum: different I mean, not only in respect of the fact that, whereas the one is the direct apprehension of a proposition, the other is the direct apprehension of a sense-datum, and that a proposition and a sense-datum are different sorts of things; but different *also*, in the sense, that the relation which you have to a proposition, when you directly apprehend it, is different from that which you have to a sense-datum, when you directly apprehend *it*. There are, I think, reasons for supposing that what I call direct apprehension of a proposition really is, in this sense, a very different sort of thing from what I call direct apprehension of a sense-datum: but I cannot tell what the difference is, if there is one; and the reasons for supposing that there is one do not seem to me to be perfectly conclusive. I must, therefore, leave undecided the question whether I am using the name *direct apprehension* in two different senses. But even if I am, I hope this need not lead to any confusion. I shall always mean by the name *either* the kind of relation which you have to a colour, when you actually see it *or* the kind of relation which you have to a proposition when you *understand* it—for instance, when you hear words which express it, and understand what they express. And if these two relations are, in fact, different, then that will only mean that there are in fact two different kinds of direct apprehension. And it is, I think, much less important to decide whether there are two different kinds—whether that which I call direct apprehension of a proposition is in fact a different kind of thing from that which I call direct apprehension of a sense-datum, than to distinguish *both* of them quite clearly, from other kinds of things, which are certainly different from either, but which might also be called ways of apprehending.

My first point about propositions is, then, that I want you to understand as clearly as possible what that way of apprehending them is, which I am going to call *direct* apprehension of them.

And my second point is this. Every proposition is, as we constantly say, a proposition *about* something or other. Some propositions may be *about* several different things; but all of them are *about* at least one thing. For instance, the proposition: Twice two are four, might be said to be *about* both the number two *and* the number four: when you believe it or apprehend it, you are apprehending something *about* the number two and also something about the number four. But the point I wish to call your attention to is this. Namely, that in the case of an immense number of the propositions which we apprehend, even at the moment when we *do* directly apprehend the whole proposition, we do *not* directly apprehend by any means all of the things which the proposition is *about*. Propositions, in fact, have this strange property: that even at the moment when we do directly apprehend the whole proposition, we need not directly apprehend *that which* the proposition is about. And in the case of immense numbers of the propositions which we directly apprehend, perhaps even the majority of them, you can, I think, easily see that this does actually happen. In *some* cases, when we directly apprehend a proposition, we do also directly apprehend the thing *about* which the proposition is. For instance, at the moment, when I am actually looking at this patch of colour, and directly apprehending it, I may also directly apprehend a proposition about it—for instance, the proposition that it *is* or exists, or that it is whitish. But obviously I can also directly apprehend propositions about it, at moments when I am *not* directly apprehending *it*. *Now*, for instance, when I am no longer directly apprehending it, I can still directly apprehend propositions *about* it—for instance, the proposition that it *was*, that I did see it just now, and so on. And it is, I think, obvious that we are constantly thus directly apprehending propositions *about* things, when we are *not* directly apprehending these things themselves. We are constantly talking and thinking *about* things, which we are *not* directly apprehending at the moment when we talk or think about them: indeed by far the greater part of our conversation and our reading is obviously *about* things which we are *not* directly apprehending when we converse or read about them: it is comparatively rarely that our conversation is confined exclusively to things which we are directly apprehending at the moment. And yet, whenever we talk or read about such things, we *are* directly apprehending propositions *about* them, though we are *not* directly apprehending the things themselves. Obviously, therefore, we do constantly directly apprehend propositions *about* things, when we are not directly apprehending these things themselves. And I want a name for this kind of relation which we have to a thing, when we do directly apprehend a proposition *about* it, but *do not* directly apprehend *it* itself. I propose to call it *indirect apprehension*. That is to say, I propose, to say that I am *now indirectly* apprehending the patch of colour which I saw just now when I looked at this envelope: meaning by that the two things that I am directly apprehending a proposition about it, but am *not* directly apprehending the thing itself. You may object to this name, on the ground that I am not now really apprehending the patch of colour at all: on the ground that to say that I have to it any relation at all, which can be called *apprehension*, is misleading. And I have a good deal of sympathy with this objection, because the very point I want to insist on is what an *immense* difference there is between this relation I have to it *now*, when I *do not* directly apprehend it, but merely directly apprehend a proposition about it, and the relation I had to it just now when I did directly apprehend it. You may say the difference is so great that they ought not to have any common name: that they ought not *both* to be called forms of apprehension. But then, great as is the difference between these two different ways of being related to a thing, there is just as great a difference between what happens when I *do* directly apprehend a proposition *about* a thing, and what happens when I do not *even* do as much as this—when I do not even think of the thing in any sense at all. So long as I am directly apprehending a proposition about a thing, I *am* in a sense conscious of that thing—I am *thinking of it or about it*, even though I am not directly apprehending it, and there is quite as great a difference between *this way* of being related to it, the apprehending of a proposition about it, and what happens when I am *not* thinking of it in any sense at all—when it is utterly out of my mind, as between *this* way of being related to it and that which I have called direct apprehension. Some name is, therefore, required for *this* way of being conscious of a thing—this way which occurs when you do directly apprehend some proposition about it, though you do not directly apprehend *it*; and I cannot think of any better name than *indirect apprehension*. You might say that I ought to use the whole long phrase: That relation which you have to a thing, when you do directly apprehend a proposition about it, and *do not* directly apprehend it. But this phrase is inconvenient, because it is so long. You might say that the short phrase 'thinking of it' would do: that this is just what we mean by thinking of a thing. But there are two objections to this. In the first place, it may be the case that this relation is the only one we have to a thing, even when we should not say that we were *merely* thinking of it, when we should say that we were doing something more than merely *thinking* of it. And in the second place, though we do often use the name 'thinking of' for this relation, we also use it for that of direct apprehension. For instance, we often say, I think, that we are thinking of a proposition, when we are directly apprehending the proposition: and so too, when I am said to be thinking of the number 2, I am, I think, very often directly apprehending the number 2. The name 'thinking of' will not, therefore, do, as an unambiguous name to distinguish the kind of relation which I want to call 'indirect apprehension' from that which I call 'direct apprehension'. And I cannot think of any better name for the purpose than 'indirect apprehension'. And, in fact, it does not much matter what name I use, provided you understand what I mean by it. I mean, then, by 'indirect apprehension' the kind of relation which you have to a thing, when you *do* directly apprehend some proposition *about* it, but *do not* directly apprehend the thing itself. And the point I want to insist on is that this is quite a different kind of relation from that which you have to a thing when you do directly apprehend it. The only connection between the two is this, that whenever you indirectly apprehend any *one* thing, you must be *directly* apprehending *something else—either* some proposition about it, or perhaps sometimes something other than a proposition.

But now by the help of what I have said about propositions, and about what occurs, when we directly apprehend them, I think I can classify and distinguish all the different sorts of relations to things, which would commonly be said to be ways of knowing them. And this is what I wish now to do.

Chapter IV

WAYS OF KNOWING

I have been occupied with doing two things: firstly with pointing out how a sort of things, which I called 'propositions', differ from things which are *not* propositions; and secondly with distinguishing two different ways of apprehending or being conscious of all sorts of different things, which I proposed to call 'direct apprehension' and 'indirect apprehension' respectively.

As regards propositions, the point which most requires to be emphasized is, I think, this: namely that a proposition is quite a different sort of thing from any image or collection of images. And this may at first sight seem to be obvious. When, for instance, you close your eyes and summon up before your mind an image of a particular colour, or of a row of colours side by side, nobody would think of saying that this image or collection of images *was* a proposition: it seems quite obvious that, whatever we do mean by a proposition, we mean by it something quite different from any such collection of images. But, if we look at the matter another way, it ceases, I think, to be quite so obvious. Consider, for instance, what happens in your mind when you believe such a proposition as *that* your hat is hanging up in the hall. We all do constantly believe things like this; and *what* you believe in such a case as this, namely, *that* your hat is hanging up in the hall, was, I said, the sort of thing I meant by a proposition: you are, in this case, believing the proposition *that* your hat is hanging up in the hall. But now, what does happen in your mind when you believe this proposition? If you look into your mind, to try to discover what is really before it, you may, I think, find it very difficult to discover anything at all except two kinds of things. You may, in the first place, discover images of words: images of the words 'My hat is hanging up in the hall'. But these, I said, cannot possibly be the proposition in the sense I meant: I said that I meant by a proposition something utterly different from any collection of words or of images of words—something which a collection of words may *mean* or *express*, but which no word or collection of words can possibly *be*. If, therefore, you are to find the proposition, you must look for something other than any images of words. But you may, I think, be unable to find anything else than this: namely a more or less vivid *image* of your hat hanging up in the hall; a more or less vivid copy, for instance, of the sense-data, you would *see*, if you saw it hanging there. It is, therefore, I think, very natural to conclude that this image—this more or less faint copy of sense-data—*is* the proposition, is *what* you believe. And this is a view which has, in fact, been taken by many philosophers. Hume, for instance, declares that *all* the perceptions of the human mind are of two sorts—impressions and ideas—and that the ideas are merely more or less faint copies of previous impressions, either themselves copies of previous impressions or else images composed of such copies, rearranged in a new way. And he held, too, that *belief* merely consisted in a particularly vivid apprehension of some such image. He entirely failed to recognize, therefore, that there ever was, either *in* or *before* the mind, any such thing as what I call a proposition. And many philosophers and psychologists still speak as if this was so. It is not, therefore, quite so obvious, as it might seem, that a proposition—namely, *what* we believe, whenever we believe anything, is something quite different from any image or collection of images. And yet, I think, you can see, on reflection, that it certainly is something quite different. Consider for example that image of your hat hanging up in the hall, and compare it with what you believe, when you believe that your hat is hanging there. The image merely consists in a more or less accurate copy *of* something else—it is something more or less like certain sense-data, which you have seen or might see. And the mere direct apprehension of this image, if vivid enough, is, it is suggested, the *same* thing as believing that your hat is hanging up in the hall. But obviously the mere direct apprehension of this image is *not* the same thing as believing that there was or is or might be in the Universe anything else at all besides the image. Merely to apprehend something which is, in fact, *like* something else is one thing: but even to suspect *that* there is in the Universe something else, either like or unlike the thing which you directly apprehend, is obviously something quite different. But surely, when you believe that your hat *is* hanging up in the hall, you are at least suspecting that there is or might be in the Universe something else besides the image which you are now directly apprehending. But if so, then, your belief that your hat is hanging up in the hall, cannot be the same thing as your direct apprehension of this image, however vivid. Nor can *what* you believe—namely the proposition that your hat is hanging up in the hall, be the same thing as the image.

This, I think, was the most important point to be emphasized with regard to the difference between propositions and other things. And with regard to the two ways of being conscious of a thing which I called direct apprehension and indirect apprehension, what I wished to emphasize was, how extremely different they are from one another. By direct apprehension I said I might possibly be meaning two different relations. I meant by it, in the first place, the kind of relation which you have to a sense-datum—a patch of colour, for instance, when you actually see it. And I meant by it also, the kind of relation which you have to a proposition, when you actually believe it; but which you may also have to a proposition, when you do not either believe or disbelieve it, but merely consider it, without either believing or disbelieving. These two relations, I said, though I proposed to call them both direct apprehension, *might* be different: it may be the case that you can never have to anything *but* a proposition that relation which I called direct apprehension of a proposition, and that you can never have *to* a proposition that relation which you have to a patch of colour when you actually see it. But, whether they differ from one another or not, I wished to call them both direct apprehension, in order to mark how extremely different they both are from that other kind of relation which I called 'indirect apprehension', and which you may have both to propositions and to anything else whatever. This relation I defined as follows: it is the relation which you have to a thing when you *do* directly apprehend some proposition *about* it, but *do not* directly apprehend the thing itself. 'Indirect apprehension' may be a bad name for this relation; but it is, I think, a relation which needs a name: for it is a perfectly definite kind of relation which we certainly do constantly have to things, and which is extremely different from either of the relations which I called direct apprehension. The most obvious sort of example of it is what happens, when, immediately after directly apprehending some sense-datum, you remember that sense-datum, or remember *that* you did just now directly apprehend it. In such a case, you are, *ex hypothesi*, no longer directly apprehending the sense-datum in question, and yet you *are*, if you directly apprehend the proposition that you did just now actually see it, directly apprehending a proposition *about* it. In this case, then, I should say that you are *now* apprehending *indirectly* the sense-datum, which you did formerly apprehend *directly*, but are now, *ex hypothesi*, no longer apprehending directly. And when I say that you apprehend a thing *indirectly*, whenever you directly apprehend any proposition *about* it, I mean the phrase—a proposition *about* so and so—to be understood in the widest possible sense. For instance I now believe *this* proposition, namely: That propositions, different from any which I have ever directly apprehended and from any which I am now directly apprehending, are at this moment being believed by Chinamen in China. In this case, I should say that I am now believing a proposition *about* those propositions that are being believed in China. I should, therefore, say that I am, at this moment, apprehending *indirectly* those propositions that are being believed in China, although I am certainly not apprehending them directly, and do not (as we should say) even know *what* propositions they are. You may say that I am not really apprehending these propositions at all; that I ought not to say, in such a case, that I am apprehending them even *indirectly*. But I certainly am, in a sense, *thinking of* them; and there is as great a difference between the relation which I have to them now, when I really am thinking of them, and that which I had to them five minutes ago, when I was not even thinking of them, as between the relation I now have to *them* and that which I *now* have to anything which I now am directly apprehending. I want a word, then, which will mark this difference: a word, which will mark the relation, which you have to a thing, when you are actually thinking of it, in however wide a sense, and which will at the same time distinguish this relation, which occurs when you *are* thinking of but are *not* directly apprehending the thing in question, from that which you have to a thing when you *are* directly apprehending it. This relation, then, is what I mean by 'indirect apprehension'; and provided you understand quite clearly what I mean, it does not much matter whether the name is a good one or not.

But there is one other point about 'indirect apprehension' which I scarcely mentioned last time, but which ought, I think, to be mentioned. I have defined it as *the* relation which you have to a thing, when you do not directly apprehend the thing itself, but *do* directly apprehend some proposition about it. But, I ought to say, that I am not sure that you may not have this very same relation to a thing even when you are *not* directly apprehending any proposition about it. My reason for doubt on this question is the following. Suppose you *now* remember a patch of colour, which you actually saw a moment ago but are not now seeing. In such a case you are certainly not directly apprehending the patch of colour itself; and you *are* apprehending it indirectly, because you are thinking of it. But are you necessarily now, while you think of it, directly apprehending any proposition about it? It is, I think, very difficult to be sure whether you are or not. If you are actually believing *that* you did just now see it, you are, of course, directly apprehending a proposition about it. And if you merely think of it *as* the patch of colour which you saw, this seems very like directly apprehending the same proposition, namely, that you did just now see it. But this does not seem quite certain: it does not seem quite certain that to think of a thing as having certain properties is the same thing as to think *that* it has these properties. There are, then, two questions. Firstly: when you think of a thing *as* the thing which has certain properties, does this amount to directly apprehending a proposition about it? I am inclined to think that it does, but I am not sure. And then secondly: Can you ever apprehend anything indirectly at all, without thinking of it at least *as* having certain properties? This question, as far as I can see, is a question which must be answered in the negative. Undoubtedly you can apprehend a thing *directly* without thinking of it *as* anything at all. But, where, as in this case, you are certainly *not* apprehending the thing itself directly, and yet *are* in some sense conscious of it—thinking of it—it seems as if you must be thinking of it *as* having certain properties. If, then, both these questions are to be answered as suggested, it would be true that you never apprehend anything indirectly, without apprehending directly some proposition about it. But the matter is, I think, so obscure that it is difficult to be sure that either question *must* be answered as suggested. So, too, when I think again of those propositions, which are being believed by people in China, which I mentioned a moment ago, I *am now* thinking of them, and I am certainly not apprehending them directly. I *am*, I think, thinking of them *as* propositions being believed in China. But am I, in merely doing this, directly apprehending some proposition about them? Is the mere thinking of them the same thing as directly apprehending some proposition about them? I am inclined to think that it is, but I am not quite sure. When, therefore, I define indirect apprehension as the relation which you have to a thing, when you do not directly apprehend the thing itself, but *do* directly apprehend some proposition about it; this definition must not be taken as meaning for certain that you *never* have this relation to a thing, *except* when you are directly apprehending some proposition about the thing. I only mean that it is the *kind* of relation, which you do have in this case, without definitely asserting that you *never* have it in other cases. The important point about indirect apprehension is that it is not direct apprehension, and yet *is* a way of being conscious of or thinking of a thing; and that it is a way of being conscious of a thing, which certainly does constantly occur when you are directly apprehending a proposition *about* a thing, though perhaps it may occur in other cases also.

But now I said that by the help of the distinction between propositions and things which are not propositions, and of the distinction between 'direct apprehension' and 'indirect apprehension', I thought I could classify all the different relations to things, which would commonly be said to be ways of *knowing* them. And this is what I shall now try to do.

You remember, we started from sense-perception; and our original question was, as to what sort of a way of knowing sense-perception *is*. Sense-perception, and all the different forms of sense-perception—seeing, hearing, feeling, smelling, etc., we should, I think, commonly say were ways of knowing[1] things. All these words —I perceive, I see, I hear, I smell, I feel, etc.—are constantly used by us to denote some sort of relation between us and something else which is *what* we perceive, or see, or hear, or feel. And we should I think say that, whenever I see anything, I do in a sense *know* the thing, which I see: that to see a thing is one way of knowing it: and so also whenever I hear anything, I do, in a sense, *know* the thing, that I hear; whenever I feel anything, I do, in a sense, *know* the thing that I feel; in short, whenever I perceive anything by any sense, I do in a sense *know* the thing that I perceive. But now besides sense-perception itself, and all the different names for different kinds of sense-perception, we also constantly use ever so many other words, of each of which we should say that it was, in the same sense, a name for a *way* of knowing things. Whenever I *remember*

[1]I do not now think this is true. I certainly often see in the street people whom I do not know; and I do not think we commonly use 'know' in such a sense that to perceive a person or a material object or a sense-datum is a way of *knowing* that person or material object or sense-datum. There is no common use of 'know' such that from the mere fact that I am seeing a person it follows that I am at that moment knowing him; although many philosophers have talked as if there were, and I myself have sometimes in these lectures used 'know' in this improper way. What Russell, in the *Problems of Philosophy* (Chapter V), calls 'knowledge by acquaintance', has no right to be called 'knowledge' at all (nor 'acquaintance' either, for that matter): it is merely identical with perception, when 'perception' is used in that sense which I have called 'direct apprehension'. On the other hand, when 'perceive' is used in the sense in which we talk of perceiving a fact or a truth (see footnote, p. 46), then 'perceive' does entail 'know'; *e.g.* if I see that a man has a beard I do (for the moment) necessarily know that he has. (1952).

anything, I do in a sense, *know* the thing that I remember; whenever I dream of anything, I do, in a sense, *know* the thing that I dream of; whenever I imagine anything, I do, in a sense, *know* the thing that I imagine; whenever I think of anything, I do, in a sense, *know* the thing that I think of; whenever I observe anything, I do, in a sense, *know* the thing that I observe. All these words, and many others, are constantly used by us to denote some sort of relation between us and something else, and we should, I think, commonly say that the relations they denoted were relations of *knowing*, *cognitive* relations, relations between a knower and something known. Philosophers, I think, do constantly use the word 'knowledge' in this wide sense: they would say that anything perceived or remembered or imagined or thought of, etc., is, at the moment when it *is* perceived or remembered or imagined or thought of, an object of knowledge. But now it seems to me that, in the case of some of these words, many different words are all used to denote exactly the same relation; and in the case of some also, the same word is used, on different occasions, to denote entirely different relations. And what I want to do is to classify the different relations which they are used to denote.

All these words, we may say, are used to express the fact that there holds at a given moment some relation—some *cognitive* relation—between a given person and a given object. And we may, to begin with, divide some at least of these relations into the four following classes. Firstly (1) some of the words in question are sometimes used to express a relation which holds between a person and an object, even at moments when the person is *not* apprehending the object either directly or indirectly; secondly (2) some of them are sometimes used *merely* to express the fact that there does hold between the person and the object at the given moment the relation of direct apprehension; (3) some of them are sometimes used *merely* to express the fact that there does hold between the person and the object at the given moment the relation of indirect apprehension; and (4) some of them, while they do assert that there holds between the person and the object at the given moment the relation of direct apprehension, *also* assert that there holds between the two some other relation besides. We may say, then, that these words, besides being some of them sometimes used *merely* to express direct apprehension or indirect apprehension—two relations about which I have already said enough: are also some of them sometimes used to express at least two new relations, (1) a relation which holds between a person and an object, at moments when he is *not* apprehending the object at all, either directly or indirectly; and (2) a relation, which while it includes direct apprehension also includes something *more* besides. And I will now illustrate these two new relations.

(1) First, then, as to the sense in which a person may be said to know a thing even at a moment when he is neither directly apprehending nor indirectly apprehending it. We all do constantly use the word 'know' itself in this sense. For instance, somebody might say of me that I know the multiplication-table, at a time when I am not thinking either directly or indirectly either of the multiplication-table itself or any part of it. And he might say it quite truly. The relation between me and the multiplication-table, which he means to express by saying that I know it, and expresses quite correctly by saying so, is in fact a relation which may hold between me and the multiplication-table, even when I am not conscious of anything at all—for instance, when I am fast asleep and not dreaming. And so too, when I say of people in general that they all do in fact know of the existence of other people beside themselves; I do not mean to say that they all are, at the moment, *thinking* of the existence of other people. What I say may be quite true, even though many of them are not at the moment apprehending either directly or indirectly the existence of any other person whatever. So too when we say of a person that he knows a certain poem by heart, we do not mean to say that he is at the moment thinking of the poem or of any part of it. And so too when we say of one friend of ours, A, that he knows or is acquainted with another friend of ours, B, we do not mean to assert that A is at the moment apprehending B either directly or indirectly. We do, therefore, constantly use the word 'know' itself, and other words, which would be said to express ways of knowing, to denote relations which may hold between a person and an object, even at moments when he is neither directly nor indirectly apprehending the object. But one thing, at least, is, I think, clear about all these relations: namely, that, whatever they are, nobody can have any of them to any object, *unless* he has *previously* apprehended the object either directly or indirectly. All cognitive relations of this type, therefore, have an essential reference to direct apprehension or indirect apprehension: none of them can be defined except by reference to one or the other. And though they may hold between us and an object at a time, when we are not apprehending either directly or indirectly the object in question, they all imply that we have at *some other* time apprehended it in one

way or the other. Some of the words then, which express cognitive relations, are used to express relations which do hold between a person and an object at moments when the person is not apprehending the object either directly or indirectly; but those relations are relations which never can hold between him and it, unless he has *previously* apprehended it either directly or indirectly. This kind of relation was the *first* of the two new kinds of relations I wished to illustrate.

(2) And the second of them was this. It was a kind of relation which never holds between a person and an object, except at a moment when he is directly apprehending the object, but which also never holds unless, *besides* merely apprehending the object, he is also at the same moment related to it in another way as well. There is one very important relation of this type—a relation which we constantly express by many different words, and which can only hold between us and a proposition—not between us and any other kind of object. It is, in fact, *the* relation which we commonly mean to express when we say without qualification that we *know* a proposition to be true—that we *know* that so and so is the case. And I will now try to explain what this relation is.

That way of knowing, which I have called the *direct apprehension* of propositions, is, it must be remembered, something which occurs just as much, when you believe a false proposition, as when you believe a true one. Suppose, for instance, that you believe your hat is hanging in the hall, when, in fact, it is not. When you believe this proposition, you *are*, in the sense I have given to the word, directly apprehending it; and in so far as you directly apprehend it, it must, I think, be admitted that you do in a sense *know* it. But obviously *only* in a sense. In *the* sense, in which we commonly use the word *know*, when we talk of knowing propositions to be true, you certainly do *not* know it, if it is false. You certainly do not really *know that* your hat is hanging in the hall, if in fact your hat is not hanging there. There is, therefore, a sense of the word *know*, in which, if you are to *know* a proposition to be true, you must, indeed, directly apprehend it, but this is not enough: several other conditions must also be fulfilled besides. In the first place, you must not only directly apprehend it; you must also believe it. And in the second place, the proposition itself must not be a false one; it must be *true*. But even these two extra conditions are not enough to constitute knowledge, in the sense I am now speaking of and in which we commonly use the word when we talk of *knowing* propositions to be true. For you may believe a proposition, and it may in fact be true, and yet you may not really *know* it. Suppose, for instance, a man believes now that it will not rain on the 20th of June, next year; and suppose that when the time comes, it actually does not rain. In that case what he believes now, when he believes it will not rain on that day, is a proposition which is, in fact, true. And yet we certainly should not admit that he now really *knows* that it will not rain. Even if we found next year that his belief was true, we should not say that proved that his present belief amounted to *knowledge*. We should be very loth to admit that he *could* now really *know* this for certain; and we should certainly say that the fact that he believed it and that it was true, did not *prove* that he *now* knows it; even though he believed it, and it was true, it yet certainly *might* be the case that he did not know it. Knowledge, therefore, in the sense in which we talk of it, when we talk of *knowing that so and so is the case*, involves *besides* the three conditions (1) that we must directly apprehend some proposition, (2) that we must not only directly apprehend it but also believe it, (3) that the proposition must be true, *also* some fourth condition. What exactly this fourth condition is, it is, I think, extremely difficult to discover. I shall presently have to say what I can about it. But for the present we may be content to recognise that there certainly is some fourth condition; and that, therefore, there is a sense of the word 'know', which involves, *beside* direct apprehension, *also* three other conditions. And this is by far the most important of all the senses of the word 'know'. I shall not give it any special name: I shall simply call it 'knowledge', or if there seems any risk of confusion between it and other relations which might be said to be ways of knowing, I will call it knowledge *proper*. But generally when I talk of 'knowing' or of 'knowledge' I shall mean this relation and this only.

We have, then, distinguished four different relations, all of which may be sometimes expressed by words which, we should say, expressed ways of knowing objects. There is first of all the kind of relation, which may hold between a person and an object, when he is not apprehending the object either directly or indirectly, but which only holds when he has *previously* apprehended it either in the one way or the other. There is secondly direct apprehension. There is thirdly indirect apprehension. And there is fourthly knowledge *proper*.

But are these four the only kind of relations which are ever expressed, by words, which, we should say, expressed ways of knowing or ways of being conscious?

A doubt arises with regard to those very words which we set out to consider—the word sense-perception itself, and the words which express different forms of sense-perception—the words to see, to hear, to feel, to smell, to taste, etc., *when* these words are applied to a material object. What relation did, in fact, hold between us and the envelope, the *material* envelope, when we all saw it? Was it any one of those four? or was it some other, different from any of those? In other words, what kind of relation is expressed by such words as perceive, observe, see, feel, *when* these are used to express some relation between us and a *material object* or *the space occupied* by a material object?

One thing seems clear to begin with, namely, that, on the view with regard to sense-data, which I have called the accepted view, the relation expressed by these words, when they express a relation between us and a material object, is *not* that of direct apprehension. We have already recognised that when you say you *see* a material object, an envelope for instance, you may mean that you see *only* a part of it. But on the accepted view with regard to sense-data, no part of the sense-data or images which you ever directly apprehend is a part of a material object; and no part of the space which you ever directly apprehend is a part of the space occupied by any material object. In so far then as you merely directly apprehend sense-data and images, you are *not* directly apprehending any part of a material object, nor any part of the space which a material object occupies. And even if, at the moment when you *see* the envelope, you *are* directly apprehending something else *beside* sense-data and images, for instance a proposition *about* the envelope, it is, I think, clear that even so nothing which you are directly apprehending is either a part of the envelope or of its surface or of the space which it occupies. If, therefore, you *see* any part of the envelope or of the space which it occupies at all, you only *see* it in quite a different sense from that in which you see the sense-data and the space which you directly apprehend. *Seeing*, as applied to sense-data, simply means direct apprehension. But as applied to material objects and the space which they occupy it must mean something quite different. And so with regard to the words perceive, observe, feel, and all the other words used to express sense-perception. They all must, on the accepted view with regard to sense-data, express on different occasions two quite different relations. When applied to sense-data they simply express direct apprehension; but when applied to material objects or their surfaces or any part of the space occupied by material objects they express something quite different.

These words then as applied to material objects, certainly do not, on the accepted view with regard to sense-data, denote direct apprehension. And it is equally plain, I think, that they do not denote two others out of the four relations which I distinguished above. They certainly do not denote any relation which can *only* hold between me and a material object, when I have previously apprehended the object either directly or indirectly. Certainly if I ever see a material object at all, I can do so without ever having apprehended it before, either directly or indirectly. The word seeing, then, as applied to material objects, certainly does not denote the first of the four relations which I distinguished above. And equally plainly it does not denote the last—it does not denote the relation which I called knowledge *proper*. For knowledge proper is a relation which you can only have to a proposition; and a material object is certainly not a proposition.

It would seem, then, that of the four relations which I distinguished, the only one which these words, as applied to material objects, can denote is that of indirect apprehension. And this is one of the alternatives we have to consider. But it is, I think, just possible that sometimes, at least, when we apply these words to material objects, we do not mean to express any one of these four relations, but another quite different one And I want now to state this alternative.

It is, I think, just possible that when I say that *you saw* the envelope, I do not mean to assert that you apprehended it even *indirectly*. I might mean merely to assert that you directly apprehended certain sense-data, which *I* know to be connected with the envelope; but not mean to assert that *you* were in any way at all aware of the envelope or of its connection with the sense-data which you saw. In this case, when *I say* that *you* saw the envelope, I must *myself* be apprehending the envelope—the material object—indirectly; but you, *when* you saw it, need not have been apprehending it at all. It is, I think, a possible view that this is all we often mean, when we say that people see material objects; and it is, I think, a very natural view to take, and one that many philosophers have taken. Namely, that, when we say that other people see trees and houses and chairs, etc., we mean only the two things (1) that *they*, the other people, merely directly apprehend certain sense-data; and (2) that *we*, when we say it, know that these sense-data are in fact connected with the material objects which we call trees and houses and chairs. And so too when I say of myself that *I saw* a tree, I may mean only to assert that at the time when I saw it I merely directly apprehended certain sense-data, though *now*, when *I* know that I saw it, I indirectly apprehend the tree with which these sense-data were in fact connected. It is, I think, a very natural view to take that this is all we mean by words like see, feel, perceive, observe, when we apply them to material objects; and I think possibly very often this may be all we mean.

But now, what I want to point out is, that if this were the *only* sense in which we ever *saw* or perceived or observed a material object at all, we could never possibly, by means of our senses, get *any knowledge of the existence* of material objects at all. For when we talk of *knowledge* of the existence of a material object we mean knowledge *proper*; and you can only *know* of the existence of a thing, *know that* it exists, in the proper sense of the word, when you are apprehending the thing in question at least indirectly. If all that ever happened when we saw or perceived or observed material objects were that we directly apprehended certain sense-data which were *in fact* connected with them; we should never, by merely seeing or perceiving or observing them in this sense, get to know that they existed at all: we could only get to know of the existence of the sense-data, which we directly apprehended; we should not even suspect the existence of any objects other than these sense-data. In those cases, therefore, where by seeing or perceiving or observing a material object, we mean a process by which we *do get to know* of their existence, this process cannot merely consist in directly apprehending certain sense-data: we must, besides doing this, also apprehend indirectly the material objects with which these sense-data are connected. So that sometimes, at all events, seeing an envelope cannot merely mean seeing certain sense-data with which it is connected; it must mean also *indirectly apprehending* this something else—the material envelope itself, *with* which these sense-data are connected.

And I think it is possible to see that something of this sort does often, at least, actually occur. Suppose, for instance, I now hold up my hand and you look at it. At the very moment, when you directly apprehend the sense-data which you do apprehend—each one of you, probably, a slightly different set—you have, I think, an obscure belief in the existence of something else, *beside* these sense-data. The sight of the sense-data is accompanied by a belief in something else, other than them. And in so far as you merely believe, however obscurely, in the existence of this something else, you are, of course, indirectly apprehending this something else, in the sense I have explained. *It*—this something else—which you thus indirectly apprehend, would, on the view I am suggesting, *be* my hand. None of the sense-data which you directly apprehend are even parts of my hand or of its surface. So that, if you see my hand at all, that means merely that you are *indirectly* apprehending it in this obscure way. That you do, when you directly apprehend certain sense-data, *often* thus believe in the existence of something else is, I think, certain. And, if this something else *is* a material object, then you really are, whenever you do it, indirectly apprehending a material object. And moreover, I think, it is difficult to be certain that you have not *always* this thought of a something else, whenever you directly apprehend any sense-data at all. So that, whenever you do anything that can properly be called seeing, or feeling, or perceiving, or observing, there is always included in the act an indirect apprehension of something other than anything which you are directly apprehending—of something, therefore, which at least *may* be a material object. And if this be so, then we might say that the seeing or perceiving of a material object consists in the *indirect* apprehension of it—that indirect apprehension of something or other other than sense-data, which occurs whenever we *directly* apprehend any sense-data. Seeing, therefore, and feeling and observing, as applied to material objects, would never mean *merely* the direct apprehension of sense-data, which were in fact connected with those objects; it would always also include the indirect apprehension of those objects with which the sense-data are connected.

But now, even if, when we directly apprehend a sense-datum, we do also indirectly apprehend something else; it by no means follows that we do ever *know* of the existence of material objects by means of our senses. It does not follow, for three reasons. In the first place, even if we do indirectly apprehend something else beside the sense-data, that only means that we *think of* something else beside them. And from the fact that you think of a thing, it by no means follows that there is any such thing as what you think of. It might be the case that there really was nothing else beside the sense-data; and that our belief that there is something else is wholly mistaken. In the second place, even though there really is something else, and our belief that there is is therefore correct, it does not follow that, because there is something else, and you believe there is, therefore you really *know* that there is. The belief in something else which accompanies the direct apprehension of sense-data might be a correct belief, but it does not follow that it amounts to *knowledge*—to what I have called knowledge *proper*. And in the third place, even if there not only *is* something else, *but* we do really *know* that there is; it does not follow that this something else is a *material* object. For instance, even if, when I look at this envelope, I *do know* that there exists something else beside the sense-data which I directly apprehend, it does not follow that I know now, or ever can know, that this something else has the properties which I attribute to it when I call it a material object. By calling it a material object, I mean to say of it at least two things, namely, that it is situated somewhere or other in space, and also that it is not a mind nor an act of consciousness. But even if, when I look at this envelope, I do *know* of the existence of something else beside the sense-data which I am directly apprehending, it does not follow that I *know* that this something else is situated anywhere in space, nor yet that it may not be a *mind* nor the act of consciousness of some mind.

Accordingly even if, when I directly apprehend certain sense-data, I do, in fact, believe in the existence of something else besides, it does not follow that I really *know* that this something else does exist; nor that, if I do know this much, I also know or ever can know that this something else is a material object. And many philosophers have expressed doubts on both these points. Some have doubted whether I can ever really know that, at the moment when the sense-data which I apprehend exist, anything else exists at all. And some, while admitting that I can *know* of the existence of *something* else beside the sense-data, have doubted whether I can know this something else to be a material object.

And one chief reason why some philosophers have held these views is, I think, that they have held certain views as to the conditions which must be satisfied if any one is ever to *know* anything at all. It must be remembered that we are now talking of *knowledge* in the sense which I called knowledge *proper*: we are now talking of *knowledge* in the sense in which mere direct apprehension is *not* knowledge, nor mere indirect apprehension either. We are talking of knowledge in the sense in which you cannot *know* anything but a fact; and in which you do not *know* a fact, unless besides merely directly apprehending a proposition which would be expressed by the same words, you *also* believe this proposition and it is true; and in which, even if you believe it and it is true, you yet *never* know it to be true, unless some other condition is satisfied *as well*. Some philosophers, then, have held views as to what the conditions are, which must be satisfied, if you are to *know* any proposition to be true. They have held that nobody ever does know a proposition to be true unless *beside* the condition that he believes it, one or other of certain other specified conditions are satisfied as well. And there are certain particular views as to what these extra conditions which must be satisfied are, which have, I think, been held by very many philosophers indeed; and which have constantly been applied by them to settle the question whether any particular person does or does not *really* know a proposition to be true, which he believes, or thinks he knows to be true. It is these particular views as to the conditions which must be satisfied, if you are ever really to *know* a proposition to be true, which have, I think, been largely responsible for *both* of the two views we are now considering: both for the view that we never really know that there exists at any moment anything else *beside* the sense-data which we are directly apprehending at that moment; and for the view, that even if we do know that *something else* exists, we never know *that* this something else is a material object. And what I propose now to do is first of all to state these views as to what is necessary for real knowledge, which have, I think, led many philosophers to doubt our knowledge of material objects; then to consider whether, supposing these views to be true, we really should be unable to *know* of the existence of material objects; and finally to consider whether these views *are* true, and, if not, what the alternative to them is.

I am now, then, going to try to state certain views as to the conditions which must be satisfied, if we are ever really to know any proposition to be true, or to be even so much as *probably* true. In other words: Some philosophers have said: Nobody ever knows any proposition to be true, or to be even probably true, *unless* the proposition in question belongs to one or other of certain specified classes. And I am going to try to state what the classes are, to which they have said a proposition must belong, if anybody is to know it to be true. The views I am going to state are I think in substance those which were held by Hume; and I think they have been more clearly stated by him than by any one else. I shall, therefore, call them Hume's views, though I shall not try to state them in precisely the same language which he used. They are, I think, extremely plausible views; and many philosophers, who would hesitate to accept them when expressly stated, yet do, I think, often argue, in particular cases, as if they were true: they argue for instance that we do not *know* of the existence of material objects at all, merely on the ground that we do not know them in any of the ways specified by Hume. These views of Hume's are, moreover, of great importance historically. Certain points in them suggested to the German philosopher, Kant, some of the most remarkable of his own views; and those remarkable views of Kant's which were suggested to him by Hume, have, I think, had more influence on the subsequent course of philosophy than have the views of all the philosophers who preceded Kant put together.

Chapter V
HUME'S THEORY

THE question which I am about to discuss is this. Under what circumstances (if any) does a man, when he believes a proposition, not merely believe it but also absolutely *know* that it is true? We are all quite certain that men do sometimes believe propositions, which they do not really *know* to be true. Sometimes they not merely believe them, but feel very certain that they are true; and yet, in spite of the fact that they feel very certain, they do not really *know* them to be so. Sometimes, for instance, when a man feels very certain indeed that something or other is true, we find out afterwards that he was quite mistaken—that after all it was not. The mere feeling of certainty, therefore, even though it be very intense, is not the same thing as knowledge—knowledge in the sense which I have called knowledge *proper*. The feeling of certainty is sometimes present, in a very intense degree, where *knowledge* proper is absent. The question is, then: What other conditions, *beside* the mere fact that a man feels very certain of a proposition, must be fulfilled, if he is to *know* that it is true? And many philosophers, by way of answer to this question, have tried to lay down rules to the following effect. They have said: A man *never* really *knows* a proposition to be true, unless, besides the mere fact that he feels certain of its truth, one or other of certain other specified conditions is also fulfilled. Hume, I said, for one, tried to lay down certain particular rules to this effect. And I proposed to begin my discussion by stating some of the rules which he laid down.

To begin with then, he divides all propositions, true and false alike, into two classes: those which assert that some particular thing has existed, does exist, or will exist, and those which do not assert the existence of anything. By propositions which do not assert the existence of anything he meant such propositions as these: Twice two are four; the three angles of a triangle are equal to two right angles; black differs from white. And he thought that the conditions which must be fulfilled, if we are to know any proposition of this kind to be true, were quite different from those which must be fulfilled if we are to know propositions asserting existence to be true. Propositions which *do not* assert existence, can, he says, be known in two ways: some can be known by *intuition* and others can be known by *demonstration*. By demonstration he means the strictly *deductive* sort of proof which is employed in mathematics: and we do all commonly suppose that mathematicians do absolutely *know* immense numbers of propositions which they have learnt in this way. Hume holds, then, that no proposition, of the sort which does not assert existence, can be really known to anybody, unless *either* it has been demonstrated; *or* it is known *intuitively*. And the sort of knowledge that he means by *intuitive* knowledge is the sort of knowledge you may have of a proposition, when, as soon as you really understand what the proposition means, you can *see* that it is true. For instance, consider this proposition, which is one of the axioms of Euclid: Things which are equal to the same thing are equal to one another. It does seem as if, as soon as you really understand what this proposition means, you can *see* that it is true. And Hume would say that this proposition was known *intuitively*; and another way of saying the same thing is to say that it is self-evident. What he means to say then, in the case of *all* propositions which do not assert existence, is that *none* of them can be *known* to be true unless they are *either* known in the way in which this one is known, *or* they have been *demonstrated*, by the strictly deductive kind of proof by which mathematical propositions are demonstrated.

But, now, he thinks that no propositions which assert the *existence* of anything, past, present or future, can be known in either of these two ways: none of them, he thinks, can be either proved *deductively* to be true, nor be known *intuitively* in the way in which it is known that: Things which are equal to the same thing are equal to one another. Neither of these two conditions can ever be fulfilled in the case of propositions which assert the existence of anything. And in their case, therefore, he proposes a different set of conditions.

He says that no man ever really *knows* a proposition which asserts the *existence* of anything, past, present or future, unless one or other of *three* conditions are fulfilled.

And the first *two* conditions, which he mentions are these.

(1) A man *may* really *know* that a thing does exist, if, at the very moment when he believes that it exists, he actually is *directly apprehending* the thing in question—directly apprehending it in the sense I have explained. And (2) A man may really *know* that a thing *did*

exist in the past, if he *did* directly apprehend it in the past and *now* remembers it.

These two are, I think, comparatively simple conditions and need no explanation. But it is otherwise with the third condition which Hume lays down. A great deal is contained in it; and I want to explain it as clearly and carefully as possible. Obviously it is far the most important of the three. For if we never really *knew* of the existence of anything at all, except in cases where one or other of the first two conditions are fulfilled, we should only know a very small part indeed of the things which we suppose ourselves to know. The things which I am now directly apprehending and have directly apprehended in the past, form but a very small part of those in the existence of which I believe. The question is then this: Under what conditions can we know of the existence of a thing (past, present or future), when *neither* of these first two conditions is fulfilled—when we are *not* directly apprehending the thing at the moment when we believe that it exists, and when also we *have not* directly apprehended it in the past?

And in order to avoid the repetition of cumbrous phrases, I will, in future, speak of this question as being the question: Under what conditions does a man know of the existence of anything which he *has never* directly apprehended? meaning by *has never* directly apprehended, *both is* not directly apprehending at the moment *and has* never directly apprehended in the past. You must please, understand, then, that when I talk of a thing which a man *has* directly apprehended, I shall mean anything whatever which he *either is* directly apprehending at the moment *or* has directly apprehended in the past; and similarly when I talk of a thing which a man *never* has directly apprehended, I shall mean anything whatever which he *neither* is directly apprehending at the moment *nor* has directly apprehended in the past.

Our question is then this: Under what conditions does a man ever really *know* of the existence of anything whatever which he has *never* directly apprehended (including under the term '*has* directly apprehended' what he *is* directly apprehending at the moment, as well as what he *has* directly apprehended in the past)?

And one main principle, which Hume means to assert, in answer to this question, is, I think, the following.

Suppose a man believes, at a given moment, in the existence, past, present or future, of some definite thing A, which he has never directly apprehended (*i.e.* is not directly apprehending now, and never has directly apprehended). Now, says Hume, whatever A may be, that man can never really *know* of the existence of A, unless he knows also that some other thing B, which he *has* directly apprehended, *would not* have existed, *unless* A *had* existed, *were* existing, or *was about to* exist as well. In other words: Suppose I am now directly apprehending or have directly apprehended some thing B with regard to which I know that it, B, would not have existed at all *unless* something else, A, had existed *before* it: then, says Hume, I may really know that A did exist before it. Or suppose again I know, with regard to B, which I have directly apprehended, that it would not have existed at all unless A had been existing simultaneously with it: *then* I may really know that A did or does exist simultaneously with it. Or suppose again, I know with regard to B, that it would not have existed at all, unless A had been *going to* exist after it: then I may really know that A did exist after it or will exist after it. But *unless* one or other of these three conditions is fulfilled, then, says Hume, I cannot possibly really *know* that A either has ever existed, does now exist, or will ever exist.

This, I think, is a correct statement of Hume's first principle. But the principle is a little complicated, and my statement of it may have been a little difficult to follow. So I will try to make it still plainer exactly what the principle is by giving particular examples. Let me, first of all, take any example whatever of a thing which I believe to exist at the present moment, but am *not* directly apprehending. I will, for instance, take my own brain. I do in fact believe now that a more or less definite sort of thing, which I call my brain, and which I am not directly apprehending, really does exist at this very moment. Well, says Hume, I cannot *really* know that my own brain is existing at this moment, *unless* I also know one or other of two things. I must *either* know that something which I *am* now directly apprehending would not be existing *unless* my brain were existing too. This is *one* alternative. For instance, I am now directly apprehending an act of consciousness of my own which I call the *hearing* of certain words—I am now hearing the words I am now speaking and am directly apprehending my hearing of them. Well then, *if* I *know*, no matter how, that this act of consciousness, this hearing, which I *am* directly apprehending, would not be existing, unless my brain were existing at the same time, then, says Hume, I *may* really know that my brain is existing now. And similarly, if I *know* that anything else whatever, which I *am* directly apprehending at this moment, would not be existing now, *unless* my brain were existing too, then I *may* really *know* that my brain is existing now. This is *one* alternative. But there is another, which Hume's theory allows. Suppose I *really* knew that something, which I did directly apprehend a moment ago, would not have existed then, unless my brain had been *going to* exist now at this moment: then also, Hume allows, I might really *know* that my brain is existing at this moment. No matter whether I could really know, or how I could really know, that the existence of anything a moment ago did entail the existence of my brain now at this moment: all Hume says is that *if* I did really know this, then I *might* know that my brain is existing now. This is the second alternative. And unless one or other of these alternatives is fulfilled, I cannot, Hume says, possibly really *know* that my brain is existing at this moment. Nobody can, he says, possibly *know* of the *present* existence of anything whatever, which he is *not* directly apprehending, unless he knows that its present existence is necessarily connected either with the existence of something which he is directly apprehending now, *or* with the existence of something, which he has directly apprehended in the past: *necessarily connected* in the sense that the directly apprehended thing *would not* have existed, *unless* the thing not directly apprehended *were* existing simultaneously with it, or had been going to exist after it.

This, then, is an example of what this first principle of Hume's means in the case of a belief concerning the *present* existence of anything, which is *not* being directly apprehended. But I want to make as plain as possible the whole of what this first principle does mean, and, therefore, at the risk of wearying you, I will give two other examples: an example of what it means in the case of a belief about the *past* existence of anything, and of what it means in the case of a belief about the *future* existence of anything.

Let us take, then, a belief about the past. I do, in fact, believe now that Julius Caesar was murdered in the Senate House at Rome nearly two thousand years ago. And I certainly did not directly apprehend this murder. Here then is a belief in the past existence of something which I have never directly apprehended. And what Hume says is this: I do not really *know* that Julius Caesar was murdered, *unless* one or other of *four* conditions is fulfilled. Either I must know that something, which I am directly apprehending *now*, would not have existed, unless Julius Caesar had been murdered. Or I must know that something which I have directly apprehended in the past, would not have existed unless Julius Caesar had been murdered before it existed. These are *two* of the conditions under which I *might* know that Julius Caesar was murdered: and, in this particular case, these are the only ones which can have been fulfilled. Obviously one or other of these *may* have been fulfilled. I have, for instance, directly apprehended in the past sense-data of many words both spoken and written, the meaning of which was that Julius Caesar was murdered. And it may be that I do really know, no matter how, that all these sense-data would not have existed, unless Julius Caesar really had been murdered. And I think we should all be inclined to agree with Hume, that, *unless* I do know this, I do not really know that Julius Caesar was murdered at all. If I do not know it in this way, it does seem that I cannot know it in any way at all. But there are two other conditions under which, according to Hume's theory, I *might* know such a past fact as that Julius Caesar was murdered. I might know it, if I had in the past directly apprehended something, which would not have been existing, *unless* the murder of Julius Caesar was taking place simultaneously with its existence. Or I might know it, if I had directly apprehended something, which would not have existed, unless the murder of Julius Caesar had been going to take place *afterwards*. We know that, in this particular case, neither of these conditions are fulfilled, because I certainly did not directly apprehend anything at all either at or before the time when Julius Caesar's murder is supposed to have taken place. But, in the case of many past events, both these two other conditions might conceivably be fulfilled. For instance, I believe now that the moon was in existence at two o'clock in the morning this day last week. I did not at that time directly apprehend the moon. But I may, for instance, have directly apprehended the moonlight coming in at my window. Well, if I *know* (no matter whether I could know) that the moonlight, which I did then directly apprehend, would not have been existing, *unless* the moon had been existing simultaneously, then, says Hume, I may really *know* now that the moon was existing at that moment. Or to take an example of the *fourth* condition. I directly apprehended the other day sense-data of the sort which we call the appearance of a bird flying in the air. But I did not watch it until it alighted anywhere; and even if I had, I should not, according to Hume, have directly apprehended the bird alighting: I should only have directly apprehended certain sense-data, which might have been connected with the bird's alighting. I did not, then, directly apprehend the bird alighting. But I may, Hume's theory allows, nevertheless know now that that very bird did alight somewhere, *if* I *know* that the sense-data, which I directly apprehended, when (as we say) I saw it flying, would not have existed then, *unless* the bird had been going to alight somewhere later on. I do not say that I could absolutely *know* this; but Hume's theory allows that *if* I do know it, then I may absolutely know now that that bird did alight somewhere. This is an example of the *fourth* condition, under which I may know now of the past existence of something which I have never directly apprehended. And *unless* one or other of these four conditions is fulfilled, nobody, says Hume, can ever absolutely *know* of the past existence of anything whatever which he has not directly apprehended. He must know, that is, either that the thing in question necessarily preceded something which he is apprehending *now*; *or* that it necessarily *preceded* something which he has apprehended in the past; or that it necessarily accompanied something which he has apprehended in the past; or that it necessarily *followed* something which he has apprehended in the past. Meaning by *necessarily* in each case merely this: that the thing directly apprehended would not have existed, *unless* the other thing, which was not directly apprehended, had preceded, or accompanied, or followed it as the case may be.

In the case, then, of a belief in the *present* existence of anything which we have not directly apprehended, there were *two* conditions, one or other of which must be fulfilled, if we are ever to know that such a belief is true; in the case of a belief about the past there are four conditions, one or other of which must be fulfilled if we are absolutely to know that the belief is true; and in the case of a belief about the future there are again only *two* conditions, one or other of which must be fulfilled.

For instance, I do believe now that five minutes hence something or other will be existing. And I cannot, says Hume, really *know* this, I cannot really know but that five minutes hence the whole Universe will have ceased to exist, except under one or other of two conditions. I must either know that something, which I am *now* directly apprehending, would not be existing now, unless *something*, at least, were going to exist five minutes hence. Or I must know that something which I have directly apprehended in the past would not have existed, unles *something*, at least, were going to exist five minutes hence. And so, too, with regard to all beliefs about particular events in the future. I do in fact believe now that the sun will rise tomorrow, and that my body, dead or alive, will be out of this room before it rises. Perhaps you will say I obviously cannot really *know* that either of these two events will occur; and I agree that I cannot absolutely *know* it. But they will do to illustrate Hume's principle. His principle is that I certainly cannot know either of these two things, *unless either* I know that something, which I am directly apprehending *now*, would not be existing now, *unless* they were going to occur; *or else* unless I know that something, which I have directly apprehended in the past, would not have existed *then*, unless they had been going to occur.

This, then is Hume's first principle. And, I think, it is obviously a very plausible one. It does seem very plausible to say: I can never know of the existence of anything which I have *not* directly apprehended, unless I know that some one thing or some set of things, which I *have* directly apprehended, would not have existed, unless the other thing, which I have *not* directly apprehended, really existed also—either before, or after, or at the same time, as the case may be.

Hume himself identifies this first principle with the principle that I cannot know of the existence of anything B, which I have *not* directly apprehended, unless I know that B is related to something or some set of things, which I have directly apprehended, by the *relation of cause and effect*. And I think the two principles really have at least this in common. Namely, if I know that any one thing A *must* have been caused by another B, then I do know that A would not have existed, unless B had existed before it. And also, if I know that any one thing A *must* have B for its effect, then I do know that A would not have existed unless B had been going to follow. But it does not follow that the two principles are identical, and it will, I think, be better to keep this discussion quite apart from the question what exactly the relation of cause and effect is.

This, then, is Hume's first principle. And he goes on to add to it a second. He now asks: Under what conditions can I know that any one thing or set of things A would not have existed, unless another, B, had existed, did exist or were about to exist also? And his first answer to this question also is, I think, extremely plausible. His answer is that nothing but *Experience* can teach me this; I cannot possibly know it except by the help of Experience. And this, so far as it goes, is an answer which has constantly been given by all sorts of philosophers. All sorts of philosophers have insisted, for instance, that I cannot possibly know that any one thing, A, would not have existed, unless another, B, had *preceded* it, except by the help of experience; and that I cannot possibly know that any one thing, A, must be followed by another, B, except by the help of experience.

How, for instance, can I know that, if I were to drop this paper, it would fall? It seems obvious to say, that I could not know this except by experience. Or how, when I see a child, can I know that it must have had two parents? It seems obvious to say that I could not know this also except by the help of experience.

But merely to say that we cannot know any such things except by the help of Experience is rather vague. And Hume tries to define more exactly what sort of Experience I must have had, in order to know that any two things are necessarily connected. And here also, I think, he does it very plausibly. I will here, to avoid being unnecessarily cumbrous, speak only of the case where what we are supposed to know is that one thing, B, must have been *preceded* by another, A. What I say with regard to this case will also apply, *mutatis mutandis*, to the other two cases: the case where what we are supposed to know is that one thing, B, must have been *accompanied* by another, A; and the case where what we are supposed to know is that one thing, B, must be or have been *followed* by another, A. I confine myself, then, for the sake of illustration, to the cases where I suppose myself to know that one thing, B, must have been *preceded* by another, A.

If, says Hume, I am ever absolutely to know this, I must constantly have observed in the past that, whenever a thing *like* B did exist, it *was* preceded by a thing *like* A. And by saying that I must *constantly* have observed this, he does not mean to say, that when I observed a thing like B, I must absolutely *always* have observed a thing like A before it. All that he means is that I must never have observed a case where a thing like B did exist, and where a thing like A certainly did *not* exist before it. If I am absolutely to *know* that B must have been preceded by A, I must, he says, have done at least this. I must have observed several cases in which, when a thing like B did exist, a thing like A did exist before it; and I must have observed no case, in which, when a thing like B did exist, a thing like A certainly did *not* exist before it.

But he adds to this a supplementary principle which is very important. The fact is we very often do not even suppose ourselves to know when a thing B exists, that it absolutely *must* have been preceded by another thing A. We often only suppose ourselves to know that it is more or less *probable* that A preceded it: often, very highly probable indeed, but sometimes only slightly probable, and sometimes with various degrees of probability between these two. And Hume thinks that by a suitable modification of his principle, he can lay down a rule for these cases also. He says we can never know that one thing, B, was even *probably* preceded by A, unless we have actually observed *some* cases (at least *one* case) in which a thing like B was preceded by a thing like A. But in order to know that B was *probably* preceded by A, we need not have observed that things like B were in the past *constantly* preceded by things like A. Even though we have observed more than one case in which a thing like B was certainly *not* preceded by a thing like A, we may still know that B in our case was *probably* preceded by A. The degree of probability will, he says, depend upon the *proportion* of the cases where we have observed a thing like B preceded by a thing like A, to those in which, when we observed a thing like B, a thing like A certainly did *not* precede it. In order to know that B was at all *probably* preceded by A, we must, when we observed a thing like B in the past, *generally* have observed that a thing like A preceded it: *generally*, in the sense that there must have been *more* cases in which a thing like A *did* precede it, than cases in which a thing like A certainly did *not* precede it. And if we have observed *many* cases in which a thing like A did precede it, and only a few in which it did not, then we may know that it is *highly* probable that A did precede B in our case.

Hume, then, lays down two rules: (1) That in order absolutely to know that B *must* have been preceded by A, I must have observed in the past that things like B were *constantly* preceded by things like A; and (2) That in order to know that *B* was *probably* preceded by A, I must have observed in the past that things like B were *generally* preceded by things like A.

And both of these two rules do, I think, at first sight seem very plausible. But let us look at them a little more closely. What they assert is this: *I*, they say, can never know that one thing B was even *probably* preceded by another A, unless *I myself* have observed cases in which things like B were preceded by things like A. *No man* can ever know that one thing B was *probably* preceded by another A, unless *that man himself* has observed cases in which things like B were preceded by things like A. They assert, therefore, that each of us can only learn things of this sort by means of *his own* experience. But is it really plausible to say this? Can I, in fact, never learn anything whatever by the experience of *other people*? Cannot I ever learn that one kind of thing has been generally preceded by another, by learning the fact that *other people* have observed that they are? It seems absurd to deny that I can learn such things by the experience of other people. And Hume himself, so far as this part of his theory is concerned, certainly does not mean to deny that I can. What he does *not* notice is that, *if* I can, then his two principles, just as he states them, cannot be true; they must be modified in some way. And the sort of way in which he meant them to be modified is, I think, the following. How, he asks, can I myself ever know that any other person ever has experienced anything whatever? This is itself a case of the very sort for which he began to lay down his rules. The fact that another person has had certain experiences is itself a thing which I myself have never directly apprehended. If, therefore, I am to know that another person really has had any particular experiences, I must know that certain things which I *have* directly apprehended, would *not* have existed unless some other person had had the experiences in question. And this, he says, I *can* only learn in the first instance by my own experience. I cannot ever learn it unless I have *myself* observed that when I hear or read certain words or directly apprehend other signs, then the statements conveyed by these words or signs are, as a general rule, true. And obviously this is a sort of thing which I could, conceivably, learn by my own experience in the way Hume lays down. If I hear statements made to the effect that I myself shall observe or have observed certain things, and if I constantly observe that, when I do hear such statements, made in a certain way and under certain conditions, then I do really see or have really seen the things which the statements asserted that I had seen or should see, I might, in this way, upon Hume's own principles, arrive at the generalisation that statements made in a certain way were as a general rule *true*. And I might, then, apply this generalisation to *all* statements made in the way and in the circumstances, in which I have myself observed that statements are generally true: I might apply it, therefore, to statements which asserted the existence of things which I myself had never seen, and might thus come to know that other people really had experienced things which I had not experienced. It is in some such way as this, I think, that Hume intended his original rules to be modified. But it must be observed that this really is a modification of the rules in question. To allow this modification is to *give up* the rules as originally stated. What the rules asserted was that I can never know that one thing B was even probably preceded by another A, unless I have *myself* observed that things like B were in the past generally preceded by things like A. And this rule must now be given up. But we may, perhaps, express the necessary modification by saying this: *I* can never know that B was even probably preceded by A, unless *either* I have *myself* observed that things like B were generally preceded by things like A; *or* unless I have myself observed that statements like some statement, which asserts that *some one* else has observed a general connection between things like B and A, are *generally* true—*i.e.* are generally either preceded or accompanied or followed by the existence of that which they assert.

Now, when this modification has been made, Hume's rules do, I think, again become plausible. Let us consider them as including this modification. What I want now to call attention to is another point about them. What they assert, you see, is that any knowledge I may have of the existence or probable existence of anything whatever that I have not directly apprehended, must be based on *observation*: either my own observations, or the observations of other people; but, if the latter, then my knowledge that any other person did observe the things in question, must itself, in the last resort, be based upon *my own* observation. And I think these rules owe their plausibility very largely to the use of this word 'observation'. We are all accustomed to think that our knowledge of what has happened, is happening, and is likely to happen is very largely based upon observation—upon observation and experiment, meaning by *experiment* merely observation under particular conditions artificially arranged. How, for instance, was it learnt that there are corpuscles in the blood? By observation, we should say. Men examined drops of blood under the microscope, and under these conditions they *observed* the bodies which are now called corpuscles: they *saw* these bodies. But now what do we mean when we say that they *observed* these things? What we *say* is that they actually *observed* the drop of blood itself, and *observed* the corpuscles in it. But, as we have seen, on the accepted theory with regard to sense-data, they did not *directly apprehend* either the drop of blood itself, or any part of it; they did not directly apprehend either the corpuscles themselves or any part of them. All that any man can ever have directly apprehended is certain sense-data, no one of which and no part of which is even a part of the material object, a drop of blood. When, therefore, we talk of *observation* in the sense in which it seems so obvious that much of our knowledge is based upon *observation*, we do *not* mean by 'observation' *direct apprehension*. We mean by *observation*, the relation which we have to the material objects themselves, *when* we directly apprehend certain sense-data: we do not mean by it the relation of *direct apprehension* which we have to the sense-data. What I *observe*, for instance, now, is the movement of my hand. But I am *not* directly apprehending the movement of my hand; I am merely directly apprehending certain sense-data, which, on the accepted theory, are not even in part identical with my hand itself or with its movements. When, therefore, we talk of knowledge that is based on observation, we do not generally mean by 'observation' direct apprehension. And when Hume himself gives instances to show how much of our knowledge is based on observation, the plausibility of his instances depends upon the fact that he means by observation what we all commonly do mean—namely, a relation to the material objects themselves, not merely the relation which we have to certain sense-data. When, for instance, he urges that it is by means of observation we learn that a stone, when dropped, will fall to the ground, or that a fire will burn; he is thinking that we have in the past actually observed stones falling and fires burning. But if we were to understand the word observation, in this sense, *in his rules themselves*, it would obviously make nonsense of them. Observation, in this sense, is a relation which we have to an object which we do *not* directly apprehend. But the very purpose of his rules is to state under what conditions we can ever know of the existence of an object, which we do *not* directly apprehend. And what they state is that we can never know of the existence of any such object unless we have previously *observed* a similar object. But obviously, even if we had previously *observed* a similar object, this could not help us at all, if 'observation' is not to mean direct apprehension. For, even when we did previously observe the similar object, we should not have directly apprehended it; and hence should not have known of its existence, unless we had again *observed* previously to it, another object similar to it, and so on *ad infinitum*. So that if I am ever to have knowledge of the existence of an object which I observe, I must have previously observed an absolutely infinite series of similar objects. To lay down such a rule as this would plainly be absurd; and it is certainly not what Hume means. In his rules, he certainly means by *observation* a relation, by which we can know of the existence of the object observed, *when* we observe it, even if we observe it for the first time. And, according to him, the *only* relation of which this is true is that of *direct apprehension*. *In his rules*, therefore, he means by 'observation' *direct apprehension*. And when we understand this they cease to be quite so plausible. What they amount to *now* is this: I can never know of the existence of any object which I have *not* directly apprehended, unless I have previously directly apprehended some object like it or know that somebody else has. Thus understood they lose the plausibility which arises from the fact that so much of our knowledge does seem to be based on previous *observation*—observation, in the sense in which we *do* observe material objects, and in which observation does *not* mean direct apprehension. And I think that the reason why they have seemed plausible to so many philosophers is largely because of this confusion between observation, in the sense in which we commonly use the word, and *direct apprehension.* But still they *have* seemed plausible. Many philosophers have, I think, consciously or unconsciously adopted them; they have argued as if these principles of Hume were true. And they *may* seem plausible, even if we understand quite clearly that by *observation* is to be meant direct apprehension and direct apprehension only. These principles have, I think, as I said, been one chief reason why many philosophers have doubted whether we ever know of the existence of any material object; and what I wish now to do is to consider whether, supposing them to be true, we *could* ever *know* of the existence of any material object. Many philosophers have held that supposing them to be true, we could not ever know of the existence of any material object—not even that it *probably* existed; and that is one chief reason why they have held that we *do not* know, even with probability, of the existence of any material object.

But, first of all, I will try to state again, as carefully as possible, exactly what the rules are.

They try to provide for two cases: (1) the case where we believe that something which we have not directly apprehended *certainly* did exist, or is existing, or will exist; and (2) the case where we believe that something which we have not directly apprehended, *probably* did exist, or is existing, or will exist.

And in the first case what they say is this. No man can ever know such a belief to be true, know, that is, that anything whatever A, which he has not directly apprehended, *certainly* did exist, or is existing or will exist, unless he knows that some thing or set of things B, which he has directly apprehended, would *certainly* not have existed, unless A had existed too, either before or at the same time or after B. And they add: And no man can ever know this last, unless *either he himself* has directly apprehended things like B *before*, and, *when* he directly apprehended them, has also directly apprehended things like A preceding or accompanying or following them as the case may be, and *also* has never found a case in which when he directly apprehended things like B, things like A certainly did *not* exist: *or* unless he knows that some other person has had direct apprehensions of this sort. And they add that, in this latter case, his knowledge that any other person has had them must *itself* be based on direct apprehensions of *his own*.

In the second case, the case where we believe that something which we have not directly apprehended *probably* exists or has existed or will exist, what Hume's rules say is this. No man can ever know any such belief to be true unless he knows that some thing B, which he *has* directly apprehended would not have existed *unless* the thing A, which he believes probably to exist, had *probably* existed also. *And* (they add) he cannot know this last unless *either* he himself *or* some other person has directly apprehended things like B before, and, *when* this happened, has *generally* directly apprehended things like A, before, or after, or at the same time; and here again, if what he relies on is the experience of *another* person, he cannot do this, unless he *knows* that that other person certainly or probably has had the experience in question, and this he cannot *know*, except where one or other of these very rules has been complied with.

These rules, you see, are rather complicated; but, I hope the general principle is clear.

Now let us consider what would follow, supposing these rules were true. I will take a particular instance. I do, in fact, believe that there are at the present moment *bones* in this hand of mine—a skeleton, of the shape with which we are probably all of us familiar from pictures of the skeleton of a hand. I do, in fact, believe, not only that there probably are, but that there *certainly* are, bones of that shape at this moment in this hand. But I am certainly not directly apprehending at this moment any of these bones. How, then, can I know, according to Hume's principles, that they even probably exist? One possible way is this. I am at this moment directly apprehending certain sense-data—the colour and shape, etc., which might be called the visible appearance of the skin of my hand. And I might have found, in the past, by direct apprehension, that visible appearances similar to these were generally connected in certain ways with other sense-data—for instance, with sense-data of the sort that I should see, if I saw the skeleton of my hand, or of the sort that I should feel if I felt the skeleton. In fact people, when they dissect a hand, do find that sense-data, similar to those which I now directly apprehend, are connected in certain ways with such sense-data as the appearance of a skeleton. Let us call the sense-data which I now see, the visible appearance of the skin of my hand. Other people have, I believe, when they dissected a hand, found that the visible appearance of the skin of a hand, which they directly apprehended at one moment, was followed by the visible appearance of a skeleton, which appeared to stand in certain spatial relations, within the same directly apprehended space, to the visible appearances of the skin which they saw just before. I have, I should explain, never dissected a hand myself, or seen one dissected. But I might according to Hume's principles, possibly have learnt that other people had experienced a connection between the visible appearance of the skin of a hand, and the visible appearance of its skeleton, such as I have just described. I might, therefore, possibly know, on the basis of *their* experience, that, if this hand were dissected, visible appearances similar to those which I now see *would*, in all probability, be followed by the visible appearance of a skeleton. And I might possibly know, too, by other experiences (I do not say I *could*) that when the visible appearance of a skeleton exists at one moment it generally exists for a considerable time before and after. I might have watched the visible appearance of a skeleton, and found that it is a sort of thing which does not quickly disappear. And I might, therefore, possibly be able to infer that since the visible appearance of a skeleton, *would* probably exist in a few moments if my hand were dissected now, it must also probably exist *already* at this moment. I might, therefore, on Hume's principles possibly know that the visible appearance of the skeleton of a hand does probably really exist now, having certain definite spatial relations, within the space which I now directly apprehend, to this visible appearance of the skin of my hand. I might possibly know this with regard to the *visible appearance* of a skeleton. And similarly I might possibly know it with regard to other sense-data; for instance, the sense-data which I should *feel*, if I touched the skeleton of a hand. It does, therefore, seem that according to Hume's principles, I might possibly know that there do exist at this moment, in connection with this visible appearance, certain other sense-data, of the sort which I should see if I saw the skeleton of a hand, or should feel if I touched it.

But now, supposing I could, according to Hume's principles, know as much as this; what would follow? Obviously the things, whose present existence I should, on this hypothesis, be able to infer would be things of the same sort as those with regard to which I gave what I called the accepted theory—they would be sense-data—they would be sense-data more or less resembling those which I should see or feel, if I saw or felt a skeleton. All that Hume's principles do seem to allow that I am able to infer is that there are *existing now*, in connection with those sense-data which I directly apprehend, other sense-data more or less like those, which I should see or feel, if I saw or felt a skeleton. If I am able to infer the existence of anything at all, even resembling the skeleton in whose existence I believe, I must, it would seem, be able to infer the existence of its *colour*—a *colour* more or less resembling that which I should see, if I directly apprehended the visible appearance of a skeleton. But many philosophers have supposed that there are insuperable objections to supposing that any such colour—the colour of the skeleton —does really exist at this moment in connection with the sense-data which I see. They have, in fact, adopted an extension of the theory which I called the accepted theory with regard to sense-data—an extension, which should be carefully distinguished from the original theory itself. The original theory asserted, you remember, that none of the sense-data, which any of us ever directly apprehend, ever exists at all *except* in that person's mind. The *extension* asserts not merely that those *same* sense-data cannot exist except in somebody's mind, but *also* that no *sense-data at all*—nothing resembling a sense-datum—can ever exist except in somebody's mind: that there cannot exist, except in somebody's mind, anything at all *like* any sense-datum that I directly apprehend. For instance, it asserts that no such thing as a colour or a sound ever exists at all, except when it is being directly apprehended by some one, or, at least, is in some one's mind. And some philosophers, Berkeley, for instance, have declared that this extension of the theory and not only the theory itself, is *self-evident*. And, if it really were so, then, of course, all discussion as to how we can know of the existence of material objects would be cut short at once. It would then be certain, not only that we can never *know* of the existence of a material object, but also that no material object can exist. For whatever we mean by a material object we do at least mean two things, namely (1) something which can exist, without being in anybody's mind, and (2) something which does, in at least one respect resemble sense-data— namely in respect of the fact that it has a *shape* and is situated in some kind of a space. If, therefore, it were self-evident, as Berkeley says, that nothing resembling a sense-datum can ever exist except in some one's mind, it would follow that no material object exists at all. But, as I said, it seems to me that this is certainly not self-evident. And most philosophers have, I think, argued as if it were not so. They have allowed that a material object which resembled sense-data in respect of having *shape*, might conceivably exist. But they have argued that we cannot *know* that it exists for the following reasons. The only way in which we could know it, is, they have said, in accordance with Hume's principles. But these principles, if they allowed us to know of it at all, would allow us to know of the existence of colours and sounds and other sense-data, in addition to shapes, which are *not* in anybody's mind. And there are the same difficulties in supposing that a colour, which I do not directly apprehend, can be part of a material object, as in supposing that one that I *do* directly apprehend can be so. Take, for instance, the supposed colour of the skeleton of my hand. Am I to suppose that the colour which it now has, is the colour which *I* should see, if my hand were dissected; or the colour which somebody else, with eyes of different power, would see? Am I to suppose that it is the colour which I should see, under a light of ten candle-power, or that which I should see under a light of a hundred candle-power? Am I to suppose that it is the colour which I should see under a yellowish light, or the different one which I should see under a bluish light? There would seem, upon Hume's theory, to be equally good reasons for supposing it to be any one of these colours; and yet it is difficult to suppose that *all* these colours do now exist at the same place inside my hand. For reasons like these, most philosophers have supposed that no colour at all can really be existing inside my hand at this moment. And since Hume's theory, *if* it gives reason for supposing that there is now in my hand a skeleton at all, seems to give reason for supposing that there is in it a *coloured* skeleton; they have supposed it can give no reason for believing that there *is* a skeleton at all. And since Hume's principles state the *only* conditions, under which I could know, even with probability, that there is a skeleton now in my hand; therefore, they conclude, I do *not* know that there even probably is one. And what applies to the present existence of the skeleton of my hand, applies equally to the existence, past, present or future, of any material object whatever. I can never know that any material object even probably exists. The only things whose existence I can know of beyond what I myself have directly apprehended are (1) the past and future contents of my own mind, including both my acts of consciousness and also all the things I directly apprehend, and (2) the contents of the minds of other people in the same sense.

This is, I think, a fair statement of one line of reasoning which has led many philosophers to suppose that I cannot possibly know of the existence of any material object. The reasoning does not seem to me to be conclusive; but it does seem to me to be plausible enough to require some sort of answer. And I will now try to give it the best answer I can.

Chapter VI

HUME'S THEORY EXAMINED

I have just been occupied mainly in stating one particular answer, which I called Hume's answer, to the following question: Under what circumstances (if any) does a man ever *know* of the existence, past, present, or future, of anything whatever, which he himself is not directly apprehending at the moment, and has not directly apprehended in the past?

And the answer to this question which I represented as given by Hume, was in two parts.

The first part was this. Let us say that the existence of one thing, A, is a *sure sign* of the existence of another thing B, whenever you can truly say: *Since* A exists, it is certain that B did exist before it, does exist at the same time, or will exist after it. And let us say that the existence of one thing, A, is a *probable sign* of the existence of another thing B, whenever you can truly say: *Since* A exists, it is *probable* that B did exist before it, does exist at the same time, or will exist after it. Well then, the first part of Hume's answer consists in saying two things: Firstly: Nobody ever knows that anything B, which he himself has not directly apprehended, *certainly* did exist, or does exist, or will exist, unless he knows that the existence of some thing or set of things, A, which he *has* directly apprehended, is a *sure sign* of the existence of B. And secondly: Nobody ever knows that anything, B, which he himself has not directly apprehended, *probably* did exist, or does exist, or will exist, unless he knows that the existence of some thing or set of things, A, which he *has* directly apprehended, is a *probable* sign of the existence of B.

This was the first part of Hume's answer to our question; and the second part was this:

Let us say that a man has experienced a *general conjunction* between *things like* A and *things like* B, if, when he has directly apprehended a thing like A in the past, he has *generally* directly apprehended a thing like B, either before or after, or at the same time. '*Conjunction*', a word which Hume himself uses, is a convenient word, because we can say that things like A are *generally conjoined* with things like B, *both* when we mean that they generally precede them, *and* when we mean that they generally follow them, *and* when we mean that they generally accompany them. Let us say, then, that a man has experienced a *general conjunction* between things like A and things like B, if, when he has directly apprehended a thing like A in the past, he has *generally* directly apprehended a thing like B also, either before or after or at the same time. Well then, if we understand the phrase 'experienced a general conjunction' in this sense, the second part of Hume's answer consists in saying this. No man, he says, ever knows that the existence of any one thing A is either a *sure sign* or even a *probable sign* of the existence of another thing B, unless *somebody* has in the past experienced a general conjunction between *things like* A and *things like* B. But obviously something more can be added to this answer. For even if somebody else has experienced a general conjunction between *things like* A and *things like* B, yet if I myself have not, and also I do not *know* that anybody else has, I shall be as far as ever from knowing that the existence of A is a sign of the existence of B. But the fact that anybody else has ever experienced anything whatever is always a fact which I myself have never directly apprehended. If, therefore, I am to know that anybody else has experienced any general conjunction, I must know that some thing A, which I *have* directly apprehended, is a *sign* that they have. And I can only know this if I *myself* have experienced a conjunction between things like A and things like the fact that somebody else has experienced the conjunction in question.

This was the second part of Hume's answer to our question. And these two rules or principles were what I tried to explain at length last time. They are, I think, very difficult to express quite accurately: I have not even tried to express them *quite* accurately even now: and yet, I think, it is very easy to see almost exactly what is meant by them, although they are so difficult to express. I will call the first the rule: That nobody can ever know of the existence of anything which he has not directly apprehended, unless he knows that something which he has directly apprehended is *a sign* of its existence. And I will call the second the rule: That nobody can ever know that the existence of any one thing A is a *sign* of the *existence* of another thing B, unless he himself (or, under certain conditions, somebody else) has experienced a *general conjunction* between *things like* A and *things like* B. And the important thing to remember about this second rule is that nobody can be said to have *experienced a conjunction* between any two things, unless he has *directly apprehended* both the things. I will call these two rules, then, Hume's first rule, and Hume's second rule. But, when I call them Hume's, I ought, perhaps, to warn you of two things. If you were to look for them in Hume, you would not find either of them expressed exactly in the form in which I have expressed them; and also you *would* find, mingled with statements which seem to be statements of these rules, other statements which mean something very different indeed, and which Hume himself does not seem to distinguish very clearly from these two rules. I do not pretend, then, that these two rules are at all a complete statement of what Hume has to say about our knowledge of the existence of things which we do not directly apprehend. All that I do mean to claim is that they certainly do express a part, and a very important part, of what he did think about this subject; and so far as I know, he was the first philosopher who did definitely think of these two rules.

But now I said that many philosophers seem to me to have been led to conclude that we cannot ever know of the existence of any material object, by the assumption, conscious or unconscious, that these rules of Hume's are true. They have, I think, argued first, with some plausibility, that, *if* these rules are true, then none of us ever knows of the existence of any material object; and *then* they have concluded that, *since* these rules *are* true, none of us does ever know that any material object exists—not even that there is the slightest probability of its existence. Both steps in this argument, I said, do seem to me plausible enough to need an answer; and I said that in this lecture I should do my best to meet it. Obviously it must be met, if at all, in one or other of two ways: you must either try to shew that, even if Hume's rules are true, we might yet know of the existence of material objects; or you must try to shew that Hume's rules are not true. I shall presently consider both of these two ways of meeting it. But first of all, I want to try to state more clearly exactly what the point at issue is.

There are, I think, two views, both very plausible and both very commonly held, which owe their plausibility, in the way I have suggested, to the assumption that Hume's rules are true.

Both of them start by admitting, as Hume does, that every man can know of the existence of things which he himself is directly apprehending at the moment, or has directly apprehended in the past and now remembers. But they hold that the only existing things which any man ever does directly apprehend are (1) his own acts of consciousness and (2) his own private sense-data and images. And, except for the possibility that some of the sense-data which we directly apprehend may not be *private* to us—the possibility, that is, that two or more of us may sometimes directly apprehend the very same sense-datum—I think they are plainly quite right so far. Nobody, I think, does ever learn by direct apprehension of the existence of anything whatever except his own acts of consciousness, on the one hand, and sense-data and images on the other: and these sense-data and images may, I think, as these views hold, be *all* of them always *private* to the person who directly apprehends them: I think this is very possibly so, only I do not feel quite sure. At all events, nobody ever does know, by direct apprehension, of the existence of anything whatever except his own acts of consciousness and the sense-data and images which he directly apprehends. As to this we are agreed. The only question is as to what things *beside* his own acts of consciousness and the sense-data and images which he directly apprehends a man can ever know to exist: and it is here that Hume's rules come in.

One of the two views I am speaking of, holds this, namely: That every man's knowledge as to what exists, or even *probably* exists, *beyond* what he himself has directly apprehended, is entirely confined to two classes of things. A man may know, it says, to a certain extent, what acts of consciousness he himself is likely to perform in the future, and what sense-data and images he is likely to directly apprehend; and so too he may be able to know that he himself has in the past, or probably has, performed certain acts of consciousness and directly apprehended certain sense-data, even though he has quite forgotten them. This is one class of things which he may know to exist, probably or certainly, by inference, according to Hume's rules. Let us say that this class consists entirely of *contents*, past and future, of his own mind—assuming, that is, that the sense-data and images which he directly apprehends are in his own mind—are *contained* in it. And the other class of things which, according to this view, a man may know to exist (probably or certainly) consists, in the same sense, entirely of the *contents of other people's minds*. A man may know, that is, that other people, beside himself, have performed, are performing, and probably will perform certain acts of consciousness; and that they also have directly apprehended, are directly apprehending and probably will directly apprehend certain sense-data. These two classes of things—certain contents past and future of his own mind—and certain contents, past, present, and future, of other people's minds, a man may know to exist, at least *probably*, even though he has not directly apprehended them, or, if he has, has quite forgotten them. *But* (this view says) nobody can ever know, even probably, that anything else whatever, not belonging to these two classes, does exist or will exist in the Universe at all. Nobody can know that there even probably has existed, does exist, or will exist in the Universe anything else whatever except certain things which are in his own mind or else in somebody else's mind. This is one view, which has, I think, been very commonly held, and which is, I think, plainly due to the assumption that Hume's rules are true. Hume's second rule states that nobody can ever know of the existence of anything which he himself has not directly apprehended, unless he has previously apprehended something *like* it. But the only existing things which any man ever has directly apprehended are things in his own mind—either his own acts of consciousness, or the sense-data and images which he has directly apprehended. It is then argued, with some plausibility, that anything else which is sufficiently *like* these to be inferred according to Hume's rule, must also be something in somebody's mind. And hence it is concluded that nobody ever does know of the existence of anything whatever except what is in somebody's mind, either his own mind or somebody else's.

This, then, is one of the two views, which seems to me to be due to the assumption that Hume's rules are true. And the second is exactly like it except in one respect. This view also holds that the only definite kinds of things which Hume's rules allow me to infer are certain contents, past and future, of my own mind and certain contents past, present, and future, of other people's minds. But it holds also that none of the events in my own mind or in other people's, which I can thus know of, are sufficient to *account for* the existence of the sense-data, which I or other people directly apprehend. This view holds, therefore, that I *can* know that *something else* exists in the Universe—because something else must have existed, in order to *cause* the existence of my own and other people's sense-data. But, it says, I cannot possibly know whether this something else, which is the cause of sense-data, is or is not in any respect *like* anything which anybody has ever directly apprehended. I cannot possibly know, for instance, whether it has shape or is situated in space or not. I cannot possibly know whether it is or is not in anybody's mind. The only means by which I can know what *sort* of a thing is likely to have caused any particular kind of thing is, by means of Hume's rules. But Hume's rules only allow me to infer the existence of certain things in my own mind and in other people's minds. I *know* that these things, which I can infer, are *not* sufficient to cause my own sense-data and other people's sense-data. I know, therefore, that *something else* must exist in the Universe. But with regard to this something else I know nothing whatever except simply that it does exist and that it causes my own and other people's sensations. I cannot possibly know that it is in the least respect similar to anything whatever which I or anybody else has ever directly apprehended.

These two views, then, I say, both deny that we can ever know of the existence of any material object—they both deny that we can ever know that any material object even *probably* exists. But curiously enough many of those who hold them have thought that they were not denying our knowledge of material objects. They have thought that, to allow that we do know of the things, which they say that we do know of, is *the same thing* as to allow that we do know of the existence of material objects. They have thought that they were not denying our power to know anything which Common Sense supposes itself to know. And what I wish now, first of all, to make plain is that both of these views *do* deny our power to know of the existence of material objects; and that in doing so they do flatly contradict Common Sense. I want to make plain how utterly and extremely different these views are from those which we take, when we do believe in the existence of material objects. And thus, at the same time, to make plain exactly what the question at issue is, when it is asked whether we can, if Hume's rules are true, ever know of the existence of any material object.

Let us take a particular instance. Look at this pencil. It is just an ordinary wooden pencil. And, when you see it, you directly apprehend a patch of brownish colour, bounded on two sides by fairly long parallel straight lines, and at the ends by much shorter lines, which, in the case of some of you, are probably curved. You directly apprehend these sense-data, and both the two views we are considering allow that, when you directly apprehend these sense-data, you may know them—these visual sense-data—to exist. But you have all often seen a pencil before; that is to say, you have directly apprehended sense-data similar to these that you are now seeing. And when you did so, you may often have directly apprehended *other sense-data* in *conjunction* with visual sense-data similar to those you are now directly apprehending. For instance, you may often have felt a pencil in your hands; and you all know the sort of sense-data you directly apprehend, when you do this—the feeling of smoothness and hardness and of a cylindrical shape. Again you have probably sometimes split a pencil in halves longwise along this line of division, and you know what sort of sense-data you would see and feel, if you looked at the pencil or felt it after doing this. Again you have probably cut one through its breadth, so, and you know what sort of sense-data, you would see and feel, if you looked at and felt the two new ends, after cutting it. These past experiences, which you may have had, of the *conjunction* of other sense-data, visual and tactual, with visual sense-data similar to those which you are now directly apprehending, are what are often called by those who hold the views I am now discussing 'routines of sensations'. And both views allow that on the ground of these past 'routines', you may, according to Hume's rules, know *now* that you *would*, if you did certain things—that is to say, if you directly apprehended the sense-data which you would directly apprehend, if you took this pencil in your hand and split it or cut it—that you *would*, that is under certain conditions, directly apprehend other sense-data, visual and tactual, of the sort to which I have referred. They allow, that is, that these sense-data, which you now directly apprehend, really are *signs* of *something* else: are *signs*, not indeed that anything else *will*, even probably, exist, but only that certain other sense-data *would* exist, *if*, in addition to the sense-data which you now directly apprehend, you were also to apprehend directly certain others. But neither view pretends that these other sense-data, of which those which you now see are in this remote way *signs*, do exist *now*. Neither view pretends that that cylindrical shape, which you would feel, if you handled the pencil, exists *now*; or that the sense-data, which you might feel or see, if you split the pencil or cut it open, exist *now*. And as regards the first view, it holds that the sense-data which you now see cannot be known by you to be a sign of the *present* existence of *anything whatever*. The pencil, so far as you mean by the pencil something which you know, even probably, to exist *now*, consists *solely* of those visual sense-data which you are now directly apprehending; *either* of these alone or, perhaps it would be said, also of any images, which you may now be directly apprehending—images of sense-data which you *would* see or feel under other circumstances. But it is not pretended that these images, even if some of them are images of what you would see or feel, if you cut the pencil open, are *inside* the pencil now. The pencil simply has no inside, so far as you know. You cannot possibly know that it has any. All that the sense-data, which you now see, are a *sign* of, is not anything which exists now, but only of certain other sense-data, which you would see or feel, *if* certain other conditions also were realised, which may never be realised.

This is what the first view holds. And the second merely adds to it this. It adds that the visual sense-data you now see really can be known to be a sign of the present existence of *something* else: not, indeed, quite strictly, of the *present* existence of anything else; since this something else can only be known as the *cause* of what you now see, and the *cause* must exist *before* the effect. But it does allow that you may know that these sense-data are a sign that *something* existed a moment ago—something different from anything which you or anybody else, so far as you know, directly apprehended at that moment. But with regard to this something else, it says, you cannot possibly know that it has any shape, or is situated anywhere in space, or that it is in any respect similar to anything which you have ever directly apprehended. You cannot know, for instance, that what causes the sense-data you see is part of a cylindrical surface, or that there is anything whatever *inside* that cylindrical surface. You could not know this, even if you had the advantages which I enjoy, and could examine the pencil both by touch and sight as closely as I can. So far as the sense-data which I directly apprehend can be known to be signs of anything having shape and occupying space at all, they can only, as the first view said, be signs of certain other sense-data, which *would* be seen or felt, under other conditions, which may perhaps never be realised: they are *not* signs of the *present* or *past* existence of anything that has shape or occupies space at all.

Now it seems to me quite plain that these views are utterly different from what we all commonly believe, when we believe in the existence of material objects. What we believe is that these sense-data which we now directly apprehend are signs of the existence of something which exists *now*, or at least did exist a moment ago—not merely of something, which *would* exist, under conditions similar to what we have experienced in the past. And we believe—we all cannot help believing, even though we may hold philosophical views to the contrary—that this something which exists now or existed a moment ago, is not merely a something which may or may not have shape or be situated in space—something with regard to which we cannot possibly tell whether it has a shape or not. We believe quite definitely that the sense-data which we now see are *signs* of the present or immediately past existence of something, which certainly has a cylindrical shape—roughly cylindrical—and which certainly has an inside. I, for instance, claim to *know* that there does exist now, or did a moment ago, not only these sense-data which I am directly apprehending—seeing and feeling—but *also* something else which I am not directly apprehending. And I claim to know not merely that this something else is the *cause* of the sense-data which I am seeing or feeling: I claim to know that this cause is situated *here*; and though by *here* I do not necessarily mean *in* the space which I directly apprehend, yet I do mean *in space*—somewhere in *some* space. And moreover I claim to know, not merely that the cause of my sensations is situated here in space, and has therefore some shape, but also roughly *what* its shape is. I claim to know that the cause of the sense-data I am now directly apprehending is part of the surface of something which is really roughly cylindrical; and that what is enclosed within this cylindrical surface is something different from what is here just outside it. It is, I think, plainly things like these that we all of us believe, when we believe in the existence of material objects. We do not always believe we know exactly what the shape of the objects is, but we do believe that they have some shape. We do take the sense-data which we directly apprehend to be *signs* of the *present*, or *immediately past* existence, of something having shape and in space: *not* merely to be signs of the *possible* future existence of something having shape and in space; *nor* merely signs of the present or immediately past existence of a bare something—something with regard to which we cannot tell whether it has shape or not.

The question is, then, whether we can, consistently with Hume's second rule, ever know that the sense-data which we directly apprehend are *signs* of the existence of a material object in this sense. And in considering this question we may as well again take this pencil as an example. If I do not know *now* that these sense-data, which I now directly apprehend, are really signs of the present or immediately past existence of a body, which I do not directly apprehend, but which is really roughly cylindrical; then, I think, I must admit that I do not ever *know* of the existence of *any* material object. If I do not know of the existence of this pencil now and here, I can hardly ever know of the existence of any material object at all. I do not suppose I have ever had better evidence for the existence of any than I have for this. Can I, then, if Hume's second rule is true, really know now that this cylindrical body, in whose existence I believe but which I *do not* directly apprehend, does, even probably, now exist, or did, even probably, exist a moment ago?

What makes it, at first sight, seem possible that I might know this, even if Hume's second rule were true, is, I think, the following circumstance. Namely, I certainly have directly apprehended in the past, *in conjunction* with sense-data similar to those which I now directly apprehend, other sense-data which were really similar, in some respects, to *parts* of the material object, in whose existence I believe. I believe, for instance, that this material object—this pencil—really is composed of a number of surfaces, similar to that which I now directly apprehend when I look at this end or feel it with my hand, in respect of the fact that they are *circular* or very nearly circular. And I have in the past, when I cut a pencil through, directly apprehended circular surfaces of this sort standing in a certain relation to sense-data similar to those which I now directly apprehend when I look at the length of the pencil. I might, therefore, it would seem, in accordance with Hume's rule, possibly know that there really exist at this moment circular surfaces standing to every point in this length which I directly apprehend in a similar relation to that in which I have found similar surfaces conjoined to points in a similar length before. I might, that is, possibly know that there really exist *at this moment*, all along this pencil a series of circular patches of colour, similar to those which I should see, if I cut it through at any point; and also a series of circular patches of smoothness and hardness, or whatever the qualities may be which I should feel, if I felt the ends, after cutting it through. Also, I or somebody else, may have sometimes examined a circular patch, similar to this, under the microscope, and have then directly apprehended colours and forms different from those which I now apprehend by the naked eye but still all enclosed in a circle. And I might, therefore, know that there really exist at this moment all along the length of this pencil, not only circular patches of colour similar to those which I should see, if I cut through the pencil, and then looked at the ends with the naked eye, but also, and *in the same place*, patches similar to those which I should see, if I looked at the ends through a microscope. It seems to me that I might, according to Hume's second rule, possibly know that these sense-data which I now directly apprehend really are signs of the present or immediately past existence of sense-data of all these kinds; are *signs* that all these sense-data really do exist *now*, though I do not directly apprehend them, and not merely that they *would* exist in the future, *if* certain other conditions were also fulfilled. I might, that is, possibly know that there really do exist now not only those sense-data which

I *do* directly apprehend, but also, in certain relations to them, immense numbers of others, which I do not directly apprehend, but similar to those which I have directly apprehended in the past in conjunction with sense-data similar to these. And these other sense-data would really be similar to parts of the material object—the pencil—in whose existence I do believe. For I do believe that there are, all along this pencil, circular surfaces, and that there are, within the circle which bounds each of these surfaces things having shapes similar to those which I should see with the naked eye, if I cut the pencil and looked at the ends: for instance, the smaller circle, of a different colour, within the larger circle, which represents the place where the lead is: I believe that there really is within this pencil, all along it, *something* similar in shape to this round surface of lead which I now see within the larger circle. And also that there really are within it, all along it, differences of structure similar in shape to those which I should see, if I cut it and examined it with a microscope. The material object, in whose present existence I believe, is, therefore, really in many respects similar to sense-data, which I *should* see in conjunction with these, which I now see, under certain circumstances; and similar also therefore, to sense-data which I have directly apprehended in conjunction with sense-data like these in the past. And Hume's second rule would, so far as I can see, allow us to infer that these sense-data, which I should see under certain circumstances, do all really exist *now*.

I might, therefore, even if Hume's second rule were true, *know of* the present existence of something very *like* in many respects to the material object, in which I believe; something consisting of parts very similar in shape, to the parts of the object which I believe to exist. I might know, that there really do exist *now* sense-data of a sort, which, according to the two views I am attacking, I can only know *would* exist under certain conditions, that are *not* now fulfilled. Hume's rule would, therefore, allow of my knowing something much more *like* what I believe, than these two views did.

But nevertheless it seems to me it would *not* allow me to know of the existence of exactly that, in which I believe—the material object, the pencil. For all these things similar in shape to parts of the pencil, which it would allow me to know of, are, it must be remembered, patches of *colour* of a certain shape, patches of *hardness*, and *smoothness or roughness* of a certain shape. And even if it might be true that there do really exist inside the pencil now colours similar to those which I should see, if I cut it open; and even if it might be true that different colours, of different sizes, might all exist in the same place: yet these patches of colour and of hardness and smoothness certainly do not constitute the *whole* of the material object in which I believe. Even if there are *here* now all sorts of colours, which I do not see, and all sorts of tactual qualities, which I do not feel, yet the pencil, in which I believe, certainly does not consist *solely* of colours and of tactual qualities: what I believe when I believe that the pencil exists is that there exists something which really is cylindrical in shape, but which does not consist *merely* of any number of patches of colour or of smoothness or hardness, or any other sort of sense-data which I have ever directly apprehended. Even if sense-data of all these kinds really are now in the same place where the pencil is—and I think there are good reasons for doubting whether they are—I certainly believe that there is in that place *something else besides*. This something else, even if it be not the *whole* material object, is certainly a *part* of it. And it seems to me that, if Hume's second rule were true, I could not possibly know of the existence of this something else. For I have never directly apprehended in the past anything whatever that was like *it*: I have only directly apprehended sense-data which had a similar *shape* to that which it has.

I think, therefore, those philosophers who argue, on the ground of Hume's principles, that nobody can ever know of the existence of any material object, are right so far as the first step in their argument is concerned. They are right in saying: *If* Hume's principles are true, nobody can ever *know* of the existence of any material object—nobody can ever know that any such object even probably exists: meaning by a material object, an object which has shape and is situated in space, but which *is not* similar, except in these respects, to any of the sense-data which we have ever directly apprehended. But are they also right in the second step of their argument? Are they also right, in concluding: *Since* Hume's principles are true, nobody ever *does* know, even probably, of the existence of any material object? In other words: Are Hume's principles true?

You see, the position we have got to is this. If Hume's principles are true, then, I have admitted, I do *not* know *now* that this pencil—the material object—exists. If, therefore, I am to prove that I *do* know that this pencil exists, I must prove, somehow, that Hume's principles, one or both of them, are *not* true. In what sort of way, by what sort of argument, can I prove this?

It seems to me that, in fact, there really is no stronger and better argument than the following. I *do* know that this pencil exists; but

I could not know this, if Hume's principles were true; *therefore*, Hume's principles, one or both of them, are false. I think this argument really is as strong and good a one as any that could be used: and I think it really is conclusive. In other words, I think that the fact that, if Hume's principles were true, I could not know of the existence of this pencil, is a *reductio ad absurdum* of those principles. But, of course, this is an argument which will not seem convincing to those who believe that the principles are true, nor yet to those who believe that I really do not know that this pencil exists. It seems like begging the question. And therefore I will try to shew that it really is a good and conclusive argument.

Let us consider what is necessary in order that an argument may be a good and conclusive one. A really conclusive argument is one which enables us to *know* that its conclusion is true. And one condition, which must be satisfied, if an argument is to enable us to know this, is that the conclusion must really follow from the premisses. Let us see, first, how my argument compares with that of my opponent in this respect.

My argument is this: I do know that this pencil exists; therefore Hume's principles are false. My opponent's argument on the contrary is: Hume's principles are true; therefore you do not know that this pencil exists. And obviously in respect of the certainty with which the conclusion follows from the premiss, these two arguments are equally good. *If* my opponent's conclusion follows from his premiss, my conclusion must certainly also follow from mine. For my opponent's conclusion does not follow from his premiss, except on one condition, namely, unless the following hypothetical proposition is true: *If* Hume's principles are true, then I do not know that this pencil exists. But if this proposition is true, then *my* conclusion also follows from my premiss. In fact, both arguments depend in this respect on exactly the same hypothetical proposition—the proposition which both I and my opponent have admitted to be true: namely that: If Hume's principles are true, then I do not know that this pencil exists. Neither conclusion follows from its premiss, unless this proposition is true; and each does follow from its premiss, if this proposition is true. And this state of things is an excellent illustration of a principle, which many philosophers are, I think, apt to forget: namely, that the mere fact that one proposition coheres with or follows from another does not by itself give us the slightest presumption in favour of its truth. My conclusion coheres with my premiss, exactly as strongly as my opponent's coheres with *his*. And yet obviously this mere fact does not give the slightest presumption in favour of either.

Both arguments, therefore, equally satisfy the first condition that is necessary to make an argument conclusive. Both equally satisfy the condition that the conclusion must follow from the premiss. What other condition, then, is necessary if an argument is to enable us to *know* that its conclusion is true?

The second condition, that is necessary, is this: Namely that we should *know* the premiss to be true. Obviously, I think, this condition must be satisfied, if the argument is to enable us to *know* that its conclusion is true. It is not sufficient merely that the premiss should *be* true, if we do not *know* that it is so. For suppose that the premiss is true, and the conclusion does follow from it, and *yet* I do not *know* that the premiss is true. How can this state of things possibly enable me to know that the conclusion is true? Obviously so long as this is the whole state of the case, I shall be just as far from *knowing* that the conclusion is true, as if I had never thought of the premiss at all. The argument may be, and is, a good argument in the sense that the conclusion does follow from the premiss, that the premiss is, in fact, true, and that, therefore the conclusion also is in fact true. But it is not a good argument in the sense that it can possibly enable either me or any one else to *know* that the conclusion is true. The mere fact that the premiss *is* true will not, by itself, enable any one whatever to know that the conclusion is so. If anybody whatever is to be enabled by the argument absolutely to *know* the conclusion, that person must himself first absolutely *know* that the premiss is true. And the same holds not only for absolute certainty but also for every degree of probability short of it. If any argument whatever is to enable me to know that its conclusion is in any degree probable, I must first know that its premiss is probable in at least the same degree. In other words, no argument is a good one, even in the sense that it enables us to know its conclusion to have any probability whatever, unless its premiss is at least as certain as its conclusion: meaning by 'certain', not merely true or probably true, but *known* to be so.

The only way, then, of deciding between my opponent's argument and mine, as to which is the better, is by deciding which premiss is known to be true. My opponent's premiss is that Hume's principles are true; and unless this premiss not merely *is* true, but is absolutely known to be so, his argument to prove that I do not know of the existence of this pencil cannot be conclusive.

Mine is that I do know of the existence of this pencil; unless this premiss not only *is* true, but is absolutely known to be so, my argument to prove that Hume's principles are false cannot be conclusive. And moreover the degree of certainty of the conclusion, in either case, supposing neither is quite certain, will be in proportion to the degree of certainty of the premiss. How is it to be decided which premiss, if either, is known? or which is the more certain?

One condition under which a premiss may be known to be true, is a condition which we have already stated. Namely, any proposition is known to be true, if we have a conclusive argument in its favour; if, that is to say, it does really follow from some premiss or set of premisses already *known* to be true. I say some premiss or *set of premisses*; and this new qualification should be noticed, because it introduces a complication. If any argument from a *single* premiss is to be conclusive, the *single* premiss must, as we have seen, be at least as certain as the conclusion: the conclusion cannot, by the help of any such argument, be known with more certainty than the premiss. But obviously in the case of a set of premisses, the conclusion may be *more* certain than any *single* one of the premisses. Here, too, however, each of the premisses must be known to be at least probable in some degree: no amount of premisses, which were not known to be probable at all, could enable us to know that the conclusion which followed from them all was even in the least degree probable. One way, therefore, in which a proposition can be known to be true, is if it follows from some premiss or set of premisses, each of which is already known to be so with some degree of certainty. And some philosophers seem to have thought that this is the only way in which any proposition can ever be known to be true. They seem to have thought, that is, that no proposition can ever be known to be true, unless it follows from some other proposition or set of propositions already known to be so.

But it is, I think, easy to see that, if this view were true, no man ever has known any proposition whatever to be in the slightest degree probable. For if I cannot know any proposition whatever to be either true or probably true, unless I have first known some other proposition, from which it follows, to be so; then, of course, I cannot have known this other proposition, unless I have first known some third proposition, before *it*; nor this third proposition, unless I have first known a fourth before it; and so on *ad infinitum*. In other words, it would follow that no man has ever known any proposition whatever to be even probably true, unless he has previously known an absolutely infinite series of other propositions. And it is quite certain that no man ever has thus known a really infinite series of propositions. If this view were true, then, neither my argument nor my opponent's argument could possibly be a good argument: neither of them could enable us to know that the conclusion was even in the least degree probable. And the same would be true of every other argument whatsoever. So that if this view—the view that we can never know any proposition whatever, unless we have a good argument for it—were true, then it would follow that we cannot ever know any proposition whatever to be true, since we never can have any good argument for it.

If, therefore, either my argument or my opponent's, or any other argument whatever, is to be a good one, it must be the case that we are capable of knowing at least *one* proposition to be true, *without* knowing any other proposition whatever from which it follows. And I propose to call this way of knowing a proposition to be true, *immediate* knowledge. And I wish to insist for a moment upon what *immediate* knowledge is. It is something utterly different from what I have called *direct apprehension*; and that is why I have chosen a different name for it, though, in fact, both of them are very often called by both names—they are both often called direct knowledge and both often called immediate knowledge. One difference between them is that *direct apprehension*, as I explained, is a relation which you may have to a proposition, equally when you believe it and when you do not, and equally when it is true and when it is false; whereas immediate knowledge is one form of the relation which I called knowledge *proper*: and knowledge *proper*, you may remember, is a relation which you never have to a proposition, unless, besides directly apprehending it, you also believe it; and unless, besides this, the proposition itself is true, *and also* some fourth condition is satisfied as well. And another difference between direct apprehension and immediate knowledge is that direct apprehension is a relation which you may have to things which are *not* propositions, whereas immediate knowledge, being a form of knowledge proper, is a relation which you can only have to propositions. For instance, at this moment, I directly apprehend the whitish colour of this paper; but I do not *immediately know* this whitish colour. When I directly apprehend it, I may *also*, if I happen to think of them, immediately know the proposition that I directly apprehend it and also the proposition that it exists. But both these propositions are something quite different from the whitish colour itself; and I may at a given moment directly apprehend a colour, without at the same time immediately knowing either proposition; although, whenever I do directly apprehend a colour or any other sense-datum, I *can, if I happen to think of them*, also *know both* the proposition that I directly apprehend it *and* also the proposition that it exists. Immediate knowledge is, therefore, something quite different from direct apprehension. And there is one other point about it which should be mentioned. I have said it is the kind of way in which you know a proposition to be true—really *know* it, not merely directly apprehend it—when you *do not* know any other proposition from which it follows. And of course, if you do not know any proposition from which it follows, then, if you know it at all, you can only know it immediately. But it is important to insist that even when you do know a proposition immediately, you *may* also at the same time know some proposition from which it follows: you may know it *both* immediately and *also* because you know some other proposition from which it follows. If, therefore, we give the name *mediate* knowledge to all cases in which you know a proposition, because you know some other from which it follows; the result is that you may at one and the same time know the same proposition *both* mediately *and* also immediately. The relation, therefore, between mediate and immediate knowledge is very different from that between direct and indirect apprehension. When you are apprehending a thing directly you are never at the same time also apprehending it indirectly; and when you are apprehending a thing indirectly, you are never at the same time also apprehending it directly. But you may, at one and the same time, *know* a proposition both mediately and immediately. Of course, cases do occur where you *only* know a proposition mediately—*only* because you know some other proposition from which it follows; but it is important to distinguish such cases from cases where, though you do know the proposition, *because* you know some other from which it follows, and therefore do know it mediately, you do not know it *only* because of this, but *also* immediately.

It is certain, then, that if any proposition whatever is ever known by us mediately, or because some other proposition is known from which it follows, some one proposition at least, must also be known by us *immediately*, or *not merely* because some other proposition is known from which it follows. And hence it follows that the conditions necessary to make an argument good and conclusive may just as well be satisfied, when the premiss is only known *immediately*, as when there are other arguments in its favour. It follows, therefore, that my argument: 'I know this pencil to exist; therefore Hume's principles are false'; may be just as good an argument as any other, even though its premiss—the premiss that I do know that this pencil exists—is only known immediately.

But is this premiss in fact known by me immediately? I am inclined to think that it is, though this might be disputed, for the following reasons. It must be noticed, that the premiss is: I know that this pencil exists. What, therefore, I am claiming to know immediately is *not*, that this pencil exists, but that I know it to exist. And it may be said: Can I possibly know immediately such a thing as this? Obviously, I cannot know *that* I know that the pencil exists, unless I do know that the pencil exists; and it might, therefore, be thought that the first proposition can only be mediately known—known *merely* because the second is known. But it is, I think, necessary to make a distinction. From the mere fact that I should not know the first, *unless* I knew the second, it does not follow that I know the first *merely* because I know the second. And, in fact, I think I do know *both* of them immediately. This might be disputed in the case of the second also. It might be said: I certainly do not know immediately that the pencil exists; for I should not know it at all, unless I were directly apprehending certain sense-data, and knew that they were signs of its existence. And of course I admit, that I should not know it, unless I were directly apprehending certain sense-data. But this is again a different thing from admitting that I do not know it immediately. For the mere fact that I should not know it, unless certain other things were happening, is quite a different thing from knowing it *only* because I know *some other proposition*. The mere direct apprehension of certain sense-data is quite a different thing from the knowledge of any proposition; and yet I am not sure that it is not by itself quite sufficient to enable me to know that the pencil exists.

But whether the exact proposition which formed my premiss, namely: I do know that this pencil exists; or only the proposition: This pencil exists; or only the proposition: The sense-data which I directly apprehend are a sign that it exists; is known by me immediately, one or other of them, I think, certainly is so. And all three of them are much more certain than any premiss which could be used to prove that they are false; and also much more certain than any other premiss which could be used to prove that they are true. That is why I say that the strongest argument to prove that Hume's principles are false is the argument from a particular case, like this in which we do know of the existence of some material object. And similarly, if the object is to prove *in general* that we do know of the existence of material objects, no argument which is really stronger can, I think, be brought forward to prove this than particular instances in which we do in fact know of the existence of such an object. I admit, however, that other arguments may be more convincing; and perhaps some of you may be able to supply me with one that is. But, however much more *convincing* it may be, it is, I think, sure to depend upon some premiss which is, in fact, less certain than the premiss that I do know of the existence of this pencil; and so, too, in the case of any arguments which can be brought forward to prove that we do not know of the existence of any material object.

Chapter VII

MATERIAL THINGS

I have now discussed a great many different points which all have a bearing upon one single question—the question: Do we, any of us, ever know of the existence of any material object? A great many philosophers have come to the conclusion that we do not. But they have used two different sorts of arguments in favour of this conclusion. Some of them have tried to prove positively that no material objects do exist; a conclusion from which it will, of course, follow that we cannot *know* of the existence of any. But I have not hitherto, except in one single instance and very briefly, tried to deal with any of the arguments used in favour of this extreme conclusion. It seems to me, in fact, that the arguments used in favour of this conclusion are not so plausible and do not appeal to nearly so many people as those used in favour of a much more modest conclusion: namely, the conclusion that, whether material objects do exist or not, we do not *know* that they exist. This is a conclusion, which, I think, commends itself very easily to a great many people. And, before I go on to consider the arguments in favour of the more extreme conclusion that *no* material objects exist, I now want, first of all, to state, as simply as I can, the arguments which seem to me the most convincing *against* this more modest and plausible conclusion. I want, in short, to make a final effort to convince you that, even if you really *do not* know of the existence of material objects, at least, you do not *know* that you do not know it.

And the first thing that needs to be done is, I think, this: namely, to make as clear and definite as possible exactly what the point at issue is. The question, as I have stated it, is this: Whether we do or do not know of the existence of material objects? And, in order to make this question quite clear and definite, it is obviously necessary to consider two points. Namely, first, what is meant by *knowing* and *not knowing*; or, in other words, what is the difference between the meaning of the assertion 'I do *know* that so and so exists', and the meaning of the assertion 'I *do not* know that so and so exists.' And, secondly, what is meant by a 'material object'. I propose to take the second point first; because the other one—the question what *knowledge* is—is obviously a much wider one, and will lead us into considerations which apply not only to our knowledge of material objects but also to our knowledge of many other things besides.

First, then, what is meant by a 'material object?' I propose to define a material object by means of three properties, one positive and the other two negative. The positive property is this. I propose to say that nothing is a material object except what is situated somewhere or other in space. Nothing can be a material object except what has position in space. I have previously spoken as if nothing could be a material object except what has *shape*. But this definition might possibly lead to misunderstanding. It is true that everything which has *shape* must have position in some space or other. But in the ordinary sense of the word 'shape', a thing might have position in space, and yet not have any shape. For instance, we should not usually say that a mere *point*—an indivisible mathematical point—had any *shape* at all. By saying, then, that every material object must have *shape*, I might be understood to mean that nothing, which merely occupied a single indivisible point, could be a material object. But I do not mean to say this. It seems to me that some material objects may, quite possibly, occupy mere points; though others, no doubt occupy lines; others occupy areas; and others occupy volumes. It is, therefore, perhaps better to say that a material object must have position in space—be situated somewhere in some space —than to say that it must have *shape*; though obviously you might say that a mere point has, in a sense, a *shape*: there is one particular shape, which is the shape of a point; a point is, in a sense, just one among figures, though we usually apply the name only to more complex figures.

The first property, then, by means of which I propose to define a material object is that it must have position in space. And this is a positive property. The other two are negative.

The first *negative* property is this. I propose to say that no sense-datum or part of a sense-datum, or collection of sense-data, is a material object or a part of one. And this needs some explanation. I have previously explained that I mean by sense-data, the coloured patches we actually see; the sounds we actually hear; the smells we actually smell; all the many different kinds of so-called sensations, which we directly apprehend when we touch things—for instance, the sensation of hardness, of softness, of smoothness, of roughness, etc.; also the so-called sensations of heat and cold—the sensation we actually feel, when we put our hands near a fire, or when we plunge them in cold water; and finally also a great many different kinds of so-called sensations, which may be called organic sensations—such as that particular kind of sense-datum, which we call the pain of a tooth-ache, or the different ones which we call the pain of a burn, or the pain of a cut. We do actually see, or hear, or smell, or feel at different times things of all these different kinds. And it might be thought that nothing ought to be called a sense-datum, except something which is or has been actually seen or heard or smelt or felt, as the case may be. For instance, it might be thought that a coloured patch ought not to be called a sense-datum, unless it is or has been actually seen by somebody; for it is only when it has been actually seen, that it has been, strictly, *given to the senses.* But now, for the purpose of defining a material object, I wish to use the term sense-datum in a much wider sense than this—a wider sense, in which the term is, in fact, very often used, and very naturally so. I wish, for instance, to say that anything which was a coloured patch, of the sort of which we directly apprehend instances, would be a sense-datum, even if it had never been actually seen; that anything which was a sound, would be a sense-datum, even if it had never been actually heard; and similarly with regard to all other classes of sense-data. This extension of the term is, I think, obviously very natural, and it has in fact constantly been made. Images are admittedly not strictly given by the senses, and yet they are very often called sense-data, because they are, in a most important respect, *of the same kind as* actual sense-data. When, for instance, in imagination or in a dream, I directly apprehend the image of a coloured patch, this image is not merely the image *of* a coloured patch, it is *itself* a coloured patch, just as much as any previously seen coloured patch, *of* which it is an image. It is usually different even in quality from any coloured patch *of* which it is an image—it is, for instance, commonly fainter, less vivid; and even if it were ever *exactly like* a previously seen coloured patch *of* which it is a copy, it would yet not be the *same thing*—numerically the same. And plainly it is quite possible that many of the coloured images which I directly apprehend are not *exactly like* any coloured patch whatever, which either I or anybody else have ever actually seen. Images, therefore, if we call them sense-data, as they often are called, are instances of sense-data, which have nevertheless never been actually given to the senses. They are called sense-data, in spite of the fact that they have not been actually given to the senses, because they obviously belong, in some *other* respect, to the same class as things which are given to the senses. This *other* respect is, I think, difficult to define; but it is perfectly easy to see what it is. A coloured image, for instance, is called a sense-datum, simply because it is a coloured patch; the image of a sound is called a sense-datum, simply because *it*—the image—is itself a sound; and similarly in all other cases. We may, therefore, extend the term sense-datum to cover all things, actual or possible, which *resemble* any sense-datum, which *has* been actually given to the senses, in the way in which a coloured image resembles a coloured patch that has been actually given to the senses. And just as we may say that every coloured image actually *is* a sense-datum, merely because it *is* a coloured patch, even though it has never been actually given to the senses; so we may say that *if* a coloured patch existed, which had never been directly apprehended at all, it *would* be a sense-datum, merely because it would be a coloured patch. It is in this extended sense that I wish to use the term sense-datum for the purpose of defining a material object. And, using the term in this sense, I say that: No sense-datum, or part of a sense-datum, or collection of sense-data, can possibly be a material object. This, you will understand, is merely an explanation of how I myself intend to use the term 'material object'. But it is important to notice it, because many philosophers have spoken as if certain collections of sense-data or 'sensations' *were* material objects. And I do not here wish to dispute that certain collections of sense-data might properly be called material objects *in a sense*. I only wish to emphasize the fact that I myself am not going to use the word material object in this sense. 'Material objects', in the sense in which I use the word, must indeed, all of them, have one property which, in the extended sense which I have given to the word, must, I think, be called a sense-datum: they must all be situated in space, and must, therefore, have the 'shape' of the part of space which they occupy—whether that shape be one of the figures which is usually called a shape, or merely what we may call the shape of a point: and every shape must, I think, according to the extended definition I have given, be admitted to be a 'sense-datum'. Every shape is a shape, and must, therefore, belong to the same class as those shapes which we directly apprehend through the senses; just as anything whatever which was a coloured patch, whether directly apprehended or not, would, in the sense I mean, be a sense-datum, merely because coloured patches are one of the sorts of things which are *sometimes* given by the senses. Every material object, then, I admit, must *have* at least one property, which is in this extended sense a sense-datum: it must have shape. But though it *has* shape, it is not itself the shape which it *has*: just as a coloured patch must have a shape, and yet the patch itself is quite a different thing from the shape which it has. And what I mean to say of all material objects is that no one of them *is* a sense-datum of any kind whatever, though they all must *have* a shape, which is a sense-datum. Anything whatever which is a sense-datum, of any kind at all, or a collection of sense-data, cannot *be* what I mean by a material object.

This is the first negative property by which I propose to define a material object. And the second is one which can be mentioned quite shortly. It is this: That no mind, and no act of consciousness can be a material object.

I propose, then, to define a material object as something which (1) does occupy space; (2) is *not* a sense-datum of any kind whatever and (3) is not a mind, nor an act of consciousness. I do not mean to say that these are the only properties which all material objects have, or which we can know them to have. On the contrary, there follows, I think, from the two last that all material objects have the important property that none of them are ever directly apprehended by us: since nothing that exists is ever directly apprehended by us except sense-data, and our own minds and acts of consciousness. And this is a property which can be expressed (though it is liable to misunderstanding) by saying that we can never know *what* a material object *is in itself*, but can only know what properties it has, or how it is related to other things. There is a sense in which we can never be said to know what a thing is in itself, unless we have either directly apprehended it, or else have directly apprehended something which is *like* it in the sense in which my acts of consciousness are *like* your acts of consciousness, and the sense-data which I directly apprehend are *like* those which you directly apprehend. And in this sense, we can, I think, never know *what* a material object is. But, of course, in another sense, we can know very well *what* material objects are: we can know, for instance, with extraordinary precision, what properties they have and how they act upon other material objects. And besides this property, that they cannot be directly apprehended, material objects all, I think, have also the important property, that they are a sort of thing which *might* exist even at times at which nobody was conscious of them. These, and perhaps other properties, do, I think, belong to all material objects. But the three properties I have mentioned are sufficient to make our question definite. It is surely a definite enough question to ask: Do we or do we not know that any object exists, which has the three properties: (1) that it does occupy space; (2) that it is not a sense-datum, or composed of sense-data of any kind whatever, (3) that it is not a mind, nor an act of consciousness? To this question many philosophers, I think, certainly have intended to give a negative answer. They have meant to assert that none of us ever does know of the existence of any object which possesses *all* these three properties together. That this negative view has been commonly held will not, I think, be disputed. What, I think, is much more likely to be said, is that the positive view—the view that we *do* know of the existence of any object, which has all these three properties together—is a purely fantastic view—a view which I personally may, perhaps, hold—but which has hardly any interest, because hardly any one does hold it. It may be said that, when people commonly believe in the existence of material objects, they are not believing in the existence of objects which have these three properties, but in something quite different. So that when I try to defend the view that we do know of the existence of objects which have these three properties, I am not defending the belief in material objects, in the sense in which that belief is commonly held—but am merely defending a view which is not commonly held at all, and which hardly anybody, except myself, has any interest in defending. I want, first of all, to show that this is not the case; to show that we all do commonly believe, in immense numbers of instances and with immense confidence, in the existence of objects having just these three properties which I have defined—having *all* three properties together.

There are four chief views, which may be held, as alternatives to this one which I wish to recommend. And I will try to show, in the case of each of them, that they really are not what we commonly believe; and that, in fact, if you realise clearly what they mean, they are very difficult to believe at all.

You have all probably often travelled in a railway-train. And you would agree that a railway-train is one specimen of the sort of things which we call material objects. And you would agree that, when you travel in a railway-train, you may, if you happen to think of it, believe in the existence of the train you are travelling in.

Let us consider what happens when you travel in one. You may be directly apprehending a great variety of different sense-data. You may actually see, for instance, certain colours and shapes, which we should describe as *appearances* of the walls, and windows, and seats, and racks of the carriage you are in, you may actually feel certain sensations of pressure from the seat you are sitting on, from the back you are leaning against, and others again from the floor you are touching with your feet; you may feel a shaking from the movement of the train; and you may actually hear a set of sounds, with which we are all very familiar as the sort of sounds which we hear when we are travelling in a train. All these sense-data you may yourself be directly apprehending. And, moreover, you may know that other people, travelling in the same train, both in the same carriage as yourself and in different carriages, are probably directly apprehending sets of sense-data more or less similar to those which you are directly apprehending. All this you may know; and besides all this you may know that certain other sense-data, which nobody is now directly apprehending *would*, under certain circumstances, be directly apprehended by you or by other people, in a certain relation to those which you are now directly apprehending. You may know, for instance, that the sense-data you are now directly apprehending—the appearances of the carriage you are in, the sensations of pressure which you feel, the shaking and the familiar sounds—are *signs* that, *if*, *after* directly apprehending these, you were to directly apprehend the sense-data which you would directly apprehend, if the train stopped, and you got out of the carriage, and examined it from outside—are signs I say that, *if* you were to directly apprehend a succession of sense-data *after* the ones you now directly apprehend, you *would* probably see that other sort of sense-data, which we call the appearances of the wheels on which your carriage was running, and of the couplings which join your carriage to other carriages in the train. You may know, too, that if you were to see the visible sense-data, which are appearances of the wheels and the couplings, you would also, *if* in succession to these, you were to directly apprehend another sort of sense-data—those namely which you would directly apprehend, if you moved up to the wheels and couplings and felt them with your hand—you may know, I say, that if *after* directly apprehending the visible appearances of the wheels and couplings you were *also* to directly apprehend a set of sense-data like these, you would, then, probably, also directly apprehend still other sense-data, namely, the sensations of coldness and hardness and smoothness, which you would get, if you felt the iron couplings, or the sensation of weight, which you would get, if you tried to lift them. You may know, I say, while you sit in the train, that the sense-data which you are at the moment directly apprehending are signs that, *if*, in succession to them, certain other sets of sense-data were to occur, you *would* probably, in succession to those, apprehend still others. The hypothesis that you may, while you sit in the train, know all this is common to *all* the five views I wish to consider; both to all the four, which I take to be mistaken, and to the one which I wish to recommend.

But now, what does the first of the four views, which I take to be mistaken, say? It says that the sort of things which I have been describing is absolutely all that you can know about the existence of the train in which you are travelling. And it says, too, that when you believe that the train exists, this sort of thing is absolutely all that you believe. It says, that is, that the existence of the train simply consists in the existence of the sense-data which you and the other people travelling in it are at the moment directly apprehending; in this together with the fact that, *if*, in succession to those, you were to directly apprehend certain others, you would, or would probably, directly apprehend still others. But to suppose that your carriage, while you sit in it, really is running on wheels, or that it really is coupled to other carriages in the train or to the engine—this, it says, is a complete mistake. You cannot possibly know that your carriage is, even probably, running on wheels: and moreover, you do not even believe that it is. If you suppose that this is part of what you believe, when you believe that you are travelling in a train, you are mistaken. All that you really believe in, and certainly all that you can possibly know, is not that there are any wheels existing at the moment, but merely that you *would*, in the future, if you were first to apprehend certain other sense-data, also directly apprehend those sense-data which we call the visible appearances of wheels, or those which you would feel, if you did that which we call touching them. But these sense-data, which you *would* directly apprehend, under other circumstances, certainly do not exist now, while you sit in the train. All that you can know to exist *now*—if such a thing can be said to exist at all—is the possibility or probability that you *would* directly apprehend these sense-data in the future under certain circumstances. So that, if you know that your carriage is running on and supported by wheels, *what* you know is that it is running on and supported by the possibility that certain sense-data should exist in the future. This possibility is what the wheels of your carriage *are*, if it has any wheels at all. And this, it is said, is not only all that you can know: it is also, according to this view, what you actually believe. To believe in the present existence of wheels on which your carriage is running is, it is said, merely to believe that you would, under certain circumstances, see the sense-data, which may be called the visible appearance of wheels, and feel those, which may be called their tactual appearance.

But now, I ask, is this, in fact, what you believe, when you believe you are travelling in a train? Do you not, in fact, believe that there really are wheels on which your carriage is running at the moment, and couplings between the carriages? That these things really exist, at the moment, even though nobody is seeing either them themselves, nor any appearances of them? And now, too, when you consider a case like this, is it not, in fact, very difficult to believe that you do not under such circumstances really *know* that the carriage is supported on wheels and is coupled to the engine? This first theory, as to our knowledge of material objects, does, I think, plainly give an utterly false account of what we do believe in ordinary life; and also, so soon as we realise clearly what it means, it is, I think, very difficult to believe that we do not, in fact, know a great deal more than it allows that we know. And yet, I believe, this theory really has been seriously held by many philosophers, and does very easily commend itself to students of philosophy. So long as it is merely presented in vague phrases such as: All that we know of material objects is the orderly succession of our own sensations; it does, in fact, sound very plausible. But, so soon as you realise what it means in particular instances like that of the train—how it means that you cannot possibly know that your carriage is, even probably, running on wheels, or coupled to other carriages—it seems to me to lose all its plausibility.

This, then, is the first of the theories, which I am arguing are mistaken.

The second is, I think, *more* plausible; but it also, when we consider particular concrete examples can, I think, be seen to be utterly different from what we believe in common life, and also very difficult to believe even now when we try to consider it philosophically. This second theory says: 'Yes: the first theory was mistaken. When you travel in a train, your carriage really does run on wheels and is coupled to other carriages, even though no one is seeing or feeling the wheels and the couplings; and you really can *know* that this is so: the wheels and the couplings really do exist at the moment when you think they do; they are not mere abstract possibilities of future sensations. *But*', this theory says, 'you must not take a hasty and unphilosophical view, as to *what* these wheels and couplings *are*. All that you can possibly know about them is simply that they are *something or other*, and that they would under certain circumstances cause you to have certain sensations. You cannot possibly know that the wheels are round, or that the couplings really join the carriages. To suppose that the couplings *join* the carriages would be to suppose that they are in space, and that there is a distance between the carriages. But this is a gross and unphilosophical view to take. Nothing but your own sensations and those of other people can be known by you to be in space or to have shape. You *do* know that there is an unknown *cause* of these sensations, a cause which does really exist now; but you cannot possibly know what sort of a thing this unknown cause is: you cannot possibly know in any instance whatever, what sort of shape it has, or whether it has any at all. The wheels and couplings, if you mean by them the now existing causes of possible future sensations, are things which you cannot know to have any shape at all, or to be at any distance in any direction either from one another or from anything else.'

This second view is, I think, more plausible than the other, because it allows that wheels and couplings are a name for something which really does exist at the moment when you think it does, and not merely a name for the abstract possibility that certain sensations might exist in the future. But this theory, I think, also ceases to seem plausible, as soon as you realise that according to it, the wheels that you know to exist are not anything that the carriage is *on*; that they are not *round*; and that the couplings are not *between* the carriages. Surely what you believe, when you sit in the carriage, is that it is *on* the wheels—*above* them, spatially related to them; that they themselves are something *round*; and that your carriage is coupled to another which is *in front of it*, spatially related to it, and that there is a distance between the two. And now, when you consider the matter philosophically, can you really believe it to be impossible that you should, when you sit in a train, really *know* that these things are, at least probably, true? It seems to me very difficult to believe that you cannot really know, under any circumstances, that your carriage really is running *on* round wheels. And yet this is what this second theory requires you to believe. Many philosophers have, I think, really believed the theory, and it also may seem very plausible so long as you merely state it in abstract terms, such as: All that we know of material objects is that they are the unknown causes of our sensations; and this is what we mean by 'material objects'. But it also seems to me to lose its plausibility, so soon as you consider what it implies in particular concrete instances.

The third mistaken view, which I wish to consider, is one which has not, I think, been held by many philosophers, but which *has* by some at least been held to be what we all commonly believe in ordinary life. And it is, I think, in some respects more plausible than either of the two last. This is the view that the sense-data or some of them which you would see and feel, if you got out and looked at the wheels and handled them, do really exist now, while you sit in the carriage, even though no one is directly apprehending them: that these sense-data are what you mean by the wheels; and that it is *on* them that the carriage is running and is supported. The plausibility of this view seems to me to rest upon the fact that it really is very difficult to believe that the sense-data which you directly apprehend at one moment do not, in some cases, still continue to exist, even when, for instance, you turn your head away, and are no longer directly apprehending them. For instance, if I now look at this hand, and turn my eyes away, I do find it very difficult to believe that just those sense-data which I just now saw, just exactly those colours—the visual appearance of the hand—are not still existing, even though neither I nor anybody else are seeing them. And moreover, at the moment when I do look at my hand, I find it very difficult to believe that the colours which I see are not *really on* the surface of the hand—in the very same place in which the surface of the hand—the material object—is. The conviction that these things are so seems to me so overwhelming, and the more so the more attentively you consider the matter, that I still do not feel sure that they really are not the case. I do not, therefore, feel at all certain that some of the coloured patches and other sense-data, which you would see and feel, if you examined the wheels, may not really be existing at the moment, when you sit in the carriage and no one is seeing them, and that they may not really be in the same place in which the wheels are. But, of course, the view that they are so, is open to the familiar objections that, *if* they are, we should apparently have to admit that many different colours were all at the same time in the same place. And, even if we could get over this difficulty, the view that they are will, I think, plainly not help us in our present problem. For the view I am now considering, is not merely that these sense-data are in the same place with the wheels, but that they *are* the wheels—that the wheels consist solely of certain sense-data, which you would directly apprehend under other circumstances. And *this* view—the view that the now existing wheels and couplings consist *solely* of sense-data, which you might directly apprehend under other circumstances, can be seen, I think, if you consider it carefully, to be just as far from what you believe in ordinary life, and just as difficult to accept as a philosophic truth, as the other two views. You do certainly believe in ordinary life that the carriage is *upon* the wheels, that the wheels are *supporting* it; and that the couplings are holding two carriages together. But consider all the sense-data, which you could possibly directly apprehend under any circumstances, if you examined the wheels and couplings. They all consist in patches of colour, and in various tactual sense-data—such so-called sensations as the hardness, smoothness, coldness, pressure or weight, which you would feel if you handled the wheels or couplings. Do you, in fact, believe that these—these alone—or any number of them are what are actually *supporting* the carriage, or connecting one carriage with the other? Obviously, if you think of it, you do not believe that the coloured patches alone would be sufficient to support the carriage or to cause the one carriage to follow the other. And there is just as great a difficulty in supposing that any of the tactual sense-data—the qualities which you would directly apprehend, if you handled the wheels and couplings—are what really *support* the carriage, or draw one carriage after the other. No doubt, the wheels only support the carriage, and the couplings only connect it with another, because they are *solid*. But it is not any solidity which you feel—which you directly apprehend—under any circumstances whatever, which does these things. The solidity which we do believe to belong to some material objects, is not identical with any sense-datum, or sort of sense-data which we ever directly apprehend. We must, therefore, I think, give up the view that the wheels—meaning by the wheels what *does* support the carriage, consist of any sense-data whatever; even if we do take the view that some sense-data are in the same place with them.

The fourth view, which may be held as an alternative to these three, and to the one which I wish to recommend, is a view, which does not, I think, easily seem plausible, but which has been held by a good many philosophers. It is the view that the wheels and couplings do really exist, when you think they do, but that they consist not of sense-data, nor yet of something unknown in its nature but of *minds*. Those who hold this view, generally, I think, hold that minds cannot have position in space at all; they hold, therefore, that the wheels are not really round, that the carriage is not really *upon* them, and that the couplings are not really *between* the carriages. And, so far as they hold this, their view is, of course, open to the same objections as the second view; namely, that it is so difficult to believe that the carriage is not really *on* the wheels—*above* them—spatially related to them, and that the wheels have not really a round shape. But it is not necessary to hold the view in this less plausible form. It might be held that the wheels really are round, and the carriage really *upon* them, although both wheels and carriage really consisted of minds; and some philosophers, I believe, have held this. But I do not propose now to try to discuss all the arguments in favour of this view. No one, I think, will maintain that it is, at first sight, very plausible, or that it is what we ordinarily believe. And the arguments used in its favour are partly of a kind, which I shall deal with later—namely, those which are supposed to show, not merely that we do not *know* of the existence of any material object, but that no material object can exist. But still I think it owes what plausibility it has, chiefly to the same arguments as those to which the other three views owe theirs; and what I am about to say will therefore apply to it to this extent.

All these four views are, then, plainly quite different from what we commonly believe. If you hold any one of them, you are holding that we do *not* know of the existence of material objects in the sense in which we all do commonly believe that we *do* know of the existence of material objects. And it follows that what we all do commonly mean by a 'material object' is just what I said—namely, an object having the three properties that it *has* position in space, and is *not* a sense-datum, *nor* a mind. So that in defending the view that we *do* know of the existence of objects having these three properties, I am defending the view which we all do in fact commonly hold—the view of Common Sense.

But now what are the reasons which have led so many philosophers to reject this Common Sense view? What reasons have led them to conclude that we never do know, even with probability, of the existence of any material object? What reasons have led them to adopt one or other of the four views which I have described? And why do some of these views so easily seem plausible?

You see, all four views have obviously something in common. They all admit that we can each of us know of the existence of *some* things which we are not directly apprehending and never have directly apprehended. And each of them lays down certain rules as to the only things of this sort, which we can know to exist, rules which are very suggestive of the reasons on which they are based. None of these four views will admit more than two alternatives. If, they say, you are to know of the existence of anything whatever which you have not directly apprehended: *Either* you must be totally incapable of knowing what sort of a thing, the thing in question is; you can only know, barely *that* it exists. This is one alternative. *Or* else, in all cases where you *can* know what sort of a thing the thing in question is, it must be a thing which is *similar*, in a strict and peculiar sense, to something which you have directly apprehended in the past. It must be *similar* to something which you have previously directly apprehended, in the strict sense in which any one colour is similar to any other colour, and in which nothing *but* a colour can be similar to a colour; in which any one sound is similar to another sound; in which any one mind or act of consciousness is *similar* to any other mind or act of consciousness. In short, you can only know of the existence of things which belong to one or other of the definite classes, to which all existing things which you directly apprehend belong. This is the second alternative. But why should anybody hold that our knowledge is strictly limited in this way? It seems to me that what really influences people to hold this, is the assumption that you can only know of the existence of any definite thing in two ways: either by direct apprehension, or by *Experience*—meaning by 'experience' what Hume meant; namely, that you have *directly apprehended* in the past *conjunctions* between things similar to something which you now directly apprehend and things similar to what you now infer. And this assumption does, I think, seem very plausible. It does seem very plausible to ask: How can I know of the existence of anything whatever, in the first instance, except by the fact that I directly apprehend it? And how can I infer the existence of any definite thing, which I have not directly apprehended, except by inference from something which I have directly apprehended? And what can possibly give me any basis for such an inference, except the fact that I have in the past directly apprehended conjunctions between things like what I now infer and things like that *from which* I now infer it?

These questions do, I think, seem very plausible. But I think there are certain arguments which can be used to diminish their plausibility. The first is one which Hume himself supplies. After laying down the principle that you cannot be justified in inferring the existence of any particular thing, except by Experience, in the sense explained, he goes on to ask: But will Experience justify the inference? And here he calls attention to a very remarkable fact. Suppose you have, in the past, constantly directly apprehended two different kinds of things in conjunction with one another; how, he asks, can you possibly be justified in inferring from this, that in a new case, where you do directly apprehend the first, but do not directly apprehend the second, that the second does nevertheless exist, or even probably exist? He points out that this inference obviously involves a gross assumption: namely, that *because* two things have gone together in the past, *therefore* it is likely that they will go together in all other cases. And how, he asks, can you possibly know that this assumption is correct? The mere fact that two things have gone together in the past, however constantly and however often, does not *absolutely prove* that they will do so, or will even probably do so, in any single other instance. It is quite *conceivable*, for instance, that even though, in the past, whenever you put your hand near a fire, you experienced a sensation of heat, yet in the future this should *never* happen again. What is there to prove that it will happen or is *likely* to happen in any single instance? Obviously you can only prove it, if you already *know* some such principle as this: namely, That when one thing has been constantly conjoined with another in the past, it *is* more likely that it will be so conjoined in any new instance, than if they had *not* been conjoined in the past. But how can you possibly know such a principle as this? It is a principle which cannot be known in any of the ways which Hume allows as possible. It is not self-evident; it cannot be deduced from anything which is self-evident; and it cannot be known by Experience, since on the contrary, Experience can never be known to prove anything whatever, unless this principle is first known to be true.

This argument of Hume's has, I think, never been answered; and I do not see how it can be answered. You may, indeed, assert that you *do* in fact know that, when two things have been conjoined in the past, they are likely to be conjoined again; and that you do know, therefore, that Experience is a sound basis for inference. But if you are going to assert this, why should you not assert also that you do know of the existence of material objects? Is the one proposition, in fact, any more certain than the other? If, on the other hand, you admit that you *do not* know that Experience is a sound basis for inference, then all your grounds for discriminating between your knowledge of material objects and your knowledge of the existence of other people or of your own future sensations, disappear. If you admit this, you must admit that you do not know of the existence of any other person beside yourself. And, then, you obviously cannot be entitled to lay down any such rule as that which I am attacking. You cannot possibly be entitled to say: No man knows of the existence of any material object. For, if you do not even know that any other man exists, how can you possibly know anything whatever as to what other men do know—or do not know? For all you know, other men, *if* they exist, *may* be able to know of the existence of material objects and of all sorts of other things. In other words, if you once accept this sceptical argument of Hume's as shewing that Experience is *not* a sufficient basis for inference, while at the same time you hold that it is the only basis you have, all attempts to lay down general propositions about the limits of human knowledge become absurd. You can only at most be entitled to lay down rules as to what you yourself do know and do not know; and even with regard to yourself you cannot possibly be entitled to assert that you may not, the very next moment, know of the existence of some material object: you can have no basis for the assertion that there is the very smallest probability that you will not know this.

This, then, is one argument which does, I think, really diminish the plausibility of the contention that we cannot know of the existence of any material object. Since what it shews is that, if we are to know that Experience itself is a sound basis for any inference whatever, we must first know a principle, which seems to have just as little certainty, if as much, as the proposition that material objects exist.

And here is another argument to the same effect. How, in fact, does any one arrive at such a principle as that which we are considering? any principle which asserts: No man can *know* of the existence of anything, unless certain conditions are fulfilled? It is, I think, obvious that no such principle is self-evident. You cannot, by merely considering the terms of such a proposition—by getting a perfectly clear and distinct idea of what it means—see at once that it must be true; in the way in which you can see, by merely considering what the proposition means, that things which are equal to the same thing are equal to one another. And if you consider how such propositions about the limits of our knowledge are, in fact, arrived at and supported, you will find, I think, that they all depend upon the consideration of particular instances, in which we do in fact seem to know or not to know particular things. They are in fact based—and this is the best basis they can have—upon an attempt to collect all the various instances, in which we obviously do know something, and all those in which we obviously do not know something, and to discover, by comparison, what conditions are common to all the cases in which we *do* know, and absent from all those in which we do not know. In fact any general principle to the effect that we can never know a particular kind of proposition, except under certain conditions, is and must be based upon an empirical induction: upon observation of the cases in which we obviously do know propositions of the kind in question, and of those in which we obviously do not, and of the circumstances which distinguish the one class from the other. But, this being so, it follows that no such general principle can have greater certainty than the particular instances upon the observation of which it is based. Unless it is obvious that, in fact, I do not know of the existence of a material object in any particular instance, no principle which asserts that I cannot know of the existence of anything except under conditions which are not fulfilled in the case of material objects, can be regarded as established. The mere fact that in any particular instance I *did* know of the existence of a material object, in spite of the fact that the conditions named were not fulfilled, would be sufficient to upset the principle and to prove that it was not true. If therefore any principle, from which it would follow that I cannot know of the existence of any material object, is to be known with certainty, it must first be known, with a greater certainty, that I do not, in fact, in any particular instance, know of one. And is this, in fact, known with any certainty? It seems to me it certainly is not. In short, the attempt to prove by means of such a principle as Hume's, that we cannot know of the existence of any material object, seems to me to be a characteristic instance of a sort of argument which is very common in philosophy: namely, an attempt to prove that a given proposition is false, by means of a principle which is, in fact, much less certain than the proposition which is supposed to be proved false by its means. It does not follow from this that all attempts to lay down general principles as to the limits of our knowledge must be hopeless and useless. It only follows that in our survey of the particular instances upon which our principle is to be based, we must be very careful not to reckon as instances of the cases where we obviously do not know something, instances in which it is by no means obvious that we do not know the thing in question. This, it seems to me, is the mistake which has been committed in this particular instance. It is not, after all, so very obvious that we do not know of the existence of material objects. And, if so, then no general principle as to the limits of knowledge, from which it would follow that we cannot know of their existence, can be any *more* obviously true. All this, I am aware, is only strictly an argument in favour of the position that we do not know that we do not know of the existence of material objects. But there is, I think, a real and important difference between this position and the dogmatic position that we *certainly do not* know of their existence. And, in practice, if not in logic, it is, I think, an important step towards the conviction that we *do* know of their existence.

May 8th 1983.

Stoke Bruerne
from a painting by Alan Firth

Dear Uncle Christopher.

In my capacity as Timothy's secretary I would like to pass on his appreciation of Dedication Dog. Timothy thinks he is splendid and endeavours to stretch his arms round him already. Evidently their ages are not as incompatible as you feared!

It was nice to see you on Friday. I am sorry I left so late & hope it didn't put you off your seminar. Enclosed (is are a) photographs of T. for you & Aunt Amy.

With love from

Ali (pp. Timothy)

The Inland Waterways Association campaigns for the restoration, retention and development of inland waterways in the British Isles and their fullest commercial and recreational use.

The Inland Waterways Association,
114 Regent's Park Road,
London NW1 8UQ.

Chapter VIII

EXISTENCE IN SPACE

I have now considered and tried to answer what seems to me to be the strongest and most plausible argument in favour of the position: That none of us ever *knows* of the existence of any material object; that we simply cannot tell at all whether any material objects exist or not. But many philosophers have not contented themselves with this position. Instead of merely asserting that we are absolutely ignorant as to whether material objects exist or not, many of them have asserted that material objects certainly do *not* exist: they have asserted that we *can* know that they do *not* exist. And I wish now to consider, and to answer as well as I can, what seem to me the most plausible arguments in favour of this position.

The first and commonest argument in favour of it is one which I have already briefly mentioned. It is this. Many philosophers seem to hold that it is quite certain that no sense-datum—nothing that is *like* a sense-datum, in the sense in which any one colour is *like* any other colour—can exist, except when it is directly apprehended by somebody. And I wish, first of all, to explain exactly what bearing this argument, if it were true, would have upon the existence of material objects.

I insisted, last time, that what I mean by a material object, and what we all commonly mean, is something which is *not* a sense-datum, nor composed of sense-data, of any kind whatever. And it might, therefore, be thought that this argument, since it only asserts that *sense-data* cannot exist except when they are directly apprehended, can have no tendency whatever to prove that material objects cannot exist. But this is not the case. For though I insisted that no material object is *itself* a sense-datum or like a sense-datum, I also insisted that every material object must be in space, or must have a *shape*—either the shape of a mere point, or some one of the figures which are more commonly called shapes. And any *shape*, I admitted, is *like* a sense-datum in the sense required: since every shape is a shape, and some shapes actually are given by the senses. The argument, therefore, applies to material objects, *because* they have shape, though for no other reason. It would follow from it, that no *shape* can exist, except when it is directly apprehended by some one. And since no material object can exist, except when its shape exists; it would follow that no material object can exist, except when its shape is being directly apprehended by some one.

But, of course, even so, it does not strictly follow from the argument, that no material object can *ever* exist *at all*, if we mean by a material object merely an object which possesses the three properties which I defined last time. It only follows that no such object can exist, except at a moment when its shape is being directly apprehended by some one. And it might be thought that *sometimes*—very often, for instance, when, as we say, we actually *see* a material object, we do directly apprehend its shape, or the shape of a part of it. And every part of a material object is itself a material object; so that, on this view, we should very often directly apprehend the shapes of material objects, and the argument would allow us to suppose that, at any moment *when* we do so, the material object in question may exist. If, therefore, we do ever directly apprehend the shape of any material object, the argument would allow, that, at such times, a material object may exist. And it might, therefore, be thought that the argument conflicts with Common Sense, *not* because it involves the denial that material objects ever exist (for, on this view, it does not), but because it involves the denial that they ever exist, *except* when we are directly apprehending their shapes—or, in other words, that they ever exist *independently* of us. I insist on this point, because the question whether material objects ever exist *at all* is very often confused with the question whether they ever exist *independently* of us; whereas obviously the two questions are really distinct, and require different arguments to settle them. Obviously, however, even if this argument merely involved the conclusion that no material object ever does exist *independently of us*, it would conflict with Common Sense most violently; for we certainly do hold that material objects constantly exist, when no man is perceiving them. But I think the conflict is, in fact, more violent still. For I think it must be admitted that we never do directly apprehend *the* shape of *any* material object. What I mean by this is that, though we do often directly apprehend shapes which are exactly *like* the shapes of some material objects, no shape which we ever directly apprehend is *numerically* the same as that of any material object: we never directly apprehend the identical lines which actually bound any material object. For instance, when you look straight at a penny, you do undoubtedly directly apprehend a roughly circular shape, which is the shape of the brown patch of colour which you directly apprehend. And no doubt, the shape of one surface of the real penny—the material object—is *also* roughly circular. But, if you were to look at the edge of the penny through a powerful microscope, the bounding line, which you would then directly apprehend, would have unevennesses in it, which were not present in the bounding line which you directly apprehended with the naked eye. And there is reason to suppose that the line which bounds the real penny is *more like* this line which you would directly apprehend under the microscope, than that which you directly apprehended with the naked eye. It follows, therefore, that the line which you directly apprehended with the naked eye is not identical with that which bounds the real penny, since it is not even exactly similar to it. But there is also reason to suppose that no line which you would see under any microscope, however powerful, is *identical* with that which bounds the real penny; since there is reason to suppose that that which bounds the real penny is *more* uneven than any which you could directly apprehend even with the most powerful microscope. No shape, therefore, which you would directly apprehend under any circumstances is *identical* with the shape of the real penny. And if none of these shapes, none of these bounding lines, are *the* shape of the penny, is there any reason to suppose that they are *the* shape of any material object whatever? No doubt, it is possible that there may be, *within* the line which bounds the real penny, other lines exactly similar both in shape and size to those which you directly apprehend with the naked eye or with different microscopes, so that *parts* of the penny really are bounded by lines *exactly like* those which you directly apprehend. But is there any reason to suppose that any line which you directly apprehend actually *is* the identical line which bounds any part of the penny? It seems to me, there is none whatever. Once you realise quite clearly, that the line, which you directly apprehend, on any occasion when you look at the penny, is *not* the identical line which bounds the surface of the real penny—the material object—which you suppose yourself to see, there is, I think, no plausibility in supposing that it *is* identical with the line which bounds some other material surface—for instance, a part of the surface of the penny. If it is not *the* line which bounds the surface of the penny, there seems no plausibility in supposing that it is *the* line which bounds some other material surface. I conclude, therefore, that none of the shapes which we ever directly apprehend are *the* shapes—the identical bounding lines—of any material object. I accept, that is, the theory that no part of the spaces, which we any of us ever directly apprehend, is identical with any part of the space in which material objects are. But, if so, then it follows from the argument we are considering, that, so far as *our* direct apprehensions are concerned, no material object ever can exist, *either* when we are perceiving it *or* when we are not. It follows that, if a material object can exist, only when some one of *us*—some man or some animal—is directly apprehending its shape or the space which it occupies, then no material object ever does exist at all.

But still, of course, it does not strictly follow from this argument, that no material object *ever* does exist. For even if we grant, as I grant, that *the* shape of a material object never is directly apprehended by any one of us—by any man, that is, or any animal—it might nevertheless be held that the shapes of all the material objects, in which we any of us ever believe, are always being perpetually directly apprehended by some one else—by God, for instance. And this is a line of argument which many philosophers have, I think, been disposed to take. They have supposed it quite certain (as we all do commonly suppose) that many things do exist, when *we* are not directly apprehending them; they have supposed that these are a kind of thing which cannot exist except when some one is directly apprehending them; and they have, therefore, inferred that some one must exist who does directly apprehend them. The argument, therefore, that no space can exist, except when it is directly apprehended by some one, does not strictly prove at all that material objects cannot exist. On the contrary, it is quite consistent with the view that all the material objects which Common Sense ever supposes to exist, really do exist—provided only that their shapes all are, whenever they exist, directly apprehended by *some* mind. This argument does not, therefore, logically, by itself, involve the denial of the existence of any material object, in which we any of us ever believe. But it is, I think, in practice, one of the strongest arguments against the existence of any of them, because, in fact, we do not commonly believe that their shapes are at all times being directly apprehended by some one. Common Sense certainly does not hold, as a certain fact, that every part of space, in which any material object is, is, at every moment, being directly apprehended by some one. It certainly holds that material objects *can* exist, even when the space in which they are is not being directly apprehended at all. And with this view of Common Sense the argument we are considering is in flat contradiction.

But now: Why should this argument appeal to any one? Why should any one think that nothing which resembles any sense-datum in the sense in which any one circular figure must resemble any other circular figure, can exist, except when it is being directly apprehended by some one?

So far as I know, there are two chief arguments advanced in favour of this position, in the case of space and spatial figures. And this is the only case which concerns us, since material objects, in the sense in which we are considering them, do not resemble any sense-datum except in respect of the fact that they occupy space and have shape.

The first argument is the one I have already mentioned, namely that used by Berkeley. It is claimed, namely, that this proposition is self-evident: that it is self-evident that no space or shape can exist except when it is being directly apprehended by some one.

And if any one does believe that this proposition is self-evident, I confess I do not quite know how to set about convincing him that it is not so. There are ever so many different arguments which might produce conviction, but, of course, none of them will be certain to do so. I will only mention the argument, which seems to me the strongest, and which has, I think, the largest share in convincing me. It is this. Any one who does hold that it is self-evident, that no space, and no shape, can exist, except when it is being directly apprehended by some one, must hold, for instance, that this room, in which we now are, is not being supported by anything; that it is not supported by walls, having a certain length and breadth and thickness; that there is, in fact, simply *nothing* below it. He must hold too, to take instances which I have used before, that there are at this moment no bones in this hand of mine; that there is nothing inside it, at all resembling the pictures of the skeleton of a hand, with which we are all of us familiar. He must hold, again, that, when he sits in a railway-train, the carriage in which he sits, is *not* supported upon wheels; that it is not supported by anything at all, either round or of any other shape. He must hold that we are *not* now nearer to St. Paul's Cathedral, than we are to Paris; and *not* nearer to the moon than we are to the sun: that, in fact, we are at no distance at all from any of these objects. He must hold that we are not now at any distance at all from New Zealand or from the North Pole; and that it is absurd to believe (as we commonly do) that London is further from these places than it is from Scotland. He must, in fact, believe ever so many propositions which contradict, what he himself constantly believes and cannot help believing in ordinary life. *Either* he must do this, or else he must believe that all these parts of space which I have mentioned are at the moment being directly apprehended by some one. That some one, for instance, is at this moment directly apprehending every part of the space occupied by any part of the structure of the walls which are supporting this room; that some one is at this moment directly apprehending every part of the space occupied at this moment by the bones of my hand; that some one is at this moment directly apprehending the whole distance between here and the North Pole. But now, I ask, are not all these propositions which I have mentioned, in fact far more certain than the supposed self-evident proposition that no part of space can exist, except when it is being directly apprehended by some one? Is it not far more certain that this room *is* supported by walls having a certain length and breadth and thickness, than that length and breadth and thickness cannot exist, unless some one is directly apprehending them? And is it not far more certain too, that there are now bones in my hand, than that anybody is directly apprehending the length and breadth and thickness of these bones? It is, I think, chiefly because all these things, and hosts of others like them, seem to me so certain, that I myself am convinced that this supposed self-evident proposition is false. Unless these Common Sense beliefs seemed so certain to me, I should not, I think, be convinced that it was false. But quite apart from the question of evidence *against* it; I confess I cannot see the smallest evidence in its favour: it does not seem to me to have any self-evidence at all. So that, even if there were not such overwhelming evidence against it, I should have thought the true conclusion with regard to it was, not that it is certainly true, but merely that it might be true—that we could not tell at all whether it was true or false.

This is all I propose to say about this first argument in favour of the proposition that no part of space can exist except when it is being directly apprehended by some one: the argument, namely, that this proposition is self-evident.

The second argument, in its favour, which I propose to mention, is one which was suggested by Kant, and which has also, I think, appealed to a great many people. It is an argument which occurred to Kant, in the course of his endeavour to answer that sceptical argument of Hume's, which I stated in my last lecture. Hume's argument, if you remember, consisted in pointing out that even if you have in the past constantly experienced the fact that the existence of one kind of thing was conjoined with that of another, it still does not follow that those two kinds of things are *always* conjoined, or indeed that they ever will be conjoined again. Even though, for instance, you have constantly found in the past that when you put a piece of paper in the fire, it was burnt, it does not, Hume says, follow from this mere fact that a piece of paper *always* has been and will be burnt, when it is put into the fire: it is quite conceivable, on the contrary, that on all occasions, except those upon which you actually saw it burnt, paper never has been and never will be burnt by a fire. In short, Hume suggests a doubt as to how you can possibly ever know *universal* propositions, of a certain kind, to be true; meaning by a *universal* proposition, a proposition which asserts that anything whatever which has some one definite property, always does, on all occasions, also have some other definite property. And the kind of universal propositions, with regard to which Hume suggests this doubt, are those which assert that anything whatever which has some definite property always has the further property that its existence is conjoined with—preceded, or accompanied, or followed by—the existence of some other definite kind of thing. For instance: the putting of a piece of paper into a fire is an act of a quite definite kind; and how, asks Hume, can you ever possibly know the *universal* proposition, that every act which has the definite property that it is the putting of a piece of paper into a fire, *always* has had, does have, and will have the other definite property that it is followed by the burning of the paper?

Now these universal propositions, with regard to which Hume suggests a doubt as to how we can know them, obviously are not mere tautologies. By a tautologous proposition, I mean a proposition like this: Everything which is round and hard, is round. This is an instance of a *universal* tautologous proposition: and it is called tautologous, because, obviously, if you have already said that a thing is both round and hard, and then go on to add that it is round, you are merely saying the *same* thing twice over. But obviously the universal propositions with regard to which Hume raises the question how we can know them, are not mere tautologies like this. The proposition: Every act, which is the putting of a piece of paper into the fire, is followed by the burning of the paper; is not a mere tautology: when you say that you did put a piece of paper into the fire, you have not already said that it was burnt; to say that it was put into the fire is not the *same* thing as to say that it was burnt. The propositions with regard to which Hume raised his question have, then, the characteristic that beside being universal, they are also *not* tautologous. And Kant gives a special name to propositions which are not tautologous: he calls them *synthetic*. Let us adopt this name. We can then say that Hume raised the question: How we can possibly know a particular kind of universal synthetic propositions?

Now Kant thought that this question, which Hume raised with regard to a particular kind of universal synthetic propositions, can be raised, with equally good ground, with regard to *all* universal synthetic propositions. With regard to all universal synthetic propositions, it is, he thought, equally difficult to see how we can possibly know them to be true. And he was thus led, by Hume's question with regard to a particular class of them, to raise the general question: How can we possibly know *any* universal synthetic proposition to be true? His answer to this question differs, with regard to details, in the case of different classes of universal synthetic propositions; and I am not here concerned to give his answer in all cases. What we are here concerned with is the answer which he gives in the case of one particular class of universal synthetic propositions. Namely propositions like this: The three angles of a triangle are always equal to two right angles. This proposition, you see, and ever so many similar ones about the properties of different spatial figures, are *universal* propositions: this one, for instance, asserts that the three angles of *every* triangle *always* are equal to two right angles. And Kant also saw (what Hume had not clearly seen) that this proposition and others like it, are not tautologous—that they really are synthetic. He thought, therefore, that there was a real difficulty in seeing how we can possibly know that universal propositions of this sort about the properties of spatial figures are true; and his answer to the question, how we can, is as follows.

He says that we could not possibly know them, if Space were anything else than a mere form in which, owing to the constitution of our minds, things appear to us. If our minds are so constituted that the angles of every triangle which appears to us are always equal to two right angles, then we may be quite certain that every triangle which ever does appear to us will have the sum of its angles equal to two right angles. If, therefore, what we mean by a triangle is merely a form in which things appear to us, it is easy to understand how we could know that *every* triangle must have its angles equal to two right angles. But if on the other hand, a triangle were a shape which a thing might have, even when we were *not* directly apprehending it, we could not possibly know that every such shape must have its angles equal to two right angles.

This, I think, is really all that Kant's argument amounts to. And it has, I think, a certain plausibility when stated vaguely and in general terms. It does sound plausible to say: We *can* know how things will *appear* to us; though we can never know what they are like in themselves. How they will *appear* to us is a thing which depends only on the constitution of our minds, and how our minds are constituted is a thing we can hope to discover. But to discover any universal synthetic propositions about what things are like in themselves, is hopelessly beyond our power.

The argument is, then, this. We can, Kant says, only know universal synthetic propositions about spatial figures, if spatial figures are merely phenomena—merely things which appear to us; and by this he means, sometimes at least, I think, things which exist only when they are directly apprehended. But we do, he thinks, know universal synthetic propositions about spatial figures. We know, for instance, that the three angles of *every* triangle are, under all circumstances, equal to two right angles. Therefore, he concludes, all spatial figures are merely things which appear to us—things which exist only when we directly apprehend them. In other words his argument to prove that spatial figures or shapes can exist only when we directly apprehend them, does not consist, like the former one, in asserting that this is self-evident; but in asserting that it must be true, because if it were not true, we could not know any universal synthetic propositions about them.

And this argument has, I think, seemed plausible to a great many people. It does, of course, follow, that *if*, as Kant says, Space is merely a form of our Sensitive Faculty—*if*, that is to say, our minds are so constituted that every triangle, which appears to us, must have its angles equal to two right angles, then, every triangle which appears to us always has had and always will have its angles equal to two right angles. This is, of course, true. But does this, in fact, explain at all, how we can *know* that this always has been and always will be the case? Obviously, it does not, unless it be first explained or be self-evident, how we can know that our minds *are* so constituted as always to give this result. But this proposition, that our minds are so constituted as always to produce the same appearances, is itself a universal synthetic proposition, of precisely the sort with regard to which Hume pointed out the difficulty in seeing how we can know them. When Kant assumes that we do know that our minds *are* so constituted, he is assuming that each of us does know not only that his own mind always has acted in a certain way, but that it always will do so; and not only this but also that the minds of all other men always have acted and always will act in this way. But how can any of us know this? Obviously it is a question which requires an answer just as much as any of those which Kant set out to answer; and yet he never even attempts to answer it: it never seems to have occurred to him to ask how we can know that *all* men's minds are so constituted as *always* to act in a certain way. And once this question is raised, I think the whole plausibility of his argument disappears.

Is it really more easy to see how you can know such a proposition as this, than how you could know such a proposition as that *all* triangles, whether directly apprehended or not, must have their angles equal to two right angles? Obviously Hume's argument applies to both propositions with equal force. From no amount of experience, which you may have had as to how your mind acted in the past, will it absolutely follow that it ever will do so again, or that it ever has done so, except in the instances which you have actually observed; nor will it follow that any other man's mind ever has acted or ever will act in the way in which yours has. And if, in spite of the fact that it does not follow, you are nevertheless able to know that all men's minds always have and always will act in this way; why should you not be able to know that *all* triangles, even if triangles are not merely appearances produced by the action of your mind, must always have their angles equal to two right angles? It is not, in fact, a bit plainer how you can know universal synthetic propositions about the action of the human mind, than how you could know them about other things; and hence the argument that anything about which you can know universal synthetic propositions must be due to the action of the human mind, entirely loses all plausibility.

I think, therefore, this argument of Kant's to prove that no part of space can exist, except when it is being directly apprehended by *us*, is no more conclusive, than the argument that it is self-evident that none can exist, except when it is being directly apprehended by *some one*. The case against the existence of material objects, so far as it rests upon the contention that no spatial figure can exist except when it is being directly apprehended, seems to me wholly inconclusive.

But I wish now to consider an entirely new and different argument to prove that material objects cannot exist. This is an argument which does not necessarily deny that spatial figures may exist when nobody is directly apprehending them. On the contrary, even if we accept it, we might still hold that this room is being supported by walls of a certain height and breadth and thickness, even though no one is directly apprehending their height and breadth and thickness; and that there really are bones in this hand of mine, even though nobody is directly apprehending the space which they occupy. We might, if we accept it, still hold that all the objects of various shapes and sizes, which we commonly suppose that we know to exist, do really exist, and are really of the shapes and sizes we suppose, even though nobody is directly apprehending these shapes and sizes. What this argument *does* profess to prove is that all these objects, even if they are of the shapes and sizes we suppose, and even if nobody is directly apprehending them, can yet not be material objects in the sense in which I am using the term, simply because they must be minds or collections of minds. That is to say, those who use it, may agree with Common Sense that when we talk of the walls which support this room, or the bones in my hand, of chairs, and tables, and railway trains, and houses, and the sun and moon and stars and earth, all these names are the names of different objects which really do exist independently *of us*; that these objects may exist, when nobody is directly apprehending them; and that they may even have the shapes and the relative positions in space which we suppose them to have: the only point as to which they necessarily disagree with Common Sense, is in holding that all these objects are minds or collections of minds. No doubt many, perhaps most, of those who hold it, would also hold that these objects cannot have shape or position in space. But the point I wish to make clear, is that the argument by itself cannot prove this. All that it can prove, by itself, if it is sound, is merely that the objects which Common Sense supposes to be material objects, are in fact minds or collections of minds: it cannot prove that, in any other respect, they are of a different sort from what Common Sense supposes them to be.

The argument I mean, is drawn from considering the relation of our own minds to our bodies. It is roughly this. It is argued, in the first place, that our own minds do manifestly act upon our bodies, and our bodies on our minds. It is argued, in the second place, that our bodies, whatever they may be, are manifestly things of a sort which *can* be acted upon by, and *can* act upon, all the other kinds of objects which we commonly suppose to be material objects. *But*, it is said, it is not possible that a mind should either act upon or be acted upon *by*, anything whatever except what is itself a mind or of the nature of a mind. And hence, it is argued, in the first place, that since our own bodies and minds obviously do interact upon one another, our bodies must be minds or of the nature of minds. And, in the second place, that since our bodies *can* interact with all other supposed material objects, and since our bodies have already been proved to be mental in their nature, all other supposed material objects must also really be mental in their nature.

And both steps in this argument have, I think, seemed plausible to great numbers of people. The essential steps are two.

The first is that our minds do really act upon our bodies, and are acted upon by them. And, as regards this step, there is hardly anything which seems more obvious to Common Sense, or is more constantly assumed by all of us. We all of us know, for instance, or suppose that we know, that the drinking of alcohol, in large quantities, does produce, very often, very marked effects upon the mind of the person who drinks it. A person who is drunk neither thinks, nor feels, nor perceives, nor wills in exactly the same way as when he is sober. The alcohol, which he has drunk, produces an effect upon his body, and the changes produced in his body cause changes in his thoughts and feelings and perceptions and volitions. So too, we all know, or think we know, that the taking of some drugs into the body will produce a temporary cessation of consciousness, or at least a very complete change in its nature: opiates will send a man to sleep —will make his mind cease, for a time, to be conscious at all; and various anæsthetics also will make his consciousness cease for a time, or will produce dreams, which are very different in nature from the perceptions which he would have had, if he had not taken the anæsthetic. All these we should commonly set down as obvious instances of an action by the body upon the mind. And, of course, there are commoner instances still. We commonly suppose that our visual perceptions—that direct apprehension of patches of colour, for instance, which we call the actual seeing of them, is caused by changes which take place in our eyes; and our direct apprehension of sounds is caused by changes which take place in our ears. We know, or suppose we know, that a blind man, who has lost his eyes, or whose eyes are in a certain state, is no longer able actually to see colours, as we see them; and we should take this as proof that the state of our eyes does produce effects upon our minds. In fact, it seems nearly as certain as anything can be that our bodies do constantly act upon our minds. And so too, it seems equally certain that our minds do very often act upon our bodies. For instance, I now make a movement with my arm. And this movement, it seems to me quite certain, was caused by the fact that I chose to move it. I should not have made it just then, unless I had chosen to do so. We all constantly distinguish between voluntary movements of our bodies, and involuntary ones: voluntary movements being those which are caused by our willing to make them, and involuntary ones those which are not caused by our own volitions. There are a certain number of changes in our bodies, which we can, it seems, most of us, almost at any moment, produce by willing them; whereas there are others, which we cannot so produce. I cannot, now, by an act of volition cause my hair to stand up on end, whereas I can move my arm as I did just now. And the influence of our wills upon our bodies, is by no means the only instance of the action of our minds upon them. Mere perceptions and thoughts also seem often to have a marked effect upon them. For instance, the mere fact that he sees a certain sight, may cause a man's body to tremble. The fact that he hears certain words and the thoughts which they suggest, may produce that change in the circulation of the blood, which we call blushing, or may cause him to shed tears—in both cases quite involuntarily. In cases like these it certainly does seem obvious that our thoughts and feelings and perceptions do cause changes in our bodies. It does, therefore, seem obvious to Common Sense both that our bodies do often act upon our minds, and that our minds do often act upon our bodies. And for my part I do not see how to dispute this. If these instances which I have given are not instances of the *action* of one thing upon another, are not instances of *causation*, it seems to me we have no better reason to say that any other instances that can be given *are* instances of action and causation. I have no better reason for saying that that light, when I look upon it, is acting upon my eyes and causing changes in them, than for saying that these changes in my eyes are acting upon my mind, and causing me to see what I do see. I have no better reason for saying that my hand is acting upon this paper, now when I push it, and causing it, the paper, to move; than for saying that my *wish* to push it (in order to give you an instance of the action of mind upon body) was what acted upon my hand and caused *it*, my hand, to move.

If, therefore, we are to reject this argument at all, we must, I think, find objections to the second step in it, *not* to this first step. This first step which merely asserts that our minds and bodies do interact, seems to me as certain as that anything does act upon or cause anything at all. If we use the words 'action' and 'cause' in their ordinary sense, it is as certain that our minds and bodies act upon and cause changes in one another, as that anything acts upon anything or causes any changes at all.

But the second step in the argument is also capable of seeming extremely plausible. This second step consists in the assertion that nothing that is a mind, or belongs to a mind—nothing that is *mental*—can possibly act upon or be acted upon by anything which is *not* mental. And the best proof how plausible this assertion may seem, is that very many philosophers have been led, on the ground that it is true, to deny that our minds and bodies ever do act upon one another. They have believed that our bodies are material objects, in the sense which I defined—that is to say that they are *not* mental in their nature. And they have been so certain that material objects, in this sense, cannot act upon a mind or upon anything mental, nor anything mental upon them, that they have concluded that our minds and bodies do *not* really act upon one another, in spite of the fact that they so obviously seem to do so. This second step in the argument, has, then, been very often held to be true, *both* by those who do believe in the existence of purely material objects, and that our bodies are such objects, *and* by those who do not. Those who hold the first view are, of course, because they hold this also, bound to deny that our bodies and minds do ever interact; whereas those who hold the second view very often regard this second step, together with the plain fact that our bodies and minds do interact, as a proof that their view is true—namely that our bodies are not material objects. The view, therefore, that a material object—an object which is not a mind—cannot possibly be acted upon or act upon a mind, has been held by very many philosophers, both of those who do believe in the existence of material objects and of those who do not. This view was held almost immediately after the beginning of modern philosophy among the disciples of Des Cartes. Some of his disciples, who never thought of questioning the existence of material objects, yet thought it so impossible that these should act upon our minds that they invented a theory which has been called 'Occasionalism': namely that, whenever certain changes occurred in our bodies, *God caused* certain corresponding changes to occur in our minds; they held, that is, that those bodily changes were not *causes* of the changes in our minds, but that they were merely *occasions*, on the occurrence of which God had arranged permanently, or definitely willed in each instance, that the mental changes should occur. And, of course, the same view, that minds and material objects cannot interact, is implied by the common modern view, that mental phenomena are events which merely happen to accompany certain material phenomena, without being either caused by or causing any. The view for instance that the mind is a mere 'epiphenomenon' attached to certain material phenomena, but incapable of influencing their course; or the view that there exists a parallelism, but no interaction, between mental and material phenomena—the view, that is, that mental phenomena regularly occur (to speak metaphorically) side by side with or parallel to material ones, but without being causally connected with them.

Let us consider this view that minds and material objects cannot interact, in relation to one quite definite theory as to their relation—a theory which is, I think, the one now commonly held, and which is, in fact, the one which I myself suppose to be true. According to this modern theory, absolutely every change which ever takes place in our minds, is accompanied by—absolutely simultaneous with—some definite change which takes place in the matter of the brain. Every different act of consciousness which you ever perform is accompanied by a different spatial arrangement of the material particles in some part of your brain; and whenever you perform a precisely similar act of consciousness, on two different occasions—if, for instance, you see a bright yellow colour on one day, and see a precisely similar bright yellow colour on the next day, or if on one day you think that twice two are four, and think the same again some other day—then, whenever this precisely similar act of consciousness recurs, it is accompanied by an arrangement of molecules in your brain precisely similar to that which accompanied it on the former occasion. There is therefore, on this view, for every different act of consciousness some configuration of the matter in a part of your brain, which occurs at absolutely the same time. And it is held too that each of these states of the matter in your brain is *caused* by some previous state of the matter in your brain, or in the nerves connected with it; and moreover that each of them has for its effect *some* subsequent state of the matter in your brain or in the nerves connected with it. It is agreed, then, according to this theory, which is, I believe, the one commonly held, that every state of consciousness is *accompanied* by some state of the brain, and that each of these accompanying brain-states is caused by and does cause some other brain-state or nerve-state. And it is worth while insisting that the brain and nerves and all their parts, are, on this view, material objects in precisely the sense I have been explaining. They are not merely collections of sense-data or possibilities of sense-data; they do actually exist, when no one is directly apprehending them—for instance, in my brain now; they are conceived as having position in space; and certainly they are not commonly conceived as being themselves minds or acts of consciousness—though the question whether they must really be so, is what we are now to consider.

Well, then, what must be asserted, on the view that minds and material objects cannot interact, is, as follows. We have it supposed, on the theory stated, that every mental act is *accompanied* by some particular brain-state. And there can be no question as to whether the mental acts are caused by the brain-states which accompany them; because, in the ordinary meaning of cause, we certainly mean by a *cause*, something which *precedes* in time, and is not simultaneous with the thing which is its effect. Our mental acts, therefore, are certainly not caused by the brain-states which *accompany* them. The only question can be as to whether that other nerve-state or brain-state, which, on this theory, *causes* the brain-state which accompanies the mental act, cannot *also* cause the mental act itself; and whether the nerve-state or brain-state which is *caused by* the brain-state which accompanies the mental act, cannot *also* be caused by the mental act itself. The view that minds and material objects cannot interact must deny this, if it denies anything. Unless it can be proved that *this* particular theory cannot be the truth, the whole argument to prove that minds and material objects cannot interact, must fail. If they *can* interact in this case, they might in any.

What argument, then, can be used to prove that a brain-state which *causes* the brain-state which accompanies a mental act, cannot also *cause* the mental act itself? and that a brain-state which is caused by the brain-state which accompanies a mental act, cannot be caused by the mental act itself?

So far as I know, there are two which are commonly used. The first is this. It is urged that a state of the brain, considered merely as a spatial arrangement of material particles, is something so utterly different in kind from a mental act, that we cannot conceive *how* the one should cause or be caused by the other. This argument, you see, if it is to be used as an argument to prove that what really causes the mental act, cannot be a brain-state, but must be another mental act, supposes that we *can* see how one mental act can cause another, though we cannot see how a brain-state should cause a mental act. And this is why it seems to me so unconvincing. I cannot see any difference between the two cases. Let us consider a case where one mental act undoubtedly does cause another. I am quite certain that, in many cases, the seeing of certain letters printed in a book, has caused me to have certain ideas of the incidents related in the book —ideas which I should not have had, if I had not seen those letters. Here, then, is an instance of the causation of one mental act by another. The seeing of printed letters in a copy of *Waverley*, has *caused* me to have ideas of the incidents which Scott meant to describe. The one mental act, the having of these ideas, is certainly an effect of the other mental act—the seeing of the printed sentences: I should not have had the ideas, had I not seen the sentences. But is it, in fact, any more easy to conceive, how that one mental act, the seeing of certain printed letters, should have caused the entirely different mental act, the imagination of certain incidents in the life of Waverley, than how either of them should have been caused by a state of my brain? It seems to me quite as easy to conceive the latter as the former. I no more understand, in the last resort, how or why the one mental act, the seeing of certain letters, should cause the imagination of certain incidents, than how or why a state of my brain should cause the seeing of the letters. All that I can be certain of in any case of mental causation—that is, of the causation of one mental act by another—seems to me to be simply that the one mental act, the effect, certainly would not have occurred, under the circumstances, unless the other had preceded it: all I can be certain of is that this is so, as a matter of fact. As to why it should be so—if by this be meant, that the fact that it must be so, can be deduced from some self-evident principle—I am in every case quite ignorant. And if the question is thus merely a question as to what is, as a matter of fact, caused by what, I can quite well conceive that it should also be true, as a matter of fact, that no mental acts would ever occur unless certain states of the brain preceded them. I cannot see why the world should not be so constituted that this should be so.

The second argument, which may be used to shew that mind and matter cannot possibly interact, is one which depends upon a different meaning of the word 'cause'—a sense, in which by a 'cause' we mean something upon the occurrence of which the effect always necessarily follows; so that, from the existence of the cause by itself it would be possible to predict with certainty that the effect must follow. Let us call a cause, of which this is true, a 'sufficient' cause—meaning by that that the mere existence of the cause is by itself a *sufficient* datum to enable us to infer the effect—that we do not need any other premises besides. Now it is widely held that *every* event in the material world has, in this sense, a *sufficient* cause in previous material events: that there is some set of previous material events from which any material event, which ever occurs, could, if we had sufficient knowledge, have been inferred with certainty. And, granted that this is so, it follows of course that every event in any one's body—in his nerves or in his brain—could have been inferred from previous material events by themselves: it follows that no knowledge of any mental events would have been necessary to enable an omniscient person to infer them. And it is, I think, often inferred from this that no mental event could have been *necessary* to produce them: that, even supposing that mental events did in fact accompany some of the material events which constitute the sufficient cause, they must yet have been something entirely superfluous and without influence on the result. But does this, in fact, follow? It seems to me quite plain, if we consider the case a little more carefully, that it does not. Granted we have a set of events from the existence of which, by themselves, it follows with absolute certainty that a certain result will follow, it by no means follows that some other event may not also be *necessary* to produce the result. The world may quite well be so constituted, that a cause which is sufficient to enable us to predict a result, should nevertheless not be sufficient to *produce* that result; it may be so constituted that the cause, which *is* sufficient for prediction, must nevertheless also, as a matter of fact, be always accompanied by some other cause, which is truly a cause, in the sense that the result would not have occurred *unless* it had existed also. Even, therefore, if we grant that every material event has a sufficient cause in previous material events, in the sense that from them alone its existence could be *predicted*; it by no means follows that in some cases mental events may not also be necessary for the *production* of the effect. And I do not see how it can possibly be proved that this is not, in fact, the case.

It seems to me, then, that both these arguments to prove that minds and material objects could not possibly interact, are inconclusive. And I know no better arguments to prove it. I conclude, then, that this particular argument to prove that material objects cannot exist, namely the argument which starts from the Common Sense fact that our minds and bodies do interact, and hence concludes that our bodies cannot be material objects, but must themselves be minds or composed of minds, is inconclusive also.

I propose to consider next some other arguments which have been held to prove that material objects do not exist—and to prove, also, that certain other things do not exist either.

Chapter IX
EXISTENCE IN TIME

I am about to consider another set of arguments, which have been used to prove that material objects cannot exist. But the interest of these arguments does not chiefly depend upon the fact that they have been used to prove this. The fact is that, *if* they proved this, they must also prove other conclusions, far more paradoxical still; and they have, in fact, been supposed by many philosophers to prove these more paradoxical conclusions. But also, quite apart from the question whether they prove any of the extremely paradoxical conclusions which they are supposed to prove, they involve questions as to the nature of the Universe, which are in any case of very great interest and not at all easy to answer.

The arguments I mean were, I believe, like one of those which I have just discussed, first suggested by the German philosopher Kant. And his suggestion of them has had an enormous influence upon the views of many subsequent philosophers. I will try to explain exactly what their nature is, by considering one particular argument of the sort, an argument which is actually used by Kant himself.

Kant himself states this argument in an extremely perplexing way.

What he seems to say is this.

It can be rigorously and conclusively proved (he seems to say) that the world must have had a beginning in time. He gives the proof, and insists that it is rigorous and conclusive. But (he seems to say) it can *also* be rigorously and conclusively proved that the world can have had *no* beginning in time, but must have existed for an absolutely infinite length of time—infinite, in the sense that the length of time in question really had *no* beginning. For this proposition also he gives the proof, and insists that *it* also is rigorous and conclusive. But (he seems to say) these two propositions contradict one another; and therefore they cannot both be true. What, then, are we to suppose? The natural thing to suppose would be that there was a mistake in one or other of the two proofs; and that, therefore, one of the two propositions is really false, and the other one true. But, Kant insists, this is certainly *not* the case. There certainly is no mistake in either of his proofs. What, then, does he conclude? Does he mean to insist that both propositions are true, in spite of the fact that they contradict one another? If his proofs really are rigorous, as he says they are, this would seem to be what he ought to conclude. Of course, in so concluding, he would be throwing overboard the Law of Contradiction, since the Law of Contradiction asserts that two contradictory propositions cannot both be true. But still, if his proofs really are rigorous, there would seem to be no alternative left. But this is not the course which he actually adopts. He clings both to the Law of Contradiction and to the rigour of his proofs; and asserts that there is another way out of the difficulty.

And so, in fact, there is. For, of course, if these two propositions really do contradict one another, and if Kant has proved rigorously that one of them must be true, he has, thereby, proved that the other one, its contradictory, must be *false*. If he has proved rigorously that the world *had* a beginning in Time, he has thereby proved that the proposition that it had *no* beginning in Time is false. Accordingly, in proving that *both* these two contradictory propositions are true, he has also proved, equally rigorously, that both of them are false. And this is the conclusion which he actually chooses to adopt. He adopts the conclusion that *both* of them are false. And of course this is just *as* legitimate a conclusion as the other one, which he rejects, namely, that both of them are true. It is just *as* legitimate; but it is also open to just as grave objections as the other. For beside the Law of Contradiction, which asserts that two contradictory propositions cannot both be true, there is another logical law, which seems just as certain, and which is called the Law of Excluded Middle: and this asserts that, if two propositions contradict one another, one or other of them *must* be true. The Law of Excluded Middle, therefore, involves the conclusion that two contradictory propositions cannot both be false. So that in asserting that both of these two propositions *are* false, Kant is throwing overboard the Law of Excluded Middle, which is just as serious a thing to do, as what he refused to do before—namely, to throw overboard the Law of Contradiction. And moreover it is to be observed that he gives the fact that he has proved both these propositions to be true, as a *reason* for concluding that they are both false. And we have seen that it actually is so. But obviously if it is a reason for concluding that they are both false, it is an equally strong reason for concluding that they are both true. And yet Kant accepts the conclusion that they are both false, and rejects the conclusion that they are both true.

I think it must be admitted that this is a very perplexing argument. And yet I think Kant certainly does seem to insist on all the points that make it perplexing. He seems to insist that he has rigorously proved that the world had a beginning in time *and* that it had *no* beginning. He seems to insist that these two propositions do contradict one another, and therefore cannot both be true. He seems to insist that they are in fact both false. And he seems to insist finally that the fact that they can be rigorously proved both to be true, is a reason for concluding that they are both false.

This argument is surely very perplexing. It seems to be utterly topsy-turvy. And yet I think it has some sense in it, though I think also that Kant himself did not see quite clearly exactly what the sense in it was. I will try to explain as clearly as I can exactly what I take the real point of it to be.

Kant seems to start, I said, by asserting that he has rigorously proved *both* of the two propositions: The world had a beginning in Time; *and*: The world had *no* beginning in Time. Now suppose we say that, instead of proving *these* two propositions, what his proofs really prove (if they prove anything at all) is the following two hypothetical propositions. Namely (1) *If* the world exists in time at all, then it must have had a beginning; and (2) *If* the world exists in time at all, then it can have had no beginning. I will presently try to shew that, *if* his proofs prove anything at all, they do prove these two hypothetical propositions. But, for the present, let us assume that this is what they do prove. How does this assumption alter the case? Obviously, I think, it alters it very much for the better. For if we say that what Kant has proved is merely these two hypotheticals, then he has *not* proved that two contradictory propositions are both of them true. For these two hypotheticals do *not* contradict one another. The assertion: *If* the world exists in time at all, it must have had a beginning; does not contradict the assertion: *If* the world exists in time at all, it cannot have had a beginning. *Both* of these two hypotheticals may perfectly well be true. All that does follow, if they are both true is, that *if* the hypothesis which occurs in each of them *were* true, *then* both of two contradictory propositions *would* be true. And this fact—the fact that *if* the hypothesis were true, it would involve the conclusion that both of two contradictory propositions were also true—is a perfectly legitimate reason for drawing one definite conclusion—namely, that the hypothesis is false. It is a perfectly legitimate reason, namely, for concluding that the world does *not* exist in time at all. That is to say, if Kant has succeeded in proving the two hypotheticals I mentioned, then he will have proved that the world does not exist in time at all. He will have proved this, because he will have proved that, *if* it did, then both of two contradictory propositions *would* be true. But we know that two contradictory propositions cannot both be true. And therefore it follows that any hypothesis, from which it would follow that they must both be true, must be false.

We see, then, that if, instead of supposing Kant to have proved both of the two contradictory propositions: The world had a beginning in time; and: The world had *no* beginning in Time; we merely suppose him to have proved both of the two hypotheticals: *If* the world is in time at all, it had a beginning; and: *If* the world is in time at all, it had no beginning, we then get a perfectly clear and straightforward argument, instead of the perplexing one which he seems to give us. And this clear and straightforward argument yields with absolute certainty the definite conclusion that the world does not exist in time at all. It yields this conclusion, that is to say, provided Kant really *has* proved the two hypotheticals in question.

And now I want to shew that Kant's two arguments, *if* they prove anything at all, *do* prove these two hypotheticals, and therefore also the conclusion that the world does not exist in Time at all. What are the arguments? The first is this. If, says Kant, the world did *not* begin to exist at a definite moment in the past, then *before* any given moment (the present moment, for instance) it must have existed at each of an absolutely infinite series of previous moments; and this, he says (for reasons which I need not mention now) is impossible. Therefore, he concludes, the world must have begun to exist at some definite moment in the past: there must have been a moment which was the first when it existed. But obviously, I think, this argument involves the proposition, that if the world exists at any moment at all, then one or other of two alternatives must be true: namely, *either* it must have existed at each of an infinite series of previous moments *or* some moment must have been the first when it existed. But the argument to prove that it is impossible that it should have existed at each of an infinite series of moments previous to any given moment proves (if it proves anything at all) that the first alternative cannot be the case. The whole argument, therefore, proves (if it proves anything at all) that if the world exists at any moment at all, then the second alternative must be true: namely, some moment must have been the first when it existed. That is to say, it proves the first of my two hypotheticals: If the world exists in time at all, it must have had a beginning.

And now let us consider the second argument. This is as follows. To say, says Kant, that the world had a beginning is to say that there was a time, previous to its beginning, when it did not exist; and this is to say that there was a time, before it began, when nothing existed at all—an absolutely empty time. But, says Kant, nothing can begin to exist in an absolutely empty time; because no part of such a time could differ from any other in a way which would explain, why after one period in it something should begin to exist, whereas previous periods had elapsed without leading to the existence of anything. Therefore, he concludes, the world cannot have had a beginning. But obviously, I think, this argument also assumes that, if the world exists at any moment at all, then there are but two possible alternatives: namely, *either* some moment was the first when it existed *or* it had no beginning at all. And here again the argument to prove that it cannot have had a first moment does prove (if it proves anything) that the first alternative cannot be the true one. The whole argument, therefore, does prove (if it proves anything) that if the world exists at any time at all, the second alternative must be the true one: namely, that it can have had no beginning. That is to say, it does prove the second of my hypotheticals.

Kant's two arguments together do, then, I think, certainly prove, if they prove anything, that, if the world existed at any time at all, both of two contradictory propositions would be true: and they prove therefore that the world cannot have existed at any time whatever.

And having simplified their results so far, we may, I think, simplify them still further. We may drop the reference to 'the world', which is, in some ways, an ambiguous word; and may say they simply prove this. Namely, that if anything whatever existed at any time whatever, both of two contradictory propositions must be true. For, suppose that anything whatever, no matter what, does exist at some moment. Then only three alternatives are possible. Either the moment at which it exists is the first moment at which anything has existed, *i.e.*, nothing has existed before it. And Kant's argument to prove that in such a case, its existence must have been preceded by empty time, and that nothing can begin to exist, if its existence has merely been preceded by empty time, will, if it proves anything, prove that this alternative is not the true one. But only two other alternatives remain. If the first moment at which the thing in question exists, is *not* the first at which anything exists, then other things must have existed before it. And with regard to these things only two alternatives are possible. Either some one of the moments at which some one of them existed, must be the first moment at which anything existed. And the same argument of Kant's, if it proves anything, will prove that this alternative cannot be the true one. Or else, before the given moment, something must have existed at each of an absolutely infinite series of previous moments. And here Kant's argument to prove that it is impossible that, before any given moment, the world should have existed at each of an absolutely infinite series of previous moments must (if it proves anything at all) prove that this alternative cannot be the true one. For Kant's argument to prove that this is impossible is not a special argument confined to some peculiar species of thing called 'the world'. It is an absolutely general argument, which can be expressed in the following way. Let us call the existence of the world at any one moment a different *fact* from its existence at any other moment, no matter whether *what* exists at the one moment is different from *what* exists at the other, or *not*. To speak in this way is, you see, quite in accordance with our ordinary use of language; for even if absolutely the same thing does exist at both of two different moments, we should yet say that its existence at the one moment was a different fact from its existence at the other: for instance, my existence now this evening, at so many minutes to nine, is a different fact from my existence at twelve noon to-day, even if the 'I' which existed at both moments is absolutely the same thing. Let us say then that the existence of the world at any one moment is a different fact from its existence at any other. Then, in the same sense, we may say that the existence of anything whatever at any one moment is a different fact either from the existence of that same thing or from the existence of anything else at any other moment. And Kant's argument is an absolutely general argument to the effect that it is impossible that, before any given moment, an absolutely infinite series of different facts, in this sense, should have elapsed—of facts, that is, each of which consists in the existence of something or other at a different moment.

We may say, then, that Kant's two arguments, if they prove anything at all, prove this: namely, that *if* anything whatever exists at any time at all, then *both* of two contradictory propositions would be true. And since it is impossible that *both* of two contradictory propositions should be true, they prove, absolutely conclusively (if they prove anything) that nothing whatever really exists at any time at all.

And I want to insist, for a moment, that this is the result, which does follow from them, if any follows; because I think both Kant himself, and others who have used similar arguments, have not seen quite clearly that exactly this *is* the result which follows. Kant infers from his argument that Time is a mere form in which things appear to us. And if he *merely* meant by this that things appeared to us to be in time, but were not, in any single case, really so, there would be no objection to his inference. His argument (as I have tried to shew) does really prove (if it proves anything) that nothing whatever can really exist in Time; but it does *not* prove that nothing can *appear* to us to be in Time: it only proves that, if anything does appear to us to be in Time, this fact itself—namely, the fact that something *does* appear to us to be in time—cannot itself really be in Time—cannot occur at any time at all: it leaves open the abstract possibility that such a fact *may* really exist, provided it does not occur *at* any time at all. But Kant himself sometimes speaks, I think, as if this were not all that he meant. He speaks as if the conclusion he meant to draw were only that anything which *does* exist in Time, must be a mere Appearance, a mere phenomenon. As if, that is to say, there was a peculiar class of things which really do exist in Time; and as if all that his arguments proved was only that things of this class must all of them be, in some sense, merely Appearances or Phenomena. I think he himself really did confuse these two views with one another: namely, the view that some things really do exist in time, but that all these things are merely Appearances—Appearances of something else which does *not* exist in Time; with the entirely inconsistent view, that nothing whatever—not even, therefore, a mere Appearance—can exist in Time. And it is, I think, largely to this confusion that his own views, and other similar views, owe their plausibility. People find it comparatively easy to admit, for various reasons, that everything which does exist in Time is a mere Appearance. And they may quite consistently do so; for there are senses of the word Appearance, in which what is a mere Appearance may exist as truly and as really as what is not. And Kant himself constantly speaks as if this were all that he did require you to admit. He speaks as if it were really true that some things did exist before others: as if, for instance, he himself had held views at one time, which he ceased to hold after he read Hume: and as if all that his arguments required him to hold, was that all these things, which have really existed before or after one another, were merely phenomena or Appearances. But once you realise quite clearly that what his arguments require you to admit, is not merely this, but that absolutely nothing ever exists in Time at all, that, therefore, nobody ever believed anything at any time, or any one thing before another, and that all statements to the effect that any one ever did do so are absolutely false—then, I think, you will find it much more difficult to admit this. That is why I wish to insist that what his arguments do prove, if they prove anything, *is* that nothing whatever, of any sort or kind, can possibly exist at any moment whatever: or, in other words, that any statement, which asserts with regard to anything whatever, whether the thing in question deserves to be called a mere Appearance or not, that it exists or has existed or will exist at any time at all, must be simply false.

Kant's arguments, therefore (if sound) do not merely prove that everything which does exist in time is a mere Appearance; on the contrary they prove that nothing exists in time at all, and therefore, that the proposition, that everything which does so exist is a mere Appearance, is a false one: since that proposition implies that some things, namely, Appearances, do so exist; whereas what Kant's arguments prove (if anything) is that *nothing* does. And moreover, they do not even prove that everything which *appears* to exist in time is a mere Appearance. This is another view which is, I think, often confused with the two former, and which yet is plainly different from both of them. The assertion that whatever *does* exist in Time is a mere appearance is often confused with the assertion that whatever *appears* to exist in Time is so; and both again are confused with the assertion that things only *appear* to exist in Time, and that nothing really does so. The third of these assertions is the only one which Kant's arguments, if sound, do really prove. And the two others stand in quite different relations to it. The first, namely, the assertion that whatever *does* exist in Time is a mere Appearance, is, as I have just said, incompatible with it: if what Kant does prove is true, *this* proposition must be false. But the second, namely, the proposition that whatever *appears* to exist in Time is a mere Appearance, is *not* proved by Kant's arguments to be either true or false. For plainly it is quite possible that what appears to exist in Time, even though it does not really do so, may nevertheless be absolutely real and *not* a mere Appearance. A stick may appear to me to be bent, when it is not really bent; but the fact that it appears to have a property, which it has not really got, does not prove for a moment that the stick itself is unreal or is a mere Appearance. And just so even if Kant has proved (and this is all he has proved, if he has proved anything) that nothing really has the property of existing in time, this goes no way at all to prove that the things which appear to have this property, may not themselves be absolutely real and not mere Appearances. All that he can have proved is that we are mistaken, if we think that they exist in time. The possibility still remains open that we are *not* mistaken, if we think that they are not mere Appearances.

What this argument of Kant's, then, proves, if it proves anything, is that nothing whatever really exists in time, because, if anything did, *both* of two contradictory propositions *would* be true. It proves just this, and neither more nor less.

And this argument, I said, was a specimen of a type of argument, of which Kant himself uses several others, and which have been much used by other philosophers since. The type of argument is this. They all really prove, if they prove anything, that nothing whatever can possibly have *some particular property*, because, if anything did have it, both of two contradictory propositions would be true. Kant himself, for instance, uses an argument which (if sound) will prove with regard to the property of existing in Space, exactly what the argument I have just stated proves with regard to the property of existing in Time. It proves, that is to say, if it is sound, that nothing whatever can possibly be situated in any part of Space, because, if anything were so situated, both of two contradictory propositions would be true. And besides these two arguments, with regard to the property of existing in Time and the property of existing in Space, Kant uses several others, with regard to other properties, which I need not mention. And, since Kant's time, the use of this type of argument has been extended enormously. Different philosophers have thought they discovered, with regard to all sorts of different properties that, *if* anything whatever had the property in question, then both of two contradictory propositions would be true. Hegel is the philosopher whose name is chiefly associated with arguments of this kind. He thought he could shew, with regard to an enormous number of different properties—properties which we commonly suppose that many things *do* have, that, if anything really had them, it must also have another contradictory property. It has, I believe, been denied with regard to Hegel, that the pairs of properties which he presents to us as implied in one another, really are absolutely contradictory, or that he thought them to be so. But it is, I think, certain that, if they are not, then the most paradoxical and striking conclusions, which he draws from the supposed fact that these properties do imply one another, certainly do not follow from that fact. He does, I think, certainly draw the conclusion that any proposition which asserts that anything really possesses one of these properties is false—or (for this is how some of his modern defenders prefer to put it) at least partially false. But unless these properties really are absolutely contradictory—unless, that is to say, any proposition which asserts that a given thing has the one, does absolutely contradict the assertion that it has the other—then it certainly does not follow that the proposition which asserts that a thing has one of them is even partially false. For, suppose we say all that Hegel has proved, or intended to prove, is that, if anything has a certain property, it must *also* have another, which appears to be, but is not really contradictory of the first. What will follow? Obviously there will not be the least reason for denying that it may be *absolutely* true that many things have *both* properties. For there is no law which asserts that a thing cannot have both of two properties, which *appear* to contradict one another, provided that they do not really do so. All that part of Hegel's philosophy, therefore, which consists in suggesting that certain common propositions, in which we assert that things have certain properties, are at least partially false—and no one will deny, I think, that he does suggest this—becomes entirely groundless, unless we suppose that his arguments, with regard to these properties, really are of the type which I am describing: that is to say, to the effect that, if anything did really possess the property in question, both of two really contradictory propositions would be true; and that therefore it cannot be absolutely true to say that anything whatever does possess the property in question. No doubt Hegel and those who use similar arguments, do often confuse *this* conclusion with the two other conclusions which I distinguished above. Namely, they confuse the conclusion: The *proposition* that a given thing *has* one of the properties in question is always a mere appearance—that is to say, it is a *proposition* which *appears* to be true, but is not really so; with the conclusion: Any*thing* which *does* have one of the properties in question, is a mere Appearance; and this again with the conclusion: Any*thing* which *appears* to have one of the properties in question, is a mere Appearance. But what I am contending is that the first of these conclusions—namely, that propositions, in which one of these properties appears as predicate of something, are merely apparently true, and not absolutely true—is certainly a part of what they take themselves to prove; and that this part of their conclusions can only really follow, if their arguments are of the type which I have described.

Now I cannot, of course, attempt to examine *all* the different arguments of this type, which different philosophers have used. What I propose to do is merely to examine those among them, which resemble the argument which I quoted from Kant in one definite respect. This argument, you may have noticed, depends on the assertion that it is impossible that an absolutely infinite series of different facts, consisting each of them in the existence of something at a different moment of Time, should have elapsed *before* a given moment. That is to say it depends on the assertion that an infinite series of a certain sort is impossible. And what I propose to do is to discuss, as well as I can, all the arguments of this type, which do thus depend on the assumption that infinite series, of some particular sort, are impossible. I choose these particular arguments, because I think that these arguments, which depend upon supposed difficulties involved in the conception of infinity, are at least as plausible as any of those by which philosophers have tried to prove that most of the propositions, which we usually suppose to be true, cannot possibly be so; and because also I think they have been actually regarded as conclusive by many more philosophers than any single other argument of the type to which they belong. And because also, I think, the notion of infinity does involve real paradoxes, and real difficulties as to what the nature of the world really is, even if it does not involve those extremely paradoxical conclusions, which, as we have seen, do, according to Kant, follow from it.

Let us take, first of all, that particular argument of Kant's with which I began, and consider it in the simplified form which I finally gave to it.

To begin with, then, we are, I think, all commonly convinced that things do exist in time. For instance, we are convinced that some things do exist now, and that other things have existed *before*, in the past, which no longer exist now. There is hardly anything of which we are, in fact, more certain than of this. And I think it is quite plain, that *if* we are right about this, then something else is certain also: namely, that *either* some moment in the past must have been the *first* moment, when anything existed, *or* there must have existed before now an absolutely infinite series of different facts, each at a different moment in the past. That one or other of these alternatives must be true is, I think, quite plain: for if *no* moment in the past was the first moment when anything existed, that means that something must have existed at a previous moment; and since this moment also cannot have been the first when anything existed, something must have existed at a moment before that; and so on *ad infinitum.*

I think, therefore, Kant is plainly quite right in supposing that, *if* anything exists in Time at all, *either* some moment must have been the first when anything existed *or* there must have existed before now an absolutely infinite series of different facts. But what he requires to prove is that if anything exists in time at all, *both* these alternatives must be true. And how is this to be done?

His argument to prove the first hypothetical, namely, that *if* anything exists in time at all, some moment *must* have been the first when anything existed consists, as I said, in an attempt to prove that the other alternative cannot be true: namely, that an infinite series of facts cannot have elapsed *before* any given moment. This, therefore, is the argument depending on the supposed difficulties of infinity. And I propose to consider this later. I wish only to point out now that, *if*, as he says, such an infinite series really is impossible then it does absolutely follow that if anything exists in time at all, there must have been a moment, *before* which nothing existed.

But even supposing he can prove this, he still requires to prove the other hypothetical, namely, that if anything exists in time at all, there *cannot* have been any moment, which was the first at which anything existed. And here, it seems to me, his proof certainly fails of absolute rigour. How can it possibly be proved with certainty that there may not have been a time in the past, before which nothing at all existed? It seems to me certainly impossible absolutely to prove this. But nevertheless it does seem to me very difficult to believe the opposite. Can you really believe, if you come to think of it, that there really was a moment, which was absolutely the first at which anything existed, and that absolutely nothing existed before it? It does seem to me almost impossible to believe this; and yet I do not know how it can be proved. Of course, if you assume that nothing can ever exist, unless there exists something before it, which *causes* it to exist, then the required result does absolutely follow. And this principle also does seem very plausible. But it does not seem absolutely certain, and I do not see how it can be proved. Though, therefore, I think there are very strong reasons for supposing that there cannot have been a moment, before which absolutely nothing existed, and though I think Common Sense would be inclined to agree with Kant that there cannot, yet I think this cannot be taken as absolutely certain. And that, therefore, for this reason alone, even if Kant's argument from the difficulties of infinity *were* conclusive, yet his whole argument—the whole argument, understood as proving *both* hypotheticals—must be regarded as inconclusive, if we take it in exactly the form in which he puts it.

But it seems to me that in this respect his argument can be mended. For though it does not seem to me quite certain, but only exceedingly probable, that there cannot have been a moment which was the first when anything existed, it does seem to me quite certain that there cannot have been a first moment of Time itself. It does seem quite certain that, however far back you go, there must always have been a time before any at which you choose to stop: that in short the length of past time must have been absolutely infinite. And so far as I can see, the fact that this is so, would have served Kant's purpose just as well as the more doubtful assumption that something *other* than time must also have existed for an infinite length of time. For his argument against the possibility of the completion of an infinite series will, I think, apply just as well to prove that there cannot have been an infinite length of past time itself, as to prove that there cannot have been an infinite series of facts in time. If, therefore, Kant's argument against the possibility of the completion of an infinite series really were sound, I think we could substitute for his original argument another argument which really does prove the same conclusion—namely, that nothing can exist in time at all.

The argument would be this. If anything exists in time, then an absolutely infinite length of time must have elapsed before its existence. This I take to be a self-evident proposition and certainly true. But, the argument goes on, it is utterly impossible that an absolutely infinite length of time should have elapsed before a given moment. And if this argument is sound, then it does follow that, if anything exists in time at all, two contradictory propositions would both be true. Hence it would follow that nothing can exist in time at all, and indeed that there can be no such thing as Time: that time is as absolute a nonentity as a round square. That is to say, this conclusion really does depend, as Kant says it does, upon the question whether an infinite series of a certain sort is possible: and if it can be shewn that such an infinite series is impossible, then the conclusion that nothing exists in time at all does follow.

And a similar argument, though not quite such a certain one can, I think, obviously be used also in the case of Space. In the case of Space, Kant's *actual* argument is, I think, obviously much more weak than in the case of Time. Here, too, what he tries to prove is that, if anything exists in space at all, *things* must exist throughout an infinite extent of space, and that it is impossible they should. And the obvious weakness of this argument is, I think, the impossibility of proving, or making it even seem very probable, that *things* must exist throughout an infinite extent of Space. It does, I think, seem highly probable, if not quite certain, that space itself, if it exists at all, must be infinite in extent: that, for instance, starting from here, in any direction, there must be an absolutely infinite series of miles in that direction. But that something must exist *in each* of those miles does not seem by any means so obvious; and so far as I know there is no reason for thinking it even probable. That the material Universe, if there is a material Universe, does extend for a *very* large number of miles in any direction from here, there is, of course, reason for thinking: but even though it extends for millions of millions of miles, there is, so far as I know, no reason for thinking that it does not *somewhere* come to an end, and that there may not be a point at some finite number of miles from here beyond which there is nothing but empty space. I think there is obviously a real difference in this respect between the cases of Space and Time. In the case of Time, as I said, it does seem to be extremely probable, though not absolutely certain, that something must have existed throughout the whole of the infinite length of past time: that, for instance, taking the infinite number of hours which have preceded this moment, *something* must have existed in each of those hours. It is, I think, very difficult to believe that this is not the case. But in the case of Space, it does seem to me quite easy to believe that the material Universe only occupies a finite number of cubic miles—finite, though, of course, very large indeed—and that beyond it there is an infinite extent of absolutely empty space—space in which there is nothing whatever. And I know of no reason why this should not be the case—if space and a material universe exist at all. Even therefore, if Kant's argument to prove that it is impossible that anything should exist in each of an absolutely infinite series of miles from this point, were sound, it seems to me that his *whole* argument lacks even plausibility, because there is no difficulty in supposing that the material Universe is, in fact, bounded in Space.

But here, too, I think, his argument may be mended if, instead of considering *what* exists *in* Space, we consider Space itself. *If* Space is Euclidean, then there must be an absolutely infinite series of miles in any direction from here: and though I suppose we must not assume it to be certain that the space which exists, and in which material objects are (*if* there is such a thing) is Euclidean, it is at least plausible to do so. And so far as I can see, Kant's argument to prove that there cannot be an infinite series of *occupied* miles in any direction from here, would do just as well to prove that there cannot be an infinite series of *empty* miles. So that we might substitute for Kant's the following argument. *If* anything exists in Euclidean Space, there must be an infinite series of miles in any direction from that thing; but it is impossible that there should be an infinite series of miles in *any* direction from a given point. Therefore, if anything did exist in Euclidean space, both of two contradictory propositions would be true. But it is impossible they should. Therefore, the hypothesis from which this would follow must be false. That is to say, nothing can exist in Euclidean space at all; and indeed there can be no such thing as Euclidean space. It must be as complete a nonentity as a round square.

It seems to me, then, that both in the case of Time and in that of Space (if we mean, by Space, Euclidean Space) there is a valid argument, on the lines suggested by Kant, which will yield the conclusion that nothing can possibly exist in Space or Time, *provided only* it can be proved that it is impossible that an infinite number of hours should have elapsed before now, and that an infinite number of miles should extend in any direction from here. *Provided* this can be proved, this conclusion is, I think, certain, because the following two hypotheticals really are certain. *namely* (1) *If* anything exists in time, an infinite number of hours must have elapsed before it existed; and (2) *If* anything exists in Euclidean Space, an infinite number of miles must extend in any direction from it.

But now can it be proved that these two things are impossible? Can it be proved that it is impossible that an absolutely infinite number of hours should have elapsed before the present moment? And impossible that space should extend for an absolutely infinite number of miles in any direction from here?

There certainly are, I think, difficulties in supposing either of these two things. Many people are, I think, inclined to agree with

Kant that these two things really are impossible. They say it is impossible to conceive a really infinite series of anything, whether of hours or minutes or days or years, or feet or yards or inches or miles; and that since it is impossible to conceive such a series, no such series really can exist. This view may, I think, be made very plausible; and I want to make it appear as plausible as possible—to bring out all the difficulties I can see in the supposition that there is an infinite series, in order to treat as fairly as possible this argument, which would, I think, prove, and which many people do really believe to prove, the extremely paradoxical conclusions that nothing really exists in Space or Time at all.

Now Kant himself seems to think that the cases of Time and Space are different. He thinks that you cannot use exactly the same argument to prove the impossibility of there being an absolutely infinite series of miles from here, as to prove that an absolutely infinite series of hours has elapsed before now. He seems, in fact, to think that you cannot prove this in the case of Space, except by reducing the case of Space, in a certain sense, to the case of Time. And his attempt to do this seems to me to be a failure. I think, therefore, that his argument in the case of Time is much the more plausible of the two. And moreover if *this* argument is inconclusive, the argument in the case of Space is certainly inconclusive also. I propose, therefore, only to consider Kant's own argument in the case of Time; and then to go on to consider other arguments which will apply to Space and Time equally.

What, then, is Kant's argument in the case of Time? He does not trouble to explain it at all elaborately, nor to make clear precisely what he means by it: he seems to think that its truth is self-evident almost without explanation.

It is simply this: That the very notion of an infinite series is one which can never be brought to an end or completed. But what we suppose, when we suppose that an infinite series of hours, or days or minutes has elapsed before now, is just that that particular series *has* come to an end now at this moment. And therefore the series in question cannot really be infinite, since it has come to an end.

Now I am inclined to think that this argument, on Kant's part, is partly a pure fallacy based on an ambiguity in the notion of end. It is quite true that when we suppose that there has been an infinite number of hours up to this moment, we do suppose that that series has come to an *end* at this moment. We suppose, therefore, that it really has got *one* end—namely, this one. But this does not at all contradict our supposition that it is infinite, for what we mean by this is merely that it has no end in the *other* direction—or, if you like to put it so, that it has no *beginning*. You see a series may have two *ends*, or if you like it, an end and a beginning; and a series will be truly infinite, even supposing that it has an end in *one* direction, provided that it has none in the other. This may be easily illustrated by one of the simplest cases of an infinite series. Consider the series of numbers 1, 2, 3, 4, 5, etc. This series has an end in one direction, since it starts with the number one. But nevertheless it is an absolutely infinite series, since an absolutely infinite number of numbers can be formed, as these are formed, by adding *one* to the preceding number. Add one to 5 and you get six; add one to six and you get 7: and similarly whatever number you take, there is plainly always *another* number greater by 1 than it is. There is, therefore, an absolutely infinite series of different numbers starting from the number 1; and this series is truly infinite, in spite of the fact that it has an end in one direction, simply because it has none in the other. It is, therefore, a pure fallacy to suppose that there cannot have been an infinite series of past hours, simply because that series has an end in one direction—has come to an end now: all that we mean by calling it infinite is that it has no end in the other direction or, in other words, no beginning.

But this fallacy, I think, is not all that there is in Kant's argument. I think he certainly meant something else besides—something which is very difficult to express accurately, but which may be put in this kind of way. He was thinking, I think, that Time, so to speak, could never have got to the present moment, if it had to pass through an absolutely infinite series of hours first. And there is, I think, certainly something plausible—something which appeals to people —in this notion. It is, I think, analogous to one of the difficulties which makes the old puzzle of Achilles and the tortoise plausible. The puzzle is this. Let us suppose that Achilles and the tortoise are to run a race; that Achilles runs ten times as fast as the tortoise; and that he starts ten yards behind him. Then, by the time Achilles has got to the point where the tortoise started, the tortoise will be a yard in front of him; because the tortoise will have run one yard, while Achilles was running ten. The tortoise will, therefore, be at the end of the eleventh yard from Achilles' starting point, by the time that Achilles is at the end of the tenth. But now, when Achilles gets to the end of the eleventh yard, the tortoise will still be a tenth of a yard in front of him. And when he has covered that tenth of a yard, the tortoise will still be a hundredth of a yard in front. And when he has covered that hundredth of a yard, the tortoise will still be a thousandth in front. And so on *ad infinitum*—absolutely *ad infinitum*. In short it seems as if Achilles never could possibly catch up the tortoise, because, before he can do so, he must have gone over an absolutely infinite series of spaces. It is true that these spaces are constantly diminishing in size; but still there does seem to be an absolutely infinite number of them; and by the time Achilles has reached any point previously occupied by the tortoise, it does seem as if the tortoise will *always* be a little in front of him. It is, I think, a difficulty analogous to this that Kant felt in the case of time. Just as it seems impossible that Achilles should ever get over an absolutely infinite series of spaces, even though these spaces are constantly diminishing in size; so, I think, it seemed to Kant impossible that time should ever have got over an absolutely infinite series of *hours*, as it must have done in order to get to the present moment. And there does seem to me to be a real difficulty here. I do not want to minimize it. But are we entitled to conclude from this apparent difficulty that the thing is really impossible? especially, when there will follow, if we do so conclude, a further conclusion, which seems so obviously false, as that nothing can exist in time at all? that there is no such thing as time? It seems to me we are certainly not—especially as it is so difficult to put the difficulty quite precisely; and Kant at least certainly does not succeed in putting it more precisely. At least I think we cannot agree to Kant's claim that he has *proved rigorously* that an infinite series of hours cannot have elapsed before now.

I shall next try to consider other arguments, drawn from the notion of infinity, against the reality of space and time, arguments which can be put more precisely; and will try to sum up upon the whole matter.

Chapter X

THE NOTION OF INFINITY

I want to get as clear as I can about the notion of infinity and its relation to Space and Time. And, first of all, I want to try to explain some preliminary points, which I think I have not made clear enough.

To begin with, then, I think we certainly all do, in ordinary life, constantly believe that there are such things as inches, feet, yards, and miles. We constantly talk about them; and we assume that we positively *know* immense numbers of propositions about them. For instance, we *know* that there are more yards between this room and Waterloo bridge than between this room and Waterloo station. We *know* that there are more miles between here and New Zealand than between here and Paris. We are sure that that blackboard is longer than it is broad; and that there are more inches along one side of it, which we call its length, than along the other which we call its breadth. If anybody, in ordinary life, were to say that Berlin is *not* further off than Paris, or that either of them is less than 100 miles off we should say he was simply ignorant of geography: that he had unquestionably made a mistake about the facts; because it is simply *a fact* that Berlin *is* further off than Paris, and that both are certainly *more* than 100 miles away.

But now, what are these inches and feet and yards and miles in the existence of which we believe so confidently? Do we, any of us, ever directly apprehend any one of them or any part of them? I ought, perhaps, to apologise for mentioning this point again, after having said so much about the difference between the space which we directly apprehend and the space in which we suppose material objects to be. But I want to make it quite plain exactly *where* the supposition that certain sorts of infinite series are impossible seems to me to conflict with Common Sense; and exactly which among all the things which we commonly believe might still be true, even if this supposition were justified. Are, then, the inches and feet and miles, in the existence of which we commonly believe, *ever* directly apprehended by us? There seems a certain paradox, at first, in saying that they are *not*. When, for instance, you look at a foot-rule, on which the inches are marked off, it does seem natural to suppose that you do, in this particular case, actually *see* any particular inch at which you look. Of course, we know that the foot-rule may not be absolutely exact, and that what is marked off on it as an inch may not be exactly an inch. But still it does seem as if, whatever the exact length of that part of the foot-rule which is marked off as an inch may be, we do, if we look straight at it, actually see *the* length which it has; and that, since this length is not much different from an inch, and we do, when we see *it*, both see a little more and a little less, we must be actually seeing *an* inch of the foot-rule, though we may not know exactly how much of what we see *is* an inch. And I do not mean to deny that we do, in such a case, actually see an inch. I think we really do, in *one* of the senses in which we commonly use the word 'seeing'. But there is, I think, great danger of confusing this sense of the word 'see', with that in which 'seeing' stands for direct apprehension. If you try to discover by introspection exactly what it is that you *see*, all that you can discover quite clearly is what you directly apprehend. You do directly apprehend a space, and it is very natural to suppose that part of *this* space is an inch: that the inch which you see really is a part of the space which you directly apprehend. But it is, I think, to say the least, extremely doubtful whether this is so. There are two chief reasons for supposing that it is doubtful. Namely: (1) That part of the foot-rule which you see, and which is an inch in length, would be seen by you equally and would still be of exactly the same length, whether you saw it with the naked eye or whether you saw it with magnifying spectacles; but the spaces which you directly apprehended in these two cases would be of *different* lengths: they cannot, therefore, *both* of them be identical with the inch of the foot-rule which you see; and there is no more reason to suppose that one of them is identical with it, than that the other is. In no particular case, therefore, is there any reason to suppose that any part of the space which you directly apprehend is *identical* with the inch that is occupied by any part of the foot-rule. And (2) it seems to be certain that every part of the space, which you directly apprehend, when you look at the foot-rule, not only seems to be, but *is* occupied by some colour; whereas there is some reason to suppose that the inch of space, which is occupied by the foot-rule, is *not* occupied by any colour. These reasons do not prove conclusively that no part of the space which you ever directly apprehend is identical with an inch of the foot-rule; but they do shew that many of the spaces which you directly apprehend, in looking at it, are *not* identical with it: and they do render it ***doubtful*** whether *any* of them is. And, if it is doubtful, whether, in looking at a foot-rule, you ever directly apprehend an inch of it; it is also doubtful whether, in looking at or touching anything whatever you ever directly apprehend either an inch or any length of *it*. It is, therefore, doubtful whether the inches, and feet, and yards, and miles, about which, in ordinary life, we talk with such confidence, are ever—either they themselves or any part of them—directly apprehended by any one of us.

Now, why I have mentioned this point is because I spoke last time as if, supposing that infinite series of certain sorts were impossible, there could be no such thing as Euclidean space at all; and as if some philosophers, and Kant among them, had actually supposed that there was no such thing. I spoke of Space in general, without distinguishing between directly apprehended spaces and the inches, feet, yards, and miles of which we speak in ordinary life. But we now see that it is certain that much of the space which we directly apprehend is *not* identical with any part of these inches or feet or miles; and that it is doubtful whether *any* of it is. And it is, I think, very important to keep the two distinct for several reasons.

In the first place, when it is argued that, because certain sorts of infinite series are impossible, therefore certain sorts of spaces cannot be real, there are two chief lines of argument which may be used. It may be argued: these spaces cannot be real, because, if they were, they would be infinite in extent, and this is impossible; or it may be argued: they cannot be real, because, if they were, they would be infinitely divisible, and this is impossible. Last time I dealt only with arguments of the first kind—arguments which say that certain sorts of spaces must be infinite *in extent*: that if, for instance, there is an Euclidean straight line a yard in length, there must lie, in the same straight line with it, an infinite number of other precisely straight lines, each of them a yard in length. This time I mean also to deal with arguments from infinite divisibility. But what I want to point out is that, in both cases, the argument against the reality of any particular piece of space, fails altogether, unless it can be shewn either that, *if* the particular piece of space is real at all, then there must be an infinite number of other pieces of the same size, *or* that the piece itself must be infinitely divisible. For instance, if it be desired to shew that no part of the side of that blackboard is really an inch long, this can only be shewn by these arguments, *if* it can be shewn that, supposing it were, there must be an infinite number of precisely similar inches in the world, *or* can be shewn that, if it were, the inch in question must be infinitely divisible. And why I say this, is, because, so far as I know, there is no reason to suppose that any part of the space *which we directly apprehend* is *either* infinitely extended *or* infinitely divisible. For instance, suppose I now consider the space which I directly apprehend in looking at this paper—the space, which *is* occupied by the whitish colour with writing on it which I directly apprehend. Part of this space, I think, undoubtedly is a square, although no square is marked out upon it; and for all I know it may be an Euclidean square. But even if it is, I know no reason to think that there are, attached to each side of this square which I directly apprehend, an infinite number of precisely similar squares; nor yet that it is itself infinitely divisible. I know no good reason for thinking that the whole of the space which I directly apprehend at any one moment is continuous with any space at all which I do *not* directly apprehend, *or* that it is infinitely divisible. That is to say, both these difficulties, if they occur at all, only occur with regard to the lines which bound parts of this paper—the material object; they do not occur, so far as I can see, with regard to any square or line or triangle or other figure which I directly apprehend in looking at the paper.

Arguments, therefore, from the supposed impossibility of infinite extent or infinite divisibility, do not, I think, go any way at all to shew that any piece of space which we directly apprehend is unreal. They do not do this, because there is no reason to suppose that any piece of space which we directly apprehend is either continuous with an infinite number of other similar pieces *or* itself infinitely divisible. It is only with regard to the inches and feet and yards and miles of which we talk in ordinary life that there is any good reason to suppose either of these two things; and these inches and yards, we have seen, are, very probably, *not* identical with any piece of space which we ever directly apprehend. *And* (this is the second point I want to call attention to) most philosophers who have used these arguments have not, I think, definitely meant them to apply to any piece of space which we directly apprehend. They have, indeed, very often not been careful to say what kind of space they were talking about. But they have, I think, generally been thinking of the inches and yards and miles of which we talk in ordinary life; though they have often confused these with pieces of space which we directly apprehend. Some philosophers, indeed, do, I think, definitely hold that even the spaces which we directly apprehend are unreal—that there simply are no such things in the Universe. But, in so far as they have distinguished these spaces from the inches and miles of which we talk in ordinary life, they have, so far as I know, never definitely tried to shew that *these*—which we directly apprehand—involve either infinite extent or infinite divisibility. The argument against *their* reality has always, I think, been drawn from different considerations.

I wish it,therefore, to be clearly understood that all that I am going to say about the infinite extent and infinite divisibility of Space is meant to apply only to the inches, feet, yards and miles, about which we talk in ordinary life: it is not meant to apply to any piece of space which we ever directly apprehend; and, so far as I can see, it does *not* apply to any such piece. The arguments about the infinity and infinite divisibility of space, which I am going to consider can only prove, if sound, such things as that there is no space between here and Charing Cross: it is only in this way that they conflict with Common Sense: they cannot prove that anything which we ever directly apprehend is unreal, because, so far as I can see, there is no reason to suppose that anybody ever has directly apprehended any part of the space between here and Charing Cross.

So much to make clear exactly what the issue is with regard to Space.

And now I want to try to make clear what it is with regard to Time.

Here, too, I think, the fundamental fact is that we do all commonly believe that there are such things as seconds, minutes, hours, days, years. We constantly talk of such things; and suppose that we absolutely *know* ever so many propositions about them. I *know*, for instance, and you all know, that I have been speaking this evening for more than five minutes. We know that the battle of Waterloo took place more than fifty years ago; and if, in common life, anybody were to suppose that it did not, we should simply say that he was ignorant of history. We should not be induced, for a moment, to suspect he might be right: we should say it was a question of fact, about which he was definitely wrong. And so, in thousands of other instances. Each of us commonly assumes that he knows thousands of absolutely true propositions about the length of time which separated different events. We never know, perhaps, *absolutely exactly how* much time elapsed between them: but we know it to be absolutely true that Queen Elizabeth did die *more* than twenty years before Queen Anne, and *less* than two hundred years; though we do not know, down to seconds and the minutest fractions of a second, *exactly* how much time elapsed between the two deaths.

But now, what *are* these seconds, minutes, days and years, about which we know so much? Is any one of them or any part of them ever directly apprehended by any one of us? Obviously this question may be asked with regard to them, just as it might be asked with regard to the inches, feet and miles, of which we talk in ordinary life. But I confess, in the case of Time, I cannot answer this question: it seems to me to be quite doubtful what the correct answer is. And I mention the point only because the fact that it is doubtful, seems to me to throw some light upon the analogous case of Space, and upon the way in which we come to know (if we do know at all) of the existence of the Space and Time of which we speak in ordinary life. In the case of Space, I said, it seems to me quite certain that we do directly apprehend pieces of space of some sort: I undoubtedly do directly apprehend patches of colour, which occupy spaces of different sizes and shapes: and I can distinguish the spaces which they occupy, from the colours which occupy them. But it is, I said, very probable that none of these directly apprehended spaces are identical with any part of the space of which we talk in ordinary life. In the case of Space, then, there was a reason for distinguishing between two sorts of space—directly apprehended space and the space of ordinary life. But in the case of Time it seems to me doubtful whether we ever directly apprehend any time at all, *either* the time of ordinary life *or* any other. Consider the cases in which, if at all, we do directly apprehend a lapse of time. We undoubtedly do directly apprehend changes of various sorts, both movements—that is to say changes of relative position in directly apprehended space—and other changes, which do not consist in movements: *e.g.* we may directly apprehend a light growing brighter, a colour changing, or a sound growing louder. It used to be supposed, and is, I think, still supposed by some people, that this is not the case. Let us take a particular instance. I can observe now the second-hand of my watch actually moving; and you all know what it looks like to *see* the second-hand moving. What I *directly apprehend* is, of course, not the second-hand *itself* nor the face of the watch *itself*: but the blackish line which I take to be an appearance of the second-hand, and the white surface which I take to be an appearance of the face of the watch. You will, please, understand, then, that I am going to talk only of these *appearances*—the blackish line and the white surface—*not* of the second-hand itself, nor of the face of the watch itself: for these latter, I think, I do *not* directly apprehend, though I *do* see or observe them. I do, then, at various moments, directly apprehend the blackish line and the white surface: no one, I think, disputes this. But it used to be thought that I never directly apprehend anything but the blackish line *at rest in one position* on the white surface; and that when I say I *see* the black line *passing over* the white surface, this does not mean that I *directly apprehend* the movement; but only that I *remember* that the black line was in a different position a moment before, and *infer* that it must have moved. It is now, however, I think, generally agreed that this is not the case: it is agreed that I do directly apprehend *the movement*. And I think you can see that what happens is in fact something quite different from the mere direct apprehension of a colour at rest combined with a memory of its being at rest formerly in several different positions. Compare this case, for instance, with what happens when I look at the hour-hand. I do there directly apprehend a line of colour at rest, and I can remember it having been in different positions previously. But certainly this is not all that happens in the case of the second-hand. I actually see the second-hand moving whereas I *do not* see the hour-hand moving; and the difference which I express in this way is certainly a difference in what I directly apprehend. The case of the second-hand is therefore a case in which I do directly apprehend a change—in this case a movement—and it would seem that this, if any, must be a case in which I directly apprehend a lapse of time. No doubt it is very difficult to decide exactly *how much* of the movement I do directly apprehend, and where direct apprehension passes into memory: but there seems no doubt that I do directly apprehend *some* movement. But do I directly apprehend any length of time which the movement occupies? I am bound to say I cannot be certain that I do. I do directly apprehend a movement; and I have no doubt that this movement *does* occupy some time. But when I examine, as carefully as I can, the whole of what I directly apprehend, I cannot clearly distinguish in this whole any *directly apprehended* element, which could be called the time which the movement occupies. I cannot be certain in fact that I do directly apprehend the time which the movement occupies in the way in which, when I look at the face of my watch, I do directly apprehend the round space which this white surface occupies. I am not sure that I *do not* directly apprehend the time; but it does seem to me that there is a great difference between space and time in respect of the ease with which we can be certain whether they are directly apprehended or not. It is, I think, quite easy to be certain that *some* space is directly apprehended; but not at all easy to be certain that *any* time is. I am not, of course, denying that we can judge *immediately* with regard to one movement, or other change, that it does take a longer time than another. If, for instance, I move my arm slowly *so*, and then fast *so*, you can, I think, know *immediately*, without inference, that the first movement took a longer time than the second. But immediate knowledge, as I insisted before, is quite a different thing from direct apprehension. And can you, in fact, be certain that you did directly apprehend any part of the time which those two movements occupied? I think it is difficult to be *certain* that you did not; but also difficult to be certain that you did. You can, I think, be quite certain that both movements did occupy time, and that the one occupied more than the other; but whether you directly apprehended any part of the time which either occupied, seems to me much less certain. And this fact, the fact that it seems so uncertain whether you do directly apprehend any time or not, seems to me calculated to weaken the objection which some people feel to admitting that any space which is not directly apprehended, can exist; or that, if any does, we can know of its existence. We have seen, in past lectures, that many people do hold that no space can exist, except when it is directly apprehended; or at least that, if it does, we cannot know of its existence. But, how, then, about Time? Is it not rather uncertain whether Time ever is directly apprehended? And are you, on that ground, going to deny that it exists at all, or that we can know of its existence? It is true that there is this difference between Time and any Space which is not directly apprehended; namely, that in the case of Time we do directly apprehend some of the *things* which occupy it, whereas, in the case of any space, which we do not directly apprehend, it is doubtful whether we ever do directly apprehend any of the things which occupy it. But the mere fact that we can be certain, in the case of Time, of the existence of something, namely a lapse of Time, with regard to which we are *not* certain that we directly apprehend it, does seem to me to weaken the presumption that we cannot know of the existence of any Space except what is directly apprehended.

In the case of Time, then, as in the case of Space, I wish to emphasize that what I mean by Time, and am going to talk about, is the seconds, minutes, hours and days of which we talk in ordinary life. And whether any part of this Time is ever directly apprehended by us I am not certain. Three different alternatives seem to me quite possible. It may be, I think, that there is a directly apprehended Time which is *not* identical with the Time of ordinary life, just as there is a directly apprehended Space, which is not identical with the Space of ordinary life. And, if there is such a Time, what I am going to say is not intended to apply to *it* at all. *Or* it may be the case that we do directly apprehend the Time of ordinary life. *Or* it may be the case that we do not directly apprehend any time at all. I cannot decide between these three alternatives. But, whichever be the truth, the Time about which I am going to speak is the time of ordinary life—the seconds, minutes, hours, days and years, of which we so constantly speak, and about which we commonly assume that we absolutely *know* so many different propositions.

What I am going to talk about, then, is the Space of ordinary life and the Time of ordinary life. That space, for instance, that there is at this moment between here and Charing Cross, and which we believe really does exist at this moment, even though nobody is directly apprehending any part of it; and the Time, for instance, which has elapsed between now and the battle of Waterloo, and which we believe certainly has elapsed, even though, perhaps, nobody has ever directly apprehended any part of it. With regard to both of these two quantities—the length of Space between here and Charing Cross and the length of Time between now and the battle of Waterloo—four different things may be argued with some plausibility. It may be argued (1) with regard to both of them, that, *if* they exist or did exist at all, there must exist also or have existed an infinite number of other quantities, of precisely the same length—or in other words that Time and Space must be infinite in extent; and it may be argued (2) that both of them must be infinitely divisible. But it may be argued also with some plausibility, that there *cannot* be an infinite number of quantities like these, and that they *cannot* be infinitely divisible. And, *if both* these arguments are sound, then it will follow that there can be no space between here and Charing Cross, and that no time can have elapsed since the battle of Waterloo. These are the arguments I am going to consider.

Let us consider first the case of infinite extent.

I gave, last time, an argument of Kant's, which involved the following proposition: Namely, that *if* one hour has elapsed before now, an infinite number of hours must have elapsed before now. And this proposition, of course, simply involves the general principle: that before *any* length of time, no matter what its length or when it occurs, there must have elapsed an infinite number of *equal* lengths of time. For there is no reason to assert it with regard to *hours*, which will not apply equally to all other lengths of time—minutes or seconds or years. And there is no reason to assert it with regard to the hour, which has just elapsed now, which will not apply equally to all other hours. Kant's argument, therefore, involves the general principle that *before any* length of time, an infinite number of equal lengths must have elapsed. And this principle may be reduced to one simpler still: namely, that before *any* length of time, there must have elapsed *one* other length equal to it. For if, before *any*, there must have been *one*, it follows that before *any* there must have been an infinite number. For to say that before any length of time there must have been *one* other equal to it, involves the proposition that, for instance, before the hour from 12 to 1 to-day there must have been *one* other hour. But, of course, the same principle involves that before this second hour, there must again have been another—a third; and involves again that before this third, there must have been a fourth, and so on *ad infinitum*. Merely to say, therefore, that before any or every length of time, there must have elapsed *one* other length equal to it, is equivalent to saying that before any or every length of time there must have elapsed an *infinite* number equal to it. This is *all* that Kant assumes. And, of course, it may be equally well assumed that *after* any or every length of time there must be *one* other equal to it, and therefore an infinite number. That is to say it may be equally well assumed that time is infinite in extent both ways—both towards the past and towards the future. And this assumption merely involves the principles that *before* any or every length of time, there must have elapsed *one* other equal to it, and that *after* any or every length of time, there must have elapsed *one* other equal to it. What are we to say of these two principles? They do seem to me to be self-evident; but I confess I do not know exactly how to set about arguing that they are self-evident. The chief thing to be done is, I think, to consider them as carefully and distinctly as possible, and then to see whether it does not seem as if they *must* be true; and to compare them with other propositions, which do seem to be certainly true, and to consider whether you have any better reason for supposing these other propositions to be true than for supposing this one to be so. Consider, for instance, the proposition that, since I began to lecture this evening, *some* time certainly has elapsed. Have you any better reason for believing this, than for believing that, if so, a length of time equal to this one must have elapsed *before* it? And that this must be true of *every* length of time equal to that which has elapsed since I began to lecture? I cannot see that you have any better reason for believing the one proposition than for believing the other. Beyond asking you to consider questions like this, all I propose to do is to consider one argument, which might be used in favour of the proposition that these two principles are not self-evident. But, before I do this, I want to call attention to one other point with regard to them—namely, that, whether they are certainly true or not, they are at least perfectly easy to *conceive*—perfectly distinct and clear and easy to understand. If you understand what is meant by any length of time at all—an hour, or a minute, or a year—it is quite easy to conceive and to understand the proposition that *both* before and after *any* minute there was or will be *another* minute. And what I wish to insist on is that, if you do understand this, you do understand what is meant by an infinite length of time. There is no obscurity, or inconceivability, or lack of clearness and distinctness about this notion. Merely to understand the assertion that *before* any minute there was another minute *is* to understand the proposition that past time was infinite in extent. Of course, there may be other propositions, implied in this one and capable of being deduced from it, which are more difficult to understand. But merely to understand this one *is* to understand the notion of infinity, though not, perhaps, all that is implied in it: and surely it is quite easy to conceive and understand at least this.

The argument I wish to mention *against* the view that it is self-evident that before any minute there must have been an infinite series of other minutes, is one which is drawn from the analogy of Space: and it is, I think, worth mentioning on other grounds. The fact is that, in the case of Space also, it does, at first sight, seem self-evident, that, if you take any straight line, of any definite length—say, a yard—there must be, in both directions from the end of that straight line, an infinite number of other straight lines, each a yard in length, in the same straight line with it. But in the case of Space, there are two *different* reasons for disputing this. In the first place, it may be disputed on the ground that it is conceivable that, if you were to start from the end of any given yard and move along in the same straight line, you would, after passing over a certain finite number of yards, come to one, beyond which there were no more: that you would simply come to an end of space. This is the alternative which is, I think, really analogous to the case of Time: and it seems to me that it is self-evident that *this* alternative is not the case. But in the case of Space, there is another alternative. Namely, in the course of the last century, mathematicians have suggested that there might be lines, really deserving to be called straight lines, which nevertheless have the apparently impossible property, that if you were to start from the end of one of them, a yard in length, and move along in the same straight line, you would, after passing over a finite number of yards, come back to the very same yard from which you started. This, I say, *appears* to be impossible; it *appears* to be obvious, that, if you are to come back to the same line from which you started the line in which you move must be a curve and *not* a straight line. And mathematicians admit, that if the yard from which you started were an *Euclidean* straight line, and if you moved from it in an Euclidean straight line, it *would* be impossible that you should ever come back to it. What they say is that many *different kinds* of straight lines are possible, and that whereas some of these cannot, in any finite number of yards, return to the point from which they started, others can. Euclidean straight lines—that is, straight lines, which have *all* the properties which Euclid supposed *all* straight lines must have, and which, till the last century, almost all mathematicians supposed all straight lines must have—cannot so return; nor can certain kinds of non-Euclidean straight lines; but *some* non-Euclidean straight lines can. Of course, you may say that no lines, except Euclidean straight lines, really deserve to be called straight lines at all: this is merely a question of words, and none of the arguments of mathematicians can settle *this* question at all, nor is it very important. What, I take it, modern mathematicians *have* proved, and what *is* important, is this. Euclid and almost all mathematicians until the last century had assumed that any line which had any one of certain definite properties must *also* have all the rest: they meant by a straight line, a line which had *all* these properties: and of course, the question whether you are to give the name only to lines which have them *all*, or also to lines which have only some of them, is, as I say, a mere question of words. But what modern mathematicians have *proved* is that Euclid was wrong in supposing that no line could have any one of these properties without having all the rest. They have proved that it is possible for a line to have *some* of them, without having others; and that hence it is possible for a line to have some of the properties, which Euclid assumed to be distinctive of straight lines, *without* having the property from which it follows that, if produced, an Euclidean straight line *cannot* in any finite number of yards return to the point from which it started. For instance: take this property: the property of being the shortest distance between two points. It is natural to suppose that any line, which *is* the shortest distance between two points, must be a straight line. But if you are going to confine the term 'straight line' to Euclidean straight lines—that is, to straight lines which have *all* the properties which Euclid supposed a straight line must have—then, it can be absolutely proved, I believe, that a line which *is* the shortest distance between two points need not be a straight line. It can be absolutely proved, for instance, that a line which *is* the shortest distance between two points might, after a finite number of yards, return to the very point from which it started. And there is, I believe, no reason yet known, why, for instance, the line, which is the shortest distance between here and Charing Cross, should not be of this nature. There is nothing to prove that it is an Euclidean straight line, nor yet that it is one of the non-Euclidean straight lines, which also have the property that they cannot in any finite length return to the point from which they started. It might *possibly* be a non-Euclidean straight line of the sort, which can, after a finite number of yards, return to the point from which it started.

It is, therefore, only if the inches and feet and miles of ordinary life are Euclidean or certain sorts of non-Euclidean straight lines, that it can be self-evident that there must, starting from any one of them, be an infinite number of others in both directions in the same straight line: and it does not seem to be self-evident, nor yet certain for any other reason, that they are Euclidean, nor yet non-Euclidean of the sort required. And it might be thought that there is a similar possibility with regard to Time. Namely, it might be thought that, if, starting from the hour which is now elapsing, namely, the hour from 9 to 10 to-night, you were to consider in order the hours preceding it, first that from 8 to 9, then that from 7 to 8, and so on, you would, after thus going over a finite number of hours—though, no doubt, a very large number—come again to this very hour from which you started—this very hour in which we are now. This, you see, would be analogous, to what, so far as can be seen, really is possible in the case of space, namely, that if, starting from this foot, you considered all the feet which are in the same straight line with it in that direction, you would, after a finite—though very large—number come back to this very foot. But there is, it seems to me, a difference between the case of Time and Space, which renders it self-evident that, even if this is possible in the case of Space, the analogous supposition is impossible in the case of Time. The supposition is that this very hour has, so to speak, preceded itself—at a certain interval. But it is, I think, self-evident owing to some peculiar property of Time that this supposition involves the supposition that this very hour, in which we are now, should have existed twice over, at two different times; and that this is impossible. There is nothing analogous to this in the case of Space: for to suppose that this foot is to the right of itself, though difficult, certainly does not involve the supposition that *it* exists twice over—that *it* exists not only here, but *also* somewhere over there.

I think, then, it is really self-evident that, before the present hour, there must have existed an infinite number of others; and that after the present hour, there will exist an infinite number of others. And so too, in the case of Space, it is, I think self-evident, that, *if* this foot is Euclidean, there must exist an infinite number of other feet in the same straight line, to the right of it, and also an infinite number of other feet, in the same straight line, to the left of it: *only* in this case, it is not self-evident, that this foot is Euclidean but only plausible to suppose so.

But, I said, plausible arguments may be brought against both these suppositions. It may be argued that *all* these infinite series are impossible. What are these arguments?

I gave you one last time. Kant, namely, seems to have thought it self-evident that an infinite number of hours cannot have elapsed before now. But it is important to observe that this argument of his only applies to this one case of infinite extent. It does not apply to either of the other three. He does *not* claim that it is self-evident that it cannot be true that an infinite series of hours *will* elapse in the future; nor that it is self-evident that there cannot be an infinite number of feet on both sides of this foot. In fact, the difficulty he seems to see is solely a difficulty as to how an absolutely infinite series of different units could have been *passed over* or have come to an end *before* a given *time*. It does not, therefore, apply to an infinite extent of future time, because there is no reason to think that *it* ever will have been passed over—or will ever come to an end; and it would only apply to infinite extent in space, if there were any reason to think that a body had by a given time *moved over* an infinite extent of space. Hence the only cases beside that of past time to which it certainly does apply is to what happens within an hour, supposing that it is infinitely divisible, or to what happens when a body moves over a yard, supposing this is infinitely divisible. So far, therefore, as what I have called *infinite extent* is concerned, Kant's argument only applies against an infinite extent of *past time*. And I do think there really is something peculiar in this case which does not apply to the other three cases. Only it does not seem to me that the matter is clear enough to entitle us o affirm, as Kant affirms, that it really is *impossible* that an infinite series of hours should have elapsed before now.

But I now come to an argument agains the possibility of an infinite extent which will apply equally to all four cases, and indeed to any infinite series whatever. It is asserted, namely, that, in the case of any infinite series, there must be exactly the same number of terms —meaning by terms, the units of which the series is composed—in some mere *part* of the whole series as in the whole series itself: that, in short, it is characteristic of every infinite series that, if you subtract from it *some* of the terms of which it is composed, there will yet be just as many terms left as there were before. Suppose, for instance, an infinite series of hours had elapsed before 9 o'clock this evening: it is asserted that, if so, then just as many hours must have elapsed before 8 o'clock: that the number of hours which had elapsed before 8 o'clock, must have been exactly the same as that which had elapsed before 9 o'clock. although by 9 o'clock one hour had been added to them. This is asserted, I believe, partly on the ground, that if you compare the series of hours before 8 o'clock, with the whole series of hours before 9 o'clock, you find that corresponding to every different hour in the latter series, there must be a different hour in the former series; a correspondence, which is expressed by saying that there is a *one-one correlation* between the two series—that to every term in the one series there corresponds one, and only one term, in the other. And why this is held may, I think, be made plainer by considering the series of numbers 1, 2, 3, 4, 5, etc., each of which is formed by adding 1 to the number before. This series is obviously an infinite series: whatever number in it you take, a new and different number can be formed by adding 1 to it: or, in other words, beyond any number in it there is another number. But now compare this series of numbers starting from 1, with the series starting from 2. The series starting from 2 is obviously infinite also. Suppose you write in a top line 1, 2, 3, 4, 5, etc., and then *under* 1, write 2, under 2, write 3, and so on. It is asserted that, in this way, corresponding to every number which can be added to the top line, a different number can be added to the bottom line: that there is, therefore, a correspondence between *every* number in the whole series starting from 1 and some different number in the series starting from 2, or in other words a one-one correlation between the two series; and that this means that there is exactly the same number of terms in both series, although there is one term, in the top series, namely, the number 1, which does not occur in the bottom series. This result seems paradoxical enough; but there follow also ever so many other results more paradoxical still. For instance, suppose you compare the whole series 1, 2, 3, 4, 5, etc., with the series of *even* numbers 2, 4, 6, 8, 10, etc. This series of even numbers is obviously infinite also and has, it is asserted, exactly the same number of terms in it as the whole series: and obviously there is just as much reason for supposing that there is a one-one correlation between these two series as between the other two. But the series of even numbers is formed by subtracting from the whole series all the *odd* numbers, namely, 1, 3, 5, 7, etc. And this series of odd numbers is itself an infinite series. It follows, therefore, that, even if you subtract from the whole series, an infinite number of terms—namely, all the odd numbers, there are still just as many left as there were before. And let us consider the case of time again. If an infinite number of years have elapsed before now, there must also have elapsed an infinite number of periods of a million years each. And there must, it is asserted, have been exactly the same number of periods of a million years, as of single years. But let us consider the first year in every period of a million years. There must obviously have been just as many of these, as there have been periods of a million years. But obviously there must have been a million times as many single years, as there have been of those years, each of which was the first in a different period of a million years. But yet, it is asserted, there must have been exactly the same number of single years, as of these first years, although there must have been also a million times as many. In other words, even if you multiply an infinite number by a million, it makes no difference: the product is just the same number as that which you had before you multiplied it.

These results, and the many similar ones, which also follow, are, I think, certainly very paradoxical. And yet they all seem to follow absolutely, if once you admit that there is a one-one correlation between the infinite series of finite whole numbers starting from 1, and the series starting from 2. If there really is a one-one correlation between these two series—if, that is to say, to *every* term in the one series there really does correspond a different term in the second—then it certainly seems to follow that there is a one-one correlation also in all the other cases. And it does *seem* to be self-evident that there *is* a one-one correlation between these two series. But at the same time it does not seem to me to be absolutely clear that this is self-evident; and hence that, if an infinite series exists at all, there *must* be a one-one correlation between the *whole* series and a mere part of itself.

But now, supposing these paradoxical results do follow from the assumption that there has been or will be an infinite series of hours, or that there is an infinite series of miles, does it follow that it is impossible there should be such an infinite series? Mr. Russell, while he insists that these paradoxical results do follow from the assumption of an infinite series, is also very anxious to argue that they constitute no argument against the existence of infinite series: that infinite series are nevertheless perfectly possible. He says that why we suppose it impossible that an infinite collection should have the same number of terms as a part of itself—impossible that, when you take some terms away from it, the same number is still left—is that we are so used to consider finite numbers only, that we suppose that what is true of finite numbers, must also be true of infinite numbers. And of course it is true of any finite number of things that, if you take one or any other number away, the number of things remaining cannot be the same as it was before. And he does, I think, succeed in shewing that there is no positive contradiction in supposing that there can have elapsed before 8 o'clock this evening exactly the same number of hours, as had elapsed before 9, even though those which had elapsed before 8 can have been only a part of those which had elapsed before 9. But there does seem to me a difficulty in supposing that this is so. And this difficulty, which, according to him, occurs, if at all, equally in the case of all infinite series, seems to me at least as great as that which, according to Kant, occurs only in the case of a particular sort of infinite series. But still, in neither case, are we, I think, justified in concluding absolutely that an infinite series of the sort in question is impossible.

I wish now just to say something about infinite divisibility; though I must cut very short what I had to say about it.

The chief reason for distinguishing carefully between this question of the infinite divisibility of Space and Time, and that of their infinite extent, is, I think, that there seems to be a very great difference between the reasons we have for supposing them to be infinitely divisible, and those which we have for supposing them to be infinite in extent. So far as we have reason for supposing them to be infinite in extent, the reason seems to be that it is self-evident they are so; and so far as I know there is no other sort of reason. But it does not seem to me to be at all self-evident that they must be infinitely divisible; and we have, I think, reasons of another sort for supposing that they are so.

There are two different senses in which it may be maintained that a yard or an hour are infinitely divisible—two different senses which are, I think, liable to be confused. It may be meant (1) that any yard and any hour may be divided into an infinite number of parts, each of which is also divisible; that there are in it an infinite number of *divisible* parts: or (2) it may be meant that each of them can be divided into an infinite number of *indivisible* elements—indivisible points in the case of space, indivisible moments in the case of Time. It is, I think, certainly commonly held that every yard and every minute is infinitely divisible in *both* senses; contains that is, *both* an infinite number of divisible parts and *also* an infinite number of indivisible parts. And so far as I can see, there is no reason whatever why *both* things should not be true, if either can be true. I mention this point because Kant assumes that it is self-evident that any finite space can be divided into an infinite number of *divisible* parts, and gives this as a reason for supposing that it cannot have *any indivisible* parts. He treats the proposition that it has an infinite number of *divisible* parts as contradicting the proposition that it has *any* *in*divisible parts; whereas, so far as I can see, there is no reason for thinking that they are contradictory at all, nor yet any clear reason for thinking that the first proposition is self-evident.

But now what reason have we for supposing that yards and minutes are infinitely divisible in *either* sense? It seems to me that the strongest reason is the same in both cases and equally strong in both cases. Namely, that in applied mathematics it is assumed that both space and time are infinitely divisible in both senses; consequences are deduced from the assumption that they are, and experience confirms the assumption, so far as it can confirm anything; since it actually turns out that the events, which *would* happen, if the assumption were correct, do actually happen. In other words the application of mathematical propositions, in which these assumptions are made, to physical science, does in ever so many instances enable us to predict future events correctly; and the general argument is that it is very unlikely that these predictions would in so many instances turn out to be correct, *if* the assumptions from which they are deduced were false.

But now what are the reasons for supposing that no yard and no hour can be infinitely divisible?

It is plain that all the paradoxical results which, as we have seen, are asserted to follow from the assumption of any infinite series, will follow, if they follow at all, from this assumption. We shall have to suppose, for instance, that every yard is composed of an infinite number of divisible parts, which are such, that, if you subtract one from them, there will be just as many as there were before. We shall have to suppose that an inch contains exactly as many divisible parts as a million miles;—also exactly as many indivisible parts. And we shall have to suppose similarly that a second contains exactly as many divisible parts as a thousand years; and also exactly as many indivisible parts: and also that there could be subtracted from both collections of parts an infinite number, and yet just as many be left as there were before.

And it also follows that the special difficulty which Kant thought to exist in the case of an infinite extent of past time, will also apply to the assumption that a body is capable of moving over any length of space—an inch or a yard or a mile—and to the assumption that any length of time is infinitely divisible. For suppose that any body does move from one end of an inch to another: it will, if the inch is infinitely divisible in both senses, have to have passed over an infinite number of divisible parts, and also an infinite number of indivisible parts; and this, that anything should *ever* get to the end of an infinite series, is just what Kant asserts to be impossible. And so too, between 8 and 9 o'clock this evening an infinite number of divisible lengths of time, and also an infinite number of indivisible moments must have elapsed: and that time could ever arrive at 9 o'clock at all, if, before doing so, it had to pass over an infinite series, is just what Kant declares to be impossible. For my part, I do not know exactly what conclusion ought to be drawn from all these arguments. They are, I think, an excellent example of the way in which philosophical arguments can make things seem uncertain, which, at first, seemed very certain. But it does seem to me that we certainly are not entitled to draw the positive conclusion, which some philosophers have drawn, to the effect that there are no such things as inches, feet, yards and miles, or as seconds, minutes, hours, and years.

Chapter XI

IS TIME REAL?

I have been trying to distinguish two different views, which I think some philosophers have held about *Time*. The first was a view which I tried to express in something like the following way. It holds, I said, that there is not really any such thing as Time at all; that nothing whatever really exists or happens *in* Time; and that, if, therefore, anybody believes that anything whatever ever happened before or after anything else, or that any two events ever happened at the same time, or that any one thing ever lasted longer than another, or that anything has existed in the past or is existing now or will exist in the future, he is simply making a mistake, because, in fact, *all* such beliefs are false. This extremely paradoxical view was one of the two views which I said I *thought* had been held about Time. And the other was a very different one. This second view admits that there is such a thing as Time; and that ever so many different things do exist in it, but it holds that all the things which ever exist in Time, and even, perhaps, Time itself, are, in some sense, mere Appearances—Appearances of something else, which does not exist in Time at all—something which has not, therefore, existed in the past, does not exist now, and will not exist in the future, but which yet *does exist* or *is real*—exists or is real 'timelessly', to use a phrase which philosophers have invented to express this idea. Both these two views do, I think, present a very strange view of the Universe; and both, I think, might be said to contradict Common Sense. The first quite plainly does so, and I do not think anyone would dispute that it does. And the second might be said to do so also, because, I think, we do find it very difficult to conceive how anything could be truly said to exist or be real at all, if it neither exists now nor ever existed in the past nor will exist in the future: the notion of *timeless* existence is certainly a very difficult one to grasp. Whatever exists at all, we should be inclined to say, must exist at some *time*. And I am not at all sure that we should not be right in saying this. But nevertheless there is, I think, an enormous difference between the two views, in respect of the *degree* to which they contradict Common Sense. It is only the first which does quite plainly and flatly contradict an enormous proportion of our ordinary beliefs. We are constantly believing (and even in saying this, that we *constantly* believe, I am, of course, presupposing that things do happen in Time—but still I think I may say *we do constantly* believe) that certain things do happen before others, and that some things are past and others present. And all these beliefs must be false, if the first view is true. But with the second view it is different. These ordinary beliefs of ours don't in any way contradict it. For they obviously only imply that ever so many things *do* exist in Time: and this might, of course, quite well be the case, even if there are *also*, some *other* most important realities which *don't* exist in Time. It is, therefore, only the first view which I have treated as contradicting Common Sense. And the question whether this first view is true or not does seem to me immensely more important than the mere question, whether, *besides* the things which *do* exist in Time, there are not *also* others which don't. The difference between what the Universe must be like, if *nothing* ever exists *at* any time at all, and what it must be like, if, as we commonly suppose, ever so many different things *do* have and *have* had temporal relations to one another, is surely immensely greater than the mere difference between supposing that everything that exists at all exists in Time, and supposing that though many things do, there are *some* which don't. This question, therefore, as to whether it is true or not that immense numbers of different things in the Universe all have temporal relations to one another, seems to me to be by far the most important question which can be raised about the relation of Time to the Universe. And indeed it seems to me to be one of the most important questions which can be raised about the Universe at all. It is, of course, only important in the particular sense which I explained in my first lecture: it is only important, if we want to know what are the characteristics which distinguish the Universe as it is, most markedly from other conceivable Universes. If we do want to know this, then surely the fact, if it is a fact, that so many things exist in Time is one of the facts about the Universe which is most worthy of notice. But, so far as I can see, the question whether this is so or not, is a question of hardly any *practical* importance. If, indeed, it were true that nothing does exist in Time, nothing whatever could have any practical importance at all. For what we mean by saying that a thing has practical importance is that it has results, in the *future*, which are important. And obviously, if there is no Time, nothing can have any results of any sort at all, good or bad. If, therefore, those philosophers who hold that there is no such thing as Time were right, the question whether they are right or not would not be inferior in practical importance to any other question whatever. It would not be *inferior*, because all questions, without exception, would be totally devoid of practical importance. But if we take the view of Common Sense, and suppose that there is such a thing as Time, and that hence some questions may have practical importance, we must, I think, admit that this particular question has hardly any. It is, no doubt, immensely important that we should all have beliefs with regard to the temporal relations of *particular* things. An enormous number of our actions are guided by such beliefs. So that if the adoption of the philosophic creed that there is no such thing as Time led us to abandon all such beliefs in ordinary life, it would be of immense practical importance which creed, upon this point, we did adopt. But I think there is no danger whatever that any philosopher, however sincerely he may adopt the philosophic opinion that there is no such thing as Time, will ever be able to divest himself of particular beliefs which contradict this opinion. He will still continue to believe, with regard to particular things, just as certainly and as often as the rest of us do, that some of them do exist before others, that some have ceased to exist and others not yet come into existence, and that the intervals of time between particular events differ in length. His actions, therefore, will be very little influenced, if at all, by his opinion on this question. I do not claim, therefore, that the question has any practical importance. And there is still another reason which might be urged for disputing its importance. It might be said that it is a wholly unimportant question, and pure waste of time to discuss it, because it is so absolutely certain which the right answer is—so absolutely certain that things do exist in time. And I admit I do think this very certain; and I admit also, that, if I thought everybody was agreed as to its certainty, I should probably not think it worth while to pay much attention to it. But, however certain it may be, surely the fact, if it be a fact, that people are *not* agreed about it, does make a difference. I confess I feel that no philosophic opinion, which is actually held by anybody whatever, however absurd it may appear and however certainly false, is wholly beneath notice. The mere fact that it is held—that somebody is sincerely convinced of its truth—seems to me to entitle it to some consideration. There is probably, in all such cases, at least some difficulty about the matter, or else nobody would hold the opinion.

And as I said, I cannot help suspecting, though I am not quite sure, that some philosophers, and those philosophers whom it is impossible not to respect, do really hold that nothing exists in time. The mere suspicion that this is so, combined with the fact that it makes such an immense difference to the Universe whether things do exist in Time or not, seems to me sufficient reason for paying attention to the question. And so I want to discuss it a little more. But what I want to do is not so much to argue directly in favour of my view on the question, as to try to define more clearly in some respects exactly what the question itself is.

The fact is there are undoubtedly philosophers who do say, most emphatically, so far as words go, that Time is *unreal*, or that Time is *not* real. And you might think that the meaning of such words is plain enough. You might think that anybody who does say this, must mean that if we believe that any one thing had ceased to exist before another came into existence, or that any one thing lasts longer than another, then we are mistaken. But there is, I think, some reason to doubt whether they always *do* mean this. You might say that, *if* they don't, then what they mean by saying that Time is unreal, can't be anything nearly so important as it would be, if they did. And I think this is so. But the fact remains that they certainly *think* that what they mean by saying that Time is unreal is something immensely important. They seem to regard it as the main problem of philosophy to settle what things are real, in the very sense in which they say that Time is not real. It seems to me, then, that whether when they say 'Time is unreal' they do mean this assertion to be understood in a sense which does contradict Common Sense, or whether they don't, it is, in any case, rather important to try to discover exactly what they do mean. If they do mean to contradict Common Sense, then obviously their view is very important, in the sense I have explained. But, if they don't, then they are implying that there is another question which may be raised about Time—a question of the utmost importance, about which I have hitherto said nothing at all. If there is such a question, then it is certainly worth while to try to discover what it is. I want, therefore, to go into the question, as to what these philosophers do mean by saying that Time is unreal. And this is a question which does not affect Time alone. We can hardly express any view about the Universe at all without making use either of the expressions 'So and so is real' or 'not real' or else certain expressions which we should naturally take to express exactly the same idea, 'So and so is a fact' or 'not a fact', 'So and so exists' or 'does not exist', 'So and so is' or 'is not', 'So and so is true' or 'not true.' I have throughout these lectures been making use of these expressions in everything I said and assuming that you would understand them. But if we raise the question as to what these expressions do mean, we shall find that there is some doubt about the matter and that it is not quite easy to say. This question as to what these expressions *mean*—what is meant by the words 'real', 'exists', 'is', 'is a fact', 'is true' is, indeed, not logically relevant to the far more important questions as to what *things* have these properties—what things are real, do exist, have being, are facts or are true. We can, for instance, all understand what is meant by the assertion 'No such person as Waverley, the hero of Scott's novel, ever did *really exist*—Waverley was not a *real* person' and we can also be sure that such an assertion is true, even if we cannot give any account of what we mean by the expressions which we use in making it—the expressions 'really exists', 'real', 'is true.' To say that it is difficult to be sure what these expressions *mean*, which is, I think, true, does not therefore imply that we cannot perfectly easily understand the meaning of sentences in which they occur, and be quite certain that some such sentences are true and others false. We can do both these things, without, in a sense, knowing exactly what these words mean. For by knowing what they mean is often meant not merely understanding sentences in which they occur, but being able to analyze them, or knowing certain truths about them—knowing, for instance, exactly how the notions which they convey are related to or distinguished from other notions. And obviously we may be quite familiar with a notion itself, it may be quite readily conveyed to us by a word, even though we cannot analyse it or say exactly how it is related to or distinguished from other notions. We may, therefore, know quite well, in one sense, what a word means, while at the same time, in another sense, we may not know what it means. We may be quite familiar with the notion it conveys, and understand sentences in which it occurs, although at the same time we are quite unable to *define* it. A very good instance of this is furnished by the words 'life', 'alive'. Who is there who does not know what is meant by saying that some men are alive and others dead, sufficiently well to be able to say with certainty in ever so many cases that some men *are* alive and others *are* dead? But yet, if you try to define the meaning of the word 'life' quite generally—to give an account of the difference between life and death, which will apply to all cases in which we say that one thing is alive and another dead, you will certainly find it extraordinarily difficult. The very same person who may know quite well that one particular man is alive and another dead, may yet be quite unable to say exactly what properties there are which are common to a living man and to all other living things—a living plant, a living cell, a living bacillus, and which at the same time do *not* belong to a dead man or to anything not living. Well, in the same way, it seems to me we do usually understand quite well the meanings of these much more fundamental expressions 'real', 'exists', 'is', 'is a fact', 'is true', and are quite well able to decide, in thousands of cases, whether sentences in which they occur are true or false, even though we do not know their meaning, in the sense of being able to define them. And that is why I say, that the question as to the definition of these words is not logically relevant to the much more important question as to which of the sentences in which they occur are true and which are false. But a great part of philosophical discussion does in fact, consist in discussions as to the meaning of words; and such discussions are very difficult to distinguish in practice from more important questions, even though they are not logically relevant to more important questions. There is, I think, no doubt that the views of philosophers as to the meaning of such words as 'real' and 'true' *has*, in fact, very much influenced their views as to what things *are* real and true. A man's views on more important questions *may*, therefore, be very much influenced by his views as to the meaning of a word. And this fact is perhaps the chief justification for entering into such questions. But whether it is the chief justification or not, there certainly is another motive for doing so, which *may* be a justification, and which, whether it is so or not, does, I think, certainly act on some people much more strongly than this one. The fact is that whether discussions as to the meaning of such words as 'real' and 'true', does or does not influence our views as to what things *are* real or true, such discussions have for some people an interest in favour of which there is certainly something to be said. For no discussion about the meaning of a word is *merely* about the meaning of a word. It always involves some discussion as to the way in which the things or notions, for which the word may stand, are distinguished from or related to one another. And every new discovery of this nature which we may make, for instance, about the notion which is conveyed by such a word as 'real' or 'true' is, you see, a new discovery which applies to the whole range of things which *are* real or true: it is, in that sense, a new discovery about properties which would belong to the Universe, even if there were no such things as words at all, and properties which are exceedingly general—which belong to an enormous number, if not to the whole, of the most important constituents of the Universe. And some general truths of this nature (I should not like to say, *all* of them) certainly are of great interest to many persons. Questions as to what 'truth' and 'falsehood' *are*, what 'reality' and 'existence' *are*, are among the questions which seem to have interested philosophers most, for their own sake. And even if such questions had no bearing on the further questions what things are true and false, real and unreal, it is, I think, difficult to say that they are not worth discussing for their own sakes.

I propose now, therefore, to discuss some points as to what these words 'real', 'exists', 'is', 'is a fact', 'is true' mean. But as I said, my chief reason for introducing the discussion at this point is that there seems to me to be a real difficulty in understanding what certain philosophers mean, when they say 'Time is unreal'; and they are philosophers whom I think it is worth while trying to understand. They seem to think, as I said, that when they say 'Time is unreal', they are expressing a most important fact about the Universe; and yet it seems doubtful whether when they say this they merely mean to express *either* of the two views which I distinguished to begin with—*either* the view that nothing exists in Time *or* the view that only some things exist in Time. They would, I think, very probably say that they are discussing *another* question, a third question distinct from either of these: a very important question which certainly ought at least to be stated, in any attempt to deal with the main problems of philosophy. And in order to shew you, why I think this is doubtful, and why I think there is a difficulty in understanding their meaning, I propose to give you some actual quotations from one of them. I propose to quote a few passages from Mr. Bradley's book called *Appearance and Reality*. Mr. Bradley is certainly one of the most eminent of living philosophers; and anything which he says, even if nobody else said it, would probably be worth attention. But Mr. Bradley does not stand alone on this particular question: there are, I think, many other philosophers who are inclined to say things more or less similar to what he says. So that there is an additional reason for trying to discover what his doctrine really is. And the quotations I am going to give will, I think, shew that there is at least some superficial difficulty in understanding it. I want to give them, too, because I think they are a good illustration of a kind of difficulty, which is constantly occurring when we study the works of philosophers—a kind of difficulty, which seems to me to be one of the greatest which does occur, and about which I think I have not hitherto said enough.

The first quotation from *Appearance and Reality* to which I wish to call your attention is from Chapter IV, entitled 'Space and Time'. It is the last sentence but one in that chapter. Here it is[1]:

'Time, like space, has most evidently proved not to be real, but to be a contradictory appearance'.

This seems to be as clear and definite as could be desired. Bradley declares that time is not real, and that it is 'an appearance'. He thinks he has proved that this is so; and his reason for thinking that it is so—the reason which he expresses by saying that time is 'contradictory'—would, if it were true, be perfectly conclusive. If it were true that from the proposition 'Time is real', there followed both of two mutually contradictory propositions, it would, of course, follow that 'Time is real' cannot possibly be true. I do not think he has succeeded in proving that 'Time is real' involves any contradiction; but to discuss whether he has proved this or not is irrelevant to my present purpose.

The next quotation which I wish to give, consists of the first three sentences of the very same chapter.[2] It is as follows:

'The object of this chapter is far from being an attempt to discuss fully the nature of space and time. It will content itself with stating our main justification for regarding them as appearance. It will explain why we deny that, *in the character which they exhibit*, they either *have* or *belong to*[3] reality.'

One reason why I call attention to these words is that here, instead of saying simply that he denies that time is real, he introduces two new phrases, saying that what he denies is that time (*in a certain character*) either 'has reality' or 'belongs to reality'. As regards the first of these two phrases, I think we may safely assume that he is using the phrase 'has reality' to mean precisely the same as the phrase 'is real': to say he denies that time 'has reality' is merely another way of saying he denies that time is real. But he implies that his other phrase '*belongs to* reality' does *not* mean the same as 'has

[1]P. 36 in the 9th impression (1930). The paging in this impression is unfortunately different from what it was in the 1st Edition (1893), but I have thought it best to give the pages of this 9th impression, which is the latest I possess. It is stated to be 'authorized and corrected', but all the four quotations I shall give appear in exactly the same words in the 1st or 2nd Edition, only with different paging.

[2]P. 30.

[3]My italics in all three cases.

reality', nor, therefore, as 'is real'. In what way, then, does denying that time belongs to reality differ from denying that time is real? This is a question which I postpone considering, till I have given you another passage in which he uses this same phrase 'belongs to reality'.

My other reason for calling attention to the present passage is that he seems here to qualify the denial that time is real by saying he denies only that time, *in the character which it exhibits*, is real. This seems plainly to imply that in some other character—some character which it actually has but does not exhibit, time may be real. But this notion that one and the same thing may, in one character, *not* be real, and in another be real, is certainly not easy to understand. Does time actually possess the 'character which it exhibits' or does it not? At first sight it seems natural to suggest that what Bradley means is that it does *not*—that it only *seems* to possess the contradictory 'character which it exhibits'. But if this were what he means, it is obvious, on a very little reflection, that the mere fact that time only *seemed* to possess a contradictory character would be no reason at all for condemning it as unreal. We must then, I think, suppose that he holds that time actually possesses the contradictory 'character which it exhibits'. But then how is it possible that one and the same thing should *both* be unreal in virtue of one character which it actually possesses, *and also*, at least possibly, real in virtue of another? I think this is plainly impossible, and that hence when Bradley supposes that time may be real 'in one character' and unreal in another, he does not mean by 'time' the same thing in both cases. And the 'time' which he supposes may possibly be real is not what we mean by 'time' at all, but something else, which does not possess any contradictory character, and which only 'corresponds', in some sense not explained, to what we all mean by 'time'. It seems quite plain that he holds that what we all mean by 'time' is something which does possess a 'contradictory' character, and therefore cannot be real.

And now I want to give two other quotations from *Appearance and Reality*, the first rather a long one, the second very short indeed.

The first occurs very near the end of Chapter XII[1], and is as follows:

'For the present' Bradley says, 'we may keep a fast hold upon this, that appearances *exist*. That is absolutely certain, and to deny it is nonsense. And whatever exists must *belong to reality*. This is also

[1]P. 114.

quite certain, and its denial once more is self-contradictory. Our appearances, no doubt, may be a beggarly show, and their nature to an unknown extent may be something which, *as it is*, is *not* true of reality. That is one thing, and it is quite another thing to speak as if these facts had no actual existence, or as if there could be anything but reality to which they might belong. And I must venture to repeat that such an idea would be sheer nonsense. What appears, for that sole reason, most indubitably *is*; and there is no possibility of conjuring its being away from it'.

The second quotation consists of a single sentence, which appeared for the first time in an Appendix to the 2nd Edition, but which still appears in an Appendix to the 9th impression (p. 493). It is as follows:

'Anything', says Bradley, 'that in any sense is, qualifies the absolute reality and so is real.'

Now we have seen that Bradley holds that time—time 'in the character which it exhibits' and which he holds to be 'contradictory', time, therefore, in the sense in which we all commonly understand that word, is 'an appearance'; and we must therefore suppose that all that he says in the first of these quotations about 'appearances' in general, is intended to apply to time. But then we find, for one thing, that he now verbally contradicts what he had formerly said; for he had formerly said that the time which is an appearance 'neither has nor belongs to reality', whereas, in the first of these last two quotations, he says that all 'appearances' (and therefore time) do 'belong to reality'. What are we to make of this apparent contradiction? We can only regard it as merely apparent—merely verbal, by supposing that he is using the phrase 'belongs to reality' in different senses on these two different occasions. But what then are the two different senses in which he is using it? I can only suppose that on the first occasion, when he said that time does *not* 'belong to reality', he was using the phrase, in spite of implying the contrary, as merely equivalent to 'has reality', i.e. to 'is real'; and that therefore when he then said time does *not* 'belong to reality', this was merely another way of saying that time is not real. And on the second occasion, when he says that all 'appearances' (and therefore time) do 'belong to reality', he perhaps means, what we have seen he holds, that there is in reality something 'corresponding to', but not identical with, time. But it is not relevant to my purpose to discuss what he means by this expression 'belongs to reality'. The only relevance to my purpose of this apparent contradiction is that it does seem to shew that Bradley is not very clear as to the meaning of the expressions which he uses, and that, therefore, there is presumably some real difficulty in getting clear about their meaning —about the meaning of 'is real', for instance, among others.

But the second point to which I wish to call attention in the first of these two quotations is that Bradley seems obviously here to be making a sharp distinction between the meaning of the expression 'is real' and that of the expression 'exists'. He said formerly, very emphatically, that time is *not* real, and now he says, perhaps even more emphatically, that the very same 'time'—time, the 'appearance'—does exist: he says that it is absolutely certain that it does, and that to deny this is nonsense. Is there not something surprising about this? It seems to me quite certain that if (as he thinks he has proved) time were really 'contradictory' (which is the only reason he has for saying that it is not real) it cannot possibly be true that time exists. If 'time is real' entails both of two mutually contradictory propositions, because time is 'contradictory', then 'time exists' must also entail both of two mutually contradictory propositions, and cannot possibly be true. But my concern now is not with the question whether what Bradley says is true, but merely with what he *means*. And the fact that he maintains that things which are not real nevertheless do exist, shows, I think, that sometimes at least he uses the expression 'is real' with a meaning different from at least one of those with which we commonly use it; for I think there is no doubt that one common usage of the expression 'is real' is such that from the mere fact that a thing exists it follows that it is real. If, therefore, his usage of 'is real' to mean something such that '*x* is real' does not follow from '*x* exists' is in accordance with some common usage, it would follow that the expression 'is real' is ambiguous. And that Bradley himself thinks that it is so, seems to be proved by my last quotation; since he there declares that whatever in any sense 'is' is real, having previously declared that time undoubtedly 'is' and yet is *not* real.

I propose, therefore, now to consider what, after all, we *do* mean by the word 'real'; what reasons there are for supposing it to be ambiguous; and how, if at all, these reasons can be answered. And I will present at once what seems to me the chief and most obvious difficulty about the matter.

I think, perhaps, the commonest usage of the word 'real' in ordinary life is that in which it is opposed to 'imaginary': as, for instance, when we say that lions and bears are *real* animals, whereas centaurs or griffins are imaginary ones; or when we say that Charles Edward was a real person, whereas Waverley is a fictitious or imaginary one. I think this is at least *one* very fundamental sense of the word, whether it is the only one or not; and I do not think anyone would say that this sense is wholly unimportant. There is certainly some great and important distinction between lions and bears and monkeys on the one hand, and centaurs and griffins and chimaeras on the other hand: the former, we are sure, are in some sense all real, whereas the latter are not real, but purely imaginary. The difference is the important one which distinguishes all mere objects of dreams, and imagination generally, from the real world. And this distinction, you see, is one which can also be perfectly naturally expressed by the use of two of the other phrases I have mentioned: we should say that bears and lions do exist, whereas centaurs and griffins do not, and never have, and that this is just what we mean by saying that the former are real, and the latter imaginary; and we might also quite naturally express the same distinction by saying that there *are* such things as bears or lions, but that there are *no* such things as griffins or chimaeras, and never have been. But with regard to *one* of the phrases I mentioned, it is not quite natural to apply it in this way: it is not *quite* natural to say that a bear or a lion is itself a *fact*, whereas a griffin is not; though, of course, we *might* say this. What we should more naturally say is that the *existence* of bears is a fact; and this distinction which we seem to make between a bear and the existence of a bear is one which we shall presently have to attend to. But, for the present, let us start with the familiar distinction between the real and the imaginary—between real animals and imaginary animals. Is there any difficulty about this distinction? Is there anything to make us doubt as to its meaning and its justice? You might think that the distinction is as clear and certain as possible; and so, in a sense, I think it is. But nevertheless, I think there *is* a difficulty about it; and I am inclined to think that this difficulty has played a very large part in philosophy. I will try to state it in the form in which it appeals most to me. I have already pointed out that to say that a centaur is not real, seems to be equivalent to saying that there is no such thing as a centaur. We should insist most strongly that there really is no such thing; that it is a pure fiction. But there is another fact, which seems at first sight to be equally clear. I certainly can imagine a centaur; we can all imagine one. And to imagine a centaur is certainly not the same thing as imagining *nothing*. On the contrary to imagine a centaur is plainly quite a different thing from imagining a griffin; whereas, it might seem, if both were nothing—pure non-entities, there would be no difference between imagining the one and the other. A centaur then, it seems, is not nothing: it is something which I do imagine. And if it is *something*, isn't that the same thing as saying that there is such a thing—that it is or has being? I certainly do imagine *something* when I imagine one; and what *is* 'something' it would seem, must *be*—there *is* such a thing as what I imagine. But it would also seem, that 'centaur' is just a name for this something which I do imagine. And it would seem, therefore, that there certainly must *be* such a thing as a centaur, else I could not imagine it. How, therefore, can we maintain our former proposition, which seemed so certain, that there is *no* such thing as a centaur?

You may think, perhaps, that all this is mere quibbling, and that the solution of the puzzle is quite easy. But I confess I do not think it is. I am as sure as you can be, that there is no such thing as a centaur: that is the side I want to take: I wish to maintain that, in the proper sense of the words, there really *is* no such thing and never has been. But I am not at all sure, how to get over the opposite argument. Mustn't you admit that, when you imagine a centaur, you are imagining *something*? Doesn't it appear that the phrase 'a centaur' is merely a name for this something, which you certainly do imagine? And can you be quite happy in maintaining that this, which is something, nevertheless has no being, that there is no such thing, that it is a pure non-entity? These three questions state the difficulty. But this difficulty, you see, if you admit that it is a difficulty, does at once seem to give some sort of a justification for one of the distinctions which Bradley makes, and an explanation of what he may possibly mean by it. Supposing we are impressed by the arguments that centaurs and griffins and chimaeras must *be*, because they *are something*—something which we imagine; one very natural way out of the difficulty—indeed the most obvious way, I think—is to suppose that there is, after all, some difference between the meaning of the word 'being' and that of the word 'reality': to maintain that though a centaur *is*, it is nevertheless not *real*. So that, in one respect, we should be maintaining about a centaur, exactly what Bradley seemed to maintain about Time: just as he seemed to say Time indubitably *is* and yet is not real; so we seem driven to say: Centaurs indubitably *are*, but yet they are certainly not real. It is true, we are not necessarily driven to agree also with Bradley's other distinctions. We should hesitate to say that a centaur exists and is a fact, because it *is*. We should be rather inclined to keep these expressions 'exists' and 'is a fact' as equivalents of 'real' in the sense in which we now distinguish 'reality' from mere 'being'. We should be inclined to say: Though centaurs *are*, they nevertheless don't exist, are not facts, and are not real; instead of saying as Bradley says: Though Time is and exists and is a fact, it is nevertheless *not real*. But once we have been driven to make a distinction between 'being' and 'reality', we cannot help, I think, feeling some doubt about these other distinctions too. It may be argued that if we admit that centaurs *are*, we must also admit that they *exist* and are facts: that to say they *are* is the same thing as to say that they exist and are facts. And there is certainly something to be said for this view. It is certainly not obvious that when we say a thing exists we do mean anything more than that it is. It may indeed be said that we seem to be contradicting Common Sense *more* violently if we say that centaurs and griffins exist than if we merely say that they are. But we do already contradict Common Sense verbally in merely saying that they *are*—in saying that there *are* such things as Centaurs. Common Sense would never admit that there *are* such things. And if we feel compelled to make *this* one violent verbal contradiction; it is difficult to be sure that we ought not also to make others. Why should we not say at once: 'There is a sense in which Centaurs both are and exist and are facts and are real; and there is another sense, in which they neither are nor exist nor are facts nor are real' without attempting to appropriate any one or more of these words to the one sense, and to keep the rest for the other? There certainly seems something to be said for this procedure, *if* we are compelled to make any distinction at all. And what the argument I have given seems to shew is that we must make some distinction: we *must* admit that in one sense, there *are* such things as Centaurs, while also we must maintain that in another there are *not*. And the important thing, of course, is to try to see how these two senses are distinguished from one another, if there *are* two such senses: to distinguish quite clearly the two different notions involved. It is comparatively unimportant what words we use to express them.

Well, then, I have stated what seems to me to be the chief difficulty as to this distinction between the real and the imaginary. The difficulty is that it seems as if we must admit that all imaginary things, in spite of being imaginary, nevertheless *are* or *have being* in a sense, simply because they are *something*, something which we imagine. Whereas, on the other hand, it is quite plain that they are nevertheless, in a sense, not real. This seems to shew that there is *some* difference which may be expressed as a difference between 'being', on the one hand, and being 'real' on the other, though it may also be expressed in many other different ways. And many philosophers have, I think, supposed that this which *seems* to be the right way out of the difficulty *is* the right way out. They have held that there really *is* such a distinction; though they have held different views as to what the precise nature of the distinction is. And I want, in the course of the next chapter, to distinguish four different views, which have, I think, been taken as to the nature of this distinction. All of these views are, I think, worth considering either because they have been commonly held or because they may possibly be true, or for both reasons at once; and they are, I think, also worth considering because the mere fact that they have been taken does shew that there really *is* a difficulty connected with this distinction between the imaginary and the real.

Chapter XII

THE MEANING OF 'REAL'

THE preceding discussion concerned the meaning of certain words. I said I proposed to raise the question: What is the meaning of the words 'real', 'exists', 'is', 'is a fact', 'is true'? But I think this was perhaps an unfortunate way of describing the question which I really wished to discuss. Obviously there can be no need for me to explain to you the meaning of the word 'real', in the sense in which it might be necessary for me to explain its meaning, if I were trying to teach English to some foreigner who did not know a word of the language. And obviously, if this *were* what I was trying to do, the means by which I began to try to do it would be perfectly absurd. All the explanations I gave were simply explanations in English: I merely used *other* English words to express what I wanted to say: and obviously, if you were foreigners who did not know a word of English, you would be none the wiser as to the meaning of 'real' after such explanations than you were before, simply because you would not understand the words which I used in my explanation any better than you understood the word 'real' itself. Of course, I am presupposing, that you do know the English language; and, since you do know it, you already know the meaning of the word 'real' just as well as you know the meaning of any of the words by the help of which I might try to explain it to you. So that the problem which I wish to raise must be quite different from this one which would arise if you did not understand English. Of course, if the word 'real' were used in philosophy in some technical sense, different from those in which it is used in ordinary life, the case would be different. I might then try to explain this technical use of the word, just as if it were a word which you had never heard before. And, of course, one possible explanation of one of the difficulties I tried to point out last time is that possibly Mr. Bradley when he says 'Time is unreal' *is* using the word 'real' in some technical sense different from any of its ordinary uses. But I do not think this is so; and, even if it were so, my object is certainly not to confine myself to explaining technical uses of these words. What I want chiefly to do is to discuss some questions with regard to the ordinary meaning of the word 'real'. But, if so, what can these questions be? If you were foreigners, who knew no English, or if I wanted to explain some special technical use of a word, what I should want to do would be merely to call up before your minds the notion or idea which is suggested by the word to those who do understand it. But since you already understand English, the mere utterance by me of the word 'real', is sufficient to do this: it is sufficient to call up before your minds the notion or notions in question. This, therefore, is certainly not all that I want to do; and therefore it was perhaps unfortunate of me to say: that I wanted to discover what the meaning of the word 'real' is. I do not want to discover this, in the sense in which a Polynesian who knew no English might want to discover it: on the contrary I already know its meaning in this sense, and you all know it, too, just as well as I do. What is it, then, that I do want to discover? What is the question which I do want to answer?

Well, it might be said, for the above reasons, that the questions which I do wish to discuss are simply not questions about the *meanings* of these words 'real', 'exists', etc., at all. They are no more questions about the meanings of those words, than a question about the anatomy of a horse, or as to the respects in which horses are similar to or different from other animals, are questions as to the meaning of the word 'horse'. Just as, if I were trying to tell you some facts about the anatomical structure of horses, I should suppose that the word 'horse' had already called up to your mind the object I was talking about, and just as, unless it had, you would not understand a word that I was saying; so I am now supposing that the word 'real' has already called up to your mind the *object* or *objects* I wish to talk about—namely the property or properties which you wish to assert that a thing possesses when you say that it *is real*—and unless the word has called up before your mind this property or properties, everything that I say will be quite unintelligible. The fact is then, that I am solely concerned with the object or property or idea, which is what is called up to your mind by the word 'real', if you understand the English language: it is solely some questions about this object or property or notion or idea that I wish to investigate. But you see there is some difficulty as to what we are to call this something, which is what is called up to your mind by the word 'real'. It is not quite natural to call it an 'object' as I have just done, as it is natural to call a horse an object: to call it an 'object' might lead you to think that what I was talking about was the objects or things which *are* real, and I want to make it quite plain that I am not talking of these at all—I am merely talking of the property which they all have in common, and which we mean to assert that they all have in common when we say that they are all real. It is more natural to call this something which I wish to talk about, a notion or idea or conception, than an object: and this also is a way of speaking that I have used: but to this way of calling it there is also an objection: there is the objection that these names can also be applied to the act which we perform, when we think of the something in question: the act which consists in having it before our minds instead of to this something which is what we have before our minds—that of which we have a notion or conception or idea; and hence if we call it an idea or notion, that might lead to the supposition that it is something which cannot *be* at all except in a mind—a view which I should be very sorry to suggest. Perhaps the most natural way of naming this something is to use the other word I used just now and to call it a property: but to this also there are objections; many people might say that 'reality', the mere being real, cannot properly be called a property at all. What, then, are we to call it? Well, you see, one very natural way of naming it is to call it the meaning of the word 'real'—'meaning' in the sense of *what is meant*; for in fact the thing I want to talk about *is* the object or property or notion or idea which is conveyed or meant by the word real, and is in that sense, its meaning. And this fact may serve to explain why I said that I was going to discuss the meaning of the word 'real': I meant that I was going to raise some questions about this notion or property, which is what is meant by the word 'real'; and some questions, too, which might be expressed in the form: What *is* this notion or property? There is, therefore, after all a sense in which the question I do want to discuss is the question: What is the meaning of the word 'real'? I do want to discuss the question: What is this notion or property, which we *mean* by the word real? But you see, the question, in this sense, is an *entirely* different question from that which would be expressed in the same words, if a Polynesian, who knew no English, asked: 'What is the meaning of the word "real"?' So far as I can see, the Polynesian's question would be simply equivalent to saying: Please, call up before my mind the notion which Englishmen express by the word 'real'. So soon as you had done this, you would have completely answered his question. Whereas this is by no means all that I want to do when I ask: What is the meaning of the word 'real'? What I want to do is to raise certain questions about the nature of this notion, which is called up by the word 'real', not merely to call it up. And, therefore, I think it was perhaps unfortunate of me to describe this question of mine as a question as to the meaning of the word 'real'. The fact that the very same words: What is the meaning of the word 'real'? may be used to express these two entirely different questions, may, I think, give rise to misunderstandings as to the precise nature and bearings of the one which I do want to raise. And I want now, by the help of this distinction, to try to point out more clearly exactly what the chief question I do want to raise is, and what its bearings are.

Obviously, even when we do know English, one question which we may raise about the meaning of the word 'real' is this. We may ask: Is the notion called up in the minds of people who do know English by the word 'real', always the same, or are there several different ones, which may be called up by it in different contexts? This is what is meant by asking whether the word 'real' is ambiguous. And I do not want to raise this question in its *whole* extent. I think there is no doubt that if you consider *all* the cases in which it is used, the word 'real' is ambiguous—that in some contexts it does call up and express a quite different notion from what it expresses in others. But I only want to raise the question as to certain particular cases. I only want to select certain cases, in which it seems to me that something particularly important is conveyed by the assertion 'So and so is real', or 'So and so is not real'; and to ask: Is what is conveyed in all *these* cases the same notion, or is it different in different cases? And you see this is, in part, a question which we cannot answer, *unless* we do know English—which we cannot answer, unless we do know the meaning of the word 'real', in the sense in which my supposed Polynesian does not know it. So far as we assert: the notion or notions in question *are* conveyed by the word 'real', we are asserting something which presupposes a knowledge of English. But I want to insist that as regards part, and the most important part of its meaning, my question is a question, which *can* be raised *without* a knowledge of English. All that it requires is that we should have before our minds the notion or notions which are in fact expressed to Englishmen by the word 'real': it does not require that we should *know* the fact that these notions are expressed to Englishmen by the word 'real'. A person may quite well investigate the differences between a horse and a donkey, without knowing at all that these objects are called 'horse' and 'donkey' in English. And similarly a person who had never heard the word 'real', might have before his mind the rough notion or notions, which are conveyed by this word to us, and might ask: Is it the same notion I have before my mind now, as I had just now, or is it a different one? And I want to insist that this part of the question—this important part, is a question which it is often really difficult to answer. You might think that it must be quite easy to see whether the notion, which you have before your mind, in one case, is or is not different from that which you have before your mind in another. If you have before your mind the notion of a horse and also the notion of a donkey, it is quite easy to see that they are different: there is no possibility of mistake. But in other cases, I think it is plain that there is a possibility of mistake: that it is very easy to make a mistake. If you ask yourself: Is the notion conveyed to my mind by the word 'real' in *that* sentence, the same as that conveyed to it by the word 'real' in *this* sentence? it is not always easy to be sure whether it is the same or not. This is a matter which is as open to question as any matter in philosophy. A man may quite easily make a mistake as to whether the thought which he is expressing in one sentence is or is not the same as what he expresses on another occasion by the same or different words. And hence it is by no means presumptuous to suggest that philosophers do make mistakes of this kind; it is no more presumptuous than to suggest that they may be wrong about other matters. A philosopher may say: When I use the word 'real', this is what I mean by it; and yet he may be wrong: what he says he means by it may not, in fact, be what he does mean by it. It may be the case that the thought which is before his mind, when he uses the word 'real', and which he expresses by it, is in fact different from that which is conveyed by the words of his definition, only that he has made the mistake of thinking they are the same. The fact, therefore, that a philosopher gives a definition of a word and says that this is the sense in which he is using the word, by no means proves that it really *is* the sense in which he is using it. It only proves that it is what he thinks he means; and what he *thinks* he means may be very different from what he *does* mean. And just as a philosopher may think that the thought which he is expressing by two different words, or by the same word on two different occasions, is the *same*, when in fact it is different; so conversely he may think that there is a difference between what he is expressing by a word on one occasion and what he expresses by the same or a different word on another, when in fact there is *no* difference—when the two thoughts, which he *thinks* are different, are, in fact, the same. Both these two mistakes may be committed by me, even when I have definitely tried to discover whether my thought on one occasion is or is not the same as my thought on another. But, of course, it is still more likely that I shall treat one thought of mine as if it were the same as another, when in fact it is different, or treat it as different, when in fact it is the same, if I have not tried to discover whether the two are or are not the same. And in both cases I may be led into serious errors. I will try to explain how. Let us call the property which I express by the word I use as predicate in one sentence 'A', and the property which I express by the word I use as predicate in another sentence 'B'. And let us suppose that it is difficult to see whether A is or is not different from B. In such a case there are two possibilities: A may in fact be different from B, or it may be the same. Let us first take the case where it is different. Here again there are two possibilities. I may have definitely tried to discover whether A is different from B or not; or I may not have tried to discover this. But in either case, whether I have tried to make this discovery or not, I shall be liable, though not equally liable, to treat A and B as if they were the same. Even if I have definitely considered the question whether they are different or not, I may have made a mistake and come to the conclusion that they are the same, when in fact they are different, simply because this happens not to be an easy thing to be sure about. In either case, therefore, I shall be liable to *treat* them as if they were the same, when in fact they are different. And by treating them as the same, what I mean is this. I may happen to know beforehand that one thing Z has the property A, and that another Y has the property B. Let us suppose I do really know both these two facts. Then knowing these facts, but not being aware that the properties A and B are different, I shall be very liable to conclude that the thing Z which has the property A also has the property B, and that the thing Y which has the property B also has A; and both these two conclusions may be very serious errors, if, *in fact*, there is an important difference between A and B. This is one kind of error into which we may fall owing to the difficulty of seeing whether the thought, which we express by the word used as predicate in one sentence, is or is not the same as that which we express by the word we use as predicate in another. But now let us take the other case. Let us suppose that A and B are in fact the same and not different. Here again, whether we have or have not expressly considered the question as to their sameness, we may be liable to treat them as different, when they are in fact the same. And the consequences which may follow will be these. We may happen to know that one thing Z has the property A, and another Y has the property B, and we may be quite right as to this. But, since we are not aware that A is the same as B, we may be led to think that the thing which has got the property A has not got the property B; and that the thing which has got the property B has not got the property A, although in fact both these two things are quite impossible, since there is no difference between A and B. We may, in short, be led to contradict ourselves without knowing it. We may, for instance, insist that a given thing exists but is not 'real', or has 'being' but does not 'exist', because we think that the property which we express by the word 'exists' is different from that which we express by the word 'real', or that that which we express by the word 'is' is different from that which we express by the word 'exists', whereas in fact the property which we have before our minds is exactly the same in both cases. This would be an instance of making a distinction without a difference—of making a merely verbal distinction, an offence of which some philosophers have often accused others and probably sometimes with justice, though I think philosophers are certainly more often guilty of the opposite offence—that of supposing that there is no difference, where there is one.

Now I think that the chief use of discussing such questions as the one I am engaged on, is because it may help us to avoid errors of both these two kinds. But I said that nevertheless the discussion of these questions is not logically relevant to the settlement of the more important questions as to what things are 'real', 'do exist', 'are facts', etc. And it might be thought that what I have just said contradicts this assertion. I have admitted that such a discussion may help us to avoid errors on these more important questions; and it might be thought that this implies that it is logically relevant to these questions. So I want to explain the distinction I have in mind. Suppose the question we want settled is: Whether elephants are real or not? And this, I think, is a question as to which, in words at all events, philosophers would differ, because, if I understand them rightly, Mr. Bradley and other philosophers would certainly *say* that elephants, as such, are not real. Suppose, then, we raise the question: Are elephants real? Can a discussion as to the meaning of the word 'real' in the sense I have explained, be logically relevant to the settlement of this question? All that such a discussion can shew us *directly* is that the property called up before us by the word 'real' in one sentence is different from or the same as that called up by it in another. Our question is therefore: Can either of these discoveries have any logical relevance to the question whether elephants have the property or properties in question? Suppose, first, that what our discussion has shewn us is that the word 'real' may be used to express two entirely different properties A and B. And let us suppose that it has also shewn us (though this is a separate point) that the possession of B does not *follow* from the possession of A. Now this result would certainly shew that it was a mistake to conclude that *because* elephants possessed the property A, they must also possess the property B. If, therefore, we had concluded that they possessed the property B, *because* they possessed A, it would shew that our *reason* was a bad one. But it could not possibly show that they did not, in fact, possess the property B: it could not prove that we were wrong in supposing them to possess the property B, as well as the property A. Our discovery that A differs from and does not imply B, could, therefore, only prevent us from making up our minds on wrong grounds. It is only in this way that it could help us to avoid an error. It would still remain an open question whether the opinion, which we had adopted, on wrong grounds, was or was not itself a wrong one. And that is why I say that the mere discovery that A and B are different from one another, is wholly irrelevant logically to the more important question as to whether any particular thing does possess A, or B, or both, or neither. And the same conclusion is, I think, equally evident, if we take the opposite case. Suppose our discussion has shewn us that the word 'real' does *not* stand for two different properties, but always for one only. This will prove absolutely that if an elephant is 'real' in one sense, it cannot possibly be unreal, in another; because it will have proved that there are *not* two different senses of the word 'real'. And if part of our ground for concluding that an elephant was unreal, was that we supposed it might be both real and unreal, it will shew that our reason for the conclusion was so far wrong; and may therefore help us indirectly to a right conclusion, by shewing that we have to choose between the two alternatives. But logically it can't settle in the least which of the two alternatives is the true one. The mere fact that an elephant can't be both real or unreal, can't possibly prove *which* of the two it is: and this fact that it can't be both, is all that our discussion as to the meaning of 'real' could possibly have shewn us.

The chief question, therefore, that I want to raise is simply as to whether the property called up before our minds by the words 'real', 'exists', 'is', 'is a fact', 'is true' on certain particular occasions is or is not the same as the property called up before our minds by those words on other particular occasions. And though I think the consideration of this question may indirectly help us to avoid errors as to what things *have* the property or properties in question, I still think it is logically quite irrelevant to all such questions. And moreover I want to insist on the point, that though the property or properties in question, are, in fact, called up before our minds by these particular words, this fact also is totally irrelevant to the question itself. It is a question which might be equally well discussed by a person who had never heard of these English words, and even, theoretically at least, without the help of any words at all.

But now let us get back to the question itself.

I am supposing that when we say 'Elephants are real animals; but griffins are not', we are asserting that elephants possess some property which griffins do not possess; and I think no one would dispute this, though they might as I said object to my use of the word 'property'. This property, therefore, which is called up before our minds by this sentence is at least *one* of the properties expressed by the word 'real'; and I think myself (though of course, this might be disputed) that *this* property is at least one of the most important properties expressed by the word 'real': I think that one of the things, which we most want to know and which it is most important to know on all sorts of occasions is whether certain things do or do not possess this property which we commonly suppose that elephants do possess and that griffins don't. But, if we admit that this is *one* of the properties expressed by the word 'real' and one of the most important, there still remains the question: are there any others different from this, and also of importance, which are expressed on other occasions by this word or the others I have mentioned? And I gave last time one reason for supposing that there is at least one such other property. The reason was this. There seems, at first sight, no doubt that, when I imagine a griffin, I am imagining something; and that if so, there is such a thing as what I imagine when I imagine a griffin: that the whole phrase 'what I imagine when I imagine a griffin' is a name of something which *is* or has being. But it also seems as if 'griffin' were merely another name for this same something; and, if so, then we must allow that there is such a thing as a griffin. But it seems quite plain that, even if we do admit this, it does not follow that griffins are 'real' in the same sense in which elephants are 'real'. But, if so, it follows that we have here two different properties before our minds, one of which may be expressed by the word 'is' or 'has being', and the other by the word 'real', one of them a property which is possessed by griffins and all imaginary things and the other a property which isn't possessed by them. And I said last time that I thought many philosophers had really supposed that this was the case—had supposed that all imaginary things really do possess some property, which may be expressed by saying that they have being, though at the same time they do not possess the property which we generally express by the word 'real'. But, if this is so, the question arises: What is the difference between these two properties? And I said I thought at least four different explanations might be given of the difference. And I want to give these explanations, not so much with the object of discussing fully whether they are right or wrong, but chiefly for the purpose of pointing out that there is a real difficulty in discovering whether the property brought before your minds by one form of words is or is not the same as that brought before your minds by another. Three at least of these explanations consist in suggesting that the property brought before our minds by the word 'real', when we say 'elephants are real and griffins are not', is identical with that brought before our minds by some other expression. But the properties brought before our minds by these three other expressions are, I think, quite obviously all of them different: this is what I mean by saying that the three explanations are different explanations. But if each of these three properties differs from the other two, it is obvious that they can't all be identical with the property which we do mean by the word 'real'. So that the mere fact that they have all been supposed to be identical with it, and that it may seem plausible to suppose them identical with it, shews that it is difficult to see whether the property expressed by 'real' is or is not identical with properties expressed in other ways.

Well, the first explanation is, I think, the one which would occur as the most obvious to any one who was asked: What is the particular difference between an elephant and a griffin, which we express by saying that the one is 'real' and the other only 'imaginary'? It is, I think, the first explanation which would occur to such a person, when once he was convinced that it would not do simply to say that the difference is that there are no such things as griffins, whereas there *are* such things as elephants. He would, I think, be inclined to say: The difference is that griffins are or exist only in the mind or in dependence on it, whereas elephants are or exist not only in the mind but independently of it. And this difference between what is only in the mind or dependent on it and what is *not* only in the mind but independent of it, is, I think, certainly a very important difference, and would therefore fully account for the importance which we attach to the distinction between the real and the imaginary. Moreover this way of stating the difference would be quite consistent with each of two different theories, the difference between which is itself important. The one theory is this: It might be held that, *when* I see an elephant, the elephant is in my mind, just as much as the griffin is when I imagine him; and that the difference between the two cases is that, whereas the elephant is sometimes in my mind, he sometimes also *is*, when he is not in any mind, whereas the griffin never is at all, except when he is in a mind. On this view, it might be said: We give the name 'real' to everything which we believe to be sometimes in a mind and sometimes *not*, and imaginary to everything which we believe to be *only* in a mind. But on the other hand, it might be held that the elephant is not ever in my mind, not even when I see him—that only my idea of him is *ever* in my mind. And then the theory would be: That all real things are things which are *never* in a mind, whereas everything that is *ever* in a mind is imaginary.

Now, to this theory, as I have stated it, there is the obvious objection that it condemns us to say that all our own mental acts—our feelings and thoughts and perceptions and desires—are just as imaginary as a griffin. My mental acts are certainly both *in* my mind and dependent on it in a sense; they *are* not at all *except* in my mind; and therefore it would seem that if everything, which is *only* in the mind or dependent on it is imaginary, my thought of a griffin is just as imaginary as the griffin himself. This is an obvious objection, and it is I think worth pointing out, because it emphasizes the extreme difference there is between the two different senses of '*in* the mind' of which I spoke before: the sense in which my mental acts themselves are in my mind, and that in which anything that I think *of* or am conscious *of* may be said to be in my mind. But, of course, this objection may be avoided, by attending to this distinction, and saying that what is imaginary is what is merely in the mind, in the sense that it *is* only when it is an *object to* the mind—*only* when someone is conscious of it. We should then have the theory that to say that a griffin is imaginary, is to say that it exists or is *only* so long as it is *an object to* some mind: we should in fact have a theory, which might be expressed by means of the formula, which I discussed before: our theory would be that the *esse* of imaginary things—the only kind of being which *they* have—is *percipi*, and that this is what distinguishes their kind of being from that which real things have. Such a theory would avoid the paradox of saying that all our mental acts are imaginary; since it may, of course be held that our mental acts do not have being only when they are perceived. But it is, I think, still exposed to one obvious objection. If, namely, we hold the proposition about sense-data, which I explained before—the proposition that all sense-data exist only when they are perceived—this theory condemns us to say that all our sense-data are purely imaginary—that they are just as imaginary as a griffin. It implies, for instance, that the coloured patches which I now actually see are purely imaginary, in the fullest sense of the word: that the most that I can mean when I say that anything is imaginary, is that it has the property which these coloured patches have—that of existing only when they are perceived. But that this is not the case can, I think, be easily perceived by a simple instance. Let us consider an imaginary person—any hero of fiction—Waverley will do as well as any other. Waverley, as we know, met Miss Flora Mac Ivor, who is also an imaginary person. And let us imagine, as we easily can, that Flora Mac Ivor's personal appearance was not exactly like that of any person who has ever really existed. Well, if that is so, when Waverley looked at Flora Mac Ivor, he directly perceived a set of sense-data, different from any that anybody has ever really directly perceived. And these sense-data, which we can imagine the imaginary Waverley to have directly perceived, are what we should naturally mean by 'imaginary' sense-data. These sense-data of Waverley's seem to be imaginary in the same sense in which a griffin is imaginary; and obviously *my* sense-data, the ones I am now directly perceiving are *not* imaginary in this sense. For this reason we cannot, I think, possibly accept the view that the distinction between the real and the imaginary is identical with the distinction between what is dependent on the mind, in the sense of being or existing only when it is an object of consciousness, and what is not so dependent. We cannot accept this view because we find that of two things, both of which are dependent on the mind in this sense—namely Waverley's sense-data when he saw Flora Mac Ivor, and my sense-data now—one may nevertheless be real and the other imaginary. That is to say, even within the class of things entirely dependent on the mind, we find the distinction between the real and the imaginary still persisting. Of course, it might be said that this distinction between what is dependent on the mind and what is not, is *one* of the distinctions, which we *sometimes* refer to by the distinction between real and unreal. And I think this may be so. Philosophers at all events often speak as if the question whether certain kinds of things are real or not were identical with the question whether they do or do not exist independently of the mind. And perhaps they may be right in so speaking. But even if they are right in doing so, what this shews is that we have to recognise *three* different properties and not two only. There will be (1) the kind of being possessed by objects entirely dependent on the mind, which are imaginary, in the sense in which Waverley's sense-data are imaginary; (2) the kind of being possessed by objects entirely dependent on the mind, which are *not* imaginary in that sense, the kind of being for instance, possessed by the sense-data which I am directly perceiving now and (3) the kind of reality which consists in being *independent* of the mind. And this theory, you see, offers no explanation at all of the difference between these first two kinds of being.

So much for this first theory as to the nature of the distinction between the real and the imaginary. The second theory is one which may, I think, be suggested in the following way. How, it may be asked, do we actually distinguish our dreams from our waking perceptions? Suppose I dream that there is a lion in my bedroom, how do I actually find out that it was only a dream, and that there wasn't a real lion there? Or how does a person in *delirium tremens* find out that the snakes which he sees are not real snakes but only imaginary ones? Well, it may be said, the way in which I may actually assure myself that there wasn't really a lion in my bedroom, is by finding in the morning that there are no such traces as would have been left by a real lion. In other words, I judge that the lion wasn't real, by the absence of some effects, such as a real lion would have produced. And similarly the man in *delirium tremens* may find out that his snakes are not real, because he finds that other people don't see them: real snakes would have the effect of making other people see them; and he concludes that they were not real, from the absence of this effect. But, of course, it need not be only by the absence of effects that we arrive at such a conclusion though, perhaps, this is the usual way; we may also judge that a thing is imaginary from the absence of certain *causes*, such as it would necessarily have had, if it had been real. Suppose, for instance, I dream that I meet a friend, whom I know to be dead or in New Zealand. I may conclude that it was only a dream, because I know that in order to be really there, he would have had to be alive or in England: I know therefore that his appearance was not preceded by *causes*, such as would have necessarily preceded it, if it had been real.

We may, therefore, say in general that one way in which we actually decide that a given thing is imaginary and not real, is by the absence of other things, which would have been connected with it (either preceding it, or following, or accompanying it) if it *had* been real. And I think there is no doubt whatever that we do sometimes decide in this way. The process I have described is a process we do actually use and which is certainly of great importance; and it might even be thought at first sight that it is *only* by a process of this type that we *ever* decide whether a thing is real or not. But in any case, whether we always decide in this way or not, it may be said, we certainly *could* always so decide: we *could* do so theoretically since it is true, as a matter of fact, that a thing which is real, *is* always connected with some thing or other with which it would not have been connected, if it had not been real; it always has *some* effect or cause or accompaniment, which it would not have had if it had been imaginary. And, so far as I can see, this *is* true. But, then, it may be said: We have here discovered a property which does belong to all real things and to no imaginary ones; and this property has two further recommendations to our notice. In the first place it is a property which we do actually use as a test in some cases, to decide whether a given thing is real or not; and in the second place, in some cases at all events, we should be totally unable to decide without its help. Unless it were the case that a thing which is real always has some connections, which it would not have had if it were unreal, we should in some cases be totally unable to decide whether a given thing was real or not; in some cases, it is certainly only by the absence of causes or effects or accompaniments, which it would have had if it were real, that we are able to decide that a thing is imaginary; and only by the presence of causes or effects or accompaniments, which it could not have had if it were imaginary, that we are able to decide that it is real. All this may, I think, be said with truth. But if so, it may be natural to ask: Why should not *this* property, which we actually *use* to decide whether a thing is real or imaginary, and which is sometimes, at least, indispensable to our decision, be the very one which we have before our minds when we say that a thing is 'real'? Why should not this property be the one which we actually mean that a thing possesses when we say that it is real? This is, I think, a very natural suggestion to make: it is very natural to suggest that here at last we have the distinction between the real and the imaginary. And many philosophers have, I think, been inclined to suppose that it is therefore the connection with other things which distinguishes a real thing from an imaginary one.

But in considering this suggestion, we must, I think, be very careful to notice exactly what the suggested property is. It must, if it is to answer our purpose, be a property which belongs to all real things, and to no imaginary ones. And the only property which the instances quoted shew to belong to all real things and no imaginary ones is precisely this: it is that of having *some* effect or cause or accompaniment, which the thing in question, would *not* have had, if it had not been real. There is nothing to shew that the effect or cause or accompaniment in question is always the *same*; that there is any one particular cause or effect or accompaniment, which always belongs to all real things and no imaginary one: on the contrary, it seems quite plain that the particular causes and effects by which we decide, are different in the case of different things. All, therefore, that our instances entitle us to predicate of *all* real things, is that each of them has *some* connection *or other*, which it would not have had, if it had not been real. This is a property which I believe all real things do possess, and, if they didn't possess it, we should very often be unable to decide whether a thing was real or imaginary. But there is, I think, a fatal objection to supposing that this is the property which we express by the word 'real'. It must be observed that the word 'real' itself occurs in the definition of this property. It is, in that sense, a *circular* definition, and though this is no objection to supposing that all real things really do have this property in addition to that which is meant by the word 'real', it is, I think, a fatal objection to supposing that this itself is *the* property meant by the word 'real'. For on further inspection we find that there would be no such property at all, unless the property conveyed by the word 'real' were something different from it: the words in which it is expressed are sheer nonsense, and stand for nothing at all, unless the word 'real' has some different meaning. We found first: 'Everything, which is real has some connection or other, which it would not have had, if it had not been real.' This is the proposition which I admit to be true, and to be by no means nonsense. But what is now suggested is this. We are asked to admit: 'To say that a thing is "real" is to say that it has some connection or other, which it would not have had, if it had not been real'. And this is what turns out to be nonsense. For if we accept this definition we are entitled to substitute for the word 'real', whenever it occurs, the supposed equivalent phrase. We may say, therefore: 'To say that a thing is "real" is to say that it has some connection or other which it would not have had, if it had not been'—what? Here we have the word 'real' itself and let us try to substitute the equivalent phrase. We begin again then: 'To say that a thing is "real" is to say that it has some connection or other which it would not have had, if it had not—had some connection or other, which it would not have had, if it had not—had some connection or other . . .'. We thus get a sentence, which can never possibly be completed, and which is pure nonsense, if anything is. And what this shews is that the property which was supposed to be the property meant by the word 'real' and which does really belong to all real things, is a property which depends for its being on *not* being *the* property meant by the word 'real'. *The* property meant by the word 'real' is a constituent part of it, enters into its constitution, and cannot therefore be identical with the whole of which it is a mere part; and unless there were such a constituent part, the whole, of which it is a part, would simply not be at all. For this reason, I think, we cannot draw any explanation of the distinction between the *real* and the imaginary, from a consideration of the above process, by which we actually often decide whether a given thing is real or imaginary. The *only* property which this process entitles us to predicate of all real things, is a property which cannot possibly be more than a property which they all possess *in addition* to their reality: it cannot possibly be the property of being real itself. This second proposed explanation of the distinction between the real and the imaginary does therefore, I think, also break down.

And the third possible explanation which I want to mention is one which is suggested by Mr. Bradley. Mr. Bradley holds that one of the properties which *he* expresses by the word 'real' is a property which has *degrees*: he constantly talks of one thing being more real or less real than another; and this conception of *degrees* of reality is one of those of which he makes most use. But he suggests also, that, where a property has degrees, the conception of *the* highest possible degree of that property is, at all events, a perfectly clear conception; and that if there is such a thing as the highest possible degree of it, and, if, also, we suppose that some thing or things possess that degree, while other things don't, we can then divide things into two classes according as they do or do not possess the highest degree of it. Now Mr. Bradley himself, I think, certainly holds that what he calls 'the Absolute' possesses the highest degree of this supposed property; whereas he holds that none of the things he calls Appearances do possess the highest degree of it; they all possess the property, he thinks, in some degree, and though some possess more of it than others, all are 'real' in this first sense, and some more 'real' than others, but no Appearance whatever has the highest possible degree of this kind of reality. We find, therefore, that according to him, one property which distinguishes the Absolute from all Appearances, is that it does possess the highest degree of this kind of reality, whereas none of them do. And, hence, it seems possible that the highest degree of the first kind of reality constitutes Mr. Bradley's second kind of reality, the kind of reality which the Absolute alone possesses and which no Appearances do possess. When he says that all Appearances are unreal, he may perhaps only mean that none of them possesses the highest degree of this first kind of reality. This therefore gives a possible explanation of the two different senses in which Mr. Bradley uses the word 'real'. In one sense of the word, 'real' certainly stands for a property which, according to him, has degrees, and this is the sense in which Time and all other Appearances, as well as the Absolute *are* 'real'. And in the other sense, 'real' may perhaps stand exclusively for the highest possible degree of this first property; and this may perhaps be the sense, in which, according to Mr. Bradley the Absolute alone is real. I don't know whether Mr. Bradley would accept this as being what he means by his second sense of 'real', as being the property which he has before his mind, but if he is right about the point that his first sense has degrees, this is at all events a possible explanation of his second sense; and, as we have seen, he certainly does hold that the Absolute *is* distinguished from Appearances, by possessing this highest possible degree, whether or not this is the distinction which he expresses by saying that it *is* real, and they are *not*. But, if this is a possible explanation of Mr. Bradley's meaning, it is also a possible explanation of *our* meaning. It is possible that when we say, as we should in ordinary life, that 'An elephant is real, and a griffin is not', the property which we really have before our minds and are ascribing to the elephant and denying to the griffin, is the highest possible degree of Mr. Bradley's first kind of reality. Mr. Bradley would, of course, say that we are wrong, if we do ascribe the highest possible degree of this first kind of reality to elephants: he certainly holds that they have not got it: elephants, according to him, are mere Appearances, and he would perhaps say also that this is not what we mean, in ordinary life, when we say that an elephant is real. But still, if, as Mr. Bradley seems to hold, griffins do have a kind of reality which has degrees, this view that elephants have the highest possible degree of this kind of reality, whereas griffins have not, may possibly be what is actually before our minds when we draw the sharp distinction between elephants and griffins which we express by saying that elephants are real and griffins are not. Here is a possible explanation of a true distinction between the 'real' and the 'imaginary', namely that both are 'real' in Mr. Bradley's first sense: but that this first kind of 'reality' has degrees; and that therefore the kind of reality which does not belong to imaginary things and does to real ones, may possibly be the highest possible degree of this first kind which belongs to both. What objection is there to this explanation? The only objections that I know of are that if you look into your mind, and try to find out what property you are attributing to griffins, if you say, as you seem forced to say, that there are such things as griffins, you find that the property in question is one which has *not* got degrees; that it is nonsense to talk of one thing having *more* being than another. And similarly that if you look into your mind and try to find out what property you are attributing to elephants, when you say that they are real, you find that this property is not the highest possible degree of any property whatever, but something merely positive. These are, I think, the obvious objections. But this question as to whether, in any important sense of the word 'real', 'real' stands either for a property which has degrees, or for one which *is* a degree of some other property, is one which I shall presently have to return to.

Chapter XIII

IMAGINATION AND MEMORY

I have begun discussing the question whether it is or is not the case that purely imaginary things, in spite of being purely imaginary, nevertheless *have* some kind of *being*; whether, for instance, supposing that griffins and centaurs and chimaeras are purely imaginary creatures, it nevertheless is not true, in a sense, that there are such things as griffins, and centaurs and chimaeras. I shall now try to finish this discussion, although I am not sure that this particular question has quite so much importance in connection with the meaning of the word 'real' as might appear at first sight.

Well, I think some philosophers certainly have supposed that all imaginary things have some kind of being, in spite of being imaginary. And I have already given one argument in favour of this view—an argument which, as I said, though it may seem to be a quibble, certainly is (so far as I can see) not quite easy to answer. But there is also another argument in its favour which I have not yet mentioned and which I wish to mention now, because the answering of it involves a distinction, which I was originally intending to assume as obvious, but which after all, I think, is by no means obvious, and which is of extreme importance in connection with this subject, and indeed, I think, in connection with the theory of knowledge generally.

The argument I mean is this.

When we imagine anything, it very often happens that we have before our minds what is sometimes called an *image*. At the present moment, for instance, when I am talking of griffins, I have before my mind a visual image more or less like pictures or statues of griffins which I have seen, though a great deal fainter. And this visual image is, of course, itself a sense-datum, in the sense that I explained. It is not of course actually given by the senses in the sense in which the patches of colour I am now seeing are given by the senses; but it is composed of patches of colour of various shapes, in exactly the same sense as they are.

Images then are one kind of sense-data; and I will assume that you know what I mean by an image. Well, many philosophers have, I think, supposed (and it is surely very natural to suppose this) that these images which we have before our minds, when we imagine things, are *what* we imagine; that indeed imagination simply consists in having images before our minds. But there is no doubt that what I am imagining now is *a* griffin. If therefore *what* I am imagining is the image which I have before my mind, it follows that this image *is* a griffin. And since there is no doubt whatever that there is such a thing as this image, it would follow that there certainly is such a thing as a griffin. In other words, it may be proposed to identify imaginary things with images; to say that any name, which is the name of an imaginary thing, is in fact no more nor less than the name of some image. And if this view were a true one, then it seems to me it would be true not only that imaginary things all have some kind of being, but also that they all exist or are real; since I think (though, of course, this might be disputed) if there is any distinction between mere being, on the one hand, and existence or reality on the other, images not only have being but also existence or reality.

This view that imaginary things are neither more nor less than images has, I think, been very commonly held or implied. Berkeley and Hume, for instance, never, I think, even suspected that there could be any difference between the two. Just as Berkeley supposed that when I say 'I ate a piece of bread and butter at tea', these words 'a piece of bread and butter' are merely a name for an idea of mine, so that in eating the bread and butter I was eating one of my own ideas; so, I think, he also supposed that when I say 'I am imagining a griffin', this name 'a griffin' is also merely a name for an *idea* of mine: and by the name 'idea', in both cases, he means merely what I have called a sense-datum or collection of sense-data. Now Hume did give different names to these two different kinds of sense-data, both of which Berkeley called 'ideas'. He proposed to give the name 'impressions' to the sense-data which I directly perceive, when I actually see or touch or taste a piece of bread and butter; and to restrict the name 'idea' to the kind of sense-data which I have just called 'images'—to the sense-data, which I directly perceive when I merely imagine 'a griffin', or to those which I directly perceive when I merely remember a piece of bread and butter, and am not actually seeing or touching or tasting it: and he supposes that these two classes of sense-data, 'impressions' on the one hand, and 'ideas' or 'images' on the other hand, are distinguished by the fact that the ideas are fainter or less vivid than the impressions. And as regards 'impressions' he does, I think, just suspect that when I said 'I ate a piece of bread and butter', the name 'a piece of bread and butter' is *not* merely a name for my impressions, but for something quite different—something which is not a sense-datum; and perhaps we might say that even Berkeley suspected this also, since what he sets himself definitely to prove is that the name is merely a name for my impressions, thus shewing that he was aware of the possibility that it might be held to be a name for something different. But neither Hume nor Berkeley, I think, shew a trace of a suspicion that there can be any corresponding difference between the 'image' which I have before my mind, when I imagine an imaginary thing, and the imaginary thing itself. Even if there is a distinction between a piece of bread and butter and my impression of a piece of bread and butter, they both, I think, always assumed that there is no distinction at all between a griffin and my idea of a griffin.

Now I think the best authorities, nowadays, would agree that this view which I have attributed to Berkeley and Hume is false. But it is such a natural view to take, that possibly many people would still be found expressly to defend it. I think, therefore, I had better try to give the best arguments I can against it; especially as I think it is extremely difficult to find really clear and conclusive arguments against it, and as I think it is also extremely difficult to realise clearly exactly what the alternative to it is, exactly what imagination can consist in, if it does not merely consist in the apprehension of images.

I want, therefore, to give the best reasons I can for supposing that, when I imagine a griffin, what I imagine is not merely the image which I have before my mind, *not* merely a sense-datum—a more or less faint and inaccurate and altered copy of pictures or statues of griffins which I have seen. What arguments can we find to prove this?

Well, first of all, there is the argument that we should naturally say that this image which is now before my mind is merely an image of a griffin, that it is not itself a griffin, and that what is merely an image of a thing, cannot be identical with the thing of which it is an image. This certainly is what we should naturally say; so that the view that this image of mine *is* a griffin does sound paradoxical. And we might also supplement this by assuming the original point in dispute and saying: It is quite plain that there *is no* such thing as a griffin; whereas it is equally plain that there *is* such a thing as my image of it; and therefore it follows that the griffin and my image of it are not identical.

And I think some weight is to be attached to both these arguments; but they would hardly be convincing, as they stand, to anyone who holds the opposite opinion. So I want to try to find others.

And the next argument I wish to bring forward is one which does not attempt to prove the point directly with regard to pure imagination, but appeals to a supposed analogy with memory. We do, of course, talk of imagination, not only where what we imagine is purely imaginary, but also when we are remembering a past scene, which did really exist in the past, and which we ourselves actually witnessed. I can now, for instance, call up by memory a scene which I actually witnessed this afternoon; and it is quite natural to say that, when I do so, I am calling it up 'in imagination'. That is to say I can dwell upon my own past experiences 'in imagination', just as well as upon what is purely imaginary. And this process, where we revive 'in imagination' what we have previously seen, is, so far as I can see, strictly analogous to *pure* imagination—imagination of what is purely imaginary—in all respects *except* that in the one case what is now imagined by me is something which *was* real, though it is not now, whereas in the other case what I now imagine is purely imaginary and never was real. We may, therefore, hope to get some light on the question, whether, in the case of pure imagination, the images which we directly perceive are or are not identical with the object imagined, by considering the corresponding question in the case of memory. When I remember a thing, is it or is it not the case, that the images which I directly perceive at the moment of memory are identical with the *object* of memory—with *what* I remember?

This is, I think, a very confusing question and calls for some distinctions which it is not at all easy to express clearly in words, even if it is easy to grasp them. And I want particularly to call attention to these distinctions.

Let me take as clear and simple an instance of memory as I can find—an instance which I used before in order to make clear the distinction between what I called direct perception of a thing, and other ways of being conscious of the same thing. Look for a moment at this piece of white paper—and please attend to the actual patch of whitish colour itself—the actual sense-datum which you certainly do directly perceive when you look at it. And now, when, I have put it out of sight, try to remember—to call up before your minds that very white patch—the sense-datum which you directly perceived a moment ago. Now you may be able to call up a visual image of it—a visual image which *is* a patch of whitish colour more or less like the one you saw just now; and if so you are now directly perceiving this *image* and can attend to it, just as you attended before to the patch of white you actually saw. It is said that some people cannot call up such images at all—that they cannot 'visualize' as it is called, and if some of you cannot do this, one of the points I want to make will be even clearer than if you can. For it is quite certain that you can, in a sense, *remember* the sense-datum which you saw just now; you know that you did see it, and can make propositions about it, as for instance, what sort of a shape it had, and you can do this *whether* you are now directly perceiving any image of it or not. And if you are not directly perceiving any image of it at all—any image, however faint, that *is* a patch of whitish colour, more or less like it, it follows that that patch of white which you *are* remembering, and are, therefore, in a sense, now still *conscious of*, cannot possibly be identical with any image which you are now directly perceiving; since in this case *ex-hypothesi* you are not directly perceiving any image at all. But let us suppose that you can visualize: that you are directly perceiving a coloured image now. And let us ask first: Is this image, which you now directly perceive identical or not identical with the whitish patch which you directly perceived a moment ago, when you were actually looking at the paper?

Now the probability is that the image you are now directly perceiving is quite obviously *not* exactly like the original sense-datum; that it obviously differs from it in certain respects, though it might be difficult to say exactly what the respects are. The most obvious way of describing one at least of the respects in which it differs, is to say, as Hume said, that it is fainter or less vivid. And I think all philosophers agree that this is normally the case: that memory images do, as a rule, differ from the original sense-data, of which they are images, and cannot, therefore possibly be absolutely identical with these original sense-data. And it might be thought, at first sight, that this admission settles our original question. For it seems obvious that, when I remember a sense-datum which I formerly saw, *what* I remember is the sense-datum which I formerly saw—*not* the image which I am now directly perceiving; and the image I am now directly perceiving is, at least as a rule, *different* from the sense-datum I formerly saw. It seems to follow that *what* I remember is as a rule *not* identical with the image which I directly perceive *when* I remember.

But, unless I am mistaken, many people would be inclined to demur to this conclusion. Such a person might, I think, be tempted to argue in something like the following way. 'I, of course, admit', he might say, 'that the coloured image now before my mind is *different* from the whitish patch which I saw just now; and that what is the case in this instance is *normally* the case. I fully admit, that is, that there is *normally* a difference between a memory-image and the original sense-datum of which it is an image. But I object to your saying that the whitish patch I just now saw is *what* I am remembering now; or that, as a rule, the original sense-datum is *what* we really remember, when we are *said* to remember it. We do, of course, so speak in ordinary life; but, when we so speak, we are, in my opinion, using language loosely; and you cannot deny that we very often do use language loosely. We continually talk, for instance, of "seeing" a chair, or a house, or a tree when in fact we are certainly *not* seeing the *whole* of these objects, but only at most a *part* of them. And, just in the same way, I may be loosely said to remember *the* patch of white I saw just now, when all that I *really* remember is a mere part of it. It seems to me that this is the case. So far as I can see, I am only really remembering now a mere *part* of what I saw just now, and *the* part of it which I do remember is, so far as I can see, absolutely identical with the image I am now directly perceiving. In short, I maintain that, of the original sense-datum which I saw just now, I only really remember just so much as is identical with the image I am now directly perceiving. And I will, therefore, in spite of what you said just now; venture to lay down this proposition: namely: That when we remember any sense-datum, which we previously saw, what we really remember is always absolutely indistinguishable from our memory-image—from the image, which we are actually directly perceiving, at the moment when we remember'. I think many people might be tempted to say this. And though, as I shall presently shew, it can be absolutely proved that what we really remember is not always identical with our memory-image, it is not, I think by any means easy to shew that this may not normally be the case. The most obvious objection to the supposition that it is normally the case, is that the memory image does not seem to differ from the original sense-datum, as this theory supposes, *merely* by being a mere *part* of it; it does not seem to differ *merely* in respect of the fact that details which were present in the original sense-datum, are absent in the image. It seems rather as if the image wholly differed in quality from the original sense-datum: as if, for instance, the colour (if it has a colour) is *all* of it fainter and therefore of a slightly different shade. Just consider whether the whitish patch you can now call up before your mind does not differ in this way from the one you saw just now. It seems, in fact, to be the case, that, so far from the image being a mere *part* of the original sense-datum, it is, normally at least, *wholly* different from it; that no part of the one is identical with any part of the other; and that all that is true as to their relation is that the image is more or less like the original sense-datum. This, I believe, is really the case; and, if so, this present theory must be utterly rejected.

But there is secondly an entirely different theory possible, which I think many people would be inclined to hold. These people would say: 'We admit that the memory image is not (as a rule, at least) identical with any part of the original sense-datum. And we admit that when we remember a past sense-datum, this sense-datum itself or parts of it, and *not* our memory-image of it, is *what* we remember. If, for instance, a person (whom we will call Mr. Smith) is now remembering the colour of a dress in a picture which he saw this afternoon, we admit that what Mr. Smith is *really* remembering is *part* at least of what he actually saw this afternoon: when we say that Mr. Smith is remembering the colour in the picture, we admit that we are asserting a relation between Mr. Smith and something which he saw this afternoon; and we admit that this something which he saw this afternoon is only *like* and not identical with the image he is *now* directly perceiving. But what we do maintain is as follows. We maintain that the only relation which does subsist now between Mr. Smith and what he saw this afternoon consists simply and solely in the two facts that he is directly perceiving an image and that this image is in fact a copy of what he saw this afternoon—more or less like it. His memory consists solely in this. It won't do, indeed, to say that his memory consists solely in his direct perception of the image. It does not; for in order that he may be properly said to be remembering what he saw this afternoon it is absolutely essential that the image which he directly perceives now should be a copy of what he saw this afternoon. But this, we maintain, is absolutely all that is essential. And hence we venture to maintain in general that: To remember is always merely to directly perceive some image, which is a copy of the thing remembered. Thus memory is always really and truly a name for a relation between the man remembering and the thing remembered—it is not merely a name for a relation between him and his memory-image; for his memory-image is, we have admitted, at least as a rule, not even partially identical with, but only similar to, the thing remembered: but we maintain that his relation to the thing remembered consists solely in the fact that the memory-image which he directly perceives is a copy of the thing remembered'.

Now, this theory also, is, I think, one which is very commonly held or implied; and I think it may seem very plausible. With regard to it also it may, I think, be absolutely proved that it is not always true; that memory does not always consist solely in this relation. But it is, I think, very difficult indeed to prove that *as a rule* there is anything more in memory. And what I want you particularly to notice about it is that it implies that we may be properly said to remember a thing, even when we are not, in a sense, in any way conscious *of* the thing remembered. And this may be thought to be an objection to it. It may be thought: Memory is obviously a name for a form of consciousness: and hence we obviously cannot be said to remember a thing, unless we are *conscious of* the thing remembered. Whereas this view maintains that memory of a thing always consists in consciousness of something else—of some other thing, which is merely an *image of* the thing remembered. But, of course, it may be said, in reply to this objection, that this is merely a question of words. It may be said: Granted that memory is a form of consciousness, why should it not be the case that one thing which we mean by being conscious of a thing, is merely the directly perceiving of some *other* thing, which is an image of, or related in some other way to, the thing of which we are said to be conscious? And I want particularly to insist on this theory, because I think a theory, of the same kind, may be, and very often is, very plausibly held not only in the case of memory, but also in the case of many other words which would be said to be names for forms of consciousness. Take, for instance, the words 'to perceive', 'to observe', 'to see', 'to hear'. We saw at the beginning of these lectures that, when I *see* this paper I am reading from, there is reason to suppose that the sense-data which I directly perceive—the black marks on a whitish ground, are not identical with any part of the paper itself. And yet what I am said, in ordinary language, to *see*, is the paper itself. And so similarly we are said to see trees, houses, and the sun and moon, when all that we in fact directly perceive are sense-data, which are not identical with any parts of these objects. Well, many people, I think, would say that what we mean by this ordinary language—what we mean by 'seeing' a tree, consists simply and solely in directly perceiving sense-data, which are in fact caused by the tree, or, at least, are signs of it. Thus, on this view, when I am said to *see* a tree, this does not mean that I am in any way conscious of the tree itself, but only that I am conscious of some sense-datum, which is, in fact, an effect or a sign of the tree. And it is, I think, very difficult indeed to prove that this is not a true account of what *normally* happens. When I walk about and *see* all sorts of objects, does anything at all happen, as a rule, except that I am conscious of sense-data, which are in fact signs of these objects, while I am not in any way at all conscious of the objects themselves? This may seem a very plausible view to take. Only, of course, it may be said that here again there is the same ambiguity about the word 'consciousness'. It may be said that to be conscious of a sense-datum, which *is* the sign of an object, is, in a sense, the same thing as to be conscious of the object in question, that this is *one* proper use of the word 'consciousness.' And indeed one view which some philosophers accuse other philosophers of holding (and with some justice, I think) is that what we call consciousness *always* consists merely in being conscious of some image or sign of the object of which we are said to be conscious: that to have an object before our minds is always merely to have our idea of it before our minds—to have before our minds an image or sign of it. This particular view, you see, cannot possibly be true, because it is obvious that the sense in which I have before my mind or am conscious of my idea—the image or sign—cannot be the same as that in which I have before my mind or am conscious of the object of which it is a sign. My consciousness of my idea cannot possibly merely consist, in my consciousness of an idea *of* that idea, and so on *ad infinitum*. But nevertheless it might be true that what we *often* mean by seeing an object, is *merely* directly perceiving a sense-datum, which *is* a sign or effect of that object; and, by remembering an object, merely directly perceiving an image, which is an image of the object. And, if this is so, then, if we maintain that 'seeing' and 'remembering' *are* names for forms of consciousness, we must admit that the word 'consciousness' is ambiguous. We must admit that when we are said to be conscious of an object, we are often, in another sense, not conscious of *it* at all. And of course, if this ambiguity does exist, it is extraordinarily important to distinguish clearly between the two different senses. And I cannot think of any clearer way of bringing out the distinction than by the instance we are now considering. It is obvious, I think, that, if when a man remembers a thing, his memory of it consists merely in directly perceiving something else—some image, which resembles the thing he is said to remember, but is not even partially identical with it, then, in a sense, he is not conscious at all of the thing remembered, when he remembers it. And I am going in future to say that if this is a true account of memory, then memory is not a form of consciousness at all. I am going in future to restrict the name consciousness to relations other than this one. Though, of course, I fully admit that this restriction may be purely arbitrary; that it may be the case that we do sometimes quite properly use the word consciousness for *this* relation as well as for others.

Well, then: I have tried to distinguish two different theories which may be held as to what happens when we remember a sense-datum, which we formerly saw. Both theories admit, what I believe every one admits, that, as a rule, the memory-image, which we are directly perceiving, when we remember, is obviously different in some respects from the original sense-datum. But the first theory maintains that it *only* differs from it as part from whole; and maintains further that, though we speak loosely as if we remembered the whole original sense-datum, all that we *really* remember of it is just so much of it as is identical with the memory-image now before our minds. This theory holds, therefore, that when we remember, *what* we really remember—the true object of memory—is quite indistinguishable from the memory-image which we are directly perceiving at the moment when we remember: that when we remember, *what* we remember simply is this image: and this theory, therefore, would fully support the original theory about pure imagination from which we started—so far as the analogy of memory *can* support any theory about pure imagination at all: it would support the theory that when I imagine a griffin, *what* I imagine, namely the griffin, is simply identical with the image which I am directly perceiving. But the second theory is quite different. *It* asserts that what I remember—even what I really remember—is *not* identical with my memory-image. But it asserts that nevertheless this memory-image is the only thing I am in any way *conscious* of when I remember. Memory, it says, is *not*, as the first theory said, merely a name for a relation between me and my memory-image: it is a name for a relation between me and a part of the original sense-datum which is not identical with the image; *but*, it says, this relation merely consists in the two facts (1) that I am conscious of the image and (2) that this image is, in fact, a copy of the original sense-datum. No other relation between me and the original sense-datum is involved: I need not be in any other sense *conscious* of the original sense-datum, when I remember it. This second theory, therefore, while it allows that the object of memory—*what* is remembered—is not identical with the memory-image: yet maintains that the object of memory is something of which we are not conscious when we remember it. While, therefore, it does not support the view that the *object* of pure imagination is identical with the image before our minds when we imagine; it would entitle us to say (so far as the analogy between memory and pure imagination may hold) that the only thing we are ever conscious of when we imagine, is some image: that, even though 'a griffin' is *not* merely a name for an image of mine, I certainly am not conscious of a griffin, when I imagine one, but *only* of my image of it. And in support of both these two theories there is the fact—the fact which has actually led to their being adopted, and which is, I think, constantly leading to difficulties in philosophy—the fact that, if we try to discover by introspection, what is before our minds when we remember or imagine, it is extraordinarily difficult to discover that anything whatever is ever before them except some image; and that even if we are convinced that something else is before them, it is still extraordinarily difficult to discover in exactly what sort of way this something else is before them. The difficulty is the same as in the case of sense-perception. When I look at this paper, *is* anything before my mind except the sense-data which I directly perceive? and if anything else is before my mind, in what sort of way is it before it? In general, I think we may say that it is extraordinarily difficult to discover by introspection that conscious processes or mental acts ever consist in anything else at all except the direct perception of sense-data, either impressions or images: we are tempted to say, as Hume said, that *all* the perceptions of the human mind are either impressions or ideas—meaning by that simply sense-data—original sense-data and copies of them. And, of course, if this were the case, then one or other of these two theories of memory *must* be true. Of course, it can be absolutely proved that this is not the case. It can be absolutely proved that we are conscious, in some sense or other, of things which are not sense-data; and that we can be conscious of sense-data, without directly perceiving them. And even those who, like Hume, assume the opposite, cannot help constantly contradicting themselves. But on the other hand, even those who are convinced that direct perception is *not* the only form of consciousness, and that sense-data are not our only objects, seem to me unable to give a really clear account as to what this other form of consciousness is; and they seem also, many of them, to be constantly liable to slip back into the assumption that after all direct perception *is* the only form of consciousness, and that sense-data are its only objects.

So much, then, in favour of these two theories. But, I said, that even if it is true that one or other of these two things is all that happens as a rule, when we remember, it can be absolutely proved that it is not *always* all that happens. And I now want to prove this.

Let us go back to our original case. You look at this piece of paper and attend to the sense-datum you directly perceive—the whitish patch of colour; and then, when you no longer see it, you try to remember it. And let us suppose you can visualize—that you can call up some image of it, however faint. Now, even if, as the first theory said, your memory of that patch might sometimes consist merely in your direct perception of the image, and even if as the second theory said, it might sometimes consist merely in this together with the fact that the image *is* in fact a copy of the original patch, it is quite obvious that something quite different may be happening now. *Now* you are not only remembering, but you know that you are remembering. And on both theories, in order to do this, you must know, in the one case, that your present image is merely a part, *not* the whole, of what you formerly saw; and, in the other case, that it is a copy, like, but different from, what you formerly saw. But this knowledge, which you now have, the knowledge that your image is *different* from the original sense-datum—in what can *this* consist? Obviously you cannot know this, without, in some sense, being conscious of the original sense-datum itself. What you know is that the original sense-datum *itself* differs from the image: obviously this is so, since the image does not differ from the image. You are, therefore, knowing something about the original sense-datum itself; and if you were *merely* conscious of the image—if this image were *all* you were conscious of, this would be quite impossible: you could not possibly know either that the image was a mere part of the original sense-datum, or that it was a copy of it, if all that you were conscious of was the image itself. Whenever, therefore, we *know* that we remember we must be conscious of the original sense-datum in some sense quite other than that of merely directly perceiving a part of it, or merely directly perceiving an image, which is, in fact, a copy of it. And this way in which we are conscious of it, when we know that we remember it, is itself obviously a kind of remembering. There certainly is therefore, a kind of remembering, which is quite other than what either of these two theories allows This kind of remembering is something which always occurs, whenever we know that we remember. And, if it occurs then, why should it not also occur in other cases? why should it not be what normally occurs, whenever we remember, even when we do not know that we are remembering? To prove that it is what normally occurs seems to me to be extraordinarily difficult; I know of no way of proving it. But the mere fact that it does *sometimes* occur, destroys, I think, the only strong reason for supposing that it is not what normally occurs. Even now, when it is occurring, it is almost impossible to discover by introspection *that* it is occurring, and exactly what it is that is occurring. You do now know that your image is different from what the original sense-datum was. You are, therefore, thinking *of* the original sense-datum itself: you are plainly not *merely* thinking of the image. The original sense-datum itself is, therefore, now, in a sense before your mind; else you could not compare it with the image and know that the two are different. But in what sense is it before your mind? You are certainly not now *directly perceiving* it; all that you are directly perceiving now is the image: and it must be remembered that the way in which I defined direct perception was simply as being the way in which you were conscious of the original sense-datum, when you actually saw it, and in which you are *not* conscious of it now. You certainly, therefore, are not now directly perceiving the original sense-datum. But in what sense, then, are you now conscious of it? All that can be said, I think, with certainty, is that you are conscious of it, in the obscure sense in which it is necessary that you should be conscious of it, in order to know that it was different from the image —different, therefore, from anything which you are directly perceiving. This obscure sort of consciousness is what I said that even those who admit its existence seem unable to give a clear account of. And I confess I can't give any clear account of it myself. I can only try to point out what it is, by pointing out that it is what occurs in this instance; when we certainly know something *about* that past sense-datum itself, though we are no longer directly perceiving it. It certainly is a thing which constantly does occur—this mere *thinking* of a thing which we are *not* directly perceiving; and it is a mental operation which is of the utmost importance. And since it is so difficult to discover it and what it is, in this instance, where it is certainly there and we are actually looking for it, it is, of course, very likely that it really is there in ever so many other instances where it is difficult absolutely to prove that it is there, and where, at the moment when it occurs, we don't happen to be looking for it. Well, what I want to suggest is that this kind of consciousness usually occurs, whenever we remember anything. That when we remember we really are usually conscious in this obscure sense of the past thing *itself*: that memory does not consist, as a rule, either *merely* in direct perception of an image, nor yet in this together *with* the fact that the image is a copy of the past thing. This, I think, is the view which would be usually accepted nowadays by the best authorities, and though I don't see how it can be proved that this kind of consciousness usually occurs when we remember, it is at all events clear that the view that it does is a possible one; and also, so far as I can see, there is nothing whatever against this view, so soon as we recognise that this kind of consciousness certainly does sometimes occur: that it does and must occur, whenever we *know* either that we ourselves are remembering or that any one else is doing so. If either of the first two theories of memory were true, then it would follow, that though acts of memory might be constantly occurring, yet nobody could ever possibly know that any such act ever did occur: nobody could ever possibly know that any image before anybody's mind *was* a part of or a copy of some previous sense-datum, although of course it might quite well often be the case that it was so, as a matter of fact. In order to *know* that memory ever occurs in either of these two suggested senses we must be able to remember previous sense-data in some other sense. The fact that we do know that memory-images are often not identical with any past sense-datum, proves that we *can* remember past sense-data, in this other sense—that the obscure kind of consciousness I have spoken of does sometimes actually occur.

But if this obscure kind of consciousness of the previous sense-datum does normally occur in memory, it follows not only that the object of memory—what is remembered—is *not* identical with any image which we may be directly perceiving, when we remember; but also that we are actually conscious of the object of memory and not only of the image. And if this is the case in memory, analogy naturally suggests that it may also be the case in pure imagination: that here, too, when I imagine a griffin, *what* I imagine is *not* identical with any image that I have before my mind; that imagination does *not* merely consist in the direct perception of images, but that we are also conscious in some other way—some way other than direct perception—of something other than the images we are directly perceiving; that this something else is what we imagine—is the griffin. How absolutely to prove that this is what happens always, or even generally, in imagination, I confess I don't know. But, as I say, I think the best authorities would now agree that it is the case; and I am going in future to assume that it is so: I am going to assume that when I imagine a griffin, any image which I may be directly perceiving is not *itself* a griffin but *only* an image *of* one, and that I am actually conscious of something other than this image. And I think the important thing is to realise that this is at least a possible view; that there is a kind of consciousness *other* than direct perception, which *may* be present in imagination, and which *may* have a different object from the object of direct perception; and also to get as clear a view as possible, by means of instances, of what this kind of consciousness is and how it differs from direct perception. I will only give one argument which seems to me again to shew that this other kind of consciousness does exist, and also to suggest, though I admit it does not absolutely prove, that it *is* present in imagination. Suppose again that you are showing a child a picture of a griffin, and that the child asks: Are griffins real? It is surely here quite obvious that the child is not asking whether the picture which it sees is real; about the reality of the picture it has no doubt at all. It is, therefore, quite plain that it is asking a question about something *other* than the picture. It is conscious in some way of something other than the picture, and this something is what it means by a griffin. But there is no reason to suppose that this something other is an image. The picture itself can here serve the same purpose as images serve on other occasions. And what I want to suggest is that the only part that images do play in imagination, is the part which the picture plays in this case. Obviously merely to see a picture of a griffin is *not* the same thing as imagining a griffin. If it were, then, in asking: Are griffins real? we should be asking: Is the picture real? which we are obviously not doing. And similarly, when we directly perceive, some image of a griffin, and ask: Are griffins real? we are no more asking whether our *image* is real, than we were asking whether the picture was real. In both cases, the sense-data which we are directly perceiving merely serve to suggest something else—something which we are not directly perceiving, and it is about this something else that we are asking our question.

I am going, therefore, to assume that the *object* of imagination—what we imagine—is *not* identical with any image which we may be directly perceiving when we imagine; and that therefore our original question as to whether imaginary objects have any kind of being, in spite of being imaginary, cannot be settled by simply identifying imaginary objects with images. I am going to assume that the argument: 'A griffin is simply a name for the image which you directly perceive, when you imagine a griffin; but there is no doubt that there is such a thing as this image; and therefore it follows that there *is* such a thing as a griffin' that this argument will not prove its point, because its first premiss 'A griffin is simply a name for the image which you directly perceive, when you imagine a griffin' is false. But, of course, even if we reject this argument, my original argument still retains its force. It may still be argued: Even if a griffin is not identical with any image of a griffin, it still remains true that a griffin *is* what you imagine, and there certainly must be such a thing as what you imagine, else you could not imagine it; and hence since there is such a thing as what you imagine, and since what you imagine is a griffin, it still follows that there is such a thing as a griffin. This is the argument I want now to try to answer.

And in order to answer it, I want to take account of an entirely new class of facts. The truth is that an exactly similar puzzle occurs in another instance—an instance which everybody admits to constitute one of the most fundamental problems of philosophy. I mean in the case of *false beliefs*, of errors or mistakes. Everybody admits that there is such a thing as believing what is not true, as making a mistake. And a question which has been much discussed by philosophers, especially recently, is: What, after all, is the difference between true and false belief, between truth and falsehood, between true beliefs and error? And if we ask this question we are liable to come upon a difficulty of exactly the same sort as when we ask what is the difference between the real and the imaginary. Indeed, everybody admits that the two questions are very closely connected, though all sorts of different views may be taken as to the precise *way* in which they are connected.

The best way I can find of putting the difficulty in the case of true and false beliefs is as follows. Suppose a man believes that God exists; and suppose his belief is true: then to say that his belief is true seems to be exactly equivalent to saying that it *is a fact* that God exists or that God's existence is a fact. If his belief *is* true, then it is a fact that God exists; and if it is not a fact that God exists, then his belief is false. And exactly the same equivalence seems to hold, whatever other belief you take instead of this one. In the case of any belief whatever, to say that that belief is true seems to be equivalent to saying that its object—what is believed in it—is a fact; if its object is not a fact, then always the belief is false. As a mere question of language I think this equivalence certainly does hold universally. Whenever we say: It is true that so and so, we can always quite naturally say instead, It is *a fact* that so and so. It seems, therefore, at first sight, perfectly natural and satisfactory to say: The difference between true and false beliefs is this, namely, that where a belief is true, there what is believed is a fact; whereas where a belief is false, there what is believed is not a fact.

But now let us look at the other side. Suppose a man believes that God exists; and suppose this belief is false. It seems, as we have seen, quite natural to say that what he believes is that God exists. And it is quite certain that when he believes this he is believing something. It seems, therefore, quite certain that there *is* such a thing as what he believes, when he believes this. But what *is* this something which is *what* he believes? It is that God exists, or, turning it another way, we may say it is 'God's existence'; since to say that a man believes in God's existence is plainly merely another way of saying that he believes that God exists. This way of putting it is indeed not open to us in the case of all beliefs: in a great many cases we can only express the *object* believed or *what* is believed by a sentence beginning with 'that' because what is believed is so complex that we cannot easily make a verbal noun of it. But this is, I think, plainly only a question of words: in every case what is believed is equivalent to what could be expressed by some verbal noun, if only it were not too complex so to express it. We may, therefore, I think, fairly take this instance of God's existence as typical of all beliefs. Exactly the same difficulty occurs with regard to all beliefs as does occur here, though in many cases we cannot express it quite so simply. And the difficulty is this. A man believes in God's existence and it seems quite plain that he is believing in something—that there is such a thing as what he believes in, and that this something is God's existence. It seems quite plain, therefore, that there *is* such a thing as God's existence, *whether* his belief is true or false. But we have just seen that if his belief is false, then God's existence is *not* a fact. And what is the difference between saying that there *is* such a thing as God's existence and that God's existence is a fact? The two expressions seem to be absolutely equivalent. If there *is* such a thing as God's existence, then it seems quite plain that God's existence *is* a fact. And if God's existence is *not* a fact, then it seems quite plain that there *is no* such thing as God's existence. We find, therefore, that the proposed way of distinguishing true from false beliefs is not quite so simple as it seemed. We proposed to say that, where a belief is false, then what is believed is *not* a fact. But it now seems to turn out, that even where a belief is false—what is believed most certainly is—there certainly *is* such a thing. And it is not quite easy to see what is the difference between saying that there is such a thing as what is believed and saying that what is believed is a fact.

Now, of course, nobody supposes that even if there *is* such a thing as what is believed in all cases equally, whether the belief is true or false, this does away with the distinction between true and false beliefs. Nobody supposes this, any more than they suppose that even if we have to admit there *are* such things as griffins and centaurs and chimaeras, this fact does away with the distinction between the real and the imaginary. Even if there *is* such a thing as *what* is believed, where a belief is false, it is certain that what is believed is *not* in that case a fact in the same sense, as it would be if the belief were true. But you see there is exactly the same reason for supposing that there *is* such a thing as God's existence, even if those who believe in it believe falsely, as there is for supposing that there is such a thing as a griffin, even if a griffin is purely imaginary. And I think the case of false belief is the clearest one, in which to raise the question whether the reason is a good one or not. I propose, therefore, to ask: Does the mere fact that people believe in God's existence, prove that there is such a thing as God's existence or not? If so, what is the difference between the assertion that there is such a thing as God's existence and the assertion that God's existence is a fact? And if not, how do you answer the argument which seems to prove that what is believed, whether truly or falsely, in any case certainly must *be*?

Chapter XIV

BELIEFS AND PROPOSITIONS

THE question which I promised to begin with now is the question what truth *is*, or what is the difference between true beliefs and false ones. And this is a question about which it seems to me to be extremely difficult either to think clearly or to speak clearly—far more difficult than in the case of any question I have yet discussed. It is, in the first place, extremely difficult to distinguish clearly and to avoid confusing the different views which may be held about it; and, in the second place, even if you do succeed in doing this, it is extremely difficult to *express* the distinctions clearly. I am afraid I shall not have succeeded in doing either—either in avoiding confusion, or in expressing myself clearly. But I must do the best I can.

One fact which is liable to introduce complications into the discussion although, so far as I can see, it is really quite irrelevant, is the fact that in the case of the commonest instances of mistaken belief—those which occur most commonly in ordinary life, and about which there is the least doubt that they *are* false beliefs—there is so often a doubt as to exactly *what* it is that is believed. You might think that we could not choose better instances, in which to investigate the essence of a false belief, than such common instances as the following. I often believe such things as that my scissors are lying on the table, when, in fact, they are not; or that my hat is hanging in the hall, when, in fact, it isn't. False beliefs of this kind do constantly occur in ordinary life; and no one doubts that they *are* false beliefs. But, as we have seen in the earlier part of these lectures, different philosophers take extremely different views as to *what* we are actually believing when we believe such things as this. There is no sort of agreement as to what scissors are, or what a table is, or what is meant by lying on a table. And though, so far as I can see, this question as to what is meant by the apparently simple proposition 'My scissors are lying on my table' is not strictly relevant to the question what is the difference between saying that it is true and saying that it is false (indeed, it seems quite plain, that, whatever its meaning may be, the difference between its being true and its being false must be the same): yet this doubt as to its meaning *might* be thought to affect the question as to what is meant by its being true, or would, I think, in any case hinder us from seeing quite as clearly as is desirable exactly what the difference is. I want, therefore, to get an instance of a false belief, in which there shall be as little doubt as possible as to exactly what it is that is believed. And in looking for an instance, which should satisfy *this* requirement, I have only been able to hit upon one, which suffers from the defect that it is a false belief, which you might say is not at all likely to be actually occurring. It is, however, a false belief of a sort which *does* quite commonly occur. And I must do the best I can with it; as I haven't been able to think of an instance which is really ideal in all respects.

Well, my instance is this. You all of you know quite well the sort of sounds—the actual sense-data which you would be hearing now if a brass-band were playing loud in this room. This kind of fact, the kind of fact which consists in the actual experience of such striking sense-data as the noise of a brass-band playing quite near you, seems to me to be a kind of fact with regard to which there is the least possibility of mistake as to their nature. And also there is no kind of fact of which each of us can be more certain than that we are or are not, at a given moment, experiencing particular sense-data of this violent nature. There is nothing of which I am more certain than that I am *not* at this moment experiencing those extremely striking and unmistakable sense-data, which I can only describe as those which I should be experiencing if a brass-band were playing loudly in this room. And you all of you, I think, know as well as I do what kind of sense-data I mean—what the noise of a brass-band is like—and that *you* are *not* now hearing these sense-data. Well, suppose that somebody somewhere were believing now that some one of us *is* now hearing the noise of a brass-band. As I say, I suppose it is not at all likely that anybody anywhere is actually making this mistake at the present moment with regard to anyone. But it is a sort of mistake which we certainly do quite often make. We often make mistakes which consist in supposing that some other person is at a given moment experiencing sense-data, which he is *not* in fact experiencing at that moment. Smith, for instance, may believe, on a particular evening, that his friend Jones has gone out to hear the band; and, if Smith is at all imaginative, he may go on to imagine what Jones would be experiencing, upon that hypothesis: he may actually represent to himself and believe that *Jones is hearing the noise of a brass-band.* Smith certainly *might* believe this of Jones; and he might easily be quite mistaken. It might be, for instance, that though Jones had told him that he was going to hear the band that evening, yet Jones had, in fact, been prevented from leaving home at all. Smith would in that case, be believing that Jones was experiencing sense-data, which Jones was *not* in fact experiencing; and surely this is a kind of mistake which does quite commonly occur. Well, similarly, it is possible that some one of our friends should be believing now that one of us is hearing the noise of a brass-band, whereas in fact we are not. And even if it isn't at all likely that anyone is believing this now of us, we all know, I think, what such a belief would be like. Let us take, then, as our instance of a false belief, the belief which some one would now be having, if he were believing *that we are now hearing the noise of a brass-band.*

Well, if anyone were believing this now, he certainly would be making a mistake. There is no doubt that his belief would be false. And it seems to me that in this case there is as little doubt as possible as to what the essence of his mistake would consist in.

Surely the whole essence of the mistake would lie simply in this, that whereas, on the one hand, he would be believing that we are hearing the noise of a brass-band, the *fact* is on the other hand that we are *not* hearing it. And similarly it is quite plain what would be necessary to make this belief of his a true one. All that would be necessary would be simply that we *should* be hearing the noise in question. If we *were* hearing it, and he believed that we were, then his belief would be true. This surely does state correctly the difference between truth and falsehood in the case of this particular belief; and what I want to ask is: Supposing that it is a correct statement of the difference, what exactly is the difference that has been stated? What does this statement mean, if we try to put it more exactly?

Well, one point seems to me plain, to begin with, and this is a point on which I wish particularly to insist. The difference between truth and falsehood, in the case of this particular belief, does we have said, depend on whether in fact we are or are *not* now hearing the noise of a brass-band. Unless, therefore we can understand the difference between these two alternatives—between our being now hearing that noise, and our *not* being now hearing it, we certainly cannot understand the difference between the truth and falsehood of this belief. This is one essential point, though it is only one. And it seems to me that as to this point there really is no doubt at all. We are *not* now hearing the noise of a brass-band; and we all, I think, can understand quite clearly in one respect the nature of the fact which I express by saying that we are not. What these words imply is that there simply is no such thing in the Universe as our being now hearing that particular kind of noise. The combination of us at this moment with the hearing of that particular kind of noise is a combination which simply has no being. There *is* no such combination. And we all do, I think, understand quite clearly what is meant by saying that there *is* no such thing. If you don't understand this, I'm afraid I can't make it any clearer. This distinction between there being such a thing as our now hearing that particular kind of noise and there being no such thing seems to me to be absolutely fundamental. And I want you to concentrate your attention upon this particular sense of the word 'being'—the sense in which there certainly *is* no such thing as our being hearing now the noise of a brass-band. In one sense, at all events, there certainly *isn't*; and we all know that there *isn't*. And we can recognise the sense in which there *isn't*. And it is this particular sense of the word 'being' that I want to get fixed. Using this sense of the word 'being' we can at once say two things about the difference between the truth and falsehood of this particular belief—the belief that we *are* now hearing the noise of a brass-band. We can say, in the first place that since the belief is false, there simply *is* not in the Universe one thing which would be in it, if the belief were true. And we can say, in the second place, that this thing, which is simply absent from the Universe since the belief is false, and which would be present, if it were true, *is* that fact, whose nature is so unmistakable—the fact which would *be*, if we were now hearing the noise of a brass-band—the fact which would consist in our actually being now hearing it.

But now these two points by themselves don't suffice to give us a perfectly satisfactory *definition* of truth and falsehood. They don't suffice to tell us absolutely definitely what property it is that we should be attributing to this belief, if we were to say that it was true, nor yet what property it is that we are attributing to it now, when we say that it is false. They don't suffice to do this for a reason which I find it very difficult to explain clearly, but which I must do my best to indicate. They do *suggest* a definition; and the definition which they suggest is as follows: To say of this belief that it is true would be to say of it that the fact to which it refers *is*—that there is such a fact in the Universe as the fact to which it refers; while to say of it that it is false is to say of it that *the fact to which it refers* simply is not —that there is no such fact in the Universe. Here we have a definition of what is meant by the truth and falsehood of this belief and a definition which I believe to be the right one; and it is a definition which *might* apply not only to this belief, but to all beliefs which we ever say are true or false. We might say quite generally: To say that a belief is true is to say always that *the fact to which it refers is* or has being, while to say of a belief that it is false is to say always, that the fact to which it refers, is not or has *no* being. But this definition is not perfectly satisfactory and definite because it leaves one point obscure: it leaves obscure what is meant by *the* fact to which a belief refers. In our particular case we happen to know what the fact to which the belief refers *is*: it is our being now hearing the noise of a brass-band, but when we say of this belief that it is false, we don't mean merely to say that we are not in fact hearing the noise of a brass-band. In merely saying this we are not attributing any property to the *belief* at all; whereas when we say that it is false, we certainly do mean to attribute to the belief itself some definite property, and that a property which it shares with other false beliefs. And it won't do to say either, that, when we say that it is false, all that we mean is simply that some fact or other is absent from the Universe. For every *different* false belief a *different* fact is absent from the Universe. And what we mean to say of each, when we say that it is false, is not merely that some *fact or other* is absent from the Universe, but that *the* fact to which it refers is so absent. But then the question is what is meant by *the* fact to which *it* refers? What *is* this relation which we call *referring to* a fact? In saying that there is such a relation, we imply that every true belief has some peculiar relation to one fact, and one fact only—every *different* true belief having the relation in question to a *different* fact. And we need to say what this relation is, in order to define perfectly satisfactorily what we mean by the fact to which a belief refers. *Can* we say what this relation is?

Well, it seems to me the only relation which quite obviously, at first sight, satisfies the requirement is as follows. Every true belief has to one fact and one fact only, *this* peculiar relation namely that we do use and have to use the *name* of the fact, in *naming* the belief. So that we might say: *The* fact to which a belief refers is always *the* fact which has the *same name* as that which we have to use in naming the belief. This, I think, is true; and I want to insist upon it, because I think this partial identity between the name of a belief and the name of the fact to which it refers often leads to confusion, and often serves to conceal the true nature of the problem which we have to face. If we want to give a name to any belief—to point out what belief it is that we are talking about, and to distinguish it from other different beliefs, we always have to do it in the following way. We can only refer to it as *the* belief *that* so and so. One belief for instance is *the* belief that 'lions exist', another is *the* belief that 'bears exist,' another is *the* belief that 'my scissors are lying on my table' and so on. The only way we have of referring to these beliefs and pointing out *which* belief it is that we are talking of is by means of one of these expressions beginning with 'that', or else by the equivalent verbal noun. Suppose, for instance, we want to talk about the belief that lions exist. How are we to refer to it? By what name are we to call it, which will show *which* belief we are talking about? Obviously its name just consists in the words I have just said: its name consists in the words 'the belief that lions exist', or in the equivalent phrase 'the belief in the existence of lions': it has absolutely no name except one or other of these two phrases: we can't refer to it, and point out which belief we mean in any other way. We can, therefore, only name beliefs by means of these expressions beginning with 'that'—'*that* lions exist', '*that* bears exist' and so on, or the equivalent verbal nouns. But, curiously enough, if we want to name *the fact to which a belief refers*—the fact which *is*, if the belief be true, and *is not* if it be false—we can only do it by means of exactly the same expressions. If the belief that lions exist be true, then there is in the Universe, some fact which would not be at all if the belief were false. But what is this fact? What is its name? Surely this fact is the fact *that lions exist*. These words 'that lions exist' constitute its name and there is no other way of referring to it than by these or some equivalent words. And these words you see are the very same words which we are obliged also to use in naming the belief. The belief *is* the belief *that lions exist*, and the fact, to which the belief refers, is the fact *that lions exist*.

It is, therefore, I think, true that *the* fact to which a belief refers is always the fact which *has the very same name* which we have to use in naming the belief. But obviously the fact that this is the case won't do as a *definition* of what we mean by the fact to which a belief refers. It cannot possibly be the case that what we mean by saying that a belief is true, is merely that there is in the Universe the fact which *has the same name*. If this were so, no belief could possibly be true, until it had a name. It must be the case therefore that there is always some *other* relation between a true belief and the fact to which it refers—some *other* relation which is *expressed by* this identity of name.

The question, therefore, which we have to face is: What *is* the relation which always holds between a true belief and the fact to which it refers? The relation which we mean by calling the fact *the* fact to which the belief refers? The relation which we express by saying that the belief does refer to the fact?

Let us try to answer this question by considering again our particular instance of a belief. In this instance, we have the advantage of knowing very clearly what the *fact* would be like, which would *be*, if the belief were true. We all know what it would be like, if we *were* now hearing the noise of a brass-band. And this fact, which certainly *isn't*, is what would *be*, if the particular belief in question were true. In order, therefore, to discover how this fact, if there were such a fact, *would* be related to the belief, we have, it might seem, only to discover what the belief itself is like. And this is where the difficulty would seem to lie. *If* some person were believing now that we are hearing the noise of a brass-band, in what would this belief of his consist? What is the correct analysis of the event that would be happening in his mind?

This is a question which it is certainly not easy to answer. But there is one very simple and natural answer to it, which suggests a correspondingly simple theory as to what is the relation between a belief and *the* fact to which it refers. And I want first, therefore, to give this simple and natural answer to the question as to the analysis of beliefs, together with the simple theory which it suggests as to the distinction between truth and falsehood.

The answer as to the analysis of beliefs is this. It says that, in the case of every belief without exception, whether it be true or whether it be false, we can always distinguish two constituents—namely, the *act* of belief, on the one hand, and the *object* of belief or what *is* believed on the other. The *act* of belief is something which is of the same nature in absolutely all cases. Whether I believe that twice two are four, or something so different as that lions exist, the *act* of belief which I perform is of exactly the same kind in both cases. What constitutes the difference between the two cases, is that the *objects* of belief are different. And we may, if we like, call the object of belief, in absolutely all cases, a '*proposition*'. Only, if we do so, we must be careful to distinguish propositions in this sense, from propositions, which consist merely in a form of *words*. 'Proposition' in the sense in which, upon this theory, the object of belief is always a proposition, is *not* a name for any mere form of words. It is a name for what is *expressed* by certain forms of words—those, namely, which, in grammar, are called 'sentences'. It is a name for what is before your mind, when you not only hear or read but *understand* a sentence. It is, in short, the *meaning* of a sentence—what is expressed or conveyed by a sentence: and is, therefore, utterly different from the sentence itself—from the mere words. And it certainly does seem, at first sight, as if there were such things as propositions in this sense; and as if whenever we believe anything we are believing some proposition. The reasons for distinguishing in every case between the act of belief on the one side, and the proposition believed on the other, seem very strong. What is quite certain is that when, for instance, one man believes that lions exist, and another man believes that bears exist, these two beliefs resemble one another in respect of the fact that they are both of them acts of belief; and also that they differ from one another in respect of the fact that one of them is the belief that lions exist and the other the belief that bears exist. But in what does this difference consist? It seems difficult to see how it can consist in anything else than that the one belief has a specific kind of relation to one object, while the other has the same kind of relation to a different object. And the natural view certainly is that the two different objects concerned are in the one case, the proposition that lions exist, and in the other, the proposition that bears exist. And if this is a true account of the difference between two different true beliefs; it is quite obvious that it is a true account of the difference between two different false beliefs. If one child believes falsely that griffins exist, and another believes falsely that centaurs exist; it is quite equally obvious here that the two beliefs resemble one another in respect of the fact that both are acts of belief, but that nevertheless, the two differ from one another in respect of the fact that one is the belief that griffins exist while the other is the belief that centaurs exist. And there is the same reason here, as in the case of true beliefs, for saying that the difference consists in the fact that the one belief has a specific relation to *the proposition* that griffins exist and the other the same relation to *the proposition* that centaurs exist.

This, then, is one theory which may be held as to the constitution of beliefs—the theory that every belief whether it be true or false always has an *object* which may be called a proposition, and that the belief simply consists in having this proposition before the mind in one particular way—in being conscious of it in the peculiar way which we call 'believing'. And what I want you to notice about this theory is that according to it, *what* is believed—the *object*—the proposition, is something which *is*—there really *is* such a thing in the Universe, *equally* whether the belief be true or false. If, for instance, we believe that lions exist, then whether this belief be true or false, there is such a thing as 'that lions exist', there is such a thing as 'the existence of lions'; because these phrases 'that lions exist', or 'The existence of lions' are a name for *what* is believed—for the proposition that is believed. But this fact creates a difficulty—for as we have seen, it is also the case that it is *only if* the belief be true, that there is such a thing as the existence of lions: if the belief be false, there is no such fact as the existence of lions. What, therefore, this theory must admit, is that, whenever a belief is *true*, there are in the Universe two quite different facts, having exactly the same name, namely (1) the *object* of the belief, the proposition that lions exist, which would be in the Universe equally, even if the belief were false, and (2) the *other* fact that lions exist, the fact, which we should usually call 'the fact that lions exist', which *is* in the Universe only if the belief be *true*. *Both* these two facts are or have being if the belief be true, in exactly the same sense; but since only one of them *is*, if the belief be false, it follows that they must be different from one another, in spite of the fact that they have exactly the same name. The fact that this theory compels us to say that, whenever a belief is true, there thus are in the Universe two different facts, having exactly *the same name*, does I think, suggest a suspicion that the theory is false. But, of course, it is not absolutely fatal to it. It might be the case that we really do thus give the same name to two quite different facts. But what I want to insist on is that the theory *must* admit that the two facts *are* different, in spite of having the *same name*: that they *only* have the same name, and that we must not be led by this into supposing that they are identical.

So much by way of explaining what this theory as to the analysis of belief is. But as I said, this theory also suggests a very simple theory as to the relation of a true belief to the fact to which *it refers*. And, in so doing, it suggests also a new theory as to what truth *is*—a new theory, not incompatible with the old one; since, whereas the former theory only pretended to define the property, which we ascribe to *beliefs* when we call them true, this only suggests that there is another property also called 'truth', which belongs *not* to *beliefs*, but only to the *objects* of belief or propositions.

What then is the theory of truth, which this theory as to the analysis of belief suggests? It is a theory which I myself formerly held, and which certainly has the advantage that it is very simple. It is simply this. It adopts the supposition that in the case of every belief, true or false, there is a proposition which is what is believed, and which certainly is. But the difference between a true and a false belief it says, consists simply in this, that where the belief is true the proposition, which is believed, besides the fact that it *is* or 'has being' also has another simple unanalysable property which may be called 'truth'. 'Truth', therefore, would, on this view, be a simple unanalysable property which is possessed by some propositions and not by others. The propositions which don't possess it, and which therefore we call false, *are* or 'have being'—just as much as those which *do*; only they just have *not* got this additional property of being 'true'. And the explanation of those two different facts having the same name, which *are* in the Universe if a belief is true, and one of which is absent if it is false, and of their relation to one another, would be simply as follows. One of these two facts, the one that *is* equally whether the belief be true or false, is of course, the proposition. And the other one, the one which *is* only if the belief be true, consists simply in the possession by the proposition of the simple property 'truth'.

We should thus have to say that the real existence of lions—the fact to which the *belief* 'that lions exist' *refers*—consists simply in the possession by the *proposition* 'that lions exist' of one simple property. And this would explain, quite simply, what we mean by saying that the fact is *the* one to which the belief refers. The belief in question *is* the belief in the proposition 'that lions exist' and hence the *truth* of that particular proposition is a fact which has to the belief a relation which no other fact has to it. The relation simply consists in the fact that this fact *is* the truth of the particular proposition which is the object of the belief. We should, of course, have to admit that we do give the same name—the name 'that lions exist' or 'the existence of lions' *both* to the mere proposition *and* to the truth of this proposition, i.e., to its possession of the simple property 'truth'. But if we have to admit, in any case, that where a belief is true, there *are* two different facts in the Universe having the same name, namely (1) the proposition and (2) the fact to which the belief refers, there seems no particular reason why this fact, which has the same name as the proposition, should not simply consist in the truth of the proposition. And as I said, this theory that truth is the name of a simple property, which belongs to some propositions and not to others, is quite consistent with our former definition of truth. Our former definition was that to say that a belief is true is to say that there *is* in the Universe *the fact* to which it refers. And we can still maintain the definition along with the new one. We should only have to admit that there are two different senses of the word 'truth', one of which applies to propositions, and the other to beliefs. And it is quite certain that there *are* at least two different senses of the word 'truth', since we certainly do say that sentences—mere forms of words—are true,[1] as well as the beliefs which they express; and no mere form of words can be true, in the same sense in which a belief is so. If, therefore, we have to admit *two* different senses of the word 'truth', one of which, can be defined by reference to the other, why should we not admit a third sense, by reference to which both the others are defined? It would only be admitting that there is (1) one ultimate sense of the word, namely that in which *some* propositions are true, and nothing but a proposition can be; and then, two derivative senses; namely (2) that in which some beliefs are true, and nothing but a belief can be, and (3) that in which some forms of words are true, and nothing but a form of words can be.

We have, then, here a theory of truth which would force us to recognise *two* ultimate and unanalysable notions or properties, the one the property of 'being' which is possessed by all propositions equally, whether true or false, and by many other things as well; and the other a property which may be called 'truth' a property which can only be possessed by propositions, and *is* only possessed by *some* among them—those which don't possess it being called 'false', though they have 'being'. This theory is, I think, a very simple and a very natural one; and I must confess I can't find any conclusive arguments against it. But yet I don't now believe that it is true, though I did formerly. And the chief objections to it—the objections which weigh with me most, though I confess I can't make either of them seem perfectly clear and convincing—are, I think, two. The first is an objection which affects only this particular theory of truth: it does not affect the theory as to the analysis of belief which this theory of truth presupposes.

It is this: namely, that the fact to which a true belief refers—the fact, which *is*, only if the belief be true, and simply has no being at all, if it be false—does not, if you think of it, seem to consist merely

[1] I see no reason now to think that we ever do call sentences or forms of words "true," except in such an archaic-sounding expression as "A true word is often spoken in jest." (1952).

in the possession of some simple property by a proposition—that is to say, by something which has being equally whether the belief be true or false. For instance, the fact that lions really do exist does not seem to consist in the possession of some simple property by the proposition which we believe, when we believe that they exist, even if we grant that there is such a thing as this proposition. The relation of the proposition to the fact doesn't seem to consist simply in the fact that the proposition is a constituent of the fact—one of the elements of which it is composed. This is an objection only to this particular theory as to the constitution of the fact to which a true belief refers. But the second objection is an objection not only to this theory but to the whole analysis of beliefs on which it rests; it is an objection to the supposition that there are such things as propositions at all, and that belief consists merely in an attitude of mind towards these supposed entities. And here again I confess I can't put the objection in any clear and convincing way. But this is the sort of objection I feel. It is that, if you consider what happens when a man entertains a false belief, it doesn't seem as if his belief consisted merely in his having a relation to some object which certainly *is*. It seems rather as if the thing he was believing, the *object* of his belief, were just *the* fact which certainly is *not*—which certainly is not, because his belief is false. This, of course, creates a difficulty, because if the object certainly is *not*—if there *is* no such thing, it is impossible for him or for anything else to have any kind of relation to it. In order that a relation may hold between two things, both the two things must certainly be; and how then is it possible for any one to believe in a thing which simply has no being? This is the difficulty, which seems to arise if you say that false belief does not consist merely in a relation between the believer or the act of belief on the one hand, and something else which certainly *is* on the other. And I confess I do not see any clear solution of the difficulty. But nevertheless I am inclined to think this is what we must say. And certain things can, I think, be said to make the view more plausible.

What I think is quite certain is that when we have before us a *sentence*—a form of words—which *seems* to express a relation between two objects, we must not always assume that the names, which seem to be names of objects between which a relation holds, are always really names of any object at all. This may be exemplified by what is happening to us in the present case. We have been conceiving, for the purpose of our illustration, the hypothesis of our being now actually hearing the noise of a brass-band. We were conceiving this when we said that this is what *would* be happening *if* the belief that we are doing so were true. We certainly *can* conceive this hypothesis: we know what it would be like if we were actually hearing the noise. And in this mere supposing—in merely conceiving an hypothesis without at all believing in it, as in the present case—exactly the same difficulty arises as in the case of false belief. 'We are now conceiving the hypothesis of our being now actually hearing a brass-band'. That *sentence*—the words I have just used—seem to state the facts. And what they seem to state is that there is a relation—the relation which we express by 'conceiving'—between *us* on the one hand, and on the other hand an object of which the name is 'our being now hearing the noise of a brass-band'. But, as we have seen and as is obvious, there *is* nothing at all which is named by this name: there *is* no such thing as our being now hearing that noise. And though you may reply: 'Yes there is such a thing; there *is the proposition* that we are now hearing that noise; *this* is what we conceive; and this most certainly *is*: the *only* thing which *is not* is the fact which would *be*, if the proposition were true'—though you may make this reply and may thus recur to the theory that there may be two different things having the same name, and that though only *one* of them *is* in the present case, yet that one most undoubtedly is: yet surely this reply is not perfectly satisfactory. In merely making it, in distinguishing between the proposition which *is*, and the fact, having the same name, which you admit, in this case, *is not* you are surely conceiving *both*: you could not even say that the fact is *not*, without conceiving it. And hence the conclusion remains that when we say: 'I am conceiving our being now hearing the noise of a brass-band'; though this statement seems to express a relation between us on the one hand, and another object having the name 'Our being now hearing the noise of a brass-band' on the other, yet sometimes at all events it does *not* do this—sometimes, at all events, the latter form of words is *not* a name for anything at all. And once you admit that this is sometimes the case, it seems to me there ceases to be any reason at all for supposing that there *ever* are those two different facts, having the same name—the proposition, on the one hand, and the fact on the other. If, in some cases, when we conceive or believe a thing, there really *is* no such thing as that which we *are said* to believe or conceive—if *sometimes* the words which we seem to use to denote the thing believed or conceived, is not really a *name* of anything at all, I think there is no reason why we should not admit that this is *always* the case in false belief, or in conception of what is purely imaginary. We should then have to say that expressions of the form 'I believe so and so', 'I conceive so and so', though they do undoubtedly express *some* fact, do *not* express any relation between *me* on the other hand and an object of which the name is the words we use to say *what* we believe or conceive. And since there seems plainly no difference, in mere analysis, between false belief and true belief, we should have to say of all belief and supposition generally, that they *never* consist in a relation between the believer and something else which *is* what is believed. Suppose, for instance, that I believe that lions exist, and that this belief is true. There *is* in this case, because the belief is true, a fact having the name 'that lions exist', but my *belief* itself does not consist in a relation between me and that fact, nor between me and any other fact having the same name. The fact that my belief is *true* does, of course, imply that there *is* a relation between me and that fact. But it is the *truth* of my belief which consists in that relation: the belief itself does *not* consist in it. Although we say 'I am believing in the existence of lions', these words 'the existence of lions' don't stand, in this expression, either for *the* fact, which *is*, nor for any fact at all to which I have a relation. They are not a name for anything at all. The whole expression 'I am believing in the existence of lions' is, of course, a name for a fact. But we cannot analyse this fact into a relation between me on the one hand, and a proposition called 'the existence of lions' on the other. This is the theory as to the analysis of belief which I wish to recommend. It may be expressed by saying that there simply are no such things as *propositions*. That belief does *not* consist, as the former theory held, in a relation between the believer, on the one hand, and another thing which may be called the proposition believed. And it seems to me that one at least of the most obvious objections to this theory can be easily answered. It might be thought that if there *are* no such things as propositions then whenever we make statements about them (as we constantly do and must do) all these statements must be nonsense. But this result does not by any means necessarily follow. Of course we can, and must, still continue to talk *as* if there were such things as propositions. We can and must continue to use such expressions as 'the proposition that lions exist', 'the proposition that 2 plus 2 equals 5'—that is to say, we can and must use *sentences*, in which these expressions occur; and many of these sentences will express a fact. For instance the sentence: 'The proposition that 2 plus 2 equals 4 is true', will still be used and will express a fact. All that our theory compels us to say is that one part of this expression, namely the words 'The proposition that 2 plus 2 equals 4', though it seems to be the name of something, is not really a name for anything at all, whereas the whole expression, 'The proposition that 2 plus 2 equals 4 is true' is a name for a fact and a most important fact; and all that our theory says is that we must not suppose that this fact can be analysed into a fact called 'the proposition that twice two are four' and a relation between this fact on the one hand and truth on the other. This is all that the theory requires. It does not require that we should discontinue the use of these expressions, which are not names for anything; or that we should suppose that sentences in which they occur can't be true.[1] On the contrary such sentences will be true just as often as before; and will often be the most convenient way of expressing important facts. Nor will they, as a rule, be misleading. They will only be misleading, if they lead us to make a mistake as to the analysis of the fact which they express, or to suppose that every expression which seems to be a name of something must be so in fact.

But this theory as to the analysis of belief is, of course, only a negative theory. It tells us that beliefs can *not* be analysed in a certain way—that they cannot be analysed into the act of belief on the one hand and the thing believed on the other—but it does not tell us how they can be analysed; and therefore, it gives us no help at all towards solving our original question—the question as to what exactly is the relation between a true belief and the *fact* to which it refers—the relation which we express by saying that the fact in question is *the* fact to which the belief refers. Possibly some positive analysis of a belief *can* be given, which would enable us to answer this question; but I know of none which seems to be perfectly clear and satisfactory. I propose, therefore, to give up the attempt to analyse beliefs. I think it must be admitted that there is a difficulty and a great difficulty in the analysis of them; and I do not know that any one would say they had a theory about the matter which was quite certainly true.

But if we thus admit that we don't know precisely what the analysis of a belief is, does it follow that we must also admit that we don't know what truth is, and what is the difference between truth and falsehood? It might seem as if it did; for how we were led into

[1]I should, of course, now say that such sentences can't be true, because our present use of "true" is such that it is nonsense to say of any *sentence*, that it is true. (See footnote p. 262). I should, therefore, substitute in this sentence and the next the words "express a truth" for the words "be true". (1952)

this discussion as to the nature of beliefs, was because we found an obscurity in our proposed definition of truth, which it seemed impossible we could entirely clear up except by discovering exactly what sort of a thing a belief is. And I think it is true that the failure to analyse belief, does mean a corresponding failure to give a complete analysis of the property we mean by 'truth'. But the point I want to insist on is that nevertheless we may know perfectly clearly and definitely, in one respect, what truth is; and that this thing which we may know about it is by far the most important and essential thing to know. In short, it seems to me that these questions as to the analysis of belief are quite irrelevant to *the* most important question as to the nature of truth. And I want to insist on this, because I think it is very easy not to distinguish clearly the different questions; and to suppose that because, in one respect, we must admit a doubt as to the nature of truth, this doubt should also throw doubt on other more important matters, which are really quite independent of it.

Let me try to state the matter quite precisely, and to explain what I think is quite certain about truth, and how this much can be certain in spite of the doubt as to the nature of belief. What I proposed to give as the definition of truth was as follows. To say that a belief is true is to say that the *fact to which it refers is* or has being; while to say that a belief is false is to say that the fact to which it refers is not—that there is no such fact. Or, to put it another way, we might say: Every belief has the property of *referring to* some particular fact, every different belief to a different fact; and *the* property which a belief has, when it is true—*the* property which we name when we call it true, is the property which can be expressed by saying that *the* fact to which it refers *is*. This is precisely what I propose to submit as the fundamental definition of truth. And the difficulty we found about it was that of defining exactly what is meant by '*referring to*', by talking of *the* fact to which a belief refers. Obviously this expression 'referring to' stands for some relation which each true belief has to one fact and to one only; and which each false belief has to no fact at all; and the difficulty was to define this relation. Well, I admit I can't define it, in the sense of analysing it completely: I don't think this can be done, without analysing belief. But obviously from the fact that we can't analyse it, it doesn't follow that we may not know perfectly well *what* the relation is; we may be perfectly well *acquainted* with it; it may be perfectly familiar to us; and we may know both that there is such a relation, and that this relation is essential to the definition of truth. And what I want to point out is that we do in this sense *know* this relation; that we are perfectly familiar with it; and that we can, therefore, perfectly well understand this definition of *truth*, though we may not be able to analyse it down to its simplest terms. Take any belief you like; it is, I think, quite plain that there is just one fact, and only one, which would have being—would be in the Universe, if the belief were true; and which would have no being—would simply *not be*, if the being were false. And as soon as we know what the belief is, we know just as well and as certainly what the fact is which in this sense corresponds with it. Any doubt as to the nature of the fact is at the same time a doubt as to the nature of the belief. If we don't know exactly what the nature of the belief is, to that extent we don't know the nature of the corresponding fact; but exactly in proportion as we *do* know the nature of the belief, we also know the nature of the corresponding fact. Take, for instance, the belief that lions exist. You may say you don't know exactly what is meant by the existence of lions—what the fact is, which would *be*, if the belief were true and would not be if it were false. But, if you don't know this, then to exactly the same extent you don't know either what the belief is—you don't know what it is to *believe* that lions exist. Or take a much more difficult instance: take a belief in a hypothetical proposition such as 'If it rains tomorrow we shan't be able to have our picnic'. It is, I admit, very difficult to be sure exactly what sort of a fact is expressed by a hypothetical sentence. Many people might say that it oughtn't to be called a fact at all. But nevertheless it is quite natural to say: It *is* a fact that *if* such and such a thing were to happen, such and such a result would follow; we use this expression as exactly equivalent to 'It is true that, if such and such a thing were to happen, such and such a result would follow', and we may be right or wrong in believing that the consequence would follow from the hypothesis, just as much as we may about anything else. And it is I think quite plain that any doubt as to the nature of the fact expressed by a hypothetical sentence, is equally a doubt as to the nature of the corresponding belief. If you don't know what fact it is that *is* when you believe truly that 'If it rains tomorrow, we shan't have our picnic' you also, and precisely to the same extent, don't know what it is to *believe* this. It is, then, I think, quite obvious that for every different belief, there is one fact and one fact only, which would *be*, if the belief were true, and would *not be*, if it were false; and that in every case we know what the fact in question is just as well or as badly as we know what the belief is. We know that this is so; and of course we could not know it, unless we were *acquainted* with the relation between the fact and the belief, in virtue of which just the one fact and one fact only corresponds to each different belief. I admit that the analysis of this relation is difficult. But any attempt to analyse it, of course, presupposes that there is such a relation and that we are acquainted with it. If we weren't acquainted with it, we couldn't even try to analyse it; and if we didn't already know that this relation is *the* relation that is essential to the defining of truth, of course our analysis, however successful, wouldn't get us any nearer to a definition of truth.

I think, therefore, that the most essential point to establish about truth is merely that every belief *does* refer, in a sense which we are perfectly familiar with, though we may not be able to define it, to *one* fact and one fact only, and that to say of a belief that it is true is merely to say that *the* fact to which it refers *is*; while to say of it that it is false is merely to say that the fact to which it refers, *is not*—that there is no such fact. Of course, this may be disputed; but what I want to insist on is that merely in saying this we are stating a clear view, and a view which may be discussed and settled, *without* entering into any questions as to the analysis of belief. And as for the reasons for believing that this is the right definition of truth, they can I think be seen as clearly as anywhere by considering our original instance. Suppose a man were believing now that we *are* hearing the noise of a brass-band. We know quite well what the fact is which *would* be if the belief were true. We also know quite well what the belief is, and that it is something utterly different from the fact, since the belief might certainly *be* at this moment, although the *fact* most certainly *is not*. And we know quite well that this belief, if it did now exist in anybody's mind, would be false. What *is* the property then which this belief (if it existed) would share with other false beliefs, and which we should mean to ascribe to it by saying that it was false? Surely this property simply consists in the fact that *the fact to which it refers*—namely our being now hearing the noise of a brass-band—has no being; and surely we do know quite well, though we may not be able to define, the exact relation between the belief and the fact, which we thus express by saying that this particular fact is *the* fact to which that particular belief *refers*?

Chapter XV

TRUE AND FALSE BELIEFS

DISCUSSION of Chapter XIV shewed that it was not quite clear to everyone in exactly what sense I was using the word 'belief'. So I should like first of all to try to make this clear. A difficulty seemed to be felt because I implied that we might and did commonly *believe* things, even when we were not quite certain or sure about them; and it was suggested that some people, at all events, would never say that they believed a thing, unless they meant that they were quite certain of it. Now it seems to me that in ordinary life we all do constantly make a distinction between merely believing a thing and being quite sure of it; and I will give an instance of the sort of occasion on which we do make this distinction. Suppose two friends of mine are talking about me, at the time of year when people go away for their holidays, and one of them asks: 'Is Moore still in London, or has he gone away for his holidays?' Surely the other might quite naturally reply, 'I *believe* he is still in London, but I am not quite sure.' Surely such language is one of the commonest possible occurrences; and everybody would understand what was meant by it. That is to say, we constantly have cases, where a man quite definitely says: I *do believe* a thing, but I am *not* quite sure of it; and we all of us, I think, understand quite well the distinction between the two states of mind referred to, the one called *merely* 'believing' and the other called 'being sure', and we know that the first may and does constantly occur, where the second is absent. It is easy to multiply similar instances quite indefinitely. For instance, you may ask a member of your family: Has the postman come yet this morning? and get the answer: I believe he has, but I'm not quite sure. And you would never suspect that the person who gave this answer was using words out of their proper senses, or was not stating truly what was the state of his own mind. He *does* really 'believe', in a quite ordinary sense of the word, that the postman has come; and yet it is equally true, that though he does believe it, he is *not* quite sure of it. Or you may go into a shop and ask: Has the parcel I ordered this morning been sent off yet? and the shopman may reply: 'I believe it has, sir, but I am not quite sure. Shall I enquire?' Have you not constantly heard people say things like this; and don't you constantly say them yourselves? I don't know how to convince you how excessively common this distinction between 'believing' and 'being certain' is, if these instances are not sufficient.

But I should be exceedingly surprised if there is a single one of you, who does not, in fact, constantly use language in this way—constantly say and say quite truly, that he does 'believe' a thing, of which he is *not* quite sure. I think, therefore, that so far as I applied the name 'belief' to a state of mind *different* from that of absolute certainty, I was using the word perfectly correctly and in one of its very commonest senses. But then it was suggested that, if 'belief' is thus to be used as a name for something short of absolute certainty, there is no difference between such belief and mere imagination. And here again it is, I think, easy to show that, as a mere question of *language* there is a distinction; that we do, in fact, often distinguish between the two. And this may be shown in the following way. Consider again the first instance I gave; where one friend of mine asks another, 'Is Moore still in London, or has he gone away for his holidays?' In such a case as this, it is, I think, quite plain that the person asked does, in a sense, imagine *both* alternatives—*both* my being in London, and my being gone away—he conceives them both, has them both before his mind; and yet in spite of this, he certainly may 'believe' the one and *not* believe the other. Instead of saying, as I first supposed: 'I believe he is still in London, but I'm not quite sure', he might answer equally naturally, 'I *don't* believe he has gone away, but I'm not quite sure'. That is to say, we certainly do say, and say quite truly that we *don't* believe things which nevertheless we *are* imagining or conceiving, even when we are using 'belief' as a name for something short of absolute certainty. This shews quite clearly that we do, in common life, very often use the name 'belief' as a name for something *intermediate*, in a sense between mere imagination on the one side and certainty on the other. Just as we often 'believe', when we are not quite sure; so we often imagine, when we neither believe in this sense, *nor* are quite sure. It is, therefore, absolutely certain that there are common senses of the words 'belief' and 'imagination', in which you may imagine a thing, which nevertheless you *don't* believe. But this, of course, does not settle *what* the difference is; it does not settle whether the difference between belief and imagination is a difference of *kind* or merely a difference of *degree*. And I think some people would be inclined to say that the difference is merely one of *degree*: that, when for instance my friend says he believes I am still in London, and *doesn't* believe that I have gone away, and is certainly imagining both alternatives, the only real difference between his attitude to the alternative which he says he believes and his attitude to the one he says he does not believe, consists in the fact that he imagines the former more strongly or more vividly. It might be suggested, that is to say, that, when in common language we make a distinction between belief which falls short of certainty and imagination, that is only because we restrict the word 'belief' to imagination which reaches a certain degree of vividness. Thus Hume suggested that the only distinction between belief and imagination lay merely in the degree of vividness; and I think a good many people would still be inclined to agree with him. And against *this* view I think it is not quite easy to find absolutely conclusive arguments. The best I can find are as follows. Take again the case where my friend believes that I am still in London, and doesn't believe that I have gone away for my holidays. So far as I can see, he might quite well be imagining both alternatives *equally* vividly, in spite of the fact that he believes the one and *dis*believes the other. Can anyone profess to be at all certain that this mightn't be the case? Indeed, so far as I can see, he might imagine the alternative which he doesn't believe *more* vividly than the one which he does. The hypothesis that I had gone away for my holidays might be the more interesting one, and he might, therefore, imagine it more vividly, in spite of the fact that he believed the other. And similarly when we imagine two alternative events, which may possibly happen to us in the future, we may desire very strongly that the one should happen rather than the other, and may imagine the one which we desire very much more vividly, and yet all the time we may not believe that it will happen, and may believe that the other one, which we don't desire and don't imagine nearly as vividly, *will* happen instead. It may be said that when we desire a thing very strongly, we can hardly help having *some* degree of belief that it will happen, and that therefore in this case it isn't true to say that we absolutely *don't* believe that it will happen. But even if this be so, it is, I think, certainly the case that we often have less belief—believe less strongly in the thing which we imagine the more vividly; so that the degree of belief *doesn't* coincide with the degree of vividness of imagination; whence it would follow that belief can't differ from *imagination merely* in degree.

It seems to me that if anyone denies this—if anyone maintains that where we have two alternatives both before the mind, and believe one and don't believe the other, or believe one more strongly than the other, the one which we believe or believe most strongly is *always* the one which we imagine the more vividly, the burden of proof rests upon him. It is by no means obvious that it is *always* so. And the case seems to me to be stronger still, if instead of comparing two alternatives, both of which are before the mind on the same occasion, we compare a case of disbelief which occurs at one time, with a case of belief which occurs at another. When I am reading a novel, I often imagine much more vividly the events which the author suggests to me, than I do imagine *now* this historical proposition that William the Conqueror came to England in 1066. Yet even when I am reading the novel, I very often don't believe in the events which I imagine so vividly, whereas I do now believe that William the Conqueror came to England in 1066. For these reasons I think it is pretty certain that the difference between belief and mere imagination is *not* merely one of degree.

There may, of course, be a similar doubt as to whether belief differs in degree only or also *in kind* from *being sure*. And here, we have, I think, to make a distinction. It is quite certain that even where we *feel* quite sure of a thing, we are sometimes mistaken; and hence I should say that mere *feeling sure* does only differ in degree from mere belief: that it is merely a name for a high degree of belief. And if therefore 'being sure' or 'being certain' is used merely as equivalent to *feeling sure*, as it sometimes is; then in that case being sure would also differ from belief only in degree. But the words *being* sure or *being* certain are sometimes used as equivalent to *knowing*, and here, it seems to me, we have not only a difference of degree but also of kind. The obvious difference between mere believing and knowing, is that you can't properly be said to *know* that a thing is so, if in fact it is not so—if you are mistaken about it. So long as you merely believe a thing, however certain of it you may feel, it is always possible you may be mistaken, whereas so soon as you *know* a thing, if you ever do, it is *never* possible you may be mistaken: and this is not a mere difference of degree but also of kind. It seems to me, however, that even where we do *know* that a thing is so, if we ever do, we always do have towards it a high degree of the very same attitude of mind, which constitutes mere belief: so that where we know we always *are* believing, though not *merely* believing; something else is happening as well which constitutes the difference in kind between belief and knowledge. We might, therefore, say that when we *know* that a thing is so (if we ever do) our knowledge consists in feeling sure that it is so, *together with* something else as well. And hence I am going to use the word 'belief' as a name for an attitude of mind, which is present even in knowledge, but is also present, where we don't know but may be mistaken, in all sorts of different degrees down from *feeling sure* to merely imagining. Perhaps this attitude is always present in *some* degree even in mere imagination; only, if it is, then we should have to say that we are believing a thing to some extent, even when we most strongly disbelieve it; since however strongly we may disbelieve it, we certainly are imagining or conceiving it. I am inclined, therefore, to think that it is *not* present always in mere imagination. But it seems to me it *is* present in some cases, where the degree of it is so slight, that we should hardly say we believed. Where a man says 'I am inclined to believe', and implies therefore that he *doesn't* actually believe, I think he really has towards the thing he says he is inclined to believe, exactly the same attitude of mind *in a very slight degree*, which, if it were a little stronger, he would express by saying that he 'believed'. I am, therefore, going to depart from common usage so far as to call such cases, cases of a very slight degree of belief; and also so far as to say that we *do* believe, though we don't *only* believe, but something else as well, even when we know. But those are, I think, the only departures from common usage in my use of the term.

So much, then, as to what I mean by 'belief'. And now I want to return to the question as to the difference between true and false belief; it being understood that false belief is a thing which can only occur in cases of *mere* belief, as distinguished from knowledge.

And as to the distinction between true and false belief, I can, I think, to begin with, state more clearly now the main points which I wanted to make last time.

Suppose that (to take the instance I gave just now) my friend believes that I *have* gone away for my holidays. There is, I think, no doubt whatever that there is at least *one* ordinary sense of the words 'true' and 'false', such that the following statements hold. We should, I think, certainly say, in the first place, that if this belief of his is *true* then I *must* have gone away for my holidays; his belief that I have gone away can't be true unless I actually have gone away: and, conversely, we should also say that *if* I *have* gone away, then this belief of his certainly *is* true; *if* I have gone away, and he believes that I have, then his belief can't be other than true. In other words, my having actually gone away for my holidays is both a *necessary* and a *sufficient* condition for the truth of this belief: the belief can't be true unless this condition is fulfilled, and it *must* be true, *if* this condition is fulfilled. Surely it is quite plain that at least one sense, in which we commonly use the word 'truth', is of such a nature that these statements are correct. And similarly we may, I think, make the following statements as to the conditions which are necessary and sufficient, if this belief is to be false. We can say: That if this belief is *false*, then I *can't* have gone away for my holidays; the belief that I have gone away can't possibly be false, *if* I *have* gone away: and, conversely, *if* I have not gone away, then the belief that I *have* gone away certainly *must* be false; if I have *not* gone away, and he believes that I *have*, his belief certainly is false. In other words, my *not* having actually gone away is both a necessary and a sufficient condition for the falsehood of this belief. The belief can't be false, unless this condition is fulfilled, and it *must* be false, *if* this condition is fulfilled. It is surely quite plain that one sense at least, in which we use the word 'false', is, of such a nature, that these statements are correct. I don't know that anyone would dispute this much, and I don't well see how it can be disputed.

We have, therefore, found a condition which is both necessary and sufficient for the truth of this belief, in at least one sense of the word 'truth', and also a condition which is both necessary and sufficient for its falsehood, in at least one sense of the word 'false'. If, therefore, we are to find a correct definition of these senses of the words 'true' and 'false' it must be a definition which does not conflict with the statement that these conditions are necessary and sufficient conditions. But the statement that these conditions are necessary and sufficient does not in itself *constitute* a definition. And I think that part of the trouble about the definition of truth and falsehood arises from the fact that people are apt to suppose that they do. We may be easily tempted to make the following assertion. We may assert: 'To say that the belief that I have gone away is *true*, is *the same thing* as to say that I have gone away: this is the very definition of what we *mean* by saying that the belief is true.' We should, in fact, in ordinary language, say that the two statements do *come to the same thing*; that the one amounts to exactly the same thing as the other. And what we *mean* by this is, of course true. The two statements do really come to the same thing, in the sense we mean. That is to say, they are strictly equivalent: provided that my friend's belief exists at all, neither can be true, unless the other is true too; neither of the facts expressed, can be a fact, unless the other is a fact also. But nevertheless it is, I think, quite plain that the two facts in question are not strictly speaking the same fact; and that to assert the one is not, strictly speaking, the same thing as to assert the other. When we assert: 'The belief that I have gone away is true', we mean to assert that this belief has some property, which it shares with other true beliefs: the possession by it of this property is the fact asserted. But in merely asserting 'I have gone away', we are not attributing any property at all to this belief—far less a property which it shares with other true beliefs. We are merely asserting a fact, which might quite well be a fact, even if no one believed it at all. Plainly I might have gone away, without my friend believing that I had; and if so, his belief would not be true, simply because it would not exist. In asserting, then, that his belief is true, I am asserting a different fact from that which I assert when I merely say that I have gone away. To say that his belief is true is *not*, therefore, strictly speaking, the same thing as to say that I have gone away.

What property is there, then, which this belief, if true, really does share with other true beliefs? Well, it seems to me we can see quite plainly that this belief, if true, has to the fact that I have gone away a certain relation, which that particular belief has to no other fact. This relation, as I admitted and tried to shew last time, is difficult to define, in the sense of analysing it: I didn't profess to be able to analyse it. But we do, I think, see this relation; we are all perfectly familiar with it; and we can, therefore, define it in the sense of pointing out what relation it is, by simply pointing out that it is *the* relation which does hold between this belief, if true, and this fact, and does not hold between this belief and any other fact. Surely you are aware of a relation which would hold between the belief that I had gone away, if true, and the fact that I had gone away—a relation which would hold, between that belief, if true, and that particular fact, and would not hold between that belief and any other fact—a relation which is expressed as I pointed out last time by the partial identity of name between the belief and the fact in question. *The* relation I mean is the relation which the belief '*that I have gone away*', if true, has to the fact '*that I have gone away*', and to no other fact; and which is expressed by the circumstance that the name of the belief is 'The belief that I have gone away' while the name of the fact is 'That I have gone away'. We may take different views as to what the exact nature of this relation is—as to how it is to be analysed, and as to how it resembles or differs from other relations; but in merely attempting to answer these questions, we do, I think, presuppose that we are already acquainted with it—that we have it before our minds; for you cannot try to determine the nature of, or to compare with other things, a thing which you have not got before your mind. Well, it seems to me that the difficulty of *defining* truth and falsehood arises chiefly from the fact that this relation, though we are all acquainted with it, has no unambiguous name; it has no *name* which is just appropriated to it alone, and which may not also be used for other relations, which are perhaps quite different from it. The moment we do give it a name, it becomes, I think, quite easy to define truth and falsehood. Let us give it a name and see how the definition turns out. I propose to call it the relation of 'correspondence'. Only, in giving it this name it must be remembered that I mean by 'correspondence' merely this particular relation which does hold between this particular belief, if true, and the fact that I have gone away, and which does not hold between that precise belief and any other fact. The name 'correspondence' is perhaps used also on other occasions for other relations quite different from this; and I don't mean for a moment to suggest that this relation for which I am using it now either resembles or is different from these other relations in any respect whatever. It must be clearly understood that I mean to use the name 'correspondence' *merely* as a name for *this* particular relation. Well then, using the name 'correspondence' *merely* as a name for this relation, we can at once assert 'To say that this belief is true is to say that there is in the Universe *a* fact to which it corresponds; and that to say that it is false is to say that there is *not* in the Universe any fact to which it corresponds'. And this statement I think, fulfils all the requirements of a definition—a definition of what we actually mean by saying that the belief is true or false. For the properties which we have now identified with truth and 'falsehood' respectively *are* properties which this belief may *share* with other true and false beliefs. We have said that to say it is true is merely to say that it does correspond to a fact; and obviously this *is* a property which may be common to it and other beliefs. The shopman's belief, for instance, that the parcel we ordered this morning has been sent off, may have the property of corresponding to a fact, just as well as this belief that I have gone away may have it. And the same is true of the property which we have now identified with the falsehood of the belief. The property which we have identified with its falsehood is merely that of not corresponding to any fact; and obviously this is a property which may belong to any number of other beliefs just as well as to this one. Moreover it follows from these definitions that the conditions which we saw to be necessary and sufficient for the truth or falsehood of this belief *are* necessary and sufficient for it: there is not only no conflict between these definitions and the statement that these conditions are necessary and sufficient, but it actually follows from the definitions that they are so. For as we have seen the relation which we are calling 'correspondence', is a relation which *does* hold between the belief 'that I have gone away', if true, and the fact that I have gone away, and which does not hold between this belief and any other fact whatever. And hence it follows that if this belief does correspond to a fact at all, then it must *be a fact* that I have gone away: that is to say, if the belief does correspond to a fact, then I *must* have gone away; the belief can't correspond to a fact, unless I have. And conversely it also follows, that *if* I have gone away, then the belief does correspond to a fact: if I have gone away, the belief *must* correspond to a fact; it can't be the case that I have gone away, and that yet the belief corresponds to no fact. It follows actually therefore, from this definition of truth, that the condition which we saw to be both necessary and sufficient for the truth of this belief is necessary and sufficient for it. And in the same way it follows from our definition of falsehood that the condition which we saw to be necessary and sufficient for its falsehood *is* necessary and sufficient for it. The only point as to which I can see any room for doubt whether these definitions do fulfil all the requirements of a definition of the words 'true' and 'false' as we should apply them to this particular belief, is that it may be doubted whether when we say that the belief is 'true' or 'false', these properties of 'corresponding to a fact' and 'not corresponding to a fact' are the properties which we actually *have before our minds* and express by those words. This is a question which can only be settled by actual inspection; and I admit that it is difficult to be quite sure what result the inspection yields. But I see no reason for answering it in the negative. I see no reason why when we say: The belief that I have gone away is true, the thought which we actually have before our minds and express by these words should *not* be the thought that: The belief in question does correspond to a fact—similarly I see no reason why when we say 'The belief that I have gone away is false' the thought which we actually have before our minds and express by these words should *not* be the thought that the belief in question does *not* correspond to any fact. However, whether *this* is so or not—whether to say that this belief is true is or is not quite strictly the *same* thing as to say that it does correspond to a fact; it is, I think, quite certain that the two expressions are strictly equivalent. When the belief is true, it certainly does correspond to a fact; and when it corresponds to a fact it certainly is true. And similarly when it is false, it certainly does not correspond to any fact; and when it does not correspond to any fact, then certainly it is false.

I want to suggest, therefore, that these definitions really are correct definitions at least of *one* common sense of the words 'true' and 'false': of the sense in which we use the words when we apply them to beliefs such as the one I have taken as an instance. And the only thing that is new about these definitions, so far as I know, is that they assign a perfectly strict and definite sense to the word 'correspondence'; they define this word by pointing out *the* relation for which it stands; namely *the* relation which certainly does hold between the belief that 'I have gone away', if that belief is true, and the *fact* that I have gone away, and which does *not* hold between that precise belief and any other fact. That there *is* such a relation, seems to me clear; and all that is new about my definitions is that they concentrate attention upon just *that* relation, and make *it* the essential point in the definitions of truth and falsehood. The use of the word 'correspondence' as a name for this relation may perhaps be misleading; and so may the word I used instead last time—the word 'referring to'. Both these words may lead you to think that the relation in question is similar to or identical with other relations that are called by the same names on other occasions. And I am particularly anxious not to suggest either that this relation is identical with or similar to any other relation or that it is not: I don't want to pronounce upon that point at all. I don't want, therefore, to insist upon the word 'correspondence'. The essential point is to concentrate attention upon the relation *itself*: to hold it before your mind, in the sense in which when I name the colour 'vermilion', you can hold before your mind the colour that I mean. If you are not acquainted with this relation in the same sort of way as you are acquainted with the colour vermilion, no amount of words will serve to explain what it is, any more than they could explain what vermilion is like to a man born blind. But, if I am right then we are all acquainted with the relation in question; and, if so, then the important point is that it is this relation itself, and not any words by which we may try to name it or to point it out, that is essential to the definition of truth and falsehood.

But now I have only claimed so far that the definitions I have given are correct definitions, or at least equivalents, for *one* of the senses in which we commonly use the words 'true' and 'false', when we apply them to beliefs. And I will drop the contention that they are actually definitions—that they are even what we actually *mean* when we say of a belief that it is true or that it is false. I don't profess to be sure that they are definitions in this sense, though, I think they are, and the important point seems to me to be merely that they *are* equivalents. All that I claim then so far is that, very often, when we say that a belief is true, a necessary and sufficient condition for its being so is simply this—that it should correspond to a fact: in the precise sense I have tried to explain. *If* it does correspond to a fact, then it is true in the sense we mean and if it does *not* correspond to a fact, then it is not true in the sense we mean. But, of course, it might be said, that though this is very often the case, it is not *always* so, and that for two different reasons. It might be said, in the first place, that in the case of absolutely *every* belief there is some other sense of the word 'true' in which it may be true, in spite of not corresponding to any fact; and similarly, that there is some other sense of the word 'true' such that a belief may fail to be 'true' in the sense in question even though it *does* correspond to a fact. This is one thing which might be said; and I am willing to allow that this may be the case. Indeed, as I shall presently explain, I think it is the case: I think that some beliefs may be true, *in a sense*, without corresponding to any fact; though I am inclined to think that this is only the case with some beliefs, not with all. And though I see no reason to think that there is any sense at all, in which a belief, which does correspond to a fact, can fail to be true; I am willing to admit that this also *may* be the case. This, then is one view which might be taken, and which I am not anxious to dispute. And another view which might be taken is that in the case of some beliefs, it is absolutely impossible that they should correspond to any fact in the sense I have explained and that yet they may be true. And this also I am willing to admit may be the case, though I know of no instance where it does seem absolutely impossible that a true belief should correspond to a fact. I have only mentioned these two views because I want to make it quite plain that I am not particularly concerned to dispute them. All that I am anxious to maintain is that *very often* when we say that a belief is true, the belief in question has the property which we mean to ascribe to it and which we express by the word 'true', if and only if it corresponds to a fact. That is the whole point of my theory of truth. And the main recommendation of this theory seems to me to lie in the fact that it does take account of and does not conflict with many millions of the most obvious facts. One such obvious fact is that my friend's belief that I have gone away for the holidays certainly will be true, in one common sense of the word, *if* and only if I actually have gone away. Another such obvious fact is that the shopman's belief that the parcel I ordered this morning has been sent off, will be true, in one common sense of the word, if and only if the parcel actually has been sent off. And obviously, if you chose, you could think of many millions of other instances as obvious as these. In millions of instances then it seems quite plain that a belief is true, in one common sense of the word, *if* and only if there is in the Universe a fact having the same name as that which we use in describing the belief—a fact standing to the belief in that peculiar relation in which the facts I have named in these two instances would obviously stand to the beliefs in question, if the beliefs were true—in short the relation which I have called 'correspondence'. It seems to me that the great defect of some other theories of truth and falsehood is that they seem to conflict with these millions of obvious facts; and I will mention two such theories which many people seem inclined to hold just now, in order to point out exactly how and why they do seem to me to conflict with them.

The first theory I wish to mention is a theory—or perhaps rather a whole set of different theories, which are advocated by some philosophers who call themselves 'Pragmatists'. The sort of thing that Pragmatists say, when they talk about truth, is that the essence of true beliefs, as distinguished from false ones, is that true beliefs 'work'. I say this is the *sort* of thing they say, because they don't always say exactly this, but sometimes other things different from and even incompatible with it; and that is one reason why I think we can hardly talk of any one theory of truth held by Pragmatists, but rather of a whole set of different theories. And another reason is that they leave it very vague, as to what they mean by saying that a belief 'works', and when they do try to explain, they often give quite different explanations in different places: sometimes they seem to say that to 'work' is the same thing as to be 'useful', sometimes that to 'work' means to lead up to some kind of satisfaction, sometimes that it means to lead, in the long run, to some kind of satisfaction, and so on. However, I think we may say, roughly, that by saying that a belief 'works', they do always mean that it leads up to some kind of satisfactory effect, though, of course, they might define the kind of satisfactory effect that is necessary differently in different places. Well then, it seems to me that Pragmatists often talk as if beliefs were true, if and *only* if they lead up to the right kind of satisfactory effect (whatever that may be) and as if no other condition were necessary for a belief to be true: some of them, perhaps, would not say that they meant this: they might say that they only meant it to apply to certain kinds of beliefs, or that they only meant it to apply to one sense of the word 'truth'. And it seems to me there are objections to their view, even if this were all that they meant. But I am not now concerned with this particular form of Pragmatism, if anyone holds it. It seems to me they certainly often talk as if their theory applied to *truth* in general, and as if, therefore, provided only that a belief led up to the right kind of satisfactory effect, it would always be 'true', in every sense of the word, no matter what kind of belief it was. But you see what this implies. It implies that my friend's belief that I had gone away for my holidays, might be true in every sense of the word, even if I had *not* gone away: that it would be thus *true*, provided only it led up to certain kinds of satisfactory results. And similarly, of course, in millions of other instances. It implies in short, that it is quite unnecessary for any belief to correspond to a fact, in the sense which I have defined, in order that it should be 'true'; and that any belief may be true in every sense of the word, *without* doing this. And that they so often seem to imply this seems to me to be the most fundamental objection to what Pragmatists *say* about truth. Whether any of them would say that they actually meant this, I don't know: I am inclined to think some of them would. But whether they would or not, it is, I think, certainly a view which they often have before their minds and are actually believing whether or not they know that they are. That is to say, they do, I think, really often hold that a belief like that of my friend's that I have gone away for my holidays, might be 'true', in *every* important sense of the word, even if I had *not* gone away.

But perhaps it should be said, in fairness to them, that they seem sometimes to mean something quite different from this—something which, though it is quite different, they don't seem to distinguish very clearly from it. And I want to mention this other view, because it brings out a point about which there is very liable to be confusion. I have already explained that all that I am really anxious to maintain is that in millions of instances and in one of the commonest and most important senses of the word 'truth' a belief is true, always if *and only* if it corresponds to a fact. That is to say I am only maintaining that this property of correspondence to a fact is a *criterion* or test of truth; not that it is the very meaning of the word 'truth'—its actual definition—though I am inclined to think that it is this, too. By a criterion or test of truth, we mean, then, a property which is always present, where truth is present, and never present where truth is not present; so that if we could discover in any particular instance whether the property in question did or did not belong to a belief, we should be able to judge from this, whether the belief was or was not true. This question as to what are the criteria or tests of truth is, of course, a question which has been much discussed by philosophers, and ever so many different criteria have been suggested. And the point I want to emphasize is that it is, of course, abstractly possible, that there may be ever so many *different* criteria, all equally good ones: that there are, in short, ever so many different properties, each of which belongs to every true belief and only to true beliefs. Well, one thing which Pragmatists seem sometimes to mean is merely that the property they talk of—the property of leading to some kind of satisfactory effect—is *a criterion* of truth. And, of course, so far as this was all they meant, their theory would not be open to the objection I just urged against it. Merely to say this would not imply that a belief might be true, even if it did not correspond to any fact. It would only imply that every belief which did lead to the right kind of satisfactory result did *also* correspond to a fact. And this, I think, is one conclusion which they actually often want to draw from their theory. They want to convince us that, wherever a belief does lead to certain kinds of satisfactory result, then it *does* correspond to a fact. And, of course, to this theory—the theory that the leading to certain kinds of satisfactory results is a *test* of truth, the objections are quite different: I shall presently have to consider them, in connection with another subject. What I want to emphasize now is how completely different this theory is, from the other one which I also attributed to them. This one merely says: The property of leading to satisfactory results always goes with the property of corresponding to a fact: wherever you have the one property you also do in fact have the other. Whereas the former one said: wherever this property of leading to satisfactory results belongs to a belief, that belief is true, *even if it does not correspond to any fact.*

So much for the Pragmatists' theory of truth. And the second theory about truth which I wish to mention because it seems to me to conflict with millions of obvious facts, is a theory which is, I think, held by Mr. Bradley among others. The theory I mean is merely a theory *about* truth and falsehood. It does not profess to give a *definition* of them, nor even a *criterion* of them. It merely lays down a universal proposition about true and false beliefs; and the proposition it lays down is this. It says: 'Absolutely every belief, without exception, is *both* partially true, and *also* partially false; no belief is *wholly* true, and none is *wholly* false; but absolutely all are *partially* both'.

Now this statement is, I think, for some reason or other, fearfully difficult to discuss. It seems to be extremely difficult to state the objections to it quite clearly and conclusively; and I am sure there must be some better way of doing it than any that I have found. The difficulty is, I think, first that it doesn't seem quite obviously, as it stands, to contradict any clear facts; and it is also very difficult to find any argument to shew quite clearly that it does. You might, indeed, take a particular instance of a belief such as I have taken: Suppose that I have gone away for my holidays, and that my friend believes that I have. It is quite plain, as we have seen, that this belief would, in such a case, be true in one common sense of the words: and I will call this the ordinary sense. Well, then, taking this as a belief which is true in the ordinary sense: we might ask: Is this belief really only partially true? Is it really partially false? And you might be disposed to say that, quite obviously the belief in question is not partially false, that it is *wholly* true. And I must admit this does seem to me fairly obvious. If I have gone away for my holidays, and what my friend believes is just that I have gone away—that and nothing more, it does seem fairly obvious that his belief is *wholly* true. And it also seems obvious that such a case might occur. It *might* be a fact that I had gone away for my holidays; surely this is a thing which might be in the Universe: and it might also be a fact that my friend believed it. You might, therefore, say: 'Here we have a case of a belief of a sort which certainly does constantly occur which is *not* partially false. And this alone is sufficient to refute the statement that *all* beliefs are partially false.'

And of course millions of other instances could be found which are *as* evident as this one. But I'm afraid this argument, as it stands, certainly wouldn't be convincing to any one who is inclined to hold Mr. Bradley's doctrine: and, I think, we must own that it isn't perfectly satisfactory: it doesn't put the matter in the clearest light. I want, therefore, to try to give another argument. And what I want to try to shew is this. It is plain that anybody who says these things: who says: Every belief is partially false must mean *something* by the word 'false'. And what I want to shew is that, *if* he is using the word 'false' in what I have called the *ordinary* sense, then, if *his* view that every belief is partially false were true, it would follow that absolutely every belief is wholly false in the same sense. If *all* beliefs were partially false, it does, I think, follow that all are *wholly* false. And hence it follows that there can never be any such fact as my having gone away for my holidays, or even as my being in London now. If any one believes that I am not in London now his belief must be *wholly* false because it can't be a fact that I am not in London. This, I think, is the conclusion which really follows from Mr. Bradley's doctrine. And I am not sure that he himself would not accept this conclusion. But to talk, as he does, as if this belief were *partially* true certainly serves to conceal the fact that this conclusion does follow. It serves to conceal the fact that in reality his doctrine is that *every* belief is, in the ordinary sense of the word, *wholly* false. And, I think, the doctrine owes its plausibility partly to the fact that this is concealed. What therefore, I want to try to bring out is that this conclusion does follow.

But, in order to do this, we must consider what he can mean by the phrase 'partially false', supposing that the word 'false' is used in its ordinary sense.

This phrase has, I think, undoubtedly one clear meaning; and I think it is clear that some beliefs really *are* partially but not wholly false. The fact is that when we talk of a belief, even when we can express it all in one sentence, the belief certainly often includes several different beliefs: when we are entertaining the belief, we are believing several different things at the same time, and some of these things may be true. For instance, you may believe that the colour of a dress which you saw in a picture this afternoon was maroon. And when you believe this you may be believing two different things at the same time. You will be believing, in the first place that the colour you saw was identical with the one you are now thinking of, whatever that may be: and of course this is one matter about which you may be right or wrong; a subsequent visit to the picture may convince you that you were mistaken as to this. But in the second place you may also be believing that the colour you are thinking of is what other people would call 'maroon'; in other words you may be entertaining a belief about the connection of the colour before your mind with a particular name—the name 'maroon'. And here again you may be right or wrong: although you may be right in thinking that the colour before your mind is the colour that you saw in the picture, you may be quite wrong in thinking that the right name for this colour is 'maroon'. I think such cases do constantly occur in which part of your belief at a given time is true and part false, although we should call the whole one belief. But now what I want to call attention to is that in such a case the whole belief taken as a whole, is just simply false in the ordinary sense of the word. Taking the whole belief to be 'that the colour you saw this afternoon is the one you now have before your mind and that the name of this colour is "maroon",' it is plain that this *whole combination* does not correspond to any fact: there is no such fact as that 'the colour before your mind is the one you saw this afternoon and that its name is "maroon".' Where, therefore, a belief is partially false, the whole belief, *as a whole*, is just simply false, in the ordinary sense of the word: and the only thing that saves it from being *wholly* false, is that a part of it is not false in this sense. But *this* part of it, which is *not* false in the ordinary sense is also a belief. And if therefore, *every* belief were partially false, there could be no part of it which was not just simply false in the ordinary sense. If, therefore, every belief were partially false, it really does follow that *every* belief must be *wholly false*. The only thing that makes it possible for *any* belief to be partially but not wholly false, is that it should have some part which is not even partially false. For it must have some part which is *not* just simply false, in the ordinary sense of the word. And we have seen that every partially false belief is just simply false in this ordinary sense. So that, if *every* belief were partially false, no belief could have any part at all which was *not* just simply false in the ordinary sense. This is the point on which the whole argument depends; and I am afraid it is not quite an easy one to see. But I think it does prove that if *every* belief were partially false, every belief must also be wholly so.

And what follows from this is that, if Mr. Bradley is using the word 'false' in its ordinary sense, then it really does follow from his doctrine that all our beliefs are *wholly* false in this ordinary sense. Of course, if he be using the word in some quite different sense, it might possibly be the case that, *in that sense*, all our beliefs were partially false and none of them wholly so. But if he is only using the word in some other than its ordinary sense, then his doctrine can form no objection to our saying that, *in* the ordinary sense of the word, many of our beliefs are *wholly* true. Indeed what we have seen is that, if any of our beliefs *are* partially false, in the ordinary sense of the word, *some* of them *must* be wholly true: there must be some which are not even partially false. And this point—the point that some of our beliefs are *wholly* true in this ordinary sense, is the point I want to insist on. This ordinary sense is certainly *a* very important sense of the word 'true', even if it is not the only important sense of that word. And I think Mr. Bradley does, in fact, mean to deny that any of our beliefs are *wholly* true, even in this ordinary sense. I think he would object to our saying that any of them are wholly true in any sense at all. I think, therefore, that this argument is in fact not merely a defence of my own doctrine, but also an attack on his.

Chapter XVI

BEING, FACT AND EXISTENCE

I have been discussing certain questions bearing on the meaning of the words 'real' and 'true', in the hope of discovering exactly what is the nature of the immensely important properties which are suggested to our minds by those words. And I want now to remind you what the point was from which we started on those discussions.

I started on them with two different objects. The first was this. We found that Mr. Bradley asserted most emphatically that Time is *not* 'real'; while on the other hand he seemed to assert, equally emphatically, that Time *does* 'exist', and indubitably '*is*'. And in combining these two assertions he certainly does not think that he is contradicting himself and talking nonsense. But he certainly is contradicting himself unless the property which he denotes by the phrase 'is real', is a different property from the one which he denotes by the phrases 'exists', and 'is'. And one of my objects was to try to discover whether this is so or not—whether he really has two different properties before his mind when he uses the one word, and when he uses the other two; and, *if* he has, what these two different properties are, and how they differ from one another. This question as to what Mr. Bradley means was one of the two questions which I wished to answer. And the second was this. I wished, partly for its own sake, and partly for the sake of the light it might throw on Mr. Bradley's meaning, to try to answer the question: What do we commonly mean by the five phrases 'is real', 'exists', 'is a fact', 'is', and 'is true'? What property or properties do those phrases commonly stand for? These two questions—the question as to Mr. Bradley's meaning, and the direct question as to the ordinary meaning of those five phrases—were the two questions I wished to answer. And I hope my discussion may at least have shewn, that there really are great difficulties in answering both questions. There are, in fact, many other difficulties besides the ones which I have pointed out and discussed. But I have already spent much more time on this discussion than I originally intended; and so now I want merely to try to state as clearly and simply as I can what I think is the correct answer to these two questions. Beginning with the question as to the ordinary meaning of the five phrases, I shall try first to point out what seems to me to be the *most important* notions or properties for which they stand; I must confine myself to the *most important*, for I cannot hope to be absolutely exhaustive. And, then, I shall try to state as briefly and clearly as possible what I take to be the real state of Mr. Bradley's mind when he says the things he does say about Time.

The most important difficulty about the meaning of the five phrases, and the strongest excuse for making a sharp distinction such as Mr. Bradley makes, still seems to me to lie in the fact from which I started—the fact that it seems as if purely imaginary things, even though they be absolutely self-contradictory like a round square, must still have some kind of *being*—must still *be* in a sense—simply because we can think and talk about them. It seems quite clear that, in a sense, there *is* not and cannot be such a thing as a round square: but, if there is not, how can I possibly think and talk about it? And I certainly can think and talk about it. I am doing so now. And not only can I make and believe propositions about it: I can make *true* propositions about it. I know that a round square, if there were such a thing, would be both round and not round: it is a fact that this is so. And now in saying that there is no such thing as a round square, I seem to imply that there *is* such a thing. It seems as if there must *be* such a thing, merely in order that it may have the property of *not* being. It seems, therefore, as if to say of anything whatever that we can mention that it absolutely *is not*, were to contradict ourselves: as if absolutely everything we can mention must *be*, must have some kind of being.

But, if we consider the analogous case of false beliefs, it seems to me to become quite clear that we can think of things which nevertheless are *not*: have no being at all. For instance, one of my friends might be believing of me now, *that I am not in London*. This is a belief which certainly might quite easily be now occurring. And yet there certainly is no such thing as my *not* being now in London. I *am* in London; and that settles the matter. As we have seen, it may be held that, *if* any friend of mine is believing this now, then there *is*, in a sense, such a thing as my *not* being now in London; it may be held that there *must* be such a thing as the object of my friend's belief—the *proposition* which he believes—and that the words 'that I am not now in London' are a name for this proposition, which undoubtedly *is*. And I don't mean now to dispute this view, though as I said, I don't think it is true. Let us grant that it *is* true. Even if it is true, it remains a fact that *one* thing, which those words *would* stand for, if his belief were true, certainly *is not*. It remains true that in *one* sense of the words there *is* no such thing as my not being now in London. In other words, even though we take the view that, where a belief is true, there are in the Universe two different things having the same name, and that, where it is false, then there is only one of those two things—even though we take this view, yet it remains a fact that, if the belief is false, there certainly is, in a sense, no such thing as my not being now in London; and that this very thing which certainly *is not*, is the very thing that we are now conceiving or imagining, even if, in order to do so, we have also at the same time to think of something else, having the same name, which certainly is. We must, therefore, I think, admit that we can, in a sense, think of things, which absolutely have no being. We must *talk* as if we did. And when we so talk and *say* that we do, we certainly do mean *something* which is a fact, by so talking. When, for instance, my friend believes that I am *not* in London, whereas in fact I am, he *is* believing that I am not in London: there is no doubt of that. That is to say this whole expression 'he believes that I am not in London' does express, or is the name for, a fact. But the solution of the difficulty seems to me to be this, namely that this whole expression does *not* merely express, as it seems to, a relation between my friend on the one hand and a fact of which the name is 'that I am not in London' on the other. It does *seem* to do this; and that is where the difficulty comes in. It does seem as if the words 'that I am not in London' *must* be a name for something to which my friend is related, something which certainly *has being*. But we must admit, I think, that these words may not really be a name for anything at all. Taken by themselves they are not a name for anything at all, although the whole expression 'he believes that I am not in London' are a name for something. This fact that single words and phrases which we use will constantly seem to be names for something, when in fact they are not names for anything at all, is what seems to me to create the whole difficulty. Owing to it, we must, in talking of this subject, constantly seem to be contradicting ourselves. And I don't think it is possible wholly to avoid this appearance of contradiction. In merely saying 'There is no such thing as a chimaera' you must seem to contradict yourself, because you seem to imply that 'a chimaera' is a name for something, whereas at the same time the very thing which you assert about this something is that it *is not*: that there is no such thing. The point to remember is that though we *must* use such expressions, and that though the whole expressions *are* names for facts, which certainly *are*, these facts cannot be analysed into a subject 'a chimaera' on the one hand, and something which is asserted of that subject on the other hand.

The question how such facts *are* to be analysed is of course another question, which presents great difficulties; and I don't pretend to be able to answer it. But what, I think, is clear is that they *can't* be analysed in the way proposed. In short we mustn't suppose that there *is* such a thing as a chimaera, merely because we can do something which we call thinking of it and making propositions about it. We aren't in fact really even mentioning a chimaera when we talk of one; we are using a word which isn't, by itself, a name for anything whatever.

I am going to say, then, in spite of the contradiction which such language seems to imply, that certain things which we can think of and talk about really have *no* being, in any sense at all. I think it is quite plain that wherever we entertain a false belief—whenever we make a mistake—there really is, in a sense, no such thing as *what* we believe in; and though such language does *seem* to contradict itself, I don't think we can express the facts at all except by the use of language which does seem to contradict itself; and if you understand what the language means, the apparent contradiction doesn't matter. And the first and most fundamental property which I wish to call attention to, as sometimes denoted by some of our five phrases, is just this one which *does* belong to *what* we believe in, whenever our belief is true, and which does *not* belong to *what* we believe in, whenever our belief is false. I propose to confine the name *being* to this property; and I think you can all see what the property in question is. If, for instance, you are believing now that I, while I look at this paper, am directly perceiving a whitish patch of colour, and, if your belief is true then there *is* such a thing as *my being now directly perceiving* a whitish patch of colour. And I think you can all understand in what sense there is such a thing. As a matter of fact, there really *is*. I *am* now directly perceiving a patch of whitish colour. But even if there weren't, you could all understand what would be meant by supposing that there *is*. This property, then, which does so plainly belong to this event (or whatever you like to call it) is the one I am going to call 'being'; and this seems to me to be the most fundamental property that can be denoted by any of our five phrases.

Another way of pointing out what this property is which I mean by 'being', and a way which does, I think, serve to make it clearer in some respects, is to say that to have being is equivalent to belonging *to the Universe*, being a constituent of the Universe, being *in* the Universe. We may say that whatever has being *is* a constituent of the Universe; and that *only* what has being can be a constituent of the Universe: to say of anything that there *is no such thing*, that it simply *is not*, is to say of it that it is not one among the constituents of the Universe, that it has no place in the Universe at all. This distinction between belonging to the Universe and not belonging to it does, I think, seem clearer in some respects than the mere distinction between being and not-being. Only, if we use this way of explaining what we mean we must recognise that the explanation is, in certain respects, inaccurate, and liable to be misunderstood. In the first place, if we say that 'to be' is equivalent to being a constituent of the Universe, this, taken strictly, would imply that it is *only* things which are constituents of the Universe which have being at all, and hence that the Universe, itself, as a whole, has no being—that there *is* no such thing. But this is perhaps absurd. It is natural to think that the Universe as a whole has being in exactly the same sense in which its constituents have it. So that, to speak quite strictly, we should perhaps have to say that the only things which have being are (1) the whole Universe itself and (2) all its constituents. For this reason alone it is not quite accurate to say that to 'be' is equivalent to 'being a constituent of the Universe'; since the Universe itself may form an exception to this rule: the Universe as a whole is certainly not a mere constituent of itself, and yet it seems as if it had being.

In the second place, if we use this conception of 'belonging to the Universe' to explain what we mean by 'being', we may be tempted to suppose that to say that a thing 'is' or 'has being' is not merely *equivalent* to but strictly the *same thing* as to say that it belongs to the Universe. And this, I think, would be also a mistake. If this were so, we should not be able to think that a thing had being, without first thinking of the Universe as a whole, and thinking that the thing in question belonged to it. But this is certainly not the case. People can think that certain things *are* and others *are not*, before they have even formed the conception of the Universe as a whole; and even when we have formed it, we certainly don't have it before our minds every time that we think that one thing *is* and another *is not*. The conception of 'being' is certainly, therefore not the *same* as that of belonging to the Universe, even though the two may be *equivalent* to the extent I pointed out. The truth is that though the conception of belonging to the Universe does seem in some ways clearer than that of being, yet the former can really only be defined by reference to the latter; not *vice versa*. If we want to say what we mean by the Universe, we can only do so by reference to the conception of 'being'—by saying, for instance, that by the Universe is meant the sum of all things which *are*, or in some such way as this. In other words, the conception of the Universe presupposes the conception of 'being', and can only be defined by reference to it; so that we cannot really define the latter by reference to the former.

And this brings me to the last respect, in which the proposal to explain 'being' by saying that it is equivalent to 'belonging to the Universe', is inaccurate and may be misleading. Suppose it really is the case, as we commonly do suppose, that besides the things which *are now* there are some things which *have been* in the past, and are *no longer* now; and others which will be in the future, but *are not yet*. It seems quite plain that, of these three classes of things, it is only those which are now that actually have, in one sense of the word, the property of 'being': of those which were, but are no longer, it is only true that they *did* have it, *not* that they have it now; and similarly of those which will be, but are not yet, it is only true that they *will* possess it, *not* that they do possess it. Of course, as we have seen, there are some philosophers who seem to think that there is nothing whatever which either has been, or is now, or will be: that everything which *has* being at all, *has* it in some timeless sense—that is to say, has *not* got it *now*, but nevertheless *has* got it; and that nothing whatever either *has* had it in the past, or will have it in the future: that in short there has been no past, is no present and will be no future. One of the things we are trying to discover is whether Mr. Bradley really does think this or not. And I don't mean now to assume that these philosophers, if any do think this, are wrong. What I want to point out is that, *supposing* they are wrong—supposing some things *have been*, which are no longer, and others *will be*, which are not yet, there does arise a difficulty as to what we are to mean by the Universe. The difficulty is this: Are we going to say or are we not, that all the things which *have been* and *will be* do belong to the Universe—are constituents of it—just as much as those which are now? I think many people would say 'Yes': that the past and future *do* belong to the Universe just as much as the present does. And I think this is certainly *one* common sense in which we use the expression 'the Universe': we do use it to include the past and future as well as the present. But if we are going to say this, then, you see, we must admit that, for still another reason 'belonging to the Universe' is *not* strictly equivalent to 'being'. For we must admit that many things, which *do* belong to the Universe, nevertheless, in a sense, *have* not got the property we mean by 'being', but only have *had* it, or *will* have it. We should have to say that to 'belong to the Universe' means, *not* to *have* now the property we call 'being', but *either* to have had it, *or* to have it now, *or* to be about to have it; and we might have further to add a fourth alternative: namely to *have* it, in some timeless sense—to *have* it in a sense which is *not* equivalent to having it now. For, as we have seen, some philosophers believe that the only sense in which anything can *be* at all is some timeless sense; and even those philosophers who believe that there has been a past, is a present, and will be a future, do many of them believe that there is *besides* a timeless sense of the word 'is'; and that beside the things which have been, are now, and will be, there are many other things also belonging to the Universe, which *are* and yet are not *now*. In other words they believe that 'being' is a property which not only *did* belong to many things, does belong to many *now*, and *will* belong to many in the future, but that it also belongs in some timeless sense to many things, to which it does *not* belong *now*. I am not at all sure, whether these philosophers are right or not. For my part, I cannot think of any instance of a thing, with regard to which it seems quite certain that it *is*, and yet also that it is not *now*. But we must I think admit that the alternative is a possible one: that the very same property called 'being' which *did* belong and *will* belong to things, to which it does *not* belong now, may also *belong* in some timeless sense to things to which it does not belong now. And hence we must admit that the phrase 'So and so *belongs* to the Universe' may mean either of four different things: it may mean *either* 'So and so *has* been', *or* 'So and so *is* now', *or* 'So and so will be', *or* 'So and so *is*, but *not* now'. For this reason I think that to explain what we mean by 'being' by saying that it is equivalent to 'belonging to the Universe' or being a constituent of it, may possibly lead to misunderstanding. If we are going to mean by 'being' a property which did and will belong to some things to which it doesn't belong *now*, then we must say that *in a sense* these things *do* not belong to the Universe, but only did or will belong to it; while in *another sense* they *do* belong to it, in spite of the fact that they *have* not got the property we mean by 'being', but only did have it or will have it. And these two senses of the phrase 'belonging to the Universe' are, I think, liable to be confused with one another. Each is also liable to be identified with the property which we mean by 'being': so that we get two different senses of the word 'being', which are liable to be confused with one another. But, apart from this possible misunderstanding, and the two others which I mentioned before, I think it does really serve to make clearer what I mean by 'being', if I say that it is equivalent to being a constituent of the Universe—if I say that in asking what things *are* and what things *are not*, we are merely asking what things really are or are not constituents of the Universe.

So much, then, to explain what I mean by the first and most fundamental property denoted by our five phrases—the one which I propose to call 'being'.

And secondly I want to consider the phrase 'is a fact', in that use of it, in which we say: It is a fact that bears exist; It is a fact that I am now talking; It is a fact that twice two are four. Obviously we do mean something immensely important by this phrase too. It is a phrase which we constantly use to express things which we particularly want to insist on. The question is: '*What* do we mean by it? Do we use it to express the very same property to which I have given the name "being" or a different one? And, if different, different in what respect?' There certainly is some difference between our *use* of this phrase, and our use of the word 'being', for, whereas it is quite natural to say 'It is a fact that bears exist', 'It is a fact that twice two are four', it is not quite natural to say 'That bears exist' *is*; or 'That twice two are four' *is*; and conversely, while it is quite natural to say that bears are constituents of the Universe, or that the number 2 is a constituent of the Universe, it is not quite natural to say that the fact that bears exist or the fact that twice two are four is a constituent of the Universe. But nevertheless I am inclined to think that this difference of usage does not really indicate any difference in the nature of the predicates or properties meant by the two phrases. So far as I can see, when we say of one thing that it is a fact, and of another that it has being or is a constituent of the Universe, the property which we mean to assert of the two things is exactly the same in both cases. The reason for the difference of usage is, I think, only that we instinctively tend to use the one phrase, when we wish to attribute the property in question to certain *kinds* of things, and the other when we wish to attribute it to *other kinds* of things. In short, the difference of usage expresses not a difference of *predicate*, but a difference in the character of the *subjects* to which it is applied. And the difference of character which leads us to make this distinction, really is, I think, one of the most fundamental differences that there is among the constituents of the Universe. We may divide all the constituents of the Universe—all things which are, into two classes, putting in one class those which we can only express by a clause beginning with 'that' or by the corresponding verbal noun, and in the other all the rest. Thus we have, in the first class, such things as 'the fact that lions exist' or (to express it by a verbal noun) 'the existence of lions', 'the fact that twice two are four', 'the fact that I am now talking', and absolutely all the immense number of facts which we thus express by phrases beginning with 'that'.

In short, this class of constituents of the Universe consists of the sort of entities which *correspond* (in the sense I explained) to true beliefs. Each true belief corresponds to one such entity; and it is *only to* entities of this sort that true beliefs do correspond. And this first class of entities—the class of entities which correspond to true beliefs, certainly constitutes I think, one of the largest and most important classes of things in the Universe. The precise respect in which they differ from all other constituents of the Universe is, I think, very difficult to define. So far as I can see, you can only point out the character which distinguishes them, by pointing out, as I have just done, that they are the class of entities which we name by calling them 'The fact that so and so', or that they are the kind of entities which correspond to true beliefs. But the difference between them and all other kinds of entities is, I think, easy to *see*, even if it is not easy to define. Surely everybody can see that the fact that a lion does exist is quite a different sort of entity from the lion himself? or the fact that twice two are four quite a different sort of entity from the number 2 itself? Of course, to say that things of this sort form a class by themselves is to say that they do, in fact, possess some common property which is not shared by other things. And hence we might say that when we use the phrase 'It is a fact that so and so', we are *not* merely attributing 'being' to the thing in question, but are *also*, as well, ascribing to it this other peculiar property, which is *not* shared by *all* the things which have being. If this were so, there would be a real difference between the property meant by 'being a fact' and the property meant by merely 'being'. But as I said, I don't think we commonly do mean to *attribute* this property when we say 'It is a fact that so and so', but only the property of being. We do instinctively use the phrase 'it is a fact' instead of 'it *is*', when we are talking of things which *have*, in fact, got this property as well as that of being: but I don't think that what we mean to say of them is that they have it. However, the question whether this is so or not, is a question of comparatively little importance. The important thing is to recognise what the property is, which makes us apply this phrase 'It is a fact that' to some things, whereas we can't apply it equally naturally to others. And I am going now, for the purposes of this discussion to restrict the name 'facts' to those constituents of the Universe and those only which have this property. Thus we shall say that the existence of lions is a fact, but that lions themselves are not facts; we shall say it is a fact that twice two are four, but that the number two itself is not a fact. And if we understand the word 'facts' in this sense it is important to notice that 'facts' are neither more nor less than what are often called 'truths'. I pointed out before that a phrase of the form 'It is *true* that so and so' can absolutely *always* be used as equivalent to the corresponding phrase of the form 'It is a *fact* that so and so'. And similarly anything which is a fact, in this sense, can always equally naturally be called 'a truth'. Instead of talking of the fact that $2+2=4$ we can equally well talk of the truth that $2+2=4$; instead of talking of the fact that lions exist, we can equally well talk of the truth that lions exist: and so on, in absolutely every case. And it is important to notice this because this property which belongs to a 'truth', and which makes it a truth, is an utterly different one from that which we have been discussing in the last two lectures—the property which belongs to '*true*' *beliefs*, and in virtue of which we call them 'true'. To say of a·truth that it is a truth is merely to say of it that it is a fact in the sense we are considering; whereas to say of an act of belief that it is 'true' is, as we saw, to say only that it *corresponds* to a fact. No one, in fact, would think of calling a true act of belief a truth: it is quite unnatural to use such language. And yet, I think, it is very common to find the two things confused.[1] It has, for instance, been very commonly supposed that truths are entirely dependent on the mind; that there could be

[1]A mistake which is perhaps even more common is that of supposing that every true proposition is a truth. This is a mistake which analogies in language would naturally lead us to make : it is natural to suppose that we should use the expression 'a truth' to mean anything that is true. But it seems to me quite plain that this is not how we in fact use the expression 'a truth'. The *fact*, with regard to any proposition, that it is true, can be quite naturally called 'a truth' ; but the fact that a given proposition is true is obviously something quite different from the proposition in question and also from the equivalent proposition that the proposition in question is true. No proposition is a truth; but in the case of every proposition which is true, the fact that it is so is a truth. (1952.)

no truths in the Universe if there were no minds in it. And, so far as I can see, the chief reason why this has been supposed, is because it has been supposed that the word 'true' stands for a property which can belong only to acts of belief, and that nothing can be a 'truth' unless it has *this* property. It is, of course, quite obvious that there could be no true beliefs in the Universe, if there were no minds in it: no act of belief could be true, unless there *were* acts of belief; and there could be no acts of belief if there were no minds, because an act of belief is an act of consciousness. It is therefore, quite obvious that the existence of *true acts of belief* is entirely dependent on the existence of mind. But the moment we realise that by a 'truth' is meant *not* a true act of belief, but merely a fact—something which corresponds to a true belief, when there are true beliefs, but which may *be* equally even when no one is believing in it, there ceases to be any reason to suppose that there could be no truths in the Universe, if there were no minds in it. It is the very reverse of obvious that there could be no facts in the Universe, if there were no minds in it. And as soon as we realise that 'a truth' is merely another name for a fact, and is something utterly different from a true act of belief, it becomes quite plainly possible that there *could* be truths in the Universe, even if there were no minds in it. For this reason it is, I think, important to notice that 'a truth' is merely another name for a fact, although the word 'true', as applied to *acts of belief*,[1] means something quite different—does *not* mean that the act of belief in question is a truth. And it is also I think, worth while to notice a connection between the phrase 'It is a fact that' and the word 'real'. To say 'It is a fact that lions exist' is obviously merely equivalent to saying 'Lions *really* do exist'. That is to say we use the word 'real', in this adverbial form, merely to express the same idea which we also express by 'It is a fact that'. Of course, though it is natural to say 'Lions *really* do exist', it is not at all natural to say 'It is *real* that lions do exist': nothing could be more unnatural. And this shows that there is some difference in the usage of the phrases 'is real' and 'is a fact'. But at the same time this use of the adverb 'really' does, I think, point to a connection between the two.

I am going, then, to use the name 'facts' simply and solely as a name for that kind of constituents of the Universe which correspond to true beliefs—for the kind of things which we express by phrases beginning with 'that'. But, of course, I don't mean to say that this

[1]And also, of course, as is much more commonly the case, as applied to propositions. (See footnote, p. 297.) (1952)

is the *only* sense in which the word 'facts' is commonly used. Philosophers, at all events, certainly sometimes use it in a wider sense: they will say for instance not merely that the existence of lions is a fact, but that a lion itself is a fact, or they will say that this whitish patch of colour—which I am now directly perceiving—this sense-datum itself—is a fact. And I don't mean to say that this wider usage is wrong: I only want to make it quite plain that I am not going to adopt it for the purposes of the present discussion. And what I think is still more important is to point out that in ordinary life, we very often use the word 'fact' in a *narrower* sense than that in which I am using it: we apply it only to *some* among the class of things which I am calling facts. The usage I am thinking of is that in which *facts* are often opposed to theories, or in which it is said that questions ought to be settled by an appeal to *the facts*. In *my* sense of the word a theory *may* be a fact, in spite of its being a mere theory; it will be a fact *if*, when anybody believes in it, his belief is true. And, so far as I can see, the chief distinction between this narrow usage of the word 'fact' and my usage of it, is that in the common usage the word is confined to those kind of facts, which we do or can absolutely *know* to be facts. It is held, that is to say, that among the many *facts*, in my sense of the word, which there are in the Universe, there are certain kinds which we can, under certain circumstances, absolutely *know* to be facts, whereas there are other kinds, which we can never (in the present state of knowledge) absolutely *know* to be facts. Thus it might be said that where a man believes in a thing, and his belief is true, yet what he believes is *not* a fact, unless it is something which some man now is capable of absolutely knowing. Whereas in my sense of the word, whenever a man believes in a thing, and his belief is true, what he believes in *is* a fact, even if nobody living could absolutely know it to be so. And, of course, my sense of the word is one of the senses in which the word is commonly used; everybody does constantly use language which implies that, when a belief is true, then what is believed in is, in a sense, a fact, whether anybody can know it to be so or not. But there certainly is also, I think, a narrower sense of the word, in which it is confined to things which are held (rightly or wrongly) to be capable of being absolutely known; and I want to make it clear that I am *not* confining it to this narrow sense.

I have, then, so far, tried to give definite meanings to two of our five phrases—the phrase 'is' or 'has being', and the phrase 'is a fact.' But the phrase I want most to consider is the phrase 'exists'. This also is certainly a phrase of the utmost importance. Nothing can well be more important than to know whether certain kinds of things do exist, or will probably exist in the future, or not: there is nothing which we are more constantly anxious to know. And the question we have to raise is: What exactly is 'existence'? What is the property which we denote by the word? Is 'to exist' simply the same thing as to be or to be a constituent of the Universe, or is it not? And, if not, how do they differ? And, as regards this question, I used to hold very strongly, what many other people are also inclined to hold, that the words 'being' and 'existence' do stand for two entirely different properties; and that though everything which exists must also 'be', yet many things which 'are' nevertheless do emphatically *not* exist. I did, in fact, actually hold this view when I began these lectures; and I have based the whole scheme of the lectures upon the distinction, having said that I would deal first with the question what sort of things exist, and then separately, as a quite distinct matter, with the question what sort of things *are*, but don't exist. But nevertheless I am inclined to think that I was wrong, and that there is no such distinction between 'being' and 'existence' as I thought there was. There is, of course, a distinction of usage, but I am inclined to think that this distinction is only of the same kind as that which I tried to explain as holding between 'being' and 'being a fact'. That is to say, when we say of a thing that it exists, we don't, I think, mean to attribute to it any property different from that of 'being'; all that we mean to say of it is simply that it *is* or is a constituent of the Universe. And the distinction of usage only comes in, because we instinctively tend to use the word 'existence' only when we mean to attribute this property to certain kinds of things and not when we mean to attribute it to *other* kinds which also, in fact, have it, and are constituents of the Universe just as much as the former. But as I said in the other case, I do not think the question whether this is so or not is really of much importance. In merely saying that there is a class of things, to which we tend to confine the word 'existence', we are, of course, saying that these things have some common property, which is *not* shared by other constituents of the Universe. And, of course, you may say, if you like (though I don't think it is strictly true) that when we say of anything that it exists we mean to say of it two things at once namely (1) that it *is*, or is a constituent of the Universe and (2) that it has this peculiar property, which does *not* belong to all the constituents of the Universe. The important thing is to recognise as clearly as possible *that* there is such a property, and *what* it is: that there is a class of things in the Universe, of which we tend to say exclusively that they exist, and how this class of things differs from other kinds of things, which do quite equally belong to the Universe, and are constituents of it, though we should not say of them that they 'exist'.

And I think the best way of doing this is to point out what are the classes of things in the Universe, of which we *cannot* quite naturally say that they 'exist'. And so far as I can see we can divide these into two classes. The first is simply the class of things which I have just called 'facts'. It is in the highest degree unnatural to say of these that they exist. No one, for instance, would think of saying that the fact that lions exist, *itself* exists; or that the fact that $2+2=4$ exists. We do, therefore, I think, certainly tend to apply the word 'existence' *only to* constituents of the Universe, *other* than facts.

But there is, it seems to me, also another class of things, which really are constituents of the Universe, in the case of which it is also unnatural, though not, perhaps, quite so unnatural, to say that they 'exist'. The class of things I mean is the class of things which Locke and Berkeley and Hume called 'general ideas' or 'abstract ideas', and which have been often called by that name by other English philosophers. This is, I think, their most familiar name.

And in order to explain quite clearly what the distinction is which seems to me to justify a distinction between 'being' and 'existing', I think it is absolutely essential to discuss the nature of 'general' or 'abstract' ideas. And this is, I think, a subject which is eminently worth discussing for its own sake too. I have hitherto said nothing at all about it. But questions as to the nature of general ideas have, in fact, played an immensely large part in philosophy. There are some philosophers who say that there are no such things at all: that general ideas are pure fictions like chimaeras or griffins. Berkeley and Hume, for instance, said this. But a majority of philosophers would, I think, say that there are such things; and *if* there are, then, I think there is no doubt that they are one of the most important kinds of things in the Universe. *If* there are any at all, there are tremendous numbers of them, and we are all constantly thinking and talking of them. But the question *what* they are, if there are such things, seems to me to be one of the most perplexing questions in philosophy. Many philosophers are constantly talking about them; but so far as I know there is no perfectly clear account of what a general idea is, and as to exactly how it differs from other constituents of the Universe. I want, therefore, to do the best I can to shew that there *are* general ideas, and what properties they have which distinguish them from other things. But, as I say, the subject seems to me to be fearfully confusing: for one thing, there seem to be so many different kinds of general ideas and it is very difficult to see what they have in common. I don't suppose, therefore, that I can make the subject really clear, but I want to do the best I can.

The first point that it is necessary to be quite clear about is that the name 'general idea' or 'abstract idea', like the name 'idea' generally, is dangerously ambiguous: it may stand for two entirely different things. I have already had occasion to insist several times on this ambiguity in the word 'idea'; but it seems to be a point which some people find it very difficult to grasp. Let us take an example. Everybody would agree that the number two, or any other number, is an abstract idea if anything is. But when I, or anybody else, *think* of the number two, two entirely different things are involved, *both* of which may be called an 'idea'. There is in the first place my mental act, the act which consists in thinking of or being conscious of or apprehending the number two; and this mental act itself may be called 'an idea'. And if we use the word in this sense, then ideas are things which can be only in the mind: they are another name for acts of consciousness. The mental act which I perform in thinking of the number 2 is, in this sense, 'an idea'; it is an idea of *mine*, and belongs exclusively to me. But obviously the number two *itself* does *not* belong exclusively to me; it is not an idea of *mine* in this sense. So that we have to recognise as something quite distinct from my mental act the thing *thought* of—the number two itself—the *object* of my act of apprehension—*what* I apprehend: and this also is often called an 'idea'. And obviously if we use the word 'idea' in this sense, then an 'idea' is a thing which can quite well *be*, without being in any mind. There may be two things, and they may really be two, even when nobody is thinking of them, or of the fact that they are two. I want, therefore, to make it quite plain that when I talk of 'general ideas' I mean, *not* acts of apprehension, but the things apprehended: *not* my act of apprehending the number two, but the number two itself, which is *what* I apprehend. With regard to the act of apprehension, the mental act, I don't wish to suggest for a moment that it doesn't exist. I think myself that *it does*, though some people would doubt this. It is only with regard to the object apprehended, that I wish to suggest that it doesn't 'exist'. The object apprehended, then, *not* the act of apprehension is what we are going to discuss; and in order to avoid confusion between the two, I think I had perhaps better not use the name 'general idea' or 'abstract idea' at all. I will use instead another name which is often used for these kind of objects, though it is not so familiar: I will call them 'universals'. What, then, I want to do is to point out what kind of things 'universals' are and that there are such things—that they are not pure fictions, like chimaeras and griffins.

And I will begin with an instance, which is not perhaps in some respects as simple as could be taken, but which I want to take, because it brings out one point which will presently be of importance. When I look at my two hands so, I directly perceive two sets of sense-data, two patches of flesh colour, of the sort of shape you all know very well, which are at a certain distance from one another. The distance, as you see, is not great, so we will say they are *near* one another. And for the sake of convenience, I will talk of these two flesh-coloured patches as *my hands*, though, as we have seen, there is reason to suppose these flesh-coloured patches are not, in fact, my hands, or any part of them. When, therefore, I talk of my *hands* you will please understand that I am talking *solely* of these two flesh-coloured patches, which I directly perceive. I don't want to assume that I have any hands at all, in the ordinary sense of the word. I want to talk solely of things which indubitably *are*; and so I want to talk only of these sense-data which I am directly perceiving, and for the sake of convenience I will call them 'my hands'. Well, then, it is a *fact*, in my sense of the word, that this hand—this flesh-coloured patch—is at this moment at a certain distance from (a distance which we will call 'near') this other hand—this other flesh-coloured patch. It is a fact that this right hand is now near this left hand. But this fact seems plainly capable of being analysed into the following constituents. When I say that it can be analysed into them, I don't mean to say that it *is* nothing more than the sum of its constituents: I think plainly it is *not*—it is not merely identical with the sum of its constituents: I only mean to say that the constituents in question *are* parts or constituents of it—that they are contained in it. The constituents I mean are these. This right hand—this sense-datum—is one of them—and the other is *what* we assert of this sense-datum, the property which we attribute to it—namely the property *of being near the left hand*. The fact is *that* the right hand is *near* the left: and we can analyse this into (1) the right hand itself—that is one thing which enters into the constitution of the fact: and (2) what is asserted of this right hand—namely the property of being now near the left. Well, this second constituent—the property of being near this left hand—is a *universal*, and one of the most indubitable instances of a universal. You see why it should be called a 'universal'. It is so called, because it is a property which can be (and is) *common* to this hand and to other things. Other things can in fact also share the property of being near this hand: other things do: this white patch which I see in looking at the paper, is also *near* this hand, and so is the coloured patch which I see in looking at the desk. All these three things have the common property of being near this hand. They are all *near* it in exactly the same sense, though, of course, each of them *also* has relations to it which the others have not got. And this property of being *near* this patch of colour, in the sense in which it is *common* both to the sense-datum of my right hand and the sense-datum of the desk and the sense-datum of the paper, really is what is commonly called a 'general' or 'abstract' idea. The relation which I mean by 'being *near*' is certainly not *identical* either with the space which I see between this hand and that, or between the hand and the desk, or between the hand and the paper. All these spaces are different. But what I mean by being 'near' is something which is absolutely identical in all three cases. We have, therefore, in this property of *being near this sense-datum*, a real instance of a 'universal' or abstract idea. And why I have begun with this instance, is because, in this case, the universal seems to me obviously to consist in the having of a relation to something which is *not* a universal. This coloured patch which I actually see, is obviously not a universal or abstract idea; nothing could be more of a *particular*. But yet the universal consists in the having of a relation—the relation of nearness—just to *this* coloured patch: the property of *being near this coloured patch* really is a property which is and may be shared in common by several different things.

We have, then, one type of universal which consists in the having of one identical relation to something which is *not* a universal. But, if we consider the following facts, we get an instance of another new sort of universal. This left hand of mine is not the only left hand in the Universe: there are ever so many other left hands, and there may even be other sense-data similar to this which I am now directly perceiving. But, in the same sense in which these things here are near my left hand, other things may be near the left hands of other people. So that there is such a property as that of *being near some left hand or other*. This, you see, is a property which these things here share with all the things that are near anybody else's left hand. All of them are near *some left hand or other*. This property also, therefore, is a universal, and it is plainly of a different type from the first one which we took. This property does not consist in the having of a specific relation to some *one* thing which is *not* a universal; but in the having of a specific relation to *some one or other* of a group of things which are not universals. And universals of this type are universals which we are constantly thinking about and talking about. Many of the very commonest words we use are names for them. For instance when we say of a man that he is a father, what we mean is that he has the relation of fatherhood to *some* human being *or other*: this is the property which is shared in common by all fathers, and obviously a great many of the commonest words are names for universals of this sort: universals which consist in the having of a certain relation to *some one or other* of a group of things which are *not* universals.

We have got, therefore, examples of two different types of universals: (1) the universal which consists in being near this hand of mine; and (2) the universal which consists in being near some left hand or other. And it might be thought that there can be no doubt at all that there *are* such things as these two universals. There certainly is, it would seem, such a thing as the property of being near *this* hand, and also such a thing as the property of being near *some hand or other*. But, in order to see why there has been doubt about the matter, we have to consider another quite different type of universal, which is involved as a constituent in both of these. Both of those properties has, as a constituent, a *relation*—the relation which I have called 'being *near*'. And most people would say that this relation is itself a 'universal': it certainly is a 'general idea'. Indeed, if this relation were *not* a universal, in at least one sense of the word, neither of these two properties could be so either. And in its case I think I shall be able to shew why Berkeley and Hume thought there were no such things as universals; and also several other points, which it is very important to notice, if we are to get really clear as to the nature of universals.

Chapter XVII

TRUTHS AND UNIVERSALS

I have said that some people are inclined to make a distinction between 'being' and 'existence' of the following kind. They hold that there are in the Universe enormous numbers of things, which undoubtedly *are*—undoubtedly have being, and which yet do *not* exist. And I was trying to explain exactly what justification there seemed to me to be for saying this.

I have said that I think there are two kinds of things, with regard to which it can be urged with some plausibility that they *are*, and yet do not *exist*. And I have been trying to explain what these two kinds of things were. The first was the class of things which I proposed last time to call 'facts' or 'truths'. And I am very anxious to make it quite clear exactly what sort of things I do mean by 'facts' or 'truths'. I admit that the word 'facts' is by no means always applied exclusively to things of the kind I mean or to what are supposed to be such. 'Facts' is a very ambiguous word, although it is so constantly used as if it were clear. It *is* quite often used simply and solely as a name for the class of things I mean; but it is also quite often used both in a wider and in a narrower sense. That is to say, it is often used as a name for kinds of things, which don't belong to the class I mean; and also often as a name for only *some* among the things which *do* belong to the class I mean. I think, therefore, it will perhaps be better if I don't use this ambiguous name 'facts', but use the name 'truths' instead. About this name 'truths' there is, I think, only one ambiguity of the same type as in the case of the name 'facts'. The name 'truths' is not too narrow, for absolutely everything which does belong to the class I mean can quite naturally be called a 'truth'; and also, with one single exception, it is not too wide, since it is quite unnatural to call anything 'a truth' except things which do belong to the class I mean—*with one single exception*. The single exception is this. We may, I think, perhaps apply the name 'a truth' not only to things of the class I mean but *also* to the forms of *words* by which we express them. When, for instance, we say 'It is a truth that twice two are four'; we may, I think, perhaps mean *either*: 'The form of words—the sentence—"Twice two are four" is a truth'; *or* we may mean that the fact which they express—the fact that twice two are four—is a truth. And there is always some danger of confusing words with what they express. But this ambiguity which attaches (if it does attach) to the expression 'a truth' is not, I think, so dangerous—so liable to lead to misunderstanding—as the ambiguities which attach to the expression 'a fact'. It will be comparatively easy to remember that when I talk of 'a truth', I never mean merely a form of words, but *always* only the kind of thing which certain forms of words express. But nevertheless the expression 'truths' is, I think, liable to lead to misunderstandings in other ways. There are two different things, other than mere forms of words, with which *truths* are liable to be confused; namely, (1) true acts of belief and (2) the kind of thing which I said some people called 'propositions', and which are also very often called 'beliefs'. The difference between these three kinds of things—(1) a truth, (2) a true act of belief, and (3) a proposition, can, I think, be easily exhibited in the following way. Take any act of belief, you like. Suppose, for instance, you see a tree in the distance and believe that it is an oak. We all know quite well what kind of thing this act of belief is—the believing that a given tree which we see is an oak. It is a sort of thing, which is constantly occurring in the minds of all of us, and with which we are perfectly familiar, though it is extremely difficult to analyse. And we know that this act of belief may occur, and may be exactly the same in its internal nature, whether it be true or false—whether the tree which we see actually is an oak or not. We all know that it is quite possible to make a mistake about a matter of this kind: we may believe that a tree is an oak *both* when it actually is one and also when it is not; and whichever be the case, our belief will be exactly the same in its nature. And this gives us our first distinction: the distinction between a truth and a true act of belief. We have seen that the act of belief is something which may occur and be just the same *both* when the tree *is* an oak, *and* when it isn't. But this shews that when the belief is true, then there is in the Universe, beside the belief, something else quite different from it—namely the fact that the tree *is* an oak. This fact, which is in the Universe, if the belief be true, and simply is not at all, if it be false, is what I call a 'truth'. And it is plainly something quite different from the true act of belief; since the act of belief may *be* in the Universe, and be exactly the same in its nature even when this 'truth' simply isn't—when, in fact, the tree is not an oak. A truth, therefore, cannot be identified with a true act of belief. And the same instance will also shew us the difference between a truth and a proposition. Those people who believe that there are such things as propositions, argue, as I explained, in the following way. They say: When I believe that a given tree, which I see, is an oak, the whole mental event which then occurs, can plainly be analysed in the following way. The whole mental event plainly resembles other acts of belief, in respect of the fact that it is an act of belief. But it also, they say, no less plainly differs from them in respect of the fact that what is believed in it is different. To believe that a given tree is an oak is obviously a different thing from believing, as we may do on another occasion, that a given tree is an ash: and the difference is, they say, that, while both are acts of belief, what is believed in the one case is that the tree is an oak, whereas what is believed in the other is that it is an ash. They propose, therefore, to distinguish, in the case of these two beliefs, between the element in respect of which they are both alike, the element which we express by saying that they are both acts of belief, and the elements in respect of which they differ; and to say that these latter elements are in the one case, the proposition that the tree is an oak and in the other the proposition that it is an ash. But it is quite plain, that, if we adopt this analysis, we must say that the proposition that the tree is an oak is something which is and is equally whether the belief be true or false. For the belief that a tree is an oak differs just as much and in exactly the same way from the belief that a tree is an ash, whether it be true or false. If, therefore, we give the name 'proposition' to the element which differentiates the two beliefs, we must say that the proposition *is* and *is* in the Universe equally whether the belief be true or false. But as we have seen, the 'truth' or 'fact' that the tree *is* an oak, is something which *is*, only if the belief be true; and hence it is quite plain that this 'truth' is something quite different from the proposition, just as it is also different from the act of belief. Whenever the act of belief occurs, the proposition also is and is in the Universe; but both act of belief and proposition may occur, without there being in the Universe any such fact or truth as that the tree is an oak. All this seems to me to be perfectly obvious, as soon as it is pointed out: it is the merest common sense to say that the fact that the tree *is* an oak is quite a different thing from my belief that it is one, and also, therefore, from what I believe, when I believe that it is one, if by '*what* I believe' we mean something which is in the

Universe equally whether my belief is true or false. And yet I think these three different things are constantly liable to be confused. As I explained, I don't now believe that there are such things as propositions at all: I don't believe that beliefs can be analysed, in this way, into the act of belief on the one hand and the proposition which is believed on the other hand. And it might be thought that if there are no such things as propositions it must be impossible to confuse anything with them. But the fact that a thing is imaginary does not, as we have seen, at all prevent us from thinking of it; and in fact we cannot help constantly both thinking and talking of imaginary things. And hence it is, I think, very easy to confuse 'truths' with these imaginary things called 'propositions', in spite of the fact that the latter are imaginary. It is therefore worth while to recognise, that whether there are such things as propositions or not, 'truths' are, in any case, quite different from them. By a 'truth', therefore, I mean something which is neither a true act of belief, nor a true proposition (supposing there is such a thing). It is something which *corresponds* to both, but is not identical with either. And to avoid all danger of its being identified with either is the chief reason for calling truths 'facts', rather than 'truths'. I really don't know which is the best name to use for them: each name may lead to misunderstanding, which the use of the other will avoid.

We have seen, then, that the sort of things I mean by 'truths' or 'facts' are quite different *both* from true acts of belief and from 'true propositions' and from true sentences or forms of words. But we have not yet seen how they differ from all the other kinds of things there may be in the Universe. It may be asked: What, after all, is the property which all truths have in common, and which is not shared by anything which is not a truth? How are we to distinguish the sort of thing you mean by a 'truth', from all the sorts of things which are not truths? And in answer to this question, I confess I don't know how to describe the property which belongs to all truths and *only* to truths: it seems to me to be a property which can be pointed out and seen, but if it can be analysed, I don't know how to analyse it. The case seems to me to be the same, as if you were asked what 'a colour' is. All of us, who are not blind, know perfectly well what a colour is, and, with regard to anything whatever which may come before our minds, we can tell, with perfect ease, whether it is a colour or not. But yet, as we shall see, it is extremely difficult to *define* what is meant by 'being a colour'—to say what the property is which belongs to all colours and only to colours. And just so with 'truths': it is, I think, quite easy to tell whether any given thing would or would not be a 'truth', in the sense I mean, supposing it had being at all and were not purely imaginary; but not at all easy to define the property common and peculiar to all truths. One way, however, of *pointing out* what the property is, is to say that a truth is one sort of thing that is expressed by a sentence. For instance, the following words, viz. 'The tree which I see is an oak' form what is called, in grammar, a *sentence*. And, if this sentence is true, then what it expresses is a truth or a fact: namely the truth or fact that the tree in question is an oak. The words 'The tree which I see', on the other hand, do not, by themselves, form a sentence; and what they express, therefore, is not a fact or a truth. It is this kind of difference —the difference that there is between a tree, on the one hand, and the fact that it is an oak, on the other—that is the difference I mean between things which are not truths and things which are. And surely it is quite easy to see that the two are quite different kinds of things? The tree itself, of course, undoubtedly is and exists and I quite admit that it might be called a 'fact'; but nobody would think of calling a tree a 'truth', whereas they might call the fact that it is an oak a truth; and this difference of language indicates the difference I mean. In other words, the grammatical difference between sentences which express a truth on the one hand and words which do *not* form sentences on the other, seems to me to correspond to a difference in the nature of the things expressed. And this difference in the nature of the things expressed, which can I think be easily seen, though I can't define it, is the difference I mean between things which are truths and things which are not. Another way of pointing out the difference is to say, as I said last time, that truths are the sort of things which correspond to true beliefs; that nothing but truths can correspond to true beliefs. Surely it is quite plain that if I believe that the tree which I see is an oak, then the whole fact that it *is* an oak corresponds to this belief in a sense in which neither the tree itself, nor what I mean by the words 'is an oak' do correspond to it? And it is surely quite plain also, that the tree itself and what I express by the words 'is an oak', can't correspond in this sense to *any* belief at all. I can't believe that the tree which I see: these words by themselves don't express anything; there can be no such belief. And similarly I can't believe that is an oak: the words 'I believe that is an oak' are nonsense if the word 'that' is being used, not as a demonstrative pronoun, but as a conjunction; and there can be no such belief. But the moment I put the tree and the property of being an oak together, the whole thing is changed. I *can* believe that the tree has the property of being an oak; and it can be a truth that the tree has this property. That the tree is an oak can be a truth, and can correspond to a belief: whereas the tree, by itself, and the property of being an oak, by itself, however real they may be, are not 'truths' and can't correspond to any belief.

I may, perhaps, be mistaken in recognising this enormous class of things which I call 'truths', and in supposing that there is some difference between them and other constituents of the Universe—some property which does belong to all of them and does not belong to any of the other constituents of the Universe. Possibly there really are no such things at all. Many philosophers don't seem to recognise them. But I think we can't help all of us constantly talking as if there were such things. And for my part, I can't help thinking, in the first place, that there are such things as true beliefs; and, in the second place, whenever I consider a true belief, no matter what the nature of the belief may be, I can't help thinking that there is always in the Universe one of these peculiar things which I call 'truths', corresponding to it.

There is another point about 'truths', which I hope will not be misunderstood. When I say that a truth is the sort of thing which corresponds to a true belief, I hope nobody will understand me to mean that there actually is a true belief corresponding to every truth. On the contrary, so far as I can see, the number of truths in the Universe is enormously greater than the number of true beliefs. We are all of us familiar with the idea that there are ever so many truths and facts, which nobody has ever known; ever so many truths that nobody has discovered yet. And this idea seems to me to be perfectly correct, although many philosophers seem to consider it a paradox. Of course, it is the case that to every truth, a true belief *might* correspond: the number of *possible* true beliefs is exactly the same as the number of *actual* truths. But most people would admit that by no means all the true beliefs which *might* occur have actually occurred. And hence the number of truths in the Universe is immensely greater than the number of actual true beliefs.

'Truths', therefore, are one of the two classes of things, with regard to which it may, I think, be plausibly urged that they *are*, but don't exist. The reason for saying so is merely that it seems rather unnatural to say 'The fact that twice two are four' exists; or to say 'the fact that lions exist' itself exists. It is quite natural to say of a lion that he exists, but it doesn't seem natural to say that his existence also exists, though it is natural to say that his existence is a fact or a truth.

What conclusion, exactly, we are to draw from the fact that this is unnatural, I will presently consider. For the present I want to go on to consider the other class of things, with regard to which it may, I think, be plausibly urged, that, though they undoubtedly *are*, they don't exist. This second class of things, I said, was the class of things that may be called 'general ideas' or 'abstract ideas', or 'universals'; and another name by which they are also often spoken of is 'concepts' or 'conceptions'. And the nature of these things might be said, by itself, to form one of the main problems of philosophy, since an enormous amount of philosophical discussion has been devoted to it.

And I am going to illustrate what I have to say about these things called 'general ideas' or 'universals' on the black-board, because I want to make it as plain as possible exactly what I am talking about, and that I am talking about things which really are.

I took last time the instance of several different things all of them at a certain distance from the same thing. And I will now illustrate these by patches of chalk on the blackboard. Let us have three patches called respectively 'B', 'C', 'D' and a fourth called 'A'. I pointed out that the property of being at a certain distance from—being spatially related to—A is a property which belongs in common to all these other three things B, C and D, and is a 'universal' or 'a general idea'; in spite of the fact that this property consists in the having of a relation to A—that is to say to something which is *not* a universal. And I pointed out that, by considering this instance, we could also think of another different type of universal. This white patch, A, is by no means the only white patch in the Universe. And just as B, C and D are near A, so other things may be near other white patches. But all the things which are near any white patch at all will have the common property of *being near some white patch or other*. This is a property which will obviously be common to an enormous number of different things in the Universe. And I said that an enormous number of our commonest words are names for universals of this type—universals which consist in the *having of a relation to some one or other* of a group of things which are not universals.

But both of these universals, I said, obviously presupposed another universal, of yet a third type—namely the *relation*, 'being at a distance from', and it is the nature of this relation that I want now to consider.

You can all of you see that B, C and D are each of them at some distance or other from A: each of them, we should say, has to A one and the same relation, in one respect—namely *the* relation of being at *a* distance from it. The question is : What exactly do we mean by saying this ? Is it true that they all do have to A the very same identical relation? Is there any one *general* relation, called 'being at a distance from', which really is common to all three cases? And, if so, what is this relation? Let us try to analyse the actual facts. It is quite plain that we do all directly perceive a space—an expanse—between A and B, another between A and C, another between A and D. And many people would, I think, be inclined to say that these spaces which we actually see are themselves *the* relations between the three pairs of terms—*the* relations of which we are thinking when we say that B, C and D are all at some distance from A. But it is obvious that each of these spaces is *different* from each of the others: this space here between A and B is not identical with this one between A and C; and neither is identical with this other one between A and D. For one thing, they are probably slightly different in length; each of them will be slightly longer or slightly shorter than either of the other two; and even if two of them should happen to be of exactly the same length, yet these two would obviously not be identical—they would not be the *same* space, but only equal to one another. And this, I think, is the reason why Berkeley and Hume denied that there are such things as general ideas at all. They said: If you try to think of *a* space, all that you can ever think of is some one particular space—a space of some one particular length and breadth and shape; it is quite impossible to think of such a thing as a space in general—a space which does not differ from other spaces; and hence they concluded that there is no such thing as a space in general. And they concluded that what was true of this general name, the name 'a space', was also true of all other general names: that all general names are, in fact, only names for *particular* ideas; that what we have before our minds when we use them, and what we express by them, is always merely some particular idea. But, of course, the first and most obvious answer to this is that we are able to think that all these three spaces *are* spaces; and that when we think this, we are not merely thinking that this one is this one, this one this one, and this one this one. We certainly can and do think that they all resemble one another in *some* respect; and *the* respect in which they are all alike is obviously *not* identical with any one of them, but *is* something common to all three. It would seem, therefore, that this thing—*the* respect in which all different spaces resemble one another—is a general idea or universal, and is obviously something of which we can think. And Hume, at least, had to admit that this is the case: he admits that we can attend to *the* respect in which different particulars resemble one another. And this admission obviously amounts to a denial of his original doctrine that there are no such things as general ideas. In admitting that we can attend to the respect in which one particular idea resembles others, he admits that we can attend to a general idea, and can, therefore, have it before our minds; so that all he is still able to maintain consistently, is merely that, whenever we do think of a general idea, we must *also* have a particular one before our minds. We must, therefore, I think admit that there *are* such things as general ideas. We can and do think of *the* respect in which these three spaces all resemble one another; this respect is obviously not identical with any one of them; and it is a general idea. But there still remains a question as to what sort of a thing this general idea is; and this seems to me to be a question which it is very difficult to answer. One way of answering it which is, I think, at first sight very tempting is this. If we consider these three spaces, the space between A and B, that between A and C, and that between A and D, one property which certainly is common to them all is that each is *one* of the *three*. Each of them is one member of this particular group of three; and this property which belongs to each of them certainly is a universal. But this property itself certainly can't be *the* one which we mean to predicate of them when we say they are all spaces. For this is a property which does not belong to any space except these three: no other space except these is a member of this particular group of three. But it is, I think, tempting and natural to suggest that *the* property which is common and peculiar to *all* spaces, is, similarly, that each of them is a member of the group consisting of all spaces. Just as these three spaces form a group, so we may suppose *all* spaces form a group; and one property which certainly is common and peculiar to all members of this group, is simply that they *are* members of it. Why should it not be the case that, just as we are able to think of this group of three spaces, we are similarly able to think of the group of all spaces, and that the property which we mean to attribute to each of them when we say it is a space, is simply and solely that it is a member of this group? This property certainly is a universal or general idea, which does belong in common to all spaces; and whether it be *the* property in question or not, it does give us an instance of a third type of universal different from either of the two which we first recognised—namely the being a member of a group of things, no one of which is itself a universal. I must confess I can't see clearly that this property may not actually be the property which we mean to attribute to a space when we say that it is a space: it seems to me possible that it really may be the only property which is both common and peculiar to every space—the only one which does belong to all spaces and does not belong to anything which is not a space. But I admit that this view may possibly involve an arrant absurdity, and I think many philosophers would say that it does for something like the following reason. They would say that the only respect in which all spaces resemble one another and differ from all other things, cannot possibly be the fact that each of them is a member of the group of spaces. For the only reason why we are able to form the idea of this group, and to distinguish between the things which do belong to it and those which don't, is simply because all the things which do belong to it already resemble one another in some *other* obvious respect, in which they differ from other things. We can only think of the group, as a whole, because we are already acquainted with this *other* property which is common and peculiar to all its members. And I admit this may be so; only I can't see clearly that it is so. My difficulty is that I can't see clearly what this other common property is, if there is one. The idea of the group of all spaces seems to me to be a fairly clear one, and I can see clearly what is meant by being a member of that group. But what is this other property which is supposed to be common to all its members? So far as I know, it can only be described as *the* respect in which they all resemble one another and differ from other things. And I admit we do know that there is some respect in which they all resemble one another and differ from other things. But if this respect is something other than belonging to the class of spaces, what is it? What sort of a thing is it? What is it like? The same difficulty occurs whenever we take any group of sense-data, and try to discover exactly what it is that is common and peculiar to all members of the group. Take, for instance, the group of colours. Every colour obviously does resemble every other colour, in some respect in which none of them resembles anything that is not a colour. But what *is* this respect in which they resemble one another and differ from other things? Here again the idea of the group of all colours seems to me to be a comparatively clear one, and I can see, I think, what is meant by being a member of that group—being one among the colours. And *this* property—the property of being one member of that group—certainly is a property which is common and peculiar to all colours: every colour does resemble every other colour in respect of the fact that it is a member of the group of colours, and nothing but a colour can resemble a colour in this respect. But is there any other property which all colours possess, and which nothing but colours possess? I can't deny that there may be; and I think it may be possible absolutely to prove that there *must* be. But I can't see the proof clearly, and I can't see what the property is. I can't then decide between these two different theories. But I wish to emphasize the great difference there is between the two. Both admit that there is a property common to all these three spaces and to all other spaces—exactly the same property *possessed* by each of them and different therefore from any one of them, and a property not possessed by anything but a space. And, in both cases, this property really is a universal or a general idea. Both theories, therefore, reject the view of Berkeley and Hume that there are no such things as general ideas. And I think this view must plainly be rejected, if only because these three spaces do plainly all possess the common and peculiar property that each is one of the three. This property is a universal or a general idea, and it is a property of which we can certainly think; and Berkeley and Hume did not, I think, even notice that there was such a property as this. But this property—the property of being one of a group of things which are not universals—is a comparatively simple and easy property to recognise. And our first theory only compels us to recognise a universal of this type as *the* property common and peculiar to all spaces: it says that the property common and peculiar to all spaces—the one which we mean by calling them all 'spaces'—simply consists in the having of a certain relation to the group of things which are spaces—the relation of being a member of that group. The only universal therefore, which we should have to recognise, on this theory, would resemble the first two that I gave in respect of the fact that it would simply consist *in the having of a certain relation to things which are not universals*. But the *other* theory which may possibly be the true one is enormously different from this. According to it the property common to all these three spaces, and which we ascribe to them when we say they all are spaces, cannot consist merely in the having of a relation to something which is *not* a universal. This theory therefore would force us to recognise an entirely new type of universal—a type of which it is very difficult to see the nature clearly.

Of the nature of this type, two different views may, I think, be taken. It may be said that it also consists in the having of a relation to something—but to a something which is, in this case, *itself* a universal and a universal of a different type from any we have hitherto considered. Or it may be said that it does not consist in the *having of a relation* to anything at all, but that there is another alternative, of which I shall have presently to try to explain the nature. But the important point—the point I want to insist on—is that, in either case, this theory would force us to recognise that there are in the Universe enormous numbers of universals, which do not consist merely in the having of a relation to something else, and which also are not relations.

This then is all I want to say at present about the nature of the universal which is *the* property common to these three different spaces—*the* property which we mean to ascribe to them when we say that they are each of them a space. I don't profess to know exactly what the nature of this common property is; though I think it is plain there is one. But we were led into this discussion by trying to discover what is the identical relation between A and B, A and C, and A and D, which we express by saying that B, C and D are each of them at a distance from A. It seemed at first sight the most obvious thing to say that this space which we actually see between A and B *is* the relation which we start from when we say that A is at a distance from B, and similarly in the other two cases; so that in order to discover *the* relation *common* to all three cases it seemed as is we needed only to discover the common property of these three spaces. But now I want to point out, what seems to me to be obvious, if you come to think of it, that this space which we actually see between A and B is not, in fact, a *relation* between them at all. The relation which A and B so obviously have to one another, and which makes us say that they are at a distance from one another, does *not* consist in this space itself; what it consists in is, I think, obviously, if you come to think of it, *not* this space itself, but the fact that this space is *between* them—that A is at one end of it, and B at the other. The space itself is not a relation at all; it is something substantive just as A and B themselves are. And what really relates A and B is the fact that this space is *between* them, that each of them has a certain relation to it. In other words, in order to give an account of this obvious relation between A and B—the relation which consists in the fact that this space is between them, we have to presuppose two *other* relations—a relation of A to this space, and a relation of B to this space—the relations which we mean by saying that A is at one end of it, and B at the other. That is to say there certainly is between A and B what I will call an indirect relation—a relation which consists in the fact that each of them has a relation to this space. And this merely *indirect* relation is, I think, the most obvious relation between them—the one of which we should generally be thinking when we say that A is at a distance from B. That is to say, it is a relation which presupposes and contains as constituents two *other* relations—namely a relation of A to this space, and a relation of B to it. And just as this whole relation between A and B is merely an *indirect* one, so it might be held that the two other relations, which are constituents of it, are in their turn merely *indirect*. For instance, it might be said that A has no direct relation to this space which lies between it and B, but that we must distinguish between A and the space which it occupies; and that its relation to the space between A and B consists in the fact that it has to the space which it occupies the relation meant by occupation, while the space which it occupies has to *this* space another relation denoted by saying that it is at one end of it. On this view the relation between A and the 'space between A and B, would itself be an indirect relation consisting in the fact that each of them has a relation to the space which A occupies. But it is, I think, plain that if we push the analysis of any indirect relation far enough, we shall always come in the end upon relations which are *not* merely indirect, but are quite *direct* relations. It is, for instance, plain, I think, that the relation of A—this white patch—to this space which it occupies is a *direct* relation: it does *not* consist in the fact that A and the space in question each of them have a relation to some third thing, but is a quite direct relation between the two. And another instance of a direct relation is the relation which I said that each of these spaces so obviously has to the group consisting of the three—the relation which we express by saying that each is one member of the group. And as regards direct relations it is, I think, quite plain that the members of two or more different pairs of terms may have exactly *the same direct* relation to one another. For instance, the relation of A to the space which it occupies is *exactly the same* as that of B or C to the spaces which they occupy: the relation meant by occupation is one and the same identical relation in each case: the relation between A and this space, does not differ from that between B and this other space, in the same way in which A differs from B, and in which this space differs from that. If, therefore, the relation which we mean by 'being at a distance from' were a *direct* relation, it would be plain that B, C and D, all really have one and the same identical relation to A. And possibly there may be some direct relation between them denoted by these words. But, if there is one, I don't think it is an obvious one; and if we want to find one identical relation, denoted by these words, which they obviously do all have to A, we must, I think, look for it in another direction. The *indirect* relation which B has to A, consisting in the fact that each is at one end of *this* space, is obviously not the same as that which C has to A, consisting in the fact that each is at one end of *this* other space. What, therefore, is *the* identical relation, if there is one, which B and C both obviously have to A? We must, I think, say that it consists in the fact that B and A are each of them at the end of *a* space, and C and A are also each of them at the end of *a* space. So that here we have a new type of indirect relation—namely an indirect relation consisting in the fact that each of two things is related to one or other of a *group* of things which are not universals. When any two things A and B are at a distance from one another, what is meant by this is that each of them is at one end of *some* space or *other*. This is a relation which really does unite all such pairs, and is absolutely and exactly the same identical relation in every case.

So far, then, we have come across six different types of universals or general ideas, which undoubtedly are in the Universe, *three* of which may be called properties, while three may be called relations. The three kinds of properties were these: (1) properties which consist in the having a relation to some *one thing* which is not a universal; (2) properties which consist in having a relation to some one or other of a group of things which are *not* universals; and (3) properties which consist in being a member of a group of things which are not universals. All these three properties you see presuppose universals of the other type—the type which I have called relations. And the three kinds of relations we found were these: (1) direct relations between two terms; (2) indirect relations between two terms, consisting in the fact that each of them has some relation to some third thing, which is not a universal; and (3) indirect relations between two terms, consisting in the fact that each of them has some relation to some one or other of a group of things which are not universals.

And having once recognised these six types of universals, we may, of course, also recognise five more. Namely (1) three kinds of properties, which consist in the having of a relation not to something which is *not* a universal, but to a universal of the types we have recognised; and (2) two kinds of indirect relations between two terms, which consist in the fact that each has some relation, *not* to something which is not a universal, but to a universal of one or other of the types we have recognised. The recognition of these new types involves complications in statement to which I have not attempted to do justice; but I don't think it's necessary to elaborate them, though it is necessary to allude to them for the sake of avoiding misunderstandings. The important point, I think, is this. We have so far recognised two main types of universals, properties and relations. But all the properties we have so far recognised consist in the having of a relation to something or other—either to *one* something, or to one or other of a group of somethings or to a whole group of somethings. And of course *the* somethings in question may be any kind of thing that there is in the Universe. They may be what I will now call particulars as distinguished from universals—things like this patch of white; they may be truths; or they may themselves be universals. But if they are universals, then, so far as we have seen hitherto, they must either themselves be properties, which consist again in the having a relation to something or other, or relations; because we have recognised no kinds of universals except these two. And similarly the third something or group of somethings which is involved in indirect relations may be any kind of thing that there is in the Universe: they also may be either particulars or truths or universals. But if they are universals, then they also must either be relations or properties which consist in the having of a relation to something or other. We may say then shortly: that we have so far recognised no universals except (1) relations and (2) properties which consist in the having of a relation to something or other. And I want to insist on this, because the question I now want to raise is: *are* there any other kinds of universals except these?

Chapter XVIII

RELATIONS, PROPERTIES AND RESEMBLANCE

I have called attention to two different kinds of 'universals' or 'general ideas', which I called respectively 'relations' and 'properties'. I want now just to give an instance, as simple as I can find, of both these two kinds of universals, in order to make as clear as possible exactly what sort of things they are, and how the two differ from one another.

Let us take these two little patches of chalk on the blackboard, which I will call 'A' and 'B'. Now it is natural to say that A has to the group consisting of the two a relation which consists in the fact that it is one of the two, or a member of the group; and that B also has to the group the same relation. It is natural to say this, and I did myself speak in this way last time. But I want now to point out that this way of speaking is not quite accurate. There is not, strictly speaking, any relation at all which consists in the fact that A is a member of that group. The fact that A is a member of that group is *not* a relation: it is a fact or a truth, and is a good instance of the sort of thing I mean by a fact or a truth. And I want to call attention to this inaccuracy of language, because I think it often gives rise to serious misunderstanding. The fact that A is a member of that group, is obviously not identical with the fact that B is so. A is a member of it, and B also is a member of it; but these are obviously two different facts, *not* one and the same. If, therefore, the relation between A and the group did really and strictly consist in the *fact* that A was a member of it, this relation would *not* be identical with any relation which B has to it: we could not say that B has to the group exactly the same relation which A has to it. And I think that this confusion—the confusion of the *fact* that A is a member of the group with the *relation* which A has to the group—is partly responsible for the view held by some philosophers that no two things can possibly have *exactly the same* relation to any third thing. What I want to maintain, and what is, I think, as clear as anything can be, is that A really has to that group precisely and identically the same relation as that which B has to it. *Both* have to it the relation which we express by the words 'is a member of': each is a member of it, in precisely and exactly the same sense. But, you see, this could not be the case if the relation between A and the group really and strictly consisted in the fact that A is a member of it and the relation between B and the group also consisted in the fact that B is a member of it, because the fact that A is a member of it is *not* identical with the fact that B is a member of it. And I am inclined to think that when some philosophers say, as they do say, that A has not and cannot have to the group A and B precisely and identically the same relation which B has to it, they are, in fact, merely thinking of this undoubted and obvious fact that the two *truths* are different. The truth that A is a member of A and B is undoubtedly and obviously different from the truth that B is a member of it. But the moment you distinguish between a truth and a relation, it is obvious that this undoubted difference between the two truths offers no obstacle whatever to the view that A and B each of them have to A and B precisely and identically the same *relation*. The relation between A and the group A and B is something which is abstracted from, and is a mere *constituent* of the whole truth or fact that A is a member of the group. And what seems to me obvious is that precisely and identically the same relation is also a constituent of the different truth or fact that B is a member of that group. We must therefore, distinguish strictly (though we don't always do so in language) between 'relations' on the one hand, and truths or facts on the other. No truth whatever is identical with a relation. But even when we have made this distinction, we are still liable to confuse relations with something else—namely with what I have called 'properties'. A has the property of being a member of the group A and B, and B also has precisely the same identical property. The property of being a member of the group A and B is, therefore, also something quite different from the truth or fact that A is a member of that group: the property is something which *does* belong both to A and to B; whereas the fact that A is a member of A and B obviously does *not* belong to B. But while this property differs from the truth or fact on the one hand, it also differs no less from the relation on the other. The *property* called 'being a member of the group A and B' is a property which does belong both to A and B; but which certainly does *not* belong to this third patch C. But, on the other hand, the relation called 'being a member' which A *has* to the group A and B, is precisely and identically the same as that which C has to the group

B and C: C is a member of the group B and C, in precisely the same sense in which A is a member of the group A and B; and yet C certainly has *not* got the property of being a member of the group A and B. We must therefore, distinguish the *relation* which A and B both have to A and B, from the property of having this *relation to A and B*, which belongs to them both. The *property* in question is a constituent of the two facts that A is a member of A and B, and that B is a member of A and B, but is not a constituent of the fact that C is a member of B and C. Whereas the *relation* expressed by 'is a member of' is a constituent of all three facts, and of millions of other facts in the Universe besides. In short, we must distinguish three very different things namely (1) the fact or truth 'that A is a member of A and B'; (2) the property 'being a member of A and B' which belongs both to A and to B, but not to C; and (3) the relation 'being a member of' which relates *both* A to A and B, *and* B to A and B, *and* C to B and C. The relation is a constituent of the property but is *not* identical with it; and the property again is a constituent of the truth or fact but is *not* identical with it. It seems to me as clear as anything can be that all these three things are different from one another, and that all three undoubtedly *are* and are in the Universe; and I want to insist on the distinction, because we are liable to call them all by the same name, and therefore, I think, to confuse them with one another. I admit that if I am mistaken with regard to this, *if* these three things are not all of them in the Universe, and *if* they are not all different from one another, then all that I have been saying and am going to say about truths and universals, is nonsense. But I must say I don't see how I can be mistaken in the matter. We can, it seems to me, distinguish perfectly clearly between the three things in question—the fact, the property, and the relation—and we can see that all of them *are*.

We have, then, here a clear and simple instance both of a relation and a property. The relation is the relation called 'being a member of'; and absolutely everything which is a member of any group whatever, has to the group of which it is a member precisely this same identical relation. The property on the other hand is the property called 'being a member of the group A and B', and this same identical property does belong both to A and to B and does *not* belong to anything whatever in the Universe except A and B. These are my instances of a 'property' and a 'relation'. But this particular relation happens to be what I called last time a *direct* relation; and I explained last time that many relations are indirect: but I don't think I need now go into the difference between direct and *indirect* relations and the difference between the two different kinds of indirect relations. All that is important to notice, for the moment, is that indirect relations are distinguished from and related to properties in exactly the same way in which direct relations are. *No* relation, whether direct or indirect, *is* identical with any property. But on the other hand every property, so far as we have yet seen, has some relation as a constituent of it. And in order to make it quite clear in what sense relations are constituents of properties, I think I must just mention the difference between the different kinds of properties which I distinguished last time. This particular property which we have just been considering, the property of being a member of the group A and B, consists in the having of a relation *to* this group. And this is an instance of *one* of the three kinds of properties which I distinguished last time—namely properties which consist in the having of a relation to some one group or collection. But just as we may have a property which consists in the having of a relation to some one group or collection, so we may have properties which consist in the having of a relation to some one thing, which is *not* a group or collection. The property of being near this patch A—a property which belongs both to B and to C and to many other things—is a property of this kind. This was a second kind of property which I distinguished last time. And both these two kinds of properties have this in common that they do consist in the having of a relation to some one thing; they differ only in respect of the fact that in the one case the thing in question is a group or collection, while in the other it isn't. But the third kind of property, which I distinguished last time, is extremely different from either of these. It consists in the having of a relation to *some one or other* of a group of things. For instance, the property called 'being a member of a group', which is equivalent to 'being a member of some group or other', is a property of this kind. And I have two reasons for wishing to call attention to properties of this kind. The first reason is that, they can't be strictly said to consist in the having of a relation to any one thing. They simply don't consist in this: they consist in the having of a relation to some one or other of a group of things, *not* to any one particular member of the group, nor yet to the group itself. The difference is, I think, quite easy to see. For instance: Every man has the property of being a son of *some* father or *other*. And this property is obviously not the same as that which consists in his being a son of his particular father. The property of being a son of some father or other is a property which he shares with all other men: but by no means all other men are sons of his particular father. But, on the other hand, the property of being a son of some father or other can also plainly not be analysed into the having the relation 'being a son of' to the whole group of fathers: he is not a son of all the fathers there are, but only of some one or other of the group. Properties of this kind, therefore, cannot be strictly said to consist in the having of a relation to any one thing, whether a group or an individual. And one reason why I wish to emphasize this is because, I am going nevertheless to speak of them as if they did. I am going for the sake of convenience, to speak of all these three kinds of properties I have just distinguished as properties which consist in the having of a relation to *something or other*. I want some common name to cover all three and I can't think of any better one than this, though I admit it is not strictly accurate. And the second reason why I want to emphasize properties of this third kind is because it is particularly easy to confuse them with relations. For instance it is extremely natural to speak of the relation which I have called 'being a member of' as the relation 'being a member of a group'. We can hardly avoid so speaking of it. And yet, strictly speaking, what the words 'being a member of a group' stand for, is a *property* and *not* a relation. By 'being a member of a group' we mean 'being a member of *some* group *or other*', and this is of course a property which does, in fact, belong to anything whatever which has the relation 'being a member of' to any group whatever. But yet I think it is quite plain that the property and the relation must be distinguished. The *relation* does not *belong* to anything whatever in the sense in which this property does: it merely *relates* two things to one another. And what relates A for instance to the group A and B is plainly not the property of being the member of *some group or other*. This property plainly does not constitute a relation between A and the particular group A and B. And what I mean by the *relation* 'being a member of' is something which really does constitute a relation between A and A and B—which really does hold between them or relate them.

I am going, then, to say that we have so far recognised two kinds of universals, namely (1) relations and (2) properties which consist in *the having of a relation to something or other*—though I admit that the latter phrase is inaccurate for the reason I stated. And the question I want now to raise is: Are there any other kinds of universals, besides these two, or are there not?

I said many people seem to suppose that there are. And in discussing whether there are or not, I think I had better start at the beginning—putting the question in the way in which it has actually presented itself in the history of philosophy. Everybody would agree that these two patches of white—the two sense-data, which any one of you directly perceives—have something in common—something which we should express by saying that they are both of them patches of white. They resemble one another not only in respect of the fact that they are patches, but also in respect of the fact that they are *white* patches. And the obvious thing to say is that what we mean when we say this, is that they both possess a property called 'whiteness'—one and the same identical property possessed by both of them—which is a universal. And many people would, I think, add that all of us, who are not blind, know quite well what whiteness is, and know, therefore what the universal is which is a common property of these two white patches.

But, if we do say this, we are, I think, liable to be making a mistake. I admit that we do know what 'whiteness' is; but the property which we most commonly mean by 'whiteness' is, it seems to me, *not* a property which belongs to these two *patches*, meaning by these patches, the *sense-data* which any one of us is now directly perceiving. We know that lilies are white, and that snow is white; and the property which is common to lilies and snow seems to me to be the property which we commonly mean by whiteness. But this property which is common to lilies and snow, is, I think, obviously a property which does *not* belong to any sense-datum. The property which is common to lilies and to snow certainly consists, in the first instance, in the *having a relation* to one or other of the *sense-data* which we call *white* patches. Three different views may be taken as to precisely what the relation is which they have to these sense-data. To begin with (and this, I think, is the natural view) we may mean, when we say that a lily is white, that a patch of white is actually *on its surface*: that is to say, we may hold that one of the sense-data which we call patches of white, has a *spatial* relation to the object which we call a lily—the relation of being spread over its surface. Or, secondly, we may say that one of the sense-data which we call patches of white is not merely on the surface of the lily but is actually a *part* of it. Both these views are, I think, very natural ones to take, and we do, I believe, habitually think of the colours which we directly perceive as being on the surface of the material objects, which we call 'white' or 'green' or 'red' or 'blue' or whatever it may be. But to both those two views, as we have seen, there is the objection, that there seems reason to think that no sense-datum ever is, in fact, either on the surface of, or a part of, any material object whatever: sense-data, when they are in space at all, are, we saw reason to think, only in a private space, belonging only to the person who directly perceives them, and having no spatial relation whatever to the space in which material objects are. Of course, even if this be so, it might be the case that when we say a lily is white, we do actually mean that a sense-datum of the kind we call a patch of white *is* on its surface: we may actually *mean* this, although we should be wrong; and I am inclined to think we do very often mean it, even when we have accepted the ordinary philosophical view that no sense-datum is ever on the surface of any material object. That is to say, we constantly, in common life hold views inconsistent with our philosophical view. But, of course, there is another thing we might mean which would be quite consistent with the ordinary philosophical view about sense-data. When we say a lily is white, what we might mean is that, in a normal light, when we are looking at the lily, it *causes* us to perceive a sense-datum of the kind which we call a patch of white. This or something similar is the only sense in which, on the ordinary philosophical view about sense-data, a lily or snow or any other material object *can* really be white at all: it can only be white, in the sense that under certain normal circumstances, it *causes us* to perceive one of the sense-data which I call 'a patch of white'. But, you see, whichever of these three views we take, the property which belongs to lilies and snow and other white objects merely consists, in the first instance, in the *having a relation* to one or other of the group of sense-data which I call 'patches of white'. And it is quite obvious that the sense-data themselves—these two white patches which I see, for instance—have *not* got *this* property. These two white patches—the actual sense-data I directly perceive—are not white, in the same sense in which lilies and snow are white. Their common property certainly does not consist in the fact that two other patches of white are on their surface, or parts of them, or caused by them.

What, then, we commonly mean by 'whiteness', seems to me to be a property which belongs to material objects, and which consists in the first instance in the having of a relation to the sense-data which I call 'patches of white', and is certainly not therefore, a property which belongs to these sense-data themselves. And when we once realise this, it makes us I think a little more doubtful as to what the property is, which *is* common to all the sense-data which I call 'patches of white', and whether we *do* know so well what this property is. The ultimate question is: What is the property which is common and peculiar to all the *sense-data*, which I call 'white patches'? And we can't settle this question by simply saying it is 'whiteness', for it certainly is not 'whiteness' in at least one ordinary sense of the term: it is not the kind of whiteness which belongs to lilies and snow and paper and other white material objects. To put the question in another way: What is the property which belongs to all *sensations* of white, and *only* to *sensations* of white? Does this property consist in their all having a common relation to some one thing? And if so what is this thing to which they all have a common relation, and what is the relation which they all have to it. And if not, what does the property consist in?

This seems to me to be an exceedingly difficult question to answer; and yet I think it is a question of the last importance, if we really want to understand what the constitution of the Universe is like: and therefore I am going to treat it as carefully as I possibly can. If we answer it in one way, we shall have to conclude that there are in the Universe enormous numbers of universals, which are *neither* relations *nor* properties which consist in the having of a relation to something or other, and which are also extremely different in their nature from what I will call 'particulars'—meaning by 'particulars' things which are *not* universals nor facts. Many philosophers seem to me constantly to assume that there are an enormous number of universals of this kind in the Universe and yet not to pay any particular attention to them, or try to give any clear account of their nature. And on the other hand many seem to assume that there are no such things at all. And though, *if* there are such things, we must all of us, be constantly thinking of them and having them before our minds, it must, I think, be admitted that we don't commonly *notice* that there are such things at all: that is to say, we do not notice that what is happening in our minds when we think of them is something very different from the mere thinking of particulars.

Now it might be said, first of all, that there is *no* property at all, which is *both* common *and* peculiar to all the sense-data which I should *call* 'white patches'. There is no doubt of course, that there are several different properties and not one only, common to them all; but what might be doubted is whether any one of them is also *peculiar* to them—belongs exclusively to them, and does *not* belong to anything which is *not* a white patch. This difficulty arises because we certainly do apply the name 'white' to many different shades, which are not perfectly pure white, and because, as you know, the colours form continuous series—they shade off into one another. That is to say, if we are going to say, as we certainly do say, that several different shades of white are all of them 'white', the question arises where we are to draw the line. For, starting from pure white, we can, for instance, get a continuous series of shades of a more and more yellowish white, passing insensibly into pure yellow; and though there is no doubt that we should call those which hardly differ at all from pure white 'whites', it is very difficult to say at what point we get to a colour which we should *not* call 'a white'. And just as we can get a continuous series of yellowish whites, passing from pure white through whitish yellows to pure yellow; so we can get a continuous series of bluish whites, passing from pure white to blue; and a continuous series of reddish whites passing from pure white to red; and so on in many different cases. And, moreover, though we might be disposed to call all yellowish whites 'whites' we should not be disposed to call all whitish yellows 'whites': we should certainly say that some of them were yellow and *not* white: and yet obviously we may get shades, with regard to which we should find it very difficult to say whether they are yellowish whites or whitish yellows; and moreover, even if we get a shade which is undoubtedly a whitish yellow and *not* a yellowish white, is it not the case that a whitish yellow always does possess the property, in virtue of which we call all whites 'whites', so that this property, in virtue of which we call all whites 'white' would not be *peculiar* to whites, but would belong also to whitish yellows, whitish blues, whitish reds and so on? We should, I think, be inclined to say that the difference between a yellowish white and a whitish yellow consists in the fact that the yellowish white is *more* white than yellow, or has more white *in* it, whereas the whitish yellow is more yellow than white—has more yellow *in* it. But this shews, you see, that we do use the word 'white' in two different senses. We can't deny that a whitish yellow, however much *more* yellow than white it may be, yet if it is white at all in any degree *is*, in a sense, white. Whereas, on the other hand, if it is hardly white at all, we should certainly class it not as a white, but as a yellow. We must, I think, recognise those two senses of the word 'white'; and if we do so, then I am inclined to think this first difficulty has been got over. We must, I think, say that in *one* sense of the word 'white', we call a patch a white patch *only* if it is *either* 'pure white' *or* nearer to pure white than it is to any other pure colour; and one question which we might try to answer is: *What* is the property which is both common and peculiar to all white patches which are white in this sense? But in another sense of the word 'white', we must, I think, admit that whitish yellows, and blues and reds, etc., however much more yellow and red and blue they may be than *white*, nevertheless *are* white, if we use this expression to mean what we often express by 'have some white *in* them'; and the question what *this* property is, will be a different one.

But the first of these two senses is certainly that in which it is most natural to use the word 'white' as applied to sense-data; and I propose, therefore, first to consider the question: 'What is the property which is both common and peculiar to all sense-data which are white in this first sense?'

Now I suggested last time that the *only* property which is *both* common and peculiar to all these patches, might be *merely* that each is a member of the group consisting of all such patches. This certainly *is a* property which is both common and peculiar to them all; and I suggested that it might be the only one. But I said there were reasons for doubting whether this is so; and I now think that it is in fact quite plain that this is *not* the *only* property common and peculiar to them all. I think this can be best seen in the following way. Absolutely any set of things in the Universe, however unlike they may be to one another, do, of course form a group. We can for instance think of a group consisting of one particular colour, one particular sound, and one particular smell. Such a group is, of course, really a group; and of all the members of it it will, of course, be true that one property is both common and peculiar to them all—the property namely of being members of that group. Each of them is a member of that group, and nothing in the Universe except one of them is a member of it. This will obviously be true of any group whatever, however arbitrarily it may be chosen. And what seems to me plain is that the group we are now considering—the group consisting of all sense-data which we should without hesitation call 'white' does differ in some way from such groups as these: all its members surely are related to one another in some way in which the members of a purely arbitrary group are *not* related: it is in some sense a natural group. But the very thing we mean by saying that it is not purely arbitrary, but natural, is that there *is* some other property, *beside* mere membership of the group, which *is* both common and peculiar to all its members. This, so far as I can see, is the only way of distinguishing a natural group from an arbitrary one; and I think there certainly is such a distinction. Of *every* natural group then, we may say that all its members must have *some* property both common and peculiar to them all, besides the mere being members of the group. And the group we are now considering is, I think certainly a *natural* group.

The question is, then: What *is* this property? And a very natural suggestion to make in answer to this question is, I think, that it can be somehow defined by means of the relation of resemblance. It certainly seems, in a sense, to be *because* all sense-data which are white *resemble* one another in a certain respect, that we class them together and think of them as a natural group. And I think there is a tendency, in some philosophers, to be content with this explanation and not to look any further. But, if we do look further, it is, I think, quite plain that this explanation certainly won't do, as it stands.

The whole subject of *resemblance* or similarity is, I think, very confusing; and I think it is worth while to go into it rather carefully.

To begin with it might be said: Take any one particular white sense-datum you like: then, all the others *do* resemble it, and that is what distinguishes them from the rest of the things in the Universe from all things that are not white in that particular sense. All other white patches do resemble our one white patch, whichever it is that we take; whereas nothing else does. Here then we have a property which is common and peculiar to them all. But, apart from another objection to which I shall presently come, there is one very obvious objection to this theory: namely that what it says is, in a sense at all events, plainly untrue. Whatever white patch you take, it is obviously not true, that nothing in the Universe except white patches resemble it at all. On the contrary absolutely everything in the Universe must resemble it *in a sense*. Absolutely everything in the Universe must resemble it in one respect at least—in respect of the fact that they are both in the Universe. That is to say, there certainly is a sense in which absolutely everything in the Universe resembles everything else: everything does resemble everything else in at least one respect. So that the property of merely resembling our one white patch, whichever patch you take, is certainly not *peculiar* to other white patches though it is common to them: so far from being peculiar to them, it is shared by them with absolutely everything else in the Universe.

But it may be said: Though this is true of *one* sense of the word resemblance, there certainly is another sense in which one thing may be quite unlike another thing—may not resemble it *at all*. We certainly do constantly speak in this way: we constantly say that one thing is quite unlike, *quite* different from another thing, and what we *mean* by this is certainly often true. There is, therefore, a sense of the word 'resemble' in which one thing may definitely *not* resemble another at all. And, for my part, I don't see my way to deny that this is true. There may possibly be more senses than one in which one thing may be *quite* unlike another. But there seems to me to be at least one, which is very important, though it is very difficult to define. One thing which we may mean when we say that one thing is quite unlike another, is, I think, that it is quite unlike it internally: that, though the two may resemble one another in respect of the fact that they have some common property—some common relation to other things, yet, *in themselves* or internally, they are quite unlike. I don't profess to be able to define what is meant by internal likeness, as distinct from external; but it seems to me something is meant, and something important, by saying this, so that it is worth while to consider whether we can answer our problem by reference to internal likeness. Suppose, then, somebody says : Take any white patch you like: every other white patch does resemble that patch *internally*, and nothing else in the Universe does. Is this true? Quite obviously it isn't. However we define internal resemblance, it is quite plain that a pure red patch does resemble a reddish white patch *internally*. So that we can't say: Take any white patch you like: then all other white patches do resemble it internally, and nothing that is not a white patch does. On the contrary, for any white patch you choose to take, there will be something, not white at all, which does resemble it internally: if your patch is a yellowish white, a pure yellow will; if a bluish white, a pure blue will, and so on. We certainly cannot, therefore, by mere reference to *internal* resemblance define a property which besides being common, is also *peculiar* to our white patches.

We have failed then to find what we require, either by considering mere resemblance, or by considering internal resemblance.

It might be next suggested that degree or closeness of internal resemblance might serve our purpose. It might be said: 'Take any white patch you like; then all the rest will have to it a closeness of internal resemblance which nothing else has: they will resemble it internally more closely than anything else in the Universe does'. But this again is obviously not true. Suppose the white patch you pitch on is very nearly, if not quite, pure white. Then obviously another patch which is distinctly white, but also a distinctly yellowish white, may have a closer internal resemblance to a whitish yellow patch, than to our pure white one. That is to say a patch which is *not* white at all, but only a whitish yellow, will resemble our yellowish white patch internally *more* closely than many patches which *are* white. And almost any white patch you choose will be subject to the same objection. It will not be true that all other white patches resemble it internally more closely than anything else in the Universe does. Here again therefore, we have failed to find a property which is *peculiar* to white patches. Closeness of internal resemblance won't serve our purpose any better than internal resemblance, or mere resemblance.

But it might be said: 'In the last two cases we failed only because we said: Take any white patch *you like*, and then nothing but white patches will resemble it internally, or will resemble it internally with the degree of closeness with which all other white patches do. If you take any white patch *you like* then these things are obviously not true. But there is *one* kind of white patch, such that, if you restrict the choice to patches of that kind, both things do become true. Absolutely pure white stands in an unique position and if you take a patch of absolutely pure white; then it is true that absolutely nothing in the Universe except white patches do resemble it internally so closely as all other white patches do.' But I can see several reasons why even this must be disputed.

For one thing it seems to me that the following is a fatal objection to it—an objection which also applies to all the other theories we have considered, though I did not mention it in their case because there were other more obvious objections to them. The objection I mean is this. We are supposed to have taken one particular patch of absolutely pure white; and we are supposing it true that all other white patches do resemble this one more closely than anything else in the Universe does. And if this is true, we really have found a property which is both common and peculiar to all other white patches *except* the absolutely pure white one we have taken. But the absolutely fatal objection to our theory just consists in this—that we must make this one exception. Even if the property we have found really were both common and peculiar to all other white patches *except* the one we have taken, yet just because it would be peculiar to them—would belong *only* to them—it follows that it would *not* belong to the one we have taken. And obviously it would not. That particular white patch does not *resemble* itself: it *is* itself—which is a very different thing. This one white patch therefore has *not* got the property which we have supposed to be common and peculiar to all the rest. And yet obviously it *has* got the property we are looking for—the one which is common and peculiar to *all* white patches. It follows, therefore, that the property we have found is *not* the one we were looking for, it is not a property which is *both* common *and* peculiar to *all* white patches. And this, you see, is an absolutely general objection to any proposal to define a property which is common and peculiar to *all* the members of a group, as consisting in any kind of resemblance to one among its members. Resemblance, of any kind whatever, *to* one of the members of the group is always necessarily a property which does *not* belong to *all* the members of the group, because it does *not* belong to the member chosen as the one which the rest resemble: the chosen member does *not* resemble itself, it *is* itself, or (if you like) is *identical* with itself. Any attempt therefore to define in this way a property both common and peculiar to the members of a group must always fail because it leaves out at least *one* member: there must be *one* member which does not possess the property in question. It may be said, of course, that this difference between resembling a thing and *being* that thing itself, is not an important one: that there is no important difference between the relation of resemblance and the relation of pure identity. But whether this is so or not, it must, I think, be admitted that there is *a* difference. What we commonly mean by resemblance is a relation which a thing certainly cannot have to *itself*: it is a relation which can *only* hold between two different things—things which are, at least, *numerically* different—are two. And hence, so long as we use the word 'resemblance' in its ordinary sense, we must, I think, definitely abandon the attempt to define a property common and peculiar to all the members of a group by means of resemblance to any one of them. This point: that we can't define the required property in this way by means of resemblance in its ordinary sense is the first point I want to make. And I think it is worth making, because I think it is often overlooked.

But, of course, this particular reason for giving up *this* theory, points to two other theories which might possibly give us what we want. The first of these is what, I think, would be naturally meant by anyone who was inclined to deny any *important* difference between identity and resemblance. Such a person might say that a thing always has to itself *some* relation which things which resemble it *also* have to it: that there is, in this sense, something *common* to the relation of resemblance and pure identity. And they might then propose to define the property we want by reference to this supposed relation which is always involved *both* in resemblance and identity, but is identical with neither. What I want to insist on is that, even if this can be done, it is not the same thing as defining the required property by means of *resemblance*. We are still entitled to say that mere *resemblance*, of whatever kind or degree, certainly won't give us the property we want. And for my part I don't see any reason to suppose that there is any such relation as this theory would require—a relation which everything always has to itself, and which is susceptible of degrees, so that those things which resemble a thing most closely internally would also have to the thing this very same relation which it has to itself, though in a less degree. But I am not prepared to prove that there is no such relation: so that we must admit this theory as one possible solution of our difficulty—a solution which nothing that I have said will exclude.

And the second theory, which still remains possible is as follows. It is the theory that the property we are looking for—the property which is common and peculiar to all whitish patches—may be merely what I will call a *disjunctive* property. It might, for instance, be said: Suppose you take any particular patch of absolutely pure white, which we will call 'A'; then a property which is *both* common and peculiar to absolutely all white patches, including A, is given in the fact that each of them *either* resembles A more closely internally than anything else in the Universe does *or* is A. This, you see, is why I call it a *disjunctive* property; namely because it consists in the having *either* of one property *or* another—*either* the resembling A with a peculiar degree of closeness or the *being* A. And it can't be denied, I think, that if all the patches of white in the Universe, except A, do resemble A internally more closely than anything else does, then this disjunctive property really is *a* property which is both common and peculiar to absolutely *all* the white patches in the Universe: each of them *either* is one of the closely resembling patches *or* it is A: this really *is* a property which does belong both to A itself and to all the rest; and it is a property which belongs to them all, even if there is nothing in common between *being* A and *resembling* A—between resemblance and identity. It does seem to me possible that there really is no property both common and peculiar to absolutely all white patches, except some such disjunctive property. I don't see any way absolutely to refute the suggestion that this may be so; and that therefore the property we want may be a purely disjunctive one.

Chapter XIX

DISJUNCTIVE AND OTHER PROPERTIES

THE point I have been trying to bring out is as follows. I have tried to show that there certainly are in the Universe two different kinds of 'universals' or 'general ideas' namely (1) relations and (2) properties which consist in the having of a relation to something or other. There certainly are in the Universe enormous numbers of different universals of both these two kinds. And I am going to assume that you now understand perfectly clearly what I mean by these two kinds of universals. Well, then: The point I have been trying to bring out was that, *beside* these two kinds, there probably also are in the Universe universals of a third quite different kind. This seems to me to be a thing which it is extremely difficult to shew quite clearly; but I think it is certainly worth while to try to do so. If it is true, if there *are* in the Universe universals of this third kind, then it is certain that they are one of the most important kinds of things that there are in it at all. *If* there are any such things at all, they are things which we all of us constantly have before our minds—things of which we are all constantly thinking and talking. But yet, if we try to give any general account of the Universe—to mention the chief kinds of things that there are in it—we are, I think, very apt not to notice these universals at all: just to overlook them and leave them out, and talk as if the Universe consisted exclusively of other kinds of things. This is true, I think, even of my first two kinds of universals—of relations, and of properties which consist in the having of a relation to something or other. Many philosophers speak as if there were in the Universe no such things even as these—as if, in short, there were no such things as universals of any kind whatever. But it is, I think, particularly true of this third kind of universals, because, in their case, it is so much more difficult to distinguish them clearly—to find them and hold them before your mind, even if you look for them.

I have been trying to give reasons for thinking that there are universals of this third kind. And I thought we might find one, if we considered one particular group of sense-data. There is a group of sense-data, which may be called patches of colour. (Under the term 'patches', as I said in footnote 1 on p. 30, I include patches of absolutely any shape or size, including even the smallest visible speck.) And, included in this group, there is a smaller group, consisting of those patches and those only, which are either pure white or, if not quite pure white, are certainly white. It was this smaller group that I chose to consider—the group consisting of all patches of colour which are certainly white, including those which are pure white.

And it was in the hope of finding a universal of my third kind that I raised the question: What property is there which belongs to all the members of this group, and to nothing else whatever in the Universe? We say, first, that one property which does undoubtedly belong to them all and to nothing else, is simply that of being members of this group; and if this were the *only* property which belonged to them all and to nothing else, we should, of course, not have found a universal of my third kind. For *this* property is only a universal of my second kind—a relational property. But I gave reasons for thinking, and it is, I think, pretty obvious, that, besides this, there is at least *one* other property which belongs to all of them and only to them. And so we proceeded to look for such a property. We did not find one. But I suggested one property, which seemed to me to come nearer to satisfying the requirement, than the others which I considered; and I want now very shortly, to state again what this property is and what is the objection to it, because I think I can state it more correctly and more plausibly than I did last time.

Every patch of yellowish white does, I think, undoubtedly resemble *every* patch of pure white more closely, *in one respect*, than *any* patch of pure yellow ever resembles *any* patch of pure white. This seems to me absolutely certain and undeniable. And we all know what name is given to the respect in question; it is in respect of its colour or shade or hue. We may say, then, that the resemblance, *in respect of colour*, between a pure white patch and a yellowish white patch, is always greater than that between a pure white patch and a pure yellow patch. In *other* respects, of course, the internal resemblance between a pure yellow and a pure white patch may be much the greater of the two. For instance we may have a pure white and a pure yellow patch of exactly the same size and shape—say, *this* shape (on the board)—and a yellowish white patch of this very different size and shape. And in that case the resemblance of the pure yellow patch to the pure white one, *in respect* both of size and of shape, will, of course, be very much *greater* than that of the yellowish white to the pure white. But, in spite of that, there is obviously *one* respect in which a yellowish white patch *always* resembles a pure white one more closely than a pure yellow one ever does—*namely* in respect of its colour or shade or hue. *Every* yellowish white patch, therefore, always does resemble any pure white patch more closely, *in respect of colour*, than any pure yellow patch *ever* resembles *any* pure white patch in that respect. And in the same way it is, I think, quite plain that *all* white patches, with the single exception of the pure whites themselves, do, *in respect of colour*, resemble *all* the pure whites more closely than anything else in the Universe resembles any pure white. This, I think, is the most obvious property which *does* belong to all of them and does not belong to anything else in the Universe: namely a certain degree of resemblance, *in respect of colour*, to *all* the pure whites. They all of them really have to the pure whites a degree of resemblance, in respect of colour, which nothing else in the Universe has. We have, therefore, found a property which does belong to all white patches, *except* the pure white ones, and which belongs to nothing else in the Universe. And it might be suggested that this is the only property, of which it is true both that all white patches possess it in common and that nothing else in the Universe does possess it. But the fatal objection to this suggestion, as we saw last time, is that the pure white patches themselves do not possess it. It is not true of them that *each* of them has, in respect of colour, a degree of resemblance to *all* the pure white patches, which nothing else in the Universe has. It is not true of them, simply because no one of them resembles *itself* at all, in any degree. Each undoubtedly has to all the *rest*—the other pure white patches—the degree of resemblance in question. But it has not got this degree of resemblance to itself, for the simple reason that it does not *resemble* itself at all, but simply *is* itself. No one of the pure white patches, therefore, has the required degree of resemblance to *all* the pure white patches: it only has it to all the *rest*, *except* itself. And we cannot, therefore, say that the property of having a certain degree of resemblance to all the pure white patches, in respect of colour, is a property which belongs to *all* white patches; simply because this property does *not* belong to all of the pure white patches themselves.

This objection however, as I said, at once suggests *another* property which really does belong to *all* white patches and to nothing else. The property I mean is this. Each of them really does have the property of *either* possessing the required degree of resemblance, in respect of colour, to all the pure white patches, *or being* a pure white patch. Of every pure white patch it *is* true that it either has the required degree of resemblance to the pure whites *or is* a pure white. This is true of all the pure whites, because each of them *is* a pure white patch, i.e. fulfils the second condition laid down in the disjunction. And it is also true of all the other white patches—all that are not pure white: it is true of them, because each of them *has* the required degree of resemblance, in respect of colour, to all the pure whites, i.e. because they fulfil the first condition laid down in the disjunction. It is true, therefore, that absolutely every white patch does fulfil one or other of the two conditions laid down in this disjunction; and hence absolutely every one of them does possess the disjunctive property of *either* resembling the pure whites in that special respect and degree *or* being a pure white. And certainly nothing else in the Universe does possess this disjunctive property: of nothing else in the Universe is it true that it either is a pure white patch *or* has the required degree of resemblance to pure white patches in respect of colour; nothing else in the Universe fulfils the condition that *either* the first *or* the second is true of it. The disjunctive property really is, therefore, a property which fulfils our requirements: it really does belong to all white patches and to nothing else. And if anyone really thinks that this is the *only* property, besides membership of the group, which belongs to all white patches and to nothing else, I confess I don't see how to prove that it isn't. I think there is probably some way of proving that it isn't, but I haven't found any. I cannot, therefore, deny that this disjunctive property *may* be the one for which we are looking. And, of course, if this is the *only* property, besides membership of the group, which does belong to them all and to nothing else, we have still failed to find a universal of my third kind. For this property, also, is only a universal of my second kind.

But most people would, I think, be inclined to say that this disjunctive property can't be the *only* one, besides membership of the group, which belongs to all the group of white patches and to nothing else. It might be claimed that it is self-evident that there is some other property common and peculiar to them all—some property which is *not* merely a disjunctive one. And though I can't feel sure whether this is so or not; it is, I think, worth while to consider what this property can be, supposing there is one.

And many people would, I think, be inclined to say not only that it is quite obvious that there is such a property but also that it is quite obvious what the property is. They would say: It obviously consists in the fact that there is *some pure white in*, or *present in*, all of them; that some amount of pure white is an *element* in all of them, or that pure white is to *some extent* an element in all of them. We certainly should naturally say of all of them, *except* the pure white ones, that there was some white *in* all of them. We should say that there was *more* white in a bluish white than in a whitish blue, and that that is what constitutes the difference between them: and again that what constitutes the difference between both of them and a pure blue, is that in a pure blue there is no white at all whereas in both of the others there is some. And if we were asked what we meant by this thing, called 'white', which is *in* all of them, we should certainly be inclined to answer that we meant 'pure white'. As to pure white patches we should be inclined to say that what constitutes the difference between them and patches which are merely white, and not pure white, is that in all the latter some other colour, as well as pure white, is present in some degree, whereas in all pure white patches pure white alone is present and no other colour is. This is, I think, the most natural account to give of the whole matter. But it presents us with several new problems. If we say: *In* every patch of bluish white or yellowish white, pure white is present in some degree, there arises first the question what *is* this thing called 'pure white'? Hitherto we have only recognised pure white *patches* or patches of pure white, and it seems obviously untrue to say that *in* every patch of bluish white a *patch* of pure white is present. It is certainly not true that every patch of bluish white contains a patch of pure white as a constituent. Apparently, therefore, we mean by 'pure white' something different from any particular patch of pure white or from the sum of them all—something which is itself a universal common to them all. And the first question we must ask is what this universal called 'pure white' *is*; whether it is or is not different from a patch of pure white, and, if different, different in what way. And then secondly we must ask what is meant by saying that it is *in* all white patches: whether this which we call 'present in' is a name for a *relation* which it has to them, or not; and if so what the relation is. And finally we shall have to ask what is meant by saying that it is in them *in different degrees*: whether what is meant is that *more* pure white is present in one than in another; or whether, on the other hand, pure white is a thing which has no degrees, and the truth of the matter is only that it is *more* present in some than in others; whether—in short—the difference in degree is a difference in the amount of pure white that is present, or a difference in the degree of its presence.

And as regards the first question, the question what the universal 'pure white' is, two very different views may be taken. I have already explained that I mean by a 'patch' a patch of absolutely any size or shape, down to, and including, the smallest visible speck—a speck, with regard to which we should be inclined to say that it has no *shape* at all, and perhaps no size either. Let us consider a patch which is larger than a mere speck—*this* patch, for instance (on the board) that is to say, any sense-datum which any one of us directly apprehends in seeing this patch on the board: and let us suppose it is absolutely pure white, though probably it isn't. It is quite obvious that any such sense-given patch is divisible into or contains other patches which are parts of it, and each of which is just as much *a* pure white patch as the whole is. Let us divide it into two parts and consider these two parts. This part obviously differs from that one in size and in shape; and they obviously also differ in one other respect, namely that this one is in a different place from that one: this one, for instance, is nearer the sense-datum which represents the edge of the board than that one is. Now one view which may be held is this. It may be held that, in spite of their difference in size and shape, and in spite of the fact that they are in two different places, the two patches themselves are *not* different, but one and the same. To speak in this way is, of course, verbally self-contradictory: if they really are two, they can't be one and the same. But the view I mean is not *self*-contradictory, though it is difficult to express it except in words which seem to be so. We might try to express it in the following way. We might say: 'There is a colour called "pure white"; and this one colour is in both these two different places at once—occupies the whole of both of them simultaneously: and why we speak, as if it were not one thing but two, is because, in this place, it *has* a different size and shape, from that which it has in this one. But yet the truth of the matter is that it is one and the same colour, which has both these two different sizes and shapes: it has the one size and shape in the one place, and the other in the other: but it is *itself* in both places at once—one and the same thing really is in both places, and has both shapes and sizes simultaneously.' And similarly, if we take one pure white speck, here, and another here, both having the same size and shape: according to this view, what we have got is not two specks of pure white, though we should and must talk as if we had; the truth of the matter is that the very same thing called 'pure white', which was formerly *not* in these two places, is now in both of them; the truth is that the thing which is visibly in this place really is the very same thing which is also in this other.

This view certainly does, I think, seem very paradoxical and it does, I think, contradict what we all of us do believe and cannot help believing every day. But the advantage of it is that it makes the universal 'pure white' something which undoubtedly is—something which we all of us actually see, and with which we are all acquainted; and leaves, therefore, no doubt *either* that there *is* such a thing *or* as to *what* it is. When you look at a pure white patch you are, according to this view, actually seeing the universal 'pure white': the universal is part of what you are directly perceiving through the sense of sight. And, as against the objection that the view is paradoxical, it may be urged that it is merely treating space as if space were exactly analogous to *time*. We do all suppose, and it seems to be true, that one and the same thing may be at one and the same place at two different times. Whenever we suppose that a thing is absolutely at rest for any length of time, we are supposing that it is *in* the same place *at two different* times. But if a thing may be in the same place at two different times, why (it may be asked) should it not be at the same time in two different places? The two suppositions are *exactly* on a par, so that *if* space *were* exactly analogous to time, it really would be so; and this is all that our theory requires us to suppose. It certainly is therefore a conceivable theory and one that is not *self*-contradictory. And I must confess I can find no absolutely conclusive objection to it. The only objection I can urge against it is that it does seem to me self-evident that that which is in *this* place here is *not* the same as that which is in this other place. Although there is no *qualitative* difference between the two, it seems to me self-evident that they *are* numerically different—that they are two and not one and the same. Or to put the same objection in another form, it seems to me self-evident that the sense-datum which occupies the whole of this space really has parts, which are different from one another: that it is not merely true that the space it occupies has parts, whereas the patch of pure white itself is indivisible, and occupies each of them. But I can only urge that these things are self-evident: I can't think of any argument to *prove* that they are true. And I think, therefore, we must admit that this paradoxical theory is one possible theory as to the nature of the universal 'pure white'.

There is only one other point which I want to add about this theory. I have talked throughout as if this one thing called 'pure white', which, according to it, is in all these different places at the same time and in every part of all of them, really would be a 'universal'. I think those who hold the theory would say that it was. And, of course, *if* it was, it would be a universal of my third kind: for it certainly is neither a relation, nor a property which consists in the having of a relation to something or other. It simply *is* this colour which we see occupying *both* the whole of this space and every part of it. But what I want to point out is that if this colour is a universal, it would seem very doubtful whether there are any things that are *not* universals in the Universe at all, *except* particular places and times. If this patch of white which we actually see is not a particular, there seems no more reason to think that anything else is, *except particular places and times*. I think this is a real difficulty about this theory. Everybody commonly talks as if there were other particulars besides particular places and times; and even those who hold this theory do so. But yet, so far as I can see, if this theory were true, and if this patch of white were a universal, there would be no reason to suppose that there are any particulars at all except particular places and times. This difficulty, and indeed the whole problem which I am now considering as to the distinction between universals and particulars, is I think, apt to be concealed by the following way of speaking. People are apt to say: 'When we talk of "this *particular* patch of white", and call it a *particular* what we mean is "the universal *considered as* occupying this particular place". What we mean by the words "*this* particular patch of white", is the universal *considered as* occupying this place; and what we mean by *that* particular patch of white is the universal *considered as* occupying *that* one. The universal *considered as* occupying the one really *is* different from the same universal considered as occupying the other. And that is how such particulars differ from their universal. It is position in space which gives particularity to these universals'. But if you come to think of it, it is I think obvious that this phrase 'pure white *considered as* occupying this place' is *either* merely a name for the universal, or it is not a name for anything at all. There is nothing at all, distinct from the universal, for which it could be a name. It is true that the *whole* sentence, 'Pure white, considered as occupying this place, is *round*', really would have a meaning, and a meaning distinct from that of the sentence, 'Pure white is round'. Its meaning would be that pure white is round *in this place*; whereas it may be square or triangular in *other places*. But it is only the two *whole* sentences which have different meanings. The phrase, 'pure white considered as occupying this place' is not by itself a name for anything at all distinct from 'pure white'. The case is analogous to what we saw before. We saw that the whole sentence 'I am imagining a chimaera' certainly has a meaning and a meaning different from that of the whole sentence 'I am imagining a griffin'. But we saw that, in spite of this, it is a mistake to suppose that the words 'a chimaera' or 'a griffin' *by themselves* are names for anything at all. Whole sentences in which they occur are very often names for facts. But these phrases by themselves are not names for anything whatever. Well, in the same way, it seems to me quite plain that the phrase 'pure white considered as occupying this place' is not a name for anything at all distinct from pure white. There *is* nothing at all in the Universe of which the name is 'pure white considered as occupying this place'. That is to say we cannot analyse the fact expressed by the sentence, 'Pure white, considered as occupying this place, is round' into a particular called 'pure white considered as occupying this place', on the one hand, and a property called 'being round' on the other; any more than we can analyse the fact expressed by 'I am imagining a griffin' into 'a griffin', on the one hand, and the property of being imagined by me on the other. In short all particulars except particular times and places, would, on this view, be something purely imaginary—as imaginary as griffins or chimaeras. All that would be true would be that one and the same universal 'pure white', would be round in one place, and square in another; large in one place, and small in another. There would be no such thing as a particular called '*the* patch of pure white in this place', which *is* round, and *not* square. All that there would be would be the universal pure white, which is *both* round and square, but which is so in different places.

Still, all this forms no fatal objection to the theory that it is one and the same thing, called 'pure white', which is in all the different places in which we say that there is a patch of pure white. And it only remains to ask: Supposing this theory were true, could it be the case that this thing called 'pure white' really is *in* or present *in* all white patches? and that its presence in them is *the* property which is common and peculiar to them all? And, so far as I can see, we must answer 'No' to this question. To begin with, it must be emphasized that, according to this theory, the thing called 'pure white' is simply not *in* patches of pure white at all: it is not in them but *identical* with them all. Every patch of pure white *is* this thing; and is one and the same patch. It is, in fact, really a mistake, on this theory, to talk of *different* patches of pure white or *every* patch of pure white at all;

there is in fact only *one* patch which is in many different places and of many different sizes and shapes. It only remains, therefore, to consider whether this thing could possibly, in any sense, be *in* the other white patches—the ones that are not pure white: *in* all the different bluish and yellowish whites, for instance. And, so far as I can see, it certainly could not be. For we have to remember that 'pure white', on this theory, is the sense-datum which we actually see when we look at a patch of pure white. And hence, if we were to suppose that it is *in* a patch of bluish white, we should have to suppose that this sense-datum, so different from bluish white, really is *contained* in *every* part of the bluish white patch. In fact the supposition would be identical with the supposition that a *patch* of pure white of exactly the same size and shape as the patch of bluish white is *contained* in every patch of bluish white; and it seems to me quite plain that this is not so.

If, therefore, we accept this theory as to the nature of pure white we have failed to find any property that is common and peculiar to *all* white patches. But supposing we reject it, on the ground that what is in *this* place is self-evidently different from and not identical with what is in *this*, although both are patches of pure white. Supposing we reject it, what is the alternative?

Well, it must be remembered, that, if we reject it, we are saying that absolutely every speck of pure white which is in one place at any one time is a *different* speck from any speck which is in a different place at the same time. We shall have thus an immense number of different specks of pure white in the Universe, each numerically *different* from all the rest, although they are all exactly alike *in quality*. And it must be remembered that it is these specks, all different from one another, which are *what we see*, when we see patches of pure white. When I see this patch of pure white here, I am not seeing the *same thing* as when I see this patch here, though both of them are patches of pure white, and exactly alike in quality. All this seems the merest Common Sense; and it really is what we all commonly suppose. But then we are to suppose also that all these different specks have some property in common, a property, which may perhaps belong also to all specks which are in any degree white, but which certainly belongs to nothing else in the Universe. And we are supposing also that this property does not consist in the mere fact that they are all members of the group containing them all, and also that it is not merely a disjunctive property. What can this property be, if there is one?

Well, it seems to me there are two different views which may be taken with regard to it. And I want to explain the difference as carefully as I can. We have seen that there are some properties which consist in the *having* of a relation to something or other. These are, in fact, the only kind of properties we have yet recognised. We took as an instance the property of *belonging* to the group A and B—being a member of that group—being one of the two patches A and B. And we saw that this is a property which belongs both to A and to B. But we saw also that to say that A is a member of the group A and B is the same thing as to say that it has the *relation* of membership to that group. And we saw that this relation is one which not only relates A and B to A and B, but also relates everything whatever which is a member of any group whatever to the group of which it is a member. The *relation* of membership therefore is something quite different from A's *having* this relation to A and B. The relation is something which C also has to B and C, and is similarly a constituent of an infinite number of other facts in the Universe besides. And, if this be realised, it is natural to ask the question: What is meant by saying that A *has* this relation to A and B? Is it not, perhaps, meant that it *has* a relation to this relation? It has, I think, been suggested that *whenever* we say of one thing A that it *has* the relation R to another B, part of what is meant by saying that it *has* this relation to B, is that it has some relation *to* this relation. And what I want to point out is that this is quite impossible. It cannot possibly be the case that part of what is meant by *having* a relation R to so-and-so is merely the *having* another relation *to* R. For obviously, if we say this, we are trying to explain the notion of *having* a relation by means of the very notion we set out to explain. If we cannot understand, to begin with, what is meant by *having* the relation R, we cannot possibly understand any better what is meant by *having* another relation *to* R. Our proposed explanation is no explanation at all. We must, therefore, insist that the notion of *having* a relation is an ultimate notion; and that it cannot possibly include as a part the *having* of another relation *to* that relation. And I want to distinguish this point clearly from another with which it is liable to be confused. It may, perhaps, be the case that whenever one thing A has any relation, R, to another thing B, it must, as a matter of fact, *also* have another relation *to* the relation R. I am not denying this; and indeed I don't see how it can be denied. All that I am insisting on is that A's *having* the relation R to B cannot possibly include its *having* this other relation *to* R. What is meant by '*having* a relation R to B' can't possibly be explained by saying that part of its meaning is the having of a certain other relation to the relation R. But why I am insisting on this point is because it follows that where a *property* consists in the having of a relation to something or other, then this property *belongs* to the thing which has it, in some sense which does not mean that it is *related* to that thing. It is, I think, worth while insisting on this point, because, if we say, 'Such and such a property *belongs* to A' it is very natural to think that what we mean by the word 'belongs' must be some relation which the property has to A. But, you see, where the property itself consists in the having of a relation to something or other, this certainly cannot be the case. The property of being a member of A and B is a property which *belongs* to A in some sense which does *not* mean that it is related to A. This follows because to say that A has this property is merely equivalent to saying that A *has* the relation of membership to A and B; and we saw that no part of what is meant by *having* a relation can possibly be the *having* a relation *to* that relation. It is quite clear, then, that properties which consist in the having of a relation to something or other, *belong* to the things of which they are properties, in some sense which does *not* consist in being related to them. And once this is realised, it is obviously possible to ask: Why should not some other things—things which do *not* consist in the having a relation to something or other—also *belong* to a given thing, in this same sense—in a sense other than that of being related to them? Or, in other words: Why should there not be properties, which do not consist in the having a relation to something or other, but which yet *belong* to things in the same sense as those which do so consist belong? Many philosophers have, I think, spoken as if there were such properties. They have spoken as if some of the things, which are called 'predicates' or 'qualities', do belong to the things of which they are predicates or qualities, in some sense which does not consist in being related to them. They have spoken as if one thing A might be 'qualified by' another B, or might have B for a predicate, and as if, in saying this, they were *not* saying that B was related to A, even though B was something which did *not* merely consist in the having of a relation to something else. Now I should not like to say that there are any properties of this kind—properties, which do *not* consist in the having of a relation to something or other, but which yet *belong* to things in some sense which does *not* mean that they are related to them. Nobody, as far as I know, has ever succeeded in pointing out any property which is quite clearly of this kind. And what, I think, is quite clear is that many of the things which are often spoken of as if they *were* properties of this kind, certainly are not so. When, for instance, *colours* are spoken of as 'secondary qualities', it is, I think, often vaguely supposed that by calling them qualities we mean that they are a sort of thing which may *belong* to the things whose qualities they are, in some sense which does not mean being related to them. There is, I think, constantly a confusion in philosophy between properties which consist in the having of a relation to something or other and the something or other in the having of a relation to which the property consists. When, for instance, an orange is said to be yellow, that certainly means merely that it has *some relation* to the colour yellow. But this property—the property of having a relation to yellow—which the orange *has*, in some sense which does not mean merely that it—this property—is related to it, is I think, very often confused with the *colour* 'yellow' itself—a thing which is *only* related to the orange, and cannot possibly belong to it in any other sense. And similarly when people talk of 'predicates' or 'adjectives', there is, I think, often a confusion of the same sort. Some people would say: There is such a thing as the *relation* of predication—the relation which a predicate always has to the thing of which it is a predicate. While others would say: There is no such thing as a *relation* of predication; the very essence of a predicate is that it *belongs* to the thing of which it is a predicate is some sense other than that of being related to it. And both parties may be right, simply because, without knowing it, they are using the word 'predicate' in different senses. The first party may mean by a predicate that *to* which an orange is said to have a relation when it is said to *be* yellow; and, in that case, there is no doubt that the predicate in *this* sense *has* a relation to the orange and only *belongs* to it because it has that relation. Whereas the second party may mean by a predicate the property of having this relation to the colour yellow; and, in that case, there is no doubt that the predicate belongs to the orange, in some sense *other* than that of being related to it. But still, once we recognise that properties, which *do* consist in the having of a relation to something or other, do *belong* to the things of which they are properties, in some sense which does *not* mean that they are related to them, it plainly becomes a *possibility* that there may be some other things in the Universe which *belong* to things in this same sense. And this *possibility* gives us the two alternatives of which I spoke in our particular case. We are supposing that there is some property which belongs to *all* sense-given white patches and *only* to them, a property which does *not* consist merely in the being a member of the group, and is *not* merely a disjunctive property; and the two alternatives are these. The one is that this property consists in their all having one and the same relation to some *one* thing—a thing which, for convenience, I will call 'W'. And the other is that there is some *one* thing, which also I may call 'W', which *belongs* to them all, in some sense which does *not* mean that it is related to them. In the latter case, the thing called 'W' would be a universal, and a universal of the third kind, for an example of which we are looking. And when we say that pure white is *in* them all or present in them all, what we should be expressing by this is *either* that W has to them all the relation in question *or* that W *belongs* to them all. And when we say that pure white is present *in* different ones among them in different degrees—that, for instance, there is *more* pure white in a bluish white than in a whitish blue—the fact which we express in this way might be of three different kinds. It might be the case that W itself was a thing which has degrees: and then we might mean either that more of W has the specific relation to one than to the other *or* that more of W *belongs* to one than to the other. Or it might be the case that W itself has no degrees, but that the relation which it has to them all (*if* there is such a relation) has degrees; and then we should mean that W has *more* of this relation to some than to others. I can see no conclusive objection to any of these suppositions. For what must be remembered is that W, on this theory, is *not* identical with any sense-datum. It is *not* what we see, when we see a patch of pure white. And what is more, it does not even *resemble* any white patch in the respect in which they, and they alone, resemble one another. For *the* respect in which they all resemble one another, and in which nothing else in the Universe resembles them, consists, according to this theory, merely in the fact that W does *belong* to them or has a special relation to them. *Ex hypothesi*, therefore, W neither belongs nor has the supposed special relation to anything else in the Universe *except* each member of the group of white patches. It follows, therefore, that W does *not* belong to itself, and has *not* got to itself the special relation which it has to each of them. And since it has not, it cannot possibly *resemble* them in the peculiar respect in which they all resemble one another. We must, therefore, recognise that W is something quite different from anything which we ever see when we look at a white patch: it is something much more different from what we see when we look at a pure white patch, than this is from a bluish white patch which is very distinctly bluish. And it is this fact that it is *so* different from any white patch we ever see which renders it possible that it should really in a sense be *in* all white patches. We saw it is quite impossible that pure white, if by pure white we mean what we see when we look at a patch of pure white, should be *in* a patch of bluish white. But there is no similar impossibility in the case of W, simply because W is so utterly different from anything that we ever see.

We have here, therefore, a theory, which so far as I can see really would give us a property which might be both common and peculiar to all white patches. And the only objection to the theory, so far as I can see, is that it is so extremely difficult to distinguish this thing which I have called 'W' and to be sure that there is such a thing at all. If there is such a thing, what is it and what is it like? How is it to be pointed out? Yet I think many philosophers have constantly presupposed, more or less vaguely, that there are such things in the Universe. And I want to put in the strongest possible way the reasons for supposing that there are. And in order to do so, we had better, I think, drop the consideration of all white patches; because I don't feel at all sure that all white patches really have any property common and peculiar to them all except a disjunctive one. It may be plausibly held that there is *only* a disjunctive property which belongs to all white patches, and only to them; so that they do not afford a very strong reason for supposing that there is any such thing as W. But if we consider absolutely pure white patches and those only, the reasons for supposing that there is such a thing seem to me very strong. It is surely undeniable that every part or point of space which is at any time occupied by a patch (if only a speck) of absolutely pure white, has, in virtue of that fact, a property which it shares with all other parts or points of space which are similarly occupied, but which belongs to nothing else whatever in the Universe. Every such part or point of space has the property of being occupied by a patch of absolutely pure white, and nothing else in the Universe has this property. But in what does this property consist? There are, so far as I can see, only two alternatives, unless we adopt the theory that there *is* some such thing as W. We must either say (1) that every such part of space is occupied by one and the same thing; that is to say, that this patch here is *not* different from this one here; that they are not two patches but only one; that the very thing which we see occupying this place, is also at the same time occupying this and this and this. And the objection to this theory, as we saw, is that it seems self-evidently untrue. Or else (2) we must say that all the different patches of pure white have nothing in common except a disjunctive property. And I will try to explain again, with reference to this particular case, exactly what I mean by this. Every patch of pure white is, of course, *exactly* similar in respect of colour to every other. So that we may say: Choose any patch you like and call it A; then it is true of all other patches, and of nothing else in the Universe, that they are exactly similar in respect of colour to A. But A is not exactly similar to itself: it *is* itself. The only property, therefore, to be got in this way that is both common and peculiar to *all* patches of pure white, is the *disjunctive* one of *either* being exactly similar to A *or* being A. Of course, instead of A, we might have taken any other patch of pure white; so that what we really get is as many different disjunctive properties as there are patches of pure white, all of which belong to every patch of pure white and to nothing else in the Universe. And the objection to this theory is that it seems so difficult to believe that all patches of pure white don't really have in common some peculiar property *other* than a merely disjunctive one. To put it in another way: we should be inclined to say that a merely disjunctive property is not really a common property at all. It seems quite evident that A really has exactly the *same* peculiar property as do all the other patches which exactly resemble it: and by this we mean that what it has in common with them does *not* merely consist in satisfying *one* of the two conditions laid down in a disjunction, while the rest only satisfy the *other* condition. You might as well suggest that men and women have absolutely nothing in common except that each of them is *either* a man *or* a woman.

It is because both of these alternatives seem so difficult to believe that we are driven to supposing that there must be some such thing as W, namely that there is some *one* thing, very different from a pure white patch, which does either *belong* to all pure white patches *or* has a certain specific relation to all of them, and which does not belong or have this relation to anything else in the Universe. This *one* thing, if there is such a thing, would of course be a thing that we are all perfectly familiar with, and have constantly before our minds. *But*—and this is the objection to the theory—I, at all events, can't succeed in distinguishing any such thing—can't succeed in holding it clearly before my mind. I can't succeed in perceiving clearly that there really is some very simple property, quite different from the patch which I *see* when I look at a pure white patch, that is both common and peculiar to all such patches. Perhaps some of you can succeed in distinguishing the property in question. Perhaps some of you, on the other hand, will say there is clearly no such thing. But, if you say this latter, you are faced with a difficulty. For it seems perfectly certain that there *is* some property common and peculiar to all pure white patches—what we express by saying that they all *are* pure white—and if you reject this theory, the only two alternaives remaining, so far as I can see, are the two I have given. You must either say that it really is *one and the same thing* which is in ever so many different places at the same time; or you must say that the *only* property common to them all is *merely* a disjunctive one—namely that each *either is* some particular one which you choose *or* is exactly similar to that one which you choose. And, for my part, I can't be satisfied with either of these two theories. In any case, there seems to me to be a difficulty about the matter. And this difficulty is simply concealed, if you merely say, as people are apt to say, that there is some property common and peculiar to all pure white patches, and talk about this property as *the* property common and peculiar to them all, and call it 'pure white', as if we all knew what it was. We do, of course, in a sense know what it is: we all have it before our minds. But, it seems to me we don't know at all which of these three utterly different kinds of things it is.

Chapter XX

ABSTRACTIONS AND BEING

In this lecture I want first of all to go over again some of the points with which I have lately been dealing, because I am afraid I did not make myself quite clear, and if the subject is worth discussing at all, it is worth while to try and get it clear. I have been dealing, for some time, with the sort of things which are often called 'universals', or 'concepts', or 'conceptions', or 'general ideas', or 'abstract ideas'. You will find, I think, that most philosophers talk of these things pretty frequently, under some name or other, and not only so, but a very large part of the work of some philosophers, particularly of Greek and mediaeval philosophers, has consisted in the discussion of theories about just these very things. Plato and Aristotle called them—or some of them—εἴδη or 'forms'; and what is called Plato's 'Theory of Ideas' is, in fact, just a theory about universals. But, in spite of all the attention that has been given to them, nobody, so far as I know, has ever succeeded in pointing out quite clearly exactly what sort of things they are, and how they differ from the other sort of things, which, in distinction from them, are often called 'particulars' or 'individuals'. And some philosophers, as I said, have even denied that there are such things as general ideas at all. Now I think there is no doubt that, *if* there are such things, they are a very important sort of thing; and I wanted, therefore, to try to make as clear as possible, *both that* there are such things, and also what sort of things they are. And I think that in many of the controversies about universals one comparatively simple distinction is overlooked. It seems to me there is no doubt at all that there really are in the Universe *two* sorts of universals which I tried to point out, namely (1) relations and (2) properties which consist in the having of a relation to something or other. It is, I think, comparatively easy to distinguish universals of both these two sorts; and if it were quite clear that they were the only sorts, the whole question about universals would, I think, be comparatively simple. But the various controversies have arisen, I think, chiefly because it has been supposed that there are universals of a third very different sort. And when people talk of universals I think they are very often thinking solely of universals of this supposed third kind. Those who have denied that there are any universals at all, have, I think, generally been thinking only of universals of this third sort: they have simply not noticed that the other two sorts certainly are universals. And similarly the other party, the defenders of universals, have, I think, often assumed too hastily that universals which are in fact merely properties which consist in the having of a relation to something or other, are universals of this third sort. Part, therefore, of the difficulty of the subject is, I think, removed by recognising clearly these two sorts of universals. But there still remain a great many cases in which there is more or less reason to think that universals of a third very different sort really are involved. And what I wanted to do was to take typical instances of the chief sorts of cases in which there does seem to me reason to suppose this, and to try to discover whether universals of this third sort are involved in them, and if so, to make as clear as possible what sort of things they are.

I took 'whiteness' as an example of one type of cases, in which it may be and is very often held that a universal of this third sort is involved. And I want briefly to sum up the points which seem to me most worthy of notice about 'whiteness'.

In the first place, I pointed out that 'whiteness', in the most ordinary sense of the word, is a name for a property which we suppose to belong to lilies and snow and other things of that sort. It is *not* a property which belongs to sense-data. And this property which we ascribe to lilies and snow undoubtedly is one which consists merely in the having of a relation to something or other. One such property, which does undoubtedly belong to lilies and snow, is the having of some sort of relation to sense-data, of the sort which may be called patches of white. And though this property may perhaps *involve* a universal of our third sort, it certainly *is* not one; and it can only involve one, if and because the sense-data, which may be called patches of white, have in their turn some other common property which either *is* or involves one.

The sense, therefore, in which lilies and snow may be white, must be strictly distinguished from the sense in which those sense-data or sensations which may be called patches of white, are white. The property called 'whiteness', which belongs to lilies and snow, does *not* belong to these sense-data; and any property called 'whiteness', which does belong to these sense-data, does *not* belong to lilies and snow.

But now if we try to find out what property is common and peculiar to the sense-data which may be called patches of white, we find that there are two different groups of sense-data, a larger and a smaller one, to which this name might be given in different senses. All patches of colour, which are in any degree whitish (however little), might claim to be 'white' in a sense. But on the other hand we certainly should not commonly call them all patches of *white*; we should restrict the name to those which definitely have, as we should say, *more* white in them than any other colour: that is to say, we *should* call a bluish white 'a white', but we should not call a whitish blue, 'a white'; we should call it 'a blue'. I have chosen to consider only the smaller group, just for this reason that, in talking of a patch of white, we should commonly mean only a member of this smaller group. But now, what is this property which all members of this smaller group possess in common, and which nothing else posesses? In considering this question, we came finally upon the suggestion that we might find out what it was, if we could find out what is the property which belongs to all patches of absolutely pure white and only to them. Of course, the property which belongs only to patches of pure white, cannot possibly be the *same* as that which belongs *not* only to them but *also* to all patches which are in any degree white. But it seems possible that the two properties may differ only in *degree*, and not in kind.

In this way, we were led to consider what property it is that is common and peculiar to all patches of absolutely pure white. And here I should like to say that I don't know for certain whether there are such things at all. It may, perhaps, be the case, for all I know, that the purest possible whites, which any of us can directly perceive are always slightly tinged *either* with yellow, *or* with blue, *or* with red, *or* with some other colour. And, if so, then the purest possible white patches would *not* form a group of patches of exactly the same shade. What I was supposing last time was that they did: it was essential to my point that the patches of which I spoke should be of *exactly the same shade*. And if the purest white patches we can get are *not* all of exactly the same shade, that fact certainly introduces a new complication into the question: What is it that is common and peculiar to all white patches? But, however that may be, whether there is or is not a group of absolutely pure white patches, such as

I supposed, the main points I wished to make with regard to them certainly do apply to countless other instances. Some of the patches of colour we directly perceive certainly are of exactly the same shade as others. And the question I wanted to raise was merely: Wherever you have a group of patches, even if only two, of exactly the same shade of colour, what property is it that belongs in common to all patches of exactly that shade and *only* to patches of exactly that shade?

Suppose, for instance, you have before you two little spots of colour of exactly the same shade, one of them square and the other round. And, since there is a doubt about pure white, let us suppose that they are both of a shade, which is a slightly creamy white. The question is then: What property is there which belongs to both of these two patches, as well as to all the other patches of exactly the same shade in the Universe, and belongs to nothing else whatever?

And one answer which may be given to this question was, we saw, as follows. It says: 'What you have before you, in such a case, is, on the one hand, two different portions of space, one round and the other square, and, on the other, something which occupies these two portions of space. You must distinguish strictly between these two portions of space, on the one hand, and what *occupies* them on the other. And if you do this, then you can say that *one and the same thing* occupies *both* of them. You are directly perceiving one single colour, which has no name appropriated to it, but which occupies *both* portions of space, both the round one and the square one: what you actually see in both of these two different places is one and the same thing. This is the truth about the matter. And it follows from this that you have no right to say that the thing which occupies the round space is round and not square. The thing which occupies the round space *is*, of course, round, but the very same thing is *also* square, because it also occupies the square place. The truth is only that it is round *in one place* and square in another; and of course in the place in which it is round it is *not* square: it can't be both round and square in exactly the same place. But it is *only* in the place in which it is round that it is *not* square: in other places it *is* square. So that the thing itself is both round and square; round in one place, and square in another'. And it follows, further, that you have no right to talk of the thing which occupies the round space as if it were a patch of this particular creamy white. By a *patch* of colour, we mean something which has got one definite size and shape, and has *not* got any other. But the thing which occupies the round space is *not* a patch of colour in this sense. It is a thing which has ever so many different sizes and shapes at the same time, though it can only have them at different places. In short this view amounts to denying that there are such things as *patches* of this particular creamy white at all. There is according to it, occupying both places, only one single thing having no special name appropriated to it, which is neither one single patch nor a collection of patches. This view, therefore really answers our question, *not* by pointing out any property which is common and peculiar to all patches of this particular shade of white; but by denying that there are any *patches* of it at all. All that it does is to point out a property which is common and peculiar to all the portions of space which we should *say* were *occupied* by patches of it: namely that of being occupied by this one single shade of white, which is what we actually see, when we *think* we see a *patch* which is of that shade. It does *not* point out any property which is common and peculiar to the *things* which occupy these portions of space; since it denies that there are any things which occupy them: it asserts that there is only *one* thing which occupies them all.

Now the only way of disputing this view, so far as I can see, is simply by denying it: simply by asserting that when I see what we should call two different patches of any particular shade, one round and the other square, we are right in so speaking. That is to say, we may assert that in such a case, it is *not* merely the two portions of space which are different, but that *what* occupies the one portion is *also* different from what occupies the other, although both are of exactly the same shade of colour. It does, in fact, seem to me to be evident that what I see occupying the one place in such a case *is* different from what I see occupying the other, that it is not one and the same thing which occupies them both. Of course, I may be wrong as to this. But, so far as I know, there is no way of proving that I am wrong. Everybody has just as good a right to take the one view as the other. There is no conclusive argument in favour of either. It is simply a matter of inspection.

But now, supposing we take the view that what occupies the round space *is* different from what occupies the square one: that what occupies the one *is* a *patch* of this particular creamy white which is round and *not* square, and what occupies the other is a *patch* of the same shade which is square and not round: we then do have to face the question: What is it that is common both to these two patches and to all the other patches of exactly the same shade of white in the Universe, but to nothing else? What is the property in virtue of which we call them all patches of that particular shade? On this view we do have a number of different things, each of which is *a* patch of that particular shade, and it seems obvious that there is some property which belongs to all of them, and only to them. What is this property?

Now, as I said, the only thing which seems quite obvious about them is that they are all exactly like one another, *in respect of their colour*, whereas nothing else in the Universe is exactly like them in this respect. And we might, therefore, endeavour to say that *the* property common and peculiar to them all consists, somehow, in this exact mutual resemblance. But there is one objection to this theory which I did not mention before. It may be held namely, that when we say that two things *resemble* one another, what we mean by this is always merely that they have some property in common. It may be held in short, that resemblance always consists in the possession of some common property—is merely another name for such possession. And if resemblance does thus consist in the possession of a common property; it is quite plain that the common property in question cannot consist in the resemblance. On this view, therefore, *the* property common and peculiar to all patches of that particular creamy white could not possibly consist in their mutual resemblance. On the contrary their mutual resemblance must consist in their having some other property in common. And we should thus apparently be driven straight to the assumption that there must be a universal of my third kind involved in the matter. We should have to suppose that there is one single thing, to which we may give a name, though it hasn't got one—let us suppose its name is 'Z'—which belongs to them all, in some sense, and does not belong to anything else in the Universe. This thing, called 'Z', would be *the* shade of colour which all patches of this particular creamy white *have*, as distinguished from the patches which have it. And we should have to suppose that what we mean when we say that they all resemble one another exactly in respect of being of that particular shade and that nothing else resembles them in this respect, is merely that Z does 'belong' to them all and to nothing else. And it is here that there comes in the distinction which I made last time as to the two different senses in which Z might *belong* to them. The distinction is, I think, really a very simple one, if only I could explain it clearly. Let us consider any fact whatever which is the fact that one thing, A, has some specific relation to another, B. Let us suppose, for instance, that one thing, A, is *different* from another, B. This fact that A is different from B may be expressed in another way by saying that A has to B the relation of difference. But, for reasons which I gave last time, it is quite plain that A's *having* to B the relation of difference, does not consist even partly in its having some other relation to the relation called 'difference'. The relation called difference *relates* A to B; and when we say that it relates them, we can't mean merely that the relation of difference is again related to them; or in other words, its relating of them does not *consist* merely in its being related to them. It follows, therefore, that A *has* to B the relation of difference in some sense which does *not* consist in its being related to that relation. The whole fact, therefore, that A differs from B, does *not include* any relation between A and difference. There may, in fact, be such a relation which is a constituent of another fact, but this other relation is not a *constituent* of the fact we are considering. The only *constituents* of the fact we are considering are A and B and 'difference', although the fact is a whole which is not identical with the sum of those constituents. But now just as one way of expressing this fact, is to say that A *has* to B the relation of difference; so another way of expressing it is to say that A has the property of differing from B, or that the property of differing from B belongs to A. Both these two forms of expression may merely express one and the same fact—namely the fact that A differs from B, a fact in which, as we have seen, no relation between A and difference is included. But this being so, when we say that the property of differing from B belongs to A, we do not necessarily mean to assert that this property has a relation to A. Here again we *might* sometimes mean this; but, when we use the expression merely to express the fact that A differs from B, we certainly are not doing so. There is, therefore, a sense of the word 'belongs' such that the fact that the property of differing from B *belongs* to A does *not* consist in this property's being *related* to A. A *has* this property, in some sense which does *not* consist in its being related to it. And similarly wherever we have a property which consists in the having of a relation to something or other, this property will *belong* to the thing which has it in some sense which does not consist in its being related to it. But once we realise this, it becomes possible to suggest that other things—things which do *not* consist in the having of a relation to something or other—may possibly *belong* to certain subjects in the same sense. As I said last time, I know no conclusive reason for supposing that this ever does actually happen. But many philosophers seem to me to have assumed that to say of certain predicates that they belong to a given subject is *not* the same thing as to say that they have a specific relation to that subject: in other words, they have assumed that to be a predicate of a subject does *not consist* in the having of any relation to that subject. And it is only by means of this analogy that I can give any sense to this supposition. By means of this analogy we can, I think, give a sense to it; and can see that it may possibly be true. It is only to suppose that what, so far as I can see, certainly is true of all properties which *do* consist in the having of a relation to something, may also be true of some other things—of some things, which do *not* consist in the having of a relation to anything. To return to our instance. Suppose that A has the property of differing from B. This is a property which consists in the having of a relation to B. And of *this* property, so far as I can see, it certainly is true that it *belongs* to A in some sense which does *not* consist in its being related to A. And the same, I think, is certainly true of *all* properties, which consist, as this one does, in the having of a relation to something or other. But, this being so, it is obviously just possible that there should be some *other* properties—properties *not* consisting in the having of a relation to anything, which do nevertheless *belong* to the subjects which possess them in the same non-relational sense. And this possibility gives us the two alternatives which are possible in our particular case. We have supposed that there is some *one* shade of colour, which we are calling Z, which *belongs*, in some sense, to all patches of the particular shade of creamy white which we so call, and to nothing else in the Universe. The question is what is meant by saying that it 'belongs' to them? And one alternative is to say that what is meant is that it has to them a specific relation, which I will call the relation of predication. The other is to say that its belonging to them does not consist in its having any relation to them at all: and this alternative I will express by calling it the theory that Z is a predicate of them. We have, then, two different theories, as to the sense in which Z may 'belong' to them. (1) is that Z is a *predicate* of them; by which I mean that it belongs to them in the *non-relational* sense I have tried to explain. And (2) that Z is not a predicate of them, but *only* has to them a *relation* which may be called the relation of predication. If the first theory were true, then *the* property common and peculiar to all patches of our particular creamy white would simply be Z itself. If the second, it would consist in Z's having to them a relation, which may be called the relation of predication. These are the two alternatives I wanted to explain. But, in either case, Z itself would be a universal of our third kind: it would itself neither be a relation, nor a property which consists in the having of a relation to anything.

Now the reason why I wished to explain this view so carefully is because, so far as I can make out, it is *the* view which most philosophers have in their minds, when they talk of *the* universal 'pure red' or 'pure white', or of *the* property which belongs in common to all patches of any one particular shade and only to them. They suppose that there is some one thing (the thing I have called 'Z') which *belongs*, in one or other of the two senses I have tried to explain, to all patches of the particular creamy white I have supposed to have that name, and to nothing else. And there is one further very important point to notice, as to the nature of this thing. Namely that, on this view, the respect in which all patches of that particular creamy white resemble one another and nothing else, is simply—that Z 'belongs' to them all. And that hence Z itself cannot possibly resemble them in *this* respect, in which they resemble one another. This follows absolutely, because Z is something which belongs to all patches of that particular shade and *only* to them, and hence cannot possibly belong to *itself*. This, I think, is a point which is very apt to be overlooked. It was a criticism directed against Plato's Theory of Ideas that, in one of its forms, it did overlook this point. When Plato suggests that universals may stand to their particulars in the relation of a model or pattern (παραδειγμα) to its copies, he is, I think, certainly thinking that it may resemble them in precisely the respect in which they all resemble one another. And it *is* very natural to think this; it is very natural, for instance, to think of the universal 'pure red' as resembling particular patches of pure red in precisely the respect in which they all resemble one another. It is, therefore, important to realise that this cannot possibly be the case. And when this is realised, it does, I think, diminish the plausibility of the whole theory that there is any such thing as Z. The objection which I feel to the theory is simply that I cannot discover any such thing. I cannot discover that I ever have it before my mind.

But, if we reject it, what is the alternative? Well, we must, in the first place, say that there is a kind of resemblance which does *not* consist in the having of a common property. And for my part I cannot see any conclusive objection to supposing that there is. To take our particular case, of two little patches of exactly the same shade of creamy white, one of them round and the other square, we can, it seems to me, distinguish between these patches *themselves* and their shapes. One of them *has* a round shape, the other a square shape; and possession of these shapes are properties which *belong* to them, and which can be distinguished from the patches which have these properties. And similarly if we suppose that, in spite of being of exactly the same shade of colour, they might yet differ in brightness; the different brightnesses would still be properties which *belong* to them; and we must distinguish between the patch which has a certain degree of brightness and the degree of brightness which it has. Our patches of creamy white then, are the things which *have* these properties of a particular shape, a particular brightness, and so on, but which themselves are different from and do not include as constituents, these properties which they have. And, this being understood, we might, I think, say that these patches *themselves* have to one another a relation which may be called *exact* resemblance, which does *not* consist in the possession of any common property. It is true that, in saying this, we should contradict common usage. For of a round patch and a square patch we should commonly say emphatically that they are not and cannot be exactly like one another, simply *because* they differ in shape. We should say they were only exactly alike *in one respect*—namely in respect of their shade of colour. But still it seems to me possible that what we *mean* by this is really, that the two patches *themselves*, as distinguished from their shapes and brightnesses, etc.—from *all* the properties which they *have*—really have to one another a relation, which does *not* consist in the possession of any common property, and which might be called exact resemblance. And this kind of resemblance, whether exact or not, might be called immediate or internal resemblance—as distinguished from that kind of resemblance, which merely consists in the possession of common properties. I can only point out what this exact immediate resemblance would be, if there is such a thing—by saying that it would be just the relation which all patches of our particular creamy white so obviously have to one another and to nothing else in the Universe, in spite of differences in size and shape and brightness and position, etc. It seems to me we certainly *can* distinguish this relation quite clearly: the only question is whether it does or does not consist in the possession of a common property.

Well, it seems to me it is quite possible it does *not* consist in the possession of a common property. And in that case we might try to define *the* property that is common and peculiar to all patches of this creamy white—*the* property in virtue of which we call them all 'Z', if we use that name—by reference to this relation of exact internal resemblance. But here comes in the difficulty which I expressed by saying that the only property to be got in this way, which really does belong to them *all* and only to them, is a disjunctive property. That is to say: Take any patch of Z you like: then, on this theory, all *other* patches of Z, and nothing else in the Universe, would have to *this* patch the supposed relation of exact internal resemblance. Exact resemblance to *this* patch would belong to all the other patches and to nothing else: but, unfortunately, it would *not* belong to this patch we have chosen, since this patch does *not resemble* itself, but *is* itself. Thus the only property which would belong to absolutely *all* patches of Z and to nothing else, would be the disjunctive one of being *either this* patch *or* exactly like it. It is as if we should say: The only property which belongs to every member of the human race and to nothing else is the disjunctive one of being *either* a man *or* a woman. All the men are men, and all the women are women: and nothing else in the Universe is *either* a man *or* a woman. So that each member of the human race, whether a man or a woman, does possess the disjunctive property of being *either* a man *or* a woman: *but* there is no other property which is both common and peculiar to them all. This does seem to me a serious objection to the proposal to define *the* property common and peculiar to all patches of Z by reference to the relation of exact internal resemblance. It seems as if they obviously had some *other* property in common which is not merely a disjunctive one. Moreover it is to be noted that on this view what one man means by 'Z' could never by any possibility be the *same* as what any other man means by it. *I* should mean by it exact resemblance to or identity with some *one* patch which *I* had directly perceived. But, in the common theory with regard to sense-data, no other man ever does directly perceive any patch which *I* directly perceive. Hence another man would mean by 'Z' exact resemblance to, or identity with, some patch which *he* has directly perceived. And since *his* patch would not be the same as my patch, what *he* meant by 'Z' would be different from what I meant by it. But nevertheless, in spite of these difficulties, I am inclined to think that this theory *may* be the true one.

This then is all that I have to say with regard to my first type of cases—the cases where, as we should say, we have two or more different things all exactly alike one another in some one respect. The problem was to discover, what is the property which is both common and peculiar to any group of things, which are thus, as we should say, exactly like one another in some respect in which nothing else is exactly like them. And I distinguished *three* different theories which might be offered as a solution of this problem. The first (1) simply consisted in denying that as a rule what we have in these cases is a number of *different* things at all. It says that what we mistake for different things, is, in fact, one and the same thing, which (if it is a colour) may be in many different places and of many different sizes and shapes and directly perceived by many different people, at one and the same time. Both the other two theories on the other hand admit that what we have to do with are really *different* things. And the first (2) says that there is always some one thing, a universal of my third kind, *not* resembling them in the respect in which they all resemble one another, which is *either* a predicate of them all and of nothing else, *or* has the relation of predication to them all and to nothing else. Whereas the last (3) says that there is a kind of resemblance which does *not* consist in the possession of any common property, and that the property common and peculiar to them all, consists in the fact that each *either* is *or* exactly resembles any one of them you like to take. And between these three theories I really don't know how to decide.

But now, there is a second type of cases, in which the first theory is obviously impossible. And this may be taken as being, so far, an argument against the first theory, though, of course, it is not a conclusive argument. It shows, at all events, that the difficulty which the first theory was designed to avoid, does recur in other cases where it cannot be avoided in the same way; and that since, in these cases, one or other of the two other theories *must* be adopted, they *may* be the right solution also in the first type of cases. Take, for instance, the group of sense-data consisting of absolutely all patches of colour, or absolutely all colours of whatever shade. Obviously all of them have some property in common, which distinguishes them from anything else in the Universe—*the* property which we mean to ascribe to them when we say that they and they alone are patches of colour or colours. Thus a patch of blue obviously has in common with a patch of yellow something which neither has in common with a sound. And here nobody can say that the sense-datum which we see occupying a portion of space, which we should say was occupied by a patch of blue, is one and the same as that which we see occupying a portion of space, which we should say was occupied by a patch of yellow. It is too obvious that a blue patch and a yellow patch are different. The first theory, therefore, cannot possibly be used to account for what is common and peculiar to all patches of colour or to all colours. And the last theory also—the theory of exact internal resemblance—needs some modification, if it is to apply to this case. It is quite obvious that a patch of yellow is *not exactly* like a patch of blue in the same sense (if any) in which any patch of Z is *exactly* like any other patch of Z. But just as we supposed that there might be a kind of *exact* resemblance which does not consist in the possession of any common properties so it seems to me there may be a kind of *resemblance*, falling short of exact resemblance, which alone is *immediate* or *internal*, that is to say, does *not* consist in the possession of any common property. Thus if we distinguish carefully between patches of colour *themselves*, and the various properties which they *have* such as size, shape, brightness, etc., we might, I think, say that every patch of colour has to every other a relation, called likeness, which nothing else in the Universe has to them, and that this is a relation which does *not* consist in the possession of any common property. In this way, by reference to this supposed relation of immediate or internal resemblance, we might in this case, as in the other, obtain a *disjunctive* property which really is common and peculiar to all patches of colour. And, in spite of the objections to supposing that the *only* property common and peculiar to them all can really be merely a *disjunctive* property of this kind, I am inclined to think that this may be the true solution. As to the application of the second theory to this case—the theory that there is some one single thing, a universal of my third kind, which is either a predicate of or has the relation of predication to, all patches of colour and to nothing else in the Universe, there are only two points I want to note. The first is that it seems to me just as difficult to distinguish this supposed thing in this case as it was in the case of the pure reds. I cannot discover that I ever have before my mind any such thing: a thing which does belong to *all* patches of colour of whatever shade and to nothing but them, and which is not a property which consists in the having of a relation to something or other. And the second point I want to notice is that in this case there seems to me no danger of supposing that the thing in question, if there is such a thing, could possibly resemble all the colours in the *same* respect in which they resemble one another. If it did, it would too obviously be itself merely one of the colours, and *not* a thing which belongs to all of them equally. The analogy of this case, therefore, makes it plainer how it might possibly be the case that *the* universal which belongs to all Z patches and only to them, might be something which does *not* resemble them in the peculiar respect in which they all resemble one another. It is surely quite plain that *the* universal which belongs to all different patches or shades of colour, and only to them (if there is such a universal), cannot resemble them in *the* peculiar respect in which they all resemble one another.

But now, finally, there is a third type of cases, in which it seems to me plainer that a universal of my third kind *is* involved, and in which it seems to me that we can perhaps distinguish this universal—hold it before our minds, and be sure that it is there, in a way in which we could not do this in either of the last two types of cases. Consider, for instance, the group formed of all collections which are collections of two things and no more—which are pairs or couples. Every pair or couple of things, no matter what the things may be, obviously has some property which belongs to all other pairs or couples and to nothing else—*the* property which we express by saying that each of them is a pair or a couple. A pair of shillings obviously has some property which also belongs to a pair of pennies, a pair of men, a pair of colours, or to the collection formed of one sound and one colour, or of one man and one penny, etc.—which belongs, in short, to all collections which are collections of two things and no more, and belongs to nothing else whatever. And here it seems to me we can perhaps see that this property does involve a universal of my third kind. The property in question does seem to consist in the fact that *the number two* belongs to every such collection and only to such a collection; and the number two itself does seem to be a universal of my third kind: something which is neither a relation, nor a property which consists in the having of a relation to something or other. And it seems to me that in this case we can perhaps distinguish the universal in question: that we can hold the number two before our minds, and see what it is, and *that* it is, in almost the same way as we can do this with any particular sense-datum that we are directly perceiving. The number two, therefore, does seem to me as good an instance as can be given of a universal of my third kind. And it also will serve very well to illustrate two points which may have seemed obscure in what I said before. In what sense does the number two *belong* to two shillings? What do we mean by saying of two shillings that they *are* two? I tried to explain that there were two different theories possible as to the sense in which universals of this kind may belong to things. The one theory I distinguished as the theory that they are predicates of them, in a *non-relational* sense; and the other as the theory that they have to them one specific relation which might be called the relation of predication. And it does seem to me that the distinction between these two theories, and the fact that both are possible, may be well brought out in this case. It surely is just possible that the number two is, in the sense I explained, a predicate of any group of two shillings. That is to say, it is surely possible that the fact that they are two is a fact which does not contain any relation as a constituent. Can anybody undertake to assert for certain that this is not so—that the verb 'are', when we say that they *are* two, does and must express a relation? But on the other hand, it seems quite possible that it does: that it expresses a peculiar relation, which might be called the relation of predication. I can't myself decide between these two alternatives, but it does seem to me that both are possible.

And the second point which this instance serves to illustrate, is what I said as to the possibility of defining the property that is common and peculiar to all the colours by reference to a kind of resemblance which I called immediate resemblance—a kind of resemblance, which does not consist in the possession of any common property. Is it possible to define the number two itself by reference to this kind of resemblance? Is it possible that after all we have *not* got, even here, a universal of my third kind? It seems to me that it is *just* possible; but there does, I think, *seem* to be a manifest difference between this case and that of the colours. The collections consisting of one sound and one colour, of one man and one penny, of one planet and one fixed star, do obviously all resemble one another in one respect—namely in respect of the fact that each of them is a collection of two things and no more. All pairs do resemble one another in this respect and nothing else does. But surely the kind of way in which all the colours resemble one another and nothing else does seems to be quite different. Does there not seem to be a difference of *kind* and not merely of degree, between these two relations, both of them *called* resemblance? Does it not seem as if the relation which every colour has to every other colour and to nothing else, was of quite a different kind from that which every pair has to every other pair and to nothing else? Those who say that resemblance *always* consists merely in the possession of a common property—is merely another name for this—might I suppose try to account for the apparent difference between the two cases by saying that the colours have many more properties in common than the pairs have. And this, I suppose, is true. But it is not, I think, true that the colours have more properties common *and peculiar* to them than the pairs have. And it is only the kind of resemblance which all the members of each group have to one another *and to nothing else*, that is here in point. I think, therefore, that those who say that resemblance always consists in the possession of a common property cannot account for the manifest difference between these two cases. And, so far as I can see, the only way to account for it is to say that the resemblance between the pairs does merely consist in the possession of a common property; whereas the resemblance between the colours, though it also is called 'resemblance', is in fact a completely different relation, which does not consist in the possession of a common property. This, therefore, would be an argument for supposing that the property common and peculiar to all *pairs must* consist in their possession of a universal of my third kind; whereas, in the case of the colours, there is no necessity to suppose this, since in their case the property common and peculiar to them all *may* be merely a disjunctive property defined by reference to immediate resemblance. And this obvious difference between the kind of way in which all colours resemble one another and the kind of way in which all groups of two things resemble one another is, I think, also illustrated by another interesting and important case. So far we have been only asking what it is that is common and peculiar to all groups that are groups of two things and no more—the property which we mean by calling them all 'groups of two', or 'pairs'. And we have decided that this property does seem to consist in the possession of a universal of my third kind—namely the number 2. And, of course, it is obvious that exactly the same argument applies to each of the other whole numbers—to 3, and 4, and 5, and 6, etc. . . . It does not seem as if all groups of three had any *immediate* resemblance to one another, any more than all groups of two have; and hence it seems as if the only kind of resemblance which they do all have to one another and to nothing else *does* consist in the possession of a common property. Each particular whole number, therefore, does seem to be a universal of my third kind. But if we raise the question: What is the property that is common and peculiar to all these different numbers, *themselves*? what is it that we mean by calling them all whole numbers? it seems to me we have again a case which is analogous to the case of the colours. The number two has, so far as I can see, an immediate resemblance to the number three, and so has every whole number to every other whole number: they have a resemblance which does *not* consist merely in the possession of a common property. So that, so far as this argument goes, there would be no reason to suppose that the property which we ascribe to them all when we call them all 'whole numbers', *does* involve a universal of my third kind: it *might* be merely a disjunctive property defined by reference to the immediate resemblance which all of them have to any one of them you like to choose. There may, for all I know, be *other* reasons for supposing that a universal of my third kind is involved in this case too. But what I want to insist on is that all the whole numbers do seem to resemble one another in a kind of way in which all groups that are groups of two things do *not* resemble one another. All whole numbers do resemble one another in the same sort of way in which all colours do, whereas all groups that are groups of two do *not* resemble one another in this way.

It seems to me, then, there are very strong reasons for supposing that each whole number—2, 3, 4, 5, etc.—is a universal of my third kind. Here at last we have a case in which universals of this kind do seem to be almost certainly involved. And there may perhaps be other cases in which it is equally certain. And moreover it seems *possible* that they may be involved also in the other cases I considered—the case of the colours, and the case of the Z's—and all similar cases. I don't see any way of deciding with certainty that they are *not* involved in these cases; although it seems to me much more doubtful whether they are so, because of the alternative possibilities. In any case, it seems pretty certain that there are *some* most important instances of universals of this third kind, and *possible* that there may be many more. We cannot, therefore, say that the *only* kinds of universals are universals of my first two kinds, namely (1) relations and (2) properties which consist in the having of a relation to something or other: we must admit, as at least a possible class, universals which are *neither* relations *nor* properties which consist in the having of a relation to something. And I wanted to draw attention to these three types of universals, partly in order to make as clear as possible what sort of things universals are, and partly because I wanted, then, to go on expressly to consider the question: What, after all, is the property which is common and peculiar to all universals? What do we mean by calling them all universals? What is it that distinguishes universals from that other sort of things which are called particulars? It seems to me that this is really an extremely difficult question, and that its difficulty is often concealed by the failure to recognise clearly the three different types of universals I have named. It is comparatively easy to give a definition which will apply to *one* of the three types; the difficulty is that the three types are so different from one another, that it is very difficult to discover any peculiar property that is really common to them all. But, as it is, I have not time to go into this question.

What I want to do, by way of conclusion, is merely to mention two very common views about universals, which seem to me to be of such a nature that it makes an enormously great difference to our view of the Universe, whether we hold them to be true or not.

The first is this. Locke constantly speaks of certain kinds of universals (I don't know whether he so speaks of *all*) as if they were the 'work of the mind'. And this view is, I think, very commonly taken, even now, with regard to *all* universals. In particular, it is very commonly taken with regard to 'relations'; it is very frequently asserted that all 'relations' are 'the work of the mind'; and if it is true of 'relations' it must, of course, be also true of all properties which consist in the having of a relation to something or other. But you see what this view implies. It implies that all universals are *created* by the mind. That, for instance, there could not possibly have been two things in the Universe, until some mind had *created* the number two; and that no two things could possibly have resembled one another until some mind had compared them and created the relation of resemblance. In this sense, it implies that all universals are *dependent* on the mind: that there cannot possibly have been any universals in the Universe, before there was a mind in it. Of course, it does not necessarily imply that they are *dependent* on the mind, in the other sense in which I have hitherto chiefly spoken of dependence. It does not necessarily imply that they can never be at all, except when some one is thinking of them. For, of course, it might be held that when once some mind had created the number two, things could in future be two, even when nobody was thinking of the number two. But, as a matter of fact, those who believe in the first kind of dependence do also, I think, generally believe in the latter. And as regards this view that all universals are 'the work of the mind' I only want to say that I can't see any shadow of reason for it. It has, I think, arisen chiefly from the failure to distinguish the two different senses of the word 'idea', of which I spoke before: namely the sense in which, when I *think* of the number two, my act of thought is an 'idea', and the sense in which what I think *of*, namely the number two itself, is an idea. We do apply the same name, 'idea' and similar names, such as 'conception', 'thought' etc., both to *acts* of thought, and to the objects thought of: it is quite natural to call the number two itself, or the relation of resemblance itself, an 'idea' or 'conception' or 'thought'; and *also* quite natural to call the *act* of thought which we perform when we think of these things an idea or conception or thought. And, for this reason, these two different things—the act of thought, and the object thought of, have I think been constantly confused. The act of thought, which we perform when we think of the number two, is of course something mental—something dependent on mind. But so soon as we realise quite clearly that the number two itself is something quite different from this act of thought, there ceases, I think, to be any reason whatever to suppose that the number two or the relation of resemblance is 'the work of the mind'. It becomes plainly quite possible that there should have been two things in the Universe, and two things which resembled one another, *before* there was any mind in it at all.

And the common-sense view about universals which I want to notice, is this. It is certain that all universals are in a sense '*abstractions*', they are 'abstract' things. Indeed, I think that, in their most proper use, these two terms are precisely equivalent: not only are all universals 'abstract', but also all 'abstract' things are universals. But many philosophers seem to suppose that when you call a thing an 'abstraction', you imply two things about it. It seems to be held, first, that in so calling it you again imply that it is the work of the mind; and this should perhaps be put down as a second separate reason why people have supposed that all universals are 'the work of the mind'. There is, of course, a psychological process called 'abstraction' and people constantly speak, I think, as if universals were a product of this process, and as if that were how they should be defined. But the true account of the matter seems to me to be this. Namely, the process of abstraction is a process by which we become aware of universals; it is our *awareness* of them which is a product of the process; not the universals themselves. And, instead of its being possible to define universals as products of the process of abstraction, it is, so far as I can see, only possible to define abstraction by reference to universals: what we mean by abstraction is just the process by which we first learn to distinguish universals, and there is no other way of defining it.

But the second thing which some philosophers seem to suppose is implied when you call a thing an abstraction, is that it is not really 'real'. They seem to suppose that to call a thing an abstraction amounts to saying that it is hardly better than a pure fiction like a griffin or chimaera; something, therefore, which need not be reckoned as one of the constituents of the Universe. And this question as to the sense, if any, in which abstractions are not 'real', brings us back to the point from which we started on this whole discussion. I will try to say as shortly as I can what seem to me to be the most important points about it.

I have distinguished three different kinds of constituents of the Universe, namely (1) particulars, (2) truths or facts, and (3) universals. And there does seem a certain amount of reason for saying that, of these three kinds of things, it is only particulars which 'exist'; that truths and universals do not exist, but *only* have *being* or *are*. It is certainly more natural to say of a particular thing that it 'exists', than to say this of the truth that twice two are four, or of the number two itself; though the usage is certainly not fixed. If, therefore, anybody chooses to say that universals don't exist, and in that sense are not 'real', I don't want to deny that this may possibly be the case. There may, I think, possibly be some property, which is what we generally mean by 'existence', which *does* belong to all particulars over and above *the* property in virtue of which we call them particulars, and which does not belong to truths or universals. I think it is doubtful whether this is the case; I think it is doubtful whether there is any property common and peculiar to all particulars, *except* that in virtue of which we call them all particulars; and hence that it is doubtful whether particulars have any kind of reality which truths and universals have not got: whether, in short, the only difference between them does not consist simply and solely in the fact that particulars *are* particulars, whereas truths and universals are not. But whether this be so or not—whether or not we ought to recognise a distinction between existence and being, *over and above* the distinction between particulars on the one hand, and truths and universals on the other—what I want to insist on is that this distinction between existence and being is in any case not nearly so important as that between the things which do have *being*, and those which simply have not got it, are purely imaginary and don't belong to the Universe at all. The property of being which certainly does belong to truths and universals *as well as* to particulars is ever so much more important than any which distinguishes them from one another. I have already explained that in talking as I have just done —in talking as if there *were* a class of things, which simply are not, have *not* got being—we do seem to contradict ourselves, but I tried to shew that the contradiction is merely verbal. And what I want to insist on is that it is this distinction, which it seems so impossible to express without a verbal contradiction, which is *the* really fundamental and important one. It is this distinction, as we saw, which is at the bottom of the distinction between truth and falsehood: there could be no important difference between truth and falsehood, but for this distinction between what is or has been or will be, and what *neither* is nor has been nor will be. And the fundamental question for philosophy is to discover whether certain things do or do not belong to the Universe in this sense. And it is, I think, this fundamental distinction which is overlooked by those who talk as if universals, because mere abstractions, were therefore pure fictions and something negligible. Those who talk in this way do, I think, really mean to degrade universals to the levels of griffins and chimaeras; but they don't see what they are doing, because they hold that even 'griffins' and 'chimaeras' are 'real' in a sense. In this way the fundamental distinction between what is and what is not comes to be slurred over; and people really hold of certain things, and may hold of almost anything, both that they *are* and, also, at the same time, that they *are not*. If you fix clearly in your mind the sense in which there certainly are no such things as griffins and chimaeras, that seems to me to give the sense in which it is important to enquire whether there are such things as universals or not. And if you do fix this sense clearly, it seems to me quite plain that there *are* such things, that universals are not in any way to be classed with griffins and chimaeras: that, on the contrary, there is *the* most fundamental difference in the Universe between the two, a difference ever so much more important than that which separates universals from particulars.

Appendix

I think now (in 1952) that Chapters XIX and XX are badly disfigured, and indeed rendered almost unintelligible in parts, by at least two bad mistakes which I made in them.

(1) The first mistake is this. In XIX, on p. 341, I actually identify two views which are in fact quite different from one another. One of the two is the view that when we have two sense-given 'patches' (using 'patch', as I have explained, in such an extended sense, that, e.g., the sense-datum of a full-stop, however small, or of a hyphen or other line, however thin, is, in my sense of the word, a patch)—two sense-given patches, I say, which are of exactly the same shade of colour as one another, and each of them of that particular shade *all over*, then, whether the two patches are of the same shape and size or of different shapes or sizes or both (e.g. one of them square and the other round), in either case the colour of the one is *identical* with the colour of the other. This first view is a view which certainly has been held by some philosophers, and which I myself still consider to be true. But the second view, with which I actually identify the view just stated, is the completely different view that, in such cases, there are not two patches at all, but only one and the same patch in different places, so that e.g. one and the same patch may be large and square in one place and small and round in another. This second view, so far as I know, has never been held by anyone, and is certainly quite untenable. I say of it, in that Chapter (p. 341), that it is 'verbally self-contradictory', but that it is not really self-contradictory, and then, by way of shewing that it is not, proceed to state the first view as if it were all that is meant by the words 'two such patches are one and the same patch'; as if, that is to say, these words meant the same as the words '*the colour of* two such patches is the same'! In fact, of course, no one would express what is meant by the latter form of words, by saying that in such cases there are not two patches, but only one. And the view that, in such cases, there are not two patches, but only one, is, of course, not only 'verbally' but really self-contradictory. The cases are defined as cases in which we have two sense-given patches; and, of course, it is self-contradictory to say that in such cases we have only one!

How I came to make this mistake I do not know. I failed, for some reason or other, to see that the colour of a patch is not identical with the patch in question; and hence I drew the absurd conclusion that, if two patches are of exactly the same colour, then they are not two patches but one and the same patch! It is owing to this mistake that, on p. 340, I make the utterly false assertion that the supposition that *in* any patch of bluish white there is some pure white, is identical with the impossible supposition that in any patch of bluish white there is contained a *patch* of pure white!

(2) A second gross mistake which I made was that of supposing anybody to hold that, in a case where we see two patches of exactly the same shade of colour, or one patch of the shade in question, this shade of colour is something which we don't see (p. 345)! This mistake was perhaps partly due to my speaking of 'what I see' when I see a white patch (p. 345), and not seeing that, in such a case, the white patch in question need not be the *only* thing I see: 'what I see' is ambiguous; it may mean 'the only thing I see' or it may mean 'all the things I see'; and I may have been misled by this ambiguity. Why should it not be the case (as I now suppose it to be) that whenever I see a white patch, of one and the same shade of white all over, I *also* see that particular shade of white, *of* which that patch happens to be? So far as I know, nobody has ever held the view that a particular shade of white, or a particular shade of any other colour, is something which I never see. Certainly, when I see a round patch of the same shade all over, I see, not only the patch, but the shade it is of, the shape it is of, and the size it is of; though I think it must be held, that when we talk of seeing these three last 'abstract' things, we are using 'see' in a somewhat different sense from that in which we use it when we talk of 'seeing' the 'concrete' patch. The view which I express in these chapters that, if there are any 'qualities' which 'belong' to a patch in the same non-relational sense in which its relational properties belong to it, then these 'qualities' must be things we never see, seems to me now to be quite absurd, and a view which nobody has ever held.

I think I was perhaps led into this mistake partly by a mistake analogous to that of overlooking the ambiguity of the phrase 'what I see'. I had certainly failed to see that when I talked of a particular shade of colour 'occupying' the area 'occupied' by the patch whose colour it is, the sense in which I talked of the colour 'occupying' that area might be different from that in which the patch 'occupies' that area. I may have thought that since the patch does 'occupy' that area, and since I certainly see the patch, its colour must be something which does not 'occupy' the area, and which I don't see.

I think I have now stated the main defects which seem to me to disfigure these two chapters, though of course these defects have consequences in several places; and I will now go on to give what I should now say about the main question which I was then trying to answer.

I was, as I said many times, trying to discover whether there were any 'universals' which were neither relations nor relational properties, but which nevertheless 'belonged' to things in the same non-relational sense in which relational properties 'belong' to things which have them; and I was mainly occupied in discussing whether colours, in the sense in which sense-data have colours, could furnish us with examples of such universals, taking as an instance the colour 'white'.

I think many philosophers are really inclined to hold that the colour 'white' itself, understood in the sense in which some sense-data are undoubtedly white, is an instance of such a universal; and, of course, if the colour 'white' then also the colours 'blue', 'green', 'red', 'yellow', 'black', 'brown', 'grey', etc. I think this view is often what is, at least vaguely, in people's minds when they call whiteness a 'quality'. There has been a tradition in philosophy to draw a distinction between 'relations' and 'qualities', as if they were different kinds of universals, and since, in general, relations have been confused with what I call 'relational properties', I think perhaps what has been vaguely in the minds of those who make this distinction is that 'qualities' (and, therefore, colours) are not relational properties, but yet 'belong' to the things which have them, in the same non-relational sense, in which relational properties belong to the things which have *them*. They are holding, I think, when they call whiteness a 'quality', that, if we say of a sense-datum 'This is white', the proposition thus expressed is not a relational proposition at all—is not a proposition which asserts of the colour 'white' that it has some relation to the sense-given patch in question; that in short the copula 'is', when 'is' is the 'is' of predication, is not a name for any relation whatever.

Now, in order to consider properly whether this view is true or false, it is, I think, absolutely necessary to take account of one very important fact. The fact I mean is the fact that two different sense-given patches, each of which can undoubtedly be properly said to 'be white', may nevertheless be of two different *shades* of white; one, for instance, may be of a slightly more creamy white than the other. There are in fact quite a number of different *shades* of white, each of which is such that any sense-datum (any sense-given patch, that is) which is *of* that shade can be properly said to be white; and I think it is pretty plain that no sense-datum can be properly said to be white at all, unless it is either *of* some particular shade of white all over (counting pure white as one of the shades) or is of a number of different shades of white in different parts of it. For the sake of simplicity, and because it is irrelevant to my present purpose, I will neglect the latter alternative, though it is of very frequent occurrence, and will confine myself to considering those white sense-data (also of frequent occurrence) which are *of exactly the same shade all over*. Every different shade of white, is, of course, a different colour, though most, if not all, of them have no name appropriated to them, and are not colours in the sense in which, e.g., 'white', 'blue', 'red', etc., are names of colours. And though each of them can be properly said to be '*a* white' or 'a particular white', none of them can possibly itself *be white* in the sense we are considering—the sense in which, not a *colour*, but a sense-given *patch* of colour or coloured *patch* may be white. No coloured patch is identical with any colour—it is merely *of* some colour; and no colour can possibly (as a patch can) be *of* a certain colour: each of them *is* a certain colour. We have, therefore, in considering the sense in which a particular sense-given patch may be *white all over*, to consider two completely different questions. We have to consider (1) what is meant by saying of a patch, which is of one and the same *shade* of white all over, that it is *of* that shade, and (2) what is meant by saying of a particular shade of white (i.e., of a colour, not a coloured patch), that it is *a shade of white*, or, to use the phrase I have just used, is '*a* white'.

I say that in considering our main question, whether colours, in the sense in which sense-data have colours, can furnish us with examples of universals which are neither relations nor relational properties, and as a particular instance, whether the colour 'white', understood in the sense in which some sense-data are undoubtedly white, is either itself such a universal or involves one, we have to consider *both* of the two completely different questions just stated. And I say so for the following reasons. (1) It seems to me quite obvious that the colour 'white' cannot *itself* be such a universal, unless in saying of a sense-datum, which is of one particular shade of white all over, that it is *of* that shade, we are attributing a non-relational property to it; and we cannot decide whether we are or not, without considering the first question just stated. (2) It also seems to me quite obvious that in saying that a sense-datum is white, we are saying that every part of it is of *some shade* of white, thus covering both the cases in which different parts are of different shades of white and the cases in which the sense-datum is of exactly the same shade all over. But, if so, then part of our main question will consist in asking our second question, namely, What is meant by saying of a *colour*, which is a shade of white, that it *is* a shade of white? If the property which we attribute to it in saying this is a non-relational property, then the colour 'white' will *involve* a property which is neither a relation nor a relational property, whether or not it is such a property *itself*: 'being *a* white', which only a *colour* can be, will be a non-relational property, whether 'being white', which only a *patch* can be, is such a property or not.

Now the answer to our first question seems to me to be that being white *is* a relational property, because being of some particular shade of white is so. And my reason for saying this latter is simply that where you have a sense-datum which is of the same shade of white all over, this colour which it *has* seems to me to be *related* to it in quite a different way from that in which its shape or its size are related to it. This (generally, and perhaps always, nameless) colour is *spread* over the whole of it. This seems to me to be what we mean by saying that it is *of* that colour *all over*. And quite certainly neither its shape nor its size are thus *spread over* the whole of it. Is not 'spread over', in this sense in which the nameless colour quite obviously is spread over the whole, the name for a relation? I cannot help thinking that it is. If so, then we have not got, in any particular shade of white, nor in white itself, an example of a property which 'belongs' to anything in some sense in which 'belongs' is not the name of a relation. Of course, the property of *being* white, and of *being* of that particular nameless shade of white, will be relational properties, and will, like all relational properties, 'belong' to that to which they belong in a non-relational sense. But, if I am right, we must distinguish strictly (as is, I think, not usually done) between the *colour* 'white', or any particular shade of white, and the relational properties of 'being white' or 'being of this particular shade'. The *colours* only belong to sense-data in the sense of having a certain relation to them; but, of course, the relational properties of *having* those colours, or *being* of those colours, 'belong' in quite a different sense.

But, if now we turn to my second question, the answer seems to me quite different. Although, as I have just said, the property of being white, which belongs to some sense-data (though not the colour 'white') seems to me to be a relational property, on the other hand, the property of being *a* white, which only belongs to colours, not to sense-data, seems to me *not* to be a relational property, but to be an example of the sort of universal we were looking for. I have to admit that I only think so, because the only possible alternative view seems to me to be that it is a disjunctive property, in which one of the disjuncts is identity and the other is defined in some way by reference to resemblance—resemblance, in this case, of course, to *colours* not, as in the cases I considered in my lectures, to coloured patches. And I simply cannot believe that it is a disjunctive property of this sort.

Index

References which seemed specially important are printed in heavier type